# MANAGING PUBLIC SAFETY TECHNOLOGY

Divided into four sections—public safety agencies, key issues like interoperability and cybercrime, management skills, and emerging trends like the transfer of military technologies to civilian agencies, *Managing Public Safety Technology* illustrates how essential managing technology is to the success of any project. Based on the authors' years of experience dealing with information systems and other tools, this book offers guidance for line personnel, supervisors, managers, and anyone dealing with public safety technology.

Designed for current or future public safety personnel, especially those in management, *Managing Public Safety Technology* can also be used for undergraduate and graduate public safety management and leadership programs.

**Jeffrey A. Rose** has an extensive background in training law enforcement officers, as well as a bachelor's degree in human resource management and a master's degree in education. He has taught numerous courses throughout the country on diverse topics, including criminal justice, administration, budgets, human resource management, and technology. He is a Captain with the San Bernardino County Sheriff Department (California), where he has been a member of the department for over 30 years. Captain Rose has worked in a variety of assignments including Corrections, Patrol, Investigations, Watch Commander, and numerous administrative and managerial positions. He is currently the Commander of one of the largest jails in the State of California, and was previously the Commander of the Emergency Operations Division and the Sheriff Regional Training Center (Academy).

**Donald C. Lacher** is Chair of the Criminal Justice Management program at the Union Institute and University. He retired at the rank of Captain from the Monrovia (California) Police Department after 31 years of honorable service, including management of both the Services and Operations Divisions. At the rank of Lieutenant he served as the Tactical Response Team Commander, Watch Commander, Detective Bureau Commander, DRE Program Coordinator, and Explorer Advisor. Captain Lacher earned a bachelor's degree in criminal justice from California State University-Los Angeles and a master's degree in organizational management from the University of La Verne. He is also a graduate of POST Center for Leadership Development-Command College.

Heretofore, there was little systematic guidance for public agency practitioners and/or educators in navigating the murky waters of publicly-funded technology procurement. Authors Lacher and Rose now provide that much-needed guidance and wisdom about this process from concept to fruition. This book is a must-read for everyone in academia and the public sector.

—**Paul Cappitelli,** *Executive Director of the California Commission on Peace Officer Standards and Training (Retired)*

This book is a must read for all public safety personnel who are tasked with a technology project. Millions of tax payer dollars are spent on public safety technology projects. This book provides practical guidelines and examples that will help you save time and money.

—**Detective Laren Leichliter,** *San Bernardino County Sheriff's Department, San Bernardino County Safety Employees' Benefit Association (President), California Peace Officer Standards and Training (POST) Commission (Chair)*

# MANAGING PUBLIC SAFETY TECHNOLOGY

Deploying Systems in Police, Courts, Corrections, and Fire Organizations

*Jeffrey A. Rose*
*Donald C. Lacher*

Routledge
Taylor & Francis Group

NEW YORK AND LONDON

First published 2017
by Routledge
711 Third Avenue, New York, NY 10017

and by Routledge
2 Park Square, Milton Park, Abingdon, Oxon, OX14 4RN

*Routledge is an imprint of the Taylor & Francis Group, an informa business*

*Library of Congress Cataloging-in-Publication Data*
A catalog record for this book has been requested

ISBN: 978-1-138-68995-4 (hbk)
ISBN: 978-0-323-29609-0 (pbk)
ISBN: 978-1-315-39786-3 (ebk)

Typeset in Bembo
by codeMantra

This book is dedicated to the men and women who have worked in the public safety field or the military and paid the ultimate sacrifice. You will never be forgotten.

A special dedication to the late Sergeant Robert Rose of the San Bernardino County Sheriff's Department. Robert was a nationally recognized expert in technology and computer crimes. He inspired and mentored many law enforcement officers that were interested in law enforcement technology. Rest in peace, Rob!

# CONTENTS

# PREFACE

This book is written for students and public safety professionals interested in technology. Public safety agencies spend thousands of dollars each year training their personnel on department specific topics like firearms, defensive tactics, fire suppression and officer safety. However, when was the last time a public safety agency sent an officer, supervisor or even a manager to a course that discusses the basic principles of project management, factors for developing a department policy or the way to manage a controversial piece of equipment like a body-worn camera? It simply doesn't happen. Public safety is integrated with technology programs and equipment, but who is actually responsible for the technology?

Typically, a chief, sheriff or department head will decide that the department needs a piece of technology or a computer program that will help the overall efficiency of the department. The task of handling this assignment usually falls to a manager or supervisor who has not been trained in the procurement process for the agency, in how to negotiate with a vendor or in how to properly conduct a needs analysis report. The sad part of this scenario is that public safety spends millions of dollars each year on technology, yet very little is spent on training personnel who are actually responsible for the technology project or equipment purchase.

An informed and educated public safety manager is not only better able to manage technology, but also is more apt to utilize technology in an effective way. Public safety personnel, specifically those in supervisor or management positions, must have a basic understanding of technology in order for a project to be successful. One only has to read the local newspaper to find a story about how the public is upset at local politicians because tax dollars were spent on a project, only to see it fail because of poor management.

The public expects and demands that public safety personnel understand and utilize technology in the performance of their jobs. Technology transcends all aspects of public safety. The general public watches television and is surrounded with innovative technology and equipment. The public expects public safety agencies to use the same type of equipment to solve crime, save lives and protect property.

This book also includes a mixture of contemporary issues facing public safety. Although the book has a primary focus on managers, the information is applicable to all public safety personnel working in law enforcement, courts, corrections and fire services. Students interested in public safety will also benefit from the information provided because it is not just a "how to" book. It is designed to give a unique perspective on management issues and on the ways technology will influence public safety in the future. The book is divided into four units of instruction with specific chapters that provide an overview of public safety technology.

The first unit of instruction provides a foundational overview of public safety organizations and the way technology plays an important role in the management of personnel and operations. This includes law enforcement, corrections, courts and fire services.

The second unit of instruction highlights popular technology concepts, programs and equipment used in public safety today. Technology like social media, body-worn cameras, biometrics, thermal imaging cameras, fire-fighting drones and predictive policing are all part of the public safety arena. The chapters in this unit are designed to give the reader an in-depth review of the specific technology being used today by public safety organizations. Unit 2 also provides practical examples of technology programs and equipment that has helped transform and keep public safety organizations in tune with private sector technology.

The third unit of instruction walks public safety personnel and criminal justice students through the process of evaluating, planning, purchasing, implementing and maintaining technology. As previously stated, public safety personnel receive very little training in this area. All of the chapters in this unit are designed to help public safety personnel navigate the process and ensure that the technology or equipment works properly and that taxpayer money is not wasted.

The final unit of instruction provides a glimpse of the future of technology in public safety, with an emphasis on the criminal justice system. New technology innovation will continue to play a crucial role for public safety managers. Equipping public safety personnel with the latest technology is vital because criminals are consistently using innovative technology to commit crimes against society. We review the latest technology concepts and ideas that hopefully will benefit future public safety organizations and the communities that they serve each and every day. This unit also includes several research papers written by command-level professionals in public safety. The papers seek to determine the future of public safety and the ways technology will inspire, transform and revolutionize their respective professions.

# ACKNOWLEDGMENTS

Collectively, we have almost seventy (70) years of law enforcement experience and we both have had some very challenging, exciting, and difficult assignments. As we reflect on our assignments, we both recall saying, "That was interesting, I should write a book about this." Those of you in public safety know exactly what we are talking about. So many wonderful experiences. Finally, we get to share some of those experiences with you.

Before we do that, we want to thank some wonderful people.

We would like to start by thanking the wonderful team at Routledge for their continued support and assistance throughout the entire book writing process: Ellen Boyle, Eve Strillacci, and Miriam Armstrong. And also Rebecca Dunn for overseeing the production of the book.

*From Jeff*
You don't write a book like this alone. Many people have helped me along the way and I wish to personally thank the following people for their contributions and support.

To my wonderful family. Thank you for your patience, support and love over the years. My beautiful wife Sandy and our children Matthew and Stephanie. To my mom and dad (Barbara and Robert) and my mother- and father-in-law (Frank and Marlene), thank you for your wisdom, love and guidance. To my brothers and sisters, Robert, John, Paula, Julie, Nick, Frank, Aubri, Debbie and many other family members and friends. Your love and support means the world to be. I can't thank you enough.

To the men and women of the San Bernardino County Sheriff's Department: I am so proud to serve in the best law enforcement agency in the country. Special thanks to Sheriffs Floyd Tidwell, Dick Williams, Gary Penrod, Rod Hoops and John McMahon.

A very special thanks to the following people for their continued support and contributions to this book: Robert Wickum, Dale Gregory, Al Daniel, Mitch Datillo, Joe Cusimano, Dave Williams, Ron Cochran, Dana Gould, Melissa Morrell, Jerry Harper, Gina Marquez,

Joanne Beard, Greg Kyritsis, Nancy Yurkoski, Kasey DeCoud, Kelly Gallagher, Greg Garland, Shannon Dicus, Paul Cappitelli, and Neil Gallucci.

To my co-author Don Lacher. Thank you for your friendship, guidance and support.

***From Don***

I would like to acknowledge my family for all of their love and support of my academic endeavours. A special thanks to my loving wife Joan. My mother-in-law Dale, our southern belle. Our kids Angela, Elizabeth, Glenn and Michelle. Our sons-in-law Bryan and Jason. Our daughter-in-law, Brialynn, and Roger, Elizabeth's significant other. Our grandchildren, Bradley, Auburn, Olivia, Colin, Tyler, Landen, Mackenzie, Austin, Madison, and Roger's daughters, Angie and Sabrina.

A special acknowledgment to our family members in Heaven, including my mother Janet, my father Wallace and Joan's father Dean. A special thanks to our family members who served our nation in war and peace: Wallace, U.S. Army Air Corps/U.S. Air Force (World War II, Korea, Laos), Dean, U.S. Army Corps/U.S. Air Force, Glenn, U.S. Army Airborne (Afghanistan), Brialynn, U.S. Army Airborne (Afghanistan), Jason, U.S. Marine Corps (Iraq, Afghanistan), Roger, U.S. Navy, and Scott, U.S. Army Ranger (Iraq).

# FOREWORD

When you travel to a foreign country, it is a good idea to try and understand the language before you make the trip. Having a basic command of the native language will make the travel experience much more pleasurable.

Conversely, being in a foreign country where everyone is speaking a different language is a daunting experience. This concept seems very basic, right?

Using this logic, it would stand to reason that public safety professionals should prepare for a journey into foreign technology territory. Unfortunately, this is usually not the case. Oftentimes, leaders find themselves thrust into a position where they suddenly have to understand the intricacies of the technology language. Simply put, one can get lost and confused in this foreign technology land without proper guidance.

This publication, *Managing Public Safety Technology: Deploying Systems in Police, Courts, Corrections and Fire Organizations*, provides this much-needed guidance. The authors' vast experience and insight in the field of public sector technology is invaluable to criminal justice academicians, students, municipal leaders and public safety professionals alike. Readers of this textbook will be better-prepared to journey into the world of technology.

Paul Cappitelli,
Executive Director (retired), California Commission on
Peace Officer Standards and Training (POST)
Captain (retired), San Bernardino County Sheriff's Department

# ACRONYMS

Throughout this book, we discuss specific terminology and vocabulary that is commonly used in the public safety field. Active practitioners will certainly understand these terms, but for the benefit of those outside of public safety, we compiled a list of the common acronyms used in the field of public safety today.

AB109—Assembly Bill 109 (California)
ACLU—American Civil Liberties Union
AFIS—Automated Fingerprint Identification System
BJA—Bureau of Justice Assistance
BWC—body-worn camera
CAD—computer aided dispatch
CAPPS—California Automated Palm Print System
CCTV—closed circuit television
CDCR—California Department of Corrections and Rehabilitation
CODIS—Combined DNA Index System
COPS—Office of Community Oriented Policing Services
DHS—Department of Homeland Security
DNA—deoxynucleic acid
DOJ—Department of Justice
FAA—Federal Aviation Administration
FBI—Federal Bureau of Investigation
GIS—geographic information system
GPS—global positioning system
HMI—human machine interface
IACP—International Association of Chiefs of Police
IAFIS—International Automated Fingerprint Identification System
IP—Internet Protocol

IT—information technology
JIMS—jail information management system
MDC—mobile data computer
NCIC—National Criminal Information Center
NIJ—National Institute of Justice
NIST—National Institute of Standards and Technology
NLECTC—National Law Enforcement and Corrections Technology Center
NTSA—National Traffic Safety Administration
OC—oleoresin capsicum
PERF—Police Executive Research Forum
POST—California Peace Officer Standards and Training
QA—quality assurance
RFI—request for information
RFP—request for proposal
RFQ—request for qualifications
RMS—records management system
SCBA—self-contained breathing apparatus
SWAT—special weapons and tactics
Title 15—California Code of Regulations Title 15 (corrections)
UAV—unmanned aircraft vehicle
USFA—United States Fire Administration
VSS—video surveillance system

# UNIT 1

# Overview of Public Safety Organizations

Unit 1 provides public safety personnel and criminal justice students with some foundational information about public safety organizations and about how technology plays an important role in the management of personnel and operations. This includes law enforcement, corrections, courts and fire services. The corresponding chapters discuss contemporary issues, current and emerging technology and the ways public safety personnel can navigate through the technology process.

This unit covers the following:

- Chapter 1—Public Safety Technology
- Chapter 2—Law Enforcement
- Chapter 3—The Court System
- Chapter 4—Corrections
- Chapter 5—Fire Services

# 1

# PUBLIC SAFETY TECHNOLOGY

"We pass bills authorizing improvements and grants. But when it comes time to pay for these programs, we'd rather put the money toward tax breaks for the wealthy than for police officers who are protecting our communities."

*—David Price*

## Learning Objectives

After reading this chapter, the student will:

- Understand the history of technology used in public safety organizations.
- Be able to explain the different types of technology used in law enforcement, courts, corrections and fire safety.
- Know and understand how technology affects public safety organizations, the criminal justice system and the community.
- Identify resources that can assist in technology projects.

## Introduction

Public safety managers play an important role when dealing with technology. Managers must research, implement and evaluate technology on a regular basis. Technology is expensive and sometimes controversial. In this chapter, we deal with the basic foundation of public safety technology and define why technology is an important aspect of law enforcement, corrections, courts and fire services. We also discuss how and why the military and the private sector have a big part in public safety organizations. This chapter also includes a list of resources that public safety managers can utilize when researching or implementing a technology project or purchasing equipment.

## Why Do We Care about Technology?

The term *technology* is defined as "the use of science in industry, engineering, etc., to invent useful things or to solve problems, a machine, piece of equipment, methods, etc., that is created by technology."[1] When we think about the word technology, we often think about science fiction movies. Movies often showcase what is possible in society. However, technology used in Hollywood can and is used in public safety agencies around the world. Technology is all around us whether we like it or not. The real question is: Does technology have a place in public safety? Why should public safety managers care about technology? Technology in public safety has evolved by the implementation of new instruments and advances in science. Technological advances like the use of a computer in a police car, biometrics, DNA, or telemedicine technology has forever changed the way public safety agencies operate. Technological advancements in public safety continue to grow at an exponential rate, much as they do for all professions.

The explosive growth of technology in the public safety field does not come without controversy. Communities across the country often debate the use of technology in public safety because technology can sometimes infringe on one's civil rights. For example, the use of unmanned aircraft or drones has created issues with law enforcement, corrections and fire services just in the last year. Opponents of drone technology argue that the drones violate their fourth amendment rights as a citizen because the drone can look into a bedroom window or monitor their daily activities.

Regardless of the controversy, technology in public safety is essential. Administrators and managers in public safety must continue to look for technology that supports their overall operational needs.

## Introduction to Public Safety Technology

Since the industrial revolution, society has become more and more dependent on technology. Technology has changed how we live our daily lives. Have you ever become upset over how much time it takes to download a document on your computer? Society expects technology to make our lives easier and more efficient. Public safety managers can and should use technology when appropriate. However, public safety involves humans and technology itself cannot replace a cop on the beat or a fireman responding to a house fire.

Over the last thirty years, our society has been transformed by the developments in technology. American and international businesses have utilized information technology to transform organizations, seek out and open new markets and firmly establish relationships with international partners. During the same time in history, public safety organizations have had to shift from draconian methods and adopt corporate models to meet the needs of their customers—the public. Mimicking our corporate cousins, the public safety sector has embarked on a crusade to channel change within their organizations.

For years, the public sector has groomed their employees to become change agents. By expanding their trust, public safety executives have encouraged their subordinates to seek innovative strategies to satisfy customers, improve efficiency and find new funding sources.

The most pivotal example is finding new technologies to improve data storage, retrieval, analysis and evaluation of services.[2] For example, law enforcement agencies are currently operating in a community policing model. In this model, law enforcement organizations develop strategies to solve problems at the neighborhood level and improve the quality of life for its inhabitants. No longer are the police relying on numbers of arrests to help reduce crime.

Arresting suspects is only one strategy in a long list of tools utilized by law enforcement to deter and reduce crime. Public safety organizations have learned that key to success is building trust, anticipating the needs of their clients and improving communication with residents. For example, public sector agencies that utilize social media are able to disseminate vital information to the public about wanted criminals, lost children, and natural or manmade disasters. In contrast, it is now common for public safety employees to find themselves being disciplined for inappropriate postings on their personal social media sites. Applicants for public safety employment many times find themselves failing the background investigation process by posting information about their past or present criminal behavior.

Throughout this book, we explore the challenges of managing technology. The technology we examine is divided into several major components: first responder technologies, communication, surveillance, data collection and retrieval and forensic analysis. We also examine the impact of transnational crime and terrorism on technology and effective responses by the technology manager.[3]

Managing and utilizing technology does present challenges to employees in the public safety sector. Technology poses significant risks to executives, managers, end users, and organizations. These risks come in two main types: technology risks and human risks. First, there is the risk that the technology does not work or improve efficiency. Other problems associated with technology implementation are projected costs versus real costs, unanticipated maintenance issues and unintended consequences of the new technology.

Human risks include resistance to using the technology. Older workers may find the onslaught of technology and constant change unsettling. Organizations who move too slowly to adapt to new technology may find that when a particular technology is implemented it may already be outdated. Examples in the arena include communication- and computer-based technologies. The main human risk to consider is the danger of new technologies to the end user and the public. Technologies utilized in law enforcement, corrections, fire services and the military can be physically dangerous to humans. Lack of training and the inability to utilize technology appropriately may cause injury to the user or the public. An example of human risk impact is the use of new technologies in use-of-force events. Managers who select and implement human risk technology sometimes fail to consider the potential cost of civil litigation by employees or defendants who are injured by application of technology.

The evolution of data collection and retrieval systems has produced astounding results. Examples include computer aided dispatching, crime mapping, and crime intelligence systems. Computer aided dispatch (CAD) is a component of the department's automated record keeping system. Call takers are able to enter vital information in real-time and store and retrieve that information later for use in solving crimes or identifying suspects. All this information is available from dispatchers or in car computer systems. Information such as vehicle license plates, suspicious persons, tattoos and other key information has vastly improved crime and problem-solving issues for communities. Combining CAD with facial recognition software and vehicle license plate reading systems have helped identify suspects committing crimes and terrorist attacks.

Area maps with different colored stickpins indicating criminal activity have been replaced by crime mapping technology. Crime mapping technology combines geographical information with crime statistics to produce usable maps to display location, dates and times and types of criminal events.[4]

Today, many law enforcement officers have laptops in their patrol cars linked to their department's CAD system. Officers routinely access their databases to retrieve vehicle registrations and driver's license information, criminal history profiles on offenders and other vital information. In California, a database known as Cal Gang allows officers to search gang membership, monikers, tattoos, vehicles and gang symbols to help solve crimes.

## What Is Your Role in Technology?

Public safety personnel are usually divided into three categories: line staff, supervisors and managers. Technology affects all three categories and is essential to their core function. Line staff *uses* the technology. They utilize the technology on a daily basis and are paramount to the overall success of any technology project. In order to gain support from the line staff, technology must be easy to use. Not every cop on the beat has extensive technical background. If the piece of equipment is too difficult to use, more than likely the officer will not use it. The equipment must also have a purpose. Does the equipment help an officer solve crime, locate stolen vehicles or process inmates inside of a correctional facility? Perhaps the equipment is used to save a life after a traffic accident. Public safety personnel can easily see the importance of the aforementioned technology; thus this type of technology will most likely be successful and used by the line staff on a regular basis.

Supervisors *use* and *provide* oversight of technology. Supervisors must understand and support technology. If the supervisor does not support the technology, his or her subordinates will generally do the same thing. The supervisor should also ensure that the technology is used properly to prevent any errors or misconduct. Supervisors can also use technology to train employees when necessary. Finally, because supervisors are usually in the field, they can use technology to analyze and plan activities. The use of crime analysis is a perfect example. As previously mentioned in this chapter, supervisors can deploy personnel to high crime areas based on crime trends or patterns.

The final category is the manager. Managers, either sworn or civilian, are the decision makers for the technology project. They are tasked with the overall responsibility to evaluate the cost of the technology versus the benefits and must ensure that the taxpayer's money is spent wisely. Managers must be able to justify the expense of any technology project or procurement when asked by the public. Managers can also use technology in the strategic planning process (data collection). Managers are also responsible for seeking out new technology. Department heads or managers often collaborate with other agency representatives and have the ability to regionalize and share the expense of technology.

## Technology Is a Force Multiplier

Technology can be expensive, and many public safety agencies are understaffed. According to a study (2010) conducted by the Police Executive Research Forum (PERF) (see Figure 1.1), more than half of the law enforcement agencies in the study stated that they had to reduce funding for technology projects.[5]

The United States employs over 760,000 police officers and spends over $100 billion on law enforcement. When the economy tanked in the mid-2010s, many agencies were forced to reduce staffing. According to a survey by PERF, 78 percent of police departments had staffing issues. Technology funding was also cut. However, as the economy gets better and law enforcement agencies get additional funding, technology is an area that can help make an impact. Technology like wearable cameras, predictive policing, cloud computing, social media and crime-fighting civic application can all have an effect on law enforcement.[6] The

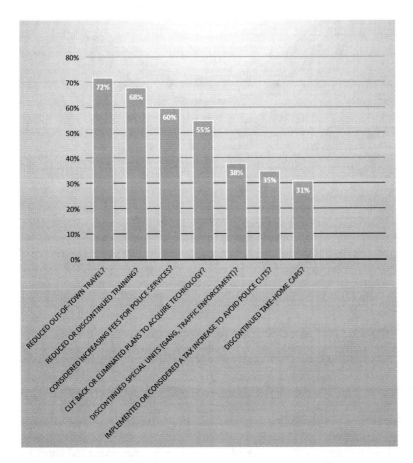

**FIGURE 1.1**  Impacts of Policies.

*Source*: Police Executive Research Forum. (2010). Is the Economic Downturn Fundamentally Changing How We Police? Critical Issues in Policing Series, Vol. 16, Washington DC: PERF.

use of technology can save on personnel costs, improve overall efficiency and reduce crime, if used properly.

William Bratton, the ex-chief of police for the Los Angeles Police Department and former commissioner for the New York Police Department, stated, "Technology is truly the key to increasing the department's effectiveness as we continue to fight and reduce crime with limited resources." He referred to technology as a "force multiplier." Under Bratton's leadership, the Los Angeles Police Department installed closed circuit television technology in the MacArthur Park area. Crime was running rampant, and the good citizens did not want to visit the park. LAPD tried to fix the issue with extra patrols, but when the extra officers were not in the park, crime continued. LAPD teamed up with General Electric and installed CCTV cameras throughout the park. The technology was a success and crime was reduced.[7]

The Los Angeles Police Department also instituted an innovative technology called COPLINK, which analyzes data or patterns and helps law enforcement identify criminals and reduce crime. The technology also allowed LAPD to share information within the department and with other agencies throughout the state of California. The use of COPLINK was a big success; officers and investigators alike were able to use the data to solve crime. After using the technology for one year, LAPD determined that it allowed them both to save money on staffing and to improve community policing because officers were able to get information quicker and move on to other calls for service.[8]

In 2003, the San Bernardino County Sheriff's Department (California) implemented mobile biometric technology. One of your authors, then-Lieutenant Jeff Rose, was assigned to a regional division called CAL-ID. This division was responsible for managing biometric technology including fingerprint live scans inside of jail facilities and latent print identification services for criminal investigations. Recognizing the need to help deputies quickly identify a suspect in the field, the San Bernardino County Sheriff's Department partnered with the Riverside County Sheriff's Department to manage the largest deployment of hand-held mobile biometric identification devices to patrol personnel in the United States. The mobile identification devices had a small fingerprint scanner and camera so the deputy could obtain a fingerprint and a photograph of a suspect within seconds. The fingerprint and photograph were electronically sent to a regional fingerprint database for processing. If the biometric data did not match, the data packet was then sent to the California Department of Justice for processing. Typically, a positive "hit" or result was sent back to the deputy within one minute. Mobile identification was an instant success, and law enforcement personnel were calling CAL-ID asking for more devices. The ability to quickly identify a suspect was evident when a San Bernardino County Sheriff's deputy stopped a subject for a vehicle code violation. The suspect had no identification and gave various names to the deputy. The deputy suspected that the driver was lying, so he used the mobile identification device. Within seconds, the driver's true identity was discovered. He was in fact lying about his name because he had a no-bail warrant for his arrest, and he was considered armed and dangerous. After he was arrested, he bragged to the deputy that he had been stopped several times by other law enforcement officers and was let go because they didn't have a way to confirm his identity in the field. Since that time, hundreds of the devices have been issued to patrol, detectives and coroner personnel across both counties.

## Innovation and Technology

Innovation transforms technology, and public safety personnel have a major part in the development process. The direction of innovative technology can be challenging, to say the least. The future of science has a direct effect on public safety technology. It can be a scary or exhilarating experience to manage constantly evolving technology. Changes in technology create vulnerabilities to a public safety agency or department. For example, millions of people across the country can utilize technology to connect with others, including criminals. As we continue to use the information grid (social media, cell phones, and so on), the more vulnerable we become to those who understand how technology works. Technology can be exploited and used against society.[9] Technology has flaws, and public safety managers must evaluate the pros and cons of any technology that is used. Regardless, new technology will always be developed, so understanding it and working past its flaws will make technology useful. The future of technology revolves around innovation. Public safety agencies must adapt to new technology and techniques. Technology provides a wide range of tools and equipment that can be utilized in law enforcement, courts, corrections and fire services. Innovative technology will always focus on ways to improve services to the public and the protection of personnel and the public at large. How important will innovative technology be in the future? Time will tell, but as technology spreads across the private sector, public safety managers must be proactive and utilize technology whenever possible.

## Technology Resources for Public Safety Agencies

There are many helpful resources available to public safety managers and other personnel. Various federal agencies provide up-to-date information on technology projects with an overall goal of assisting local public safety personnel. In some cases, private companies are funded by federal agencies to research and develop technology projects or to address emerging trends that may impact public safety. The following is a short list of government agencies that may be of assistance to public safety managers throughout the United States.

### *National Institute of Justice*

The National Institute of Justice (NIJ) is the research, development and evaluation agency of the U.S. Department of Justice. NIJ has six strategic challenges:

- Fostering science-based criminal justice practices by supporting scientific research to ensure the safety of families, neighborhoods and communities.
- Translating knowledge to practice by disseminating scientific research to criminal justice professionals in the hopes of preventing or reducing crime.
- Advancing technology to build a more effective, fair and efficient criminal justice system through technology.
- Working across disciplines by connecting physical, forensic and social sciences to reduce crime and promote justice.

- Bolstering the research infrastructure by supporting young scholars, encouraging researchers from a broad array of disciplines to apply their work to criminal justice and increasing the availability of research findings and data.
- Adopting a global perspective by understanding crime in its social context with the United States and around the world.[10]

The National Institute of Justice supports research, evaluation and development projects in the following areas:

- Causes and correlates of crime
- Crime prevention and control
- Prevention of violence and victimization
- Forensic sciences
- Corrections practice and policy, including community corrections
- Law enforcement effectiveness, legitimacy, accountability and safety
- Courts and adjudication[11]

## National Law Enforcement and Corrections Technology Center

The National Law Enforcement and Corrections Technology Center (NLECTC) is part of the National Institute of Justice and is the conduit between research and criminal justice professionals in the field for technology issues. NLECTC works with criminal justice professionals to identify urgent and emerging technology needs. They sponsor research and development or identify best practices to address those needs.[12]

## U.S. Fire Administration

The U.S. Fire Administration provides information on fire services, including various technology-related projects and programs. The U.S. Fire Administration is an entity of the U.S. Department of Homeland Security's Federal Emergency Management Agency.[13]

## The Federal Bureau of Investigation

The Federal Bureau of Investigation is a great resource for public safety managers interested in technology. The FBI provides research on current and emerging technology projects and equipment along with statistical data that can be helpful for public safety managers looking to fund a technology project in her or her jurisdiction. With an estimated readership of over 200,000 criminal justice professionals each month, the *FBI Law Enforcement Bulletin* is a monthly publication that should be required reading for all public safety personnel. Topics include homeland security, law enforcement, corrections, courts, training and technology.[14]

## Office of Community Oriented Policing Services (COPS)

The Office of Community Oriented Policing Services (COPS) is the component of the U.S. Department of Justice responsible for advancing the practice of community policing by the nation's state, local, territorial and tribal law enforcement agencies through information and grant resources. Community policing begins with a commitment to building trust and mutual respect between police and communities. It is critical to public safety, ensuring that all stakeholders work together to address our nation's crime challenges. When police and communities collaborate, they more effectively address underlying issues, change negative behavioral patterns and allocate resources. The COPS office awards grants to hire community policing professionals, develop and test innovative policing strategies and provide training and technical assistance to community members, local government leaders and all levels of law enforcement. Since 1994, the COPS Office has invested more than $14 billion to help advance community policing.[15]

The aforementioned list can be a valuable resource for public safety managers, but perhaps the most important resource when evaluating or even discussing a technology project is your neighboring public safety agency. Public safety agencies across the country are embarking on innovative technology projects like body cameras, thermal cameras, downlink cameras and integrated data systems that link multiple agencies with information within seconds. Many agencies have already implemented successful projects and thus can be a wealth of information. Public safety personnel, at any level, should always reach out to other agencies for help and guidance. Sharing of criminal intelligence and crime trends is the backbone of any law enforcement agency so why not share information on technology? New public safety personnel or students reading this book should also do some research and see what your local agency is doing in the area of technology. There is no sense in reinventing the wheel. Public safety is not a competition. If someone has already done something that works, jump on board and make your community safer.

## The Cost of Technology

Emerging technologies are very expensive. Public safety organizations rely on two main funding sources: pilot test agreements and government grants. Pilot test agreements are between private vendors wishing to test their emerging technologies by partnering with public safety agencies. In these partnerships, vendors test their new products and in turn allow the agency to continue to use the technology after the pilot test is completed. The arrangements are a win–win situation for both the vendor and the organization. Results from the experiment and endorsements from the host agency reap significant rewards for the vendor when selling their technology on the open market.

Grants are offered to the public safety sector by federal and state governments and by private and non-profit organizations. Many agencies have applied and received technology grants to improve their service to the public. In bleak economic times, public sector agencies will be forced to seek more grants, just to manage maintenance costs for the technology they already possess. Over the years, public safety organizations have sought out personnel with excellent writing skills to research and write grants to enhance their technology capabilities. Organizations such as the International Association of Chiefs of Police lend expertise to law enforcement agencies to help them obtain grants for emerging technologies.

In 2013, the U.S. Commerce Department, Nation Telecommunications and Information Administration, awarded $116 million dollars in grants to fire departments. The grant was funded to help fire departments plan for upgrades in the National Public

Safety Broadband Network. The program helps fire departments across the nation to better communicate with their peers and allied agencies during future disasters or terrorist attacks.[16]

## The Military and Homeland Security Technology

Much of the cutting-edge technology today was developed for use by the military. Government research and development programs have revolutionized law enforcement, corrections, courts and the fire service. For many years, technology designed to detect biological, chemical and nuclear threats was developed and refined for the protection of military personnel on the battlefield. The September 11, 2001, attacks brought the battlefield within our borders, and a new war on terror was launched. The threat of a future biological, chemical or nuclear attack by terror cells is now a real threat in the United States.

Certainly in this century, the September 11, 2011, attacks on America caused a paradigm shift in the public safety sector arena. The one positive result was the desire by federal agencies to share information on extremists with local and state law enforcement. The military began working closely with civilian law enforcement by providing training and sharing military technology. Law enforcement and fire organizations throughout the country reaped untold benefits from the military. The military virtually gave away expensive technology, including automatic firearms, ballistic gear, night-vision equipment, infrared technology, biohazard equipment, armored vehicles and helicopters.

Many public and private entities have installed or improved existing remote camera technology to prevent crime or to identify suspects involved in criminal offenses or terrorist acts. On April 15, 2013, a bomb exploded in the city of Boston. Two brothers who were radicalized Islamists placed two bombs along the Boston Marathon route, wounding onlookers and killing three. Later, the two suspects also killed a university police officer. During a shootout with police, one of the suspects was killed. The other suspect was captured after an altercation with police. Photographs taken from surveillance technology and cell phones helped federal agents identify the two bombing suspects.[17]

## Chapter Summary

Technology poses multifaceted challenges for public safety managers. They are tasked with identifying and implementing emerging technologies to enhance the mission of their organization. Law enforcement, fire, courts, corrections and homeland security managers face real threats worldwide. In the case of law enforcement, managers who learned to effectively manage peace officers and crime scenes now find themselves managing techno-savvy civilians who are motivated differently than cops. In the downward trends of the economy, public safety managers will face budgetary and funding issues. However, public safety managers can receive help from a variety of resources, including the Office of Community Oriented Policing Services (COPS) and the National Institute of Justice (NIJ). The great thing about the public safety profession is that its membership is dedicated to providing a valuable service to the community. Sharing information about technology is the standard across the country. Public safety managers should always reach out to other agencies and learn about new and innovative technology that may help their own agency build better relationships with the community, improve operational efficiency and, more importantly, save lives.

## Key Words or Terminology

| | | |
|---|---|---|
| technology | public safety | private sector |
| terrorism | corrections | law enforcement |
| fire services | funding | line staff |
| supervisor | manager | CCTV |
| NIJ | COPS | FBI |
| courts | grants | innovation |
| mobile biometric technology | | |

## Discussion Questions

1. Prepare a timeline of the implementation of technology at your local public safety agency since 2000. If you work in public safety, please use your own agency. How did the events of the 911 attacks change or modify the technology needs?
2. Research an example of a military technology adapted to law enforcement, corrections or the fire service. Discuss the key elements of this technology. What are the advantages and disadvantages of this technology in your career field?
3. Compare and contrast the roles of the executive, manager and first-line supervisor in technology management. How are they similar? How do they differ?
4. Research the various government agencies that can help with technology research, purchasing and implementation. What did you learn from your research?

## Notes

1  The Merriam-Webster online dictionary. Retrieved June 1, 2013, from www.merriam-webster.com.
2  Lacher, D. (2014). *Contemporary issues in criminal justice management* (1st ed.). San Diego, CA: Cognella Books.
3  Ibid.
4  Schmalleger, F. & Worrall, J. (2010). *Policing today,* Upper Saddle River, NJ: Pearson Education.
5  (2010). Is the economic downturn fundamentally changing how we police? *Critical Issues in Policing Series, vol. 16.* Washington DC: Police Executive Research Forum.
6  Newcombe, T. (2014). *Force multiplier: police seek effective uses of technology.* Retrieved from www.governing.com/templates/gov_print_article?id+275216341.
7  Davis, P. (2007). *Technology serves as force multiplier.* Retrieved from www.officer.com/article/10249729/technology-serves-as-a-force-multiplier.
8  Ibid.
9  Goodman, M. (2015). *Future crimes.* New York: Doubleday.
10  (2015). *About NIJ.* National Institute of Justice. Retrieved from www.nij.gov/about/pages/welcome.aspx.
11  Ibid.
12  (2016). *About NLECTC.* National Law Enforcement and Corrections Center. Retrieved from www.justnet.org/about_NLECTC.html.

13 (2016). *About the U.S. Fire Administration.* United States Fire Administration. Retrieved from www.usfa.fema.gov/about/index.html.

14 (2015). *A history.* Federal Bureau of Investigation. Retrieved from www.leb.fbi.gov/in-each-issue/a-history.

15 (2016). *About.* Office of Community Oriented Policing Services. Retrieved from www.cops.usdoj.gov/about.

16 (2013). *More than $116 million awarded to assist states in FirstNet planning.* National Telecommunications and Information Administration. United States Department of Commerce. Washington, DC: U.S. Government Printing Office.

17 (2013). *Boston Marathon terror attack: Fact sheet.* CNN Library. Retrieved from www.cnn.com/2013/06/03/us/boston-marathon-terror-attack-fast-facts/index.html.

# 2

# LAW ENFORCEMENT

"The police are the public and the public are the
police; the police being only members of the public
who are paid to give full time attention to duties which
are incumbent on every citizen in the interests of
community welfare and existence."

—*Sir Robert Peel*

## Learning Objectives

After reading this chapter, the student will:

- Compare and contrast nineteenth-century Peelian Principles and contemporary polic-
  ing ideals.
- Define the basic terminology of police technology.
- Discuss how advances and trends in police technology will improve efficiency in fight-
  ing crime.
- Analyze how technology is transforming policing.
- Explore the historical aspects of police technology.

## Introduction

In this chapter, we examine the three main technological impacts on policing. The first
impact provides the reader with a historical perspective of policing and explains how law
enforcement theory is blended with our collective experiences. We discuss how technology
has changed over the years and examine its overall impact on the way law enforcement
serves the public, solves problems and prevents crime.

Secondly, we explore how contemporary technological issues impact the industry today.
We explore the impact on law enforcement organizations and examine their coping

strategies, including the economic challenges they face to maintain current technology levels. We also become acquainted with the strategies that law enforcement organizations are employing to reduce personnel costs by using technology more efficiently.

Lastly, we survey current and emerging technologies that impact law enforcement organizations. Many of these technologies are discussed later in the book. Also, in this chapter, you hear from a number of law enforcement management experts who live with and use technology every day.

## Law Enforcement—A Historical Perspective

Many experts agree that the Industrial Revolution in Great Britain (1760–1850) was the catalyst for the advancement of modern technology. Advances in agriculture spurred by the development of metal tools and machines increased the English food supply.[1] The surplus in the food supply coupled with improvement in the textile industry drove profits. As profit margins increased, so did worldwide commerce. The eighteenth century saw Europe experience a population shift that was driven by the decrease in death rates, an explosion in the birth rate, the elimination of plagues, and the increase in food production. Workers moved *en masse* to factories from the fields to seek work. Towns and settlements sprang up around factories. As the population increased, social conditions sank and crime and poverty flourished.[2]

In 1829, Sir Robert Peel introduced to the English Parliament a list of guideline principles called the Metropolitan Police Act. The act reorganized the police forces in London as one efficient and paid body of officers. In 1833, the New York Police department adopted Peel's principles.[3]

Today, well over a hundred years later, these principles still hold true in policing. Many of the principles are affected by technology. For example, one of the principles concerns crime records. Police agencies around the world routinely write and store police reports and other types of records. Technology has dramatically changed how law enforcement stores and manages police records. The principles are:

- The police must be stable and organized along military lines.
- The police must be under government control.
- The absence of crime will best prove the efficiency of the police.
- The distribution of crime news is essential.
- The deployment of police strength, both by time and area, is essential.
- No quality is more indispensable to policemen than a perfect command of temper. A quiet, determined manner has more effect than violent action.
- Good appearance commands respect.
- The selection and training of proper persons are at the root of efficient law enforcement.
- Police security demands that every officer be given an identifying number.
- Police headquarters should be centrally located and easily accessible to the people.
- Policemen should be hired on a probationary basis before permanent assignment.
- Police crime records are necessary to the best distribution of police strength.[4]

**FIGURE 2.1**  Sir Robert Peel.

*Source*: Wikimedia Commons. Retrieved from www.commons.wikimedia.org/wiki/file:sir_robert_peel_2nd_
bt_by_henry_william_p... Public domain.

The industrial age and factory era in America mirrored the British experience. Famines, particularly in Ireland, brought thousands of immigrants to the United States seeking a better life. The resulting crime and poverty challenged American law enforcement and the political and social systems of the day. Policing in America followed the traditions set by England. New York and Philadelphia established full-time police departments with paid officers. The Civil War and the expansion in the west established a need for professional lawmen to battle cattle thieves. Modern technologies such as the railroad and the telegraph improved the efficiency of town marshals and sheriffs across the country. While much of the eighteenth-century law enforcement patrolled towns and cities on foot and horseback, Spillman Technologies reported that the Akron, Ohio, Police Department used the first police vehicle in 1899. In 1920, the New York Police Department introduced motor vehicles to improve police response times. In 1928, the Detroit Police Department added one-way radios in their police vehicles, and in 1934 the Boston Police Department was the first agency to use two-way radio systems, which enhanced police communications.[5]

Thus, a new era in police philosophy was born as other agencies utilized motorized police vehicles and had instant communication. However, one interesting communications tool overlapped the police radio. Many American police agencies utilized British policing concepts, which included the call box. For example, in 1860, the Washington, D.C., Metropolitan Police Department established a call box system in our nation's capital.

**FIGURE 2.2** Call Box in Washington, D.C., 1911–1920.

*Source*: United States Library of Congress. Retrieved from www.hdl.loc.gov/loc.pnp/hec.03392. Public domain.

As early as 1848, the boxes were illuminated with gas lights, and by 1926 there were 12,371 call boxes covering the District of Columbia. Prior to electricity, the boxes contained pointers so the officer could order an ambulance or a paddy wagon or report a fire. The boxes were sealed and opened by an officer using a key. He could flip a switch to notify his command that all was well. Policemen of the time rotated to a new box on every beat every thirty minutes. In 1910, the boxes contained telephone lines that allowed the officer to speak to the precinct sergeant. Today, more than 700 nonoperational call boxes can be found in Washington, D.C.[6]

The significance of the police subculture of call boxes is vividly depicted in Joseph Wambaugh's Bumper Morgan character in his novel and film, *The Blue Knight*. Officer William Morgan, or "Bumper," is of the old breed. He is a foot beat officer in Los Angeles. He maintains the peace in a rundown part of town, where he frequently solves problems associated with winos, pimps, prostitutes, junkies and thieves. His sergeant assigns him to drive a patrol car against his wishes. Bumper tells a character in the book that he never got a good call on his police radio. Bumper would rather visit his call boxes to conduct police business.[7]

There were many other inventions that have helped law enforcement agencies over the years. They include:

- Multi-shot pistol—Introduced by Samuel Colt in the 1850s.
- Adjustable handcuffs—Invented by W.V. Adams in 1862.
- Modern day polygraph—1930.
- Radar is introduced and used in law enforcement in 1948.
- The New Orleans Police Department uses a data processing machine that summarizes arrests and warrants in 1955.
- Side-handle baton—1958.
- First computer-aided dispatch—1960s.
- National Law Enforcement Telecommunications System—1966.
- FBI National Crime Information Center—1967.
- ATT introduces 911 for emergency calls to public safety—1968.
- The Taser was introduced to law enforcement in the 1960s.
- Body armor—1970s.
- Pepper spray—1982.[8]

## Who Is Using Technology?—PERF Survey

In 2012, the Police Executive Research Forum (PERF) published an in-depth study on the widespread use of technology in law enforcement.

> PERF is a professional organization of progressive chief executives of city, county and state law enforcement agencies. Since 1976, PERF has developed and published some of the leading literature in the law enforcement field. Public safety managers should take the time to visit the PERF website and read the various literature and comprehensive studies. For more information, visit www.policeforum.org.

The PERF study involved numerous interviews from over 100 police chiefs and leaders in the field. The study discussed the various experiences with technology and their views of the future of technology. The study also explains how technology makes law enforcement more efficient and benefits the community. Chuck Wexler, the executive director of PERF, wrote the following:[9]

**TABLE 2.1** Letter from PERF Executive Director Chuck Wexler

---

I don't think I'm guilty of overstatement in saying that policing in the United States has undergone a fundamental transformation in just the last 30 or 40 years. Policing today bears very little resemblance to the policing of the 1970s. For those of us who have been watching this happen day by day, the differences are simply stunning.

Back then, police officers thought they were doing a fine job if they responded quickly to calls for service and investigated crimes thoroughly. Today's police departments have given themselves a much larger and more important mission: working with their communities to solve crime problems, and in so doing, actually preventing crimes from being committed, and reducing crime rates.

What's more, today's police have proved that they can succeed in fulfilling this bold new mission. According to the FBI's Uniform Crime Reports, violent crime rates nationwide have declined 47 percent since the early 1990s.[1] In many cities, the changes have been even more dramatic. New York City had 536 homicides in 2010, compared to more than 2,200 in 1990. Washington, DC—once called the murder capital of the world—had 132 murders in 2010, compared to 479 in 1991.

Technology undoubtedly played a big role in helping police to bring crime rates down. CompStat would not have been possible without accurate, timely information about where and when crimes are being committed, and computers made it possible to gather crime data on a weekly or daily basis.

The police chiefs who participated in the PERF Executive Session on Technology have made it clear that we are just beginning to realize the impact that technology will have on the effectiveness of policing.

We expect to see a new Age of Technology in policing over the next 10 to 20 years, as the technologies that we currently are testing really take hold, and new technologies that we aren't even aware of yet become available.

Furthermore, police chiefs tell us that the economic downturn that began in 2008 is making policing technology more important, to the extent that it can help officers be more effective and efficient.

Because of tight budgets in all levels of government, many police departments are being forced to lay off officers or let attrition bring down their staffing levels over time. Some chiefs are reporting success in using various technologies to mitigate the effects of a shrinking workforce. At the same time, we know from another Critical Issues survey that police departments are cutting back on technology spending because of budget cuts.

Consider just one type of technology: license plate readers (LPRs). PERF's survey showed that 71 percent of responding agencies already have LPRs. But typically, an agency has only a few vehicles equipped with the devices, and they are used for certain limited purposes, such as finding stolen cars or vehicles that have multiple parking violations and can be booted or towed.

But our survey found that almost every police agency expects to acquire or increase their use of LPRs in coming years, and that five years from now, on average they expect to have 25 percent of their cars equipped with LPRs. Think of the implications of that for helping police to quickly locate wanted persons or vehicles that have been linked to serious crimes.

No doubt there will be challenges in the Age of Technology. For example, 80 percent of our survey respondents told us they expect to increase the practice of placing GPS devices on crime suspects' vehicles. But the U.S. Supreme Court is currently considering a case that will decide whether GPS tracking of cars violates the Fourth Amendment ban on unreasonable searches and seizures. So at the moment, we don't know whether this is one technology that will be restricted by the courts.

But I expect that the setbacks will be far outnumbered by the advances, especially as police find ways to use multiple technologies in concert with each other. For example, in Camden, N.J., where the police force was cut nearly in half due to a budget crisis, technology is a force-multiplier. Camden police are using Compstat to identify crime hot spots, and then directing patrol officers to drive through the hot-spot areas fairly often, in order to establish a police presence and reduce the opportunities for crime. In addition, GPS devices on the squad cars automatically provide data on how often each police car travels through a hot-spot area. If a hot spot is not getting enough attention in the form of patrol car visits, the computer can be set to automatically send a notification to officers or supervisors.

The challenges of the coming decade in policing will include identifying technologies that are most effective (and cost-effective) in reducing crime, and training officers to use those technologies properly.

---

[1]www.fbi/gov/about-us/cjis/ucr/crime-in-the-u.s./2010/crime-in-the-u.s.-2010/tables/10tbl01.xls

*Source*: Police Executive Research Forum. (2012). *How Are Innovations in Technology Transforming Policing?* Critical Issues in Policing Series. Washington, DC: PERF.

In 2011, PERF surveyed more than 70 law enforcement agencies about their current technologies, best practices and lessons learned. The following are the results of the survey.

### Predictive Policing

Seventy percent of the law enforcement agencies were already using some type of predictive policing program, which was defined as information technology used to predict or prevent crime. Ninety percent intended to increase the use of predictive policing in the next five years.[10]

### In-Car Video Technology

The survey also discussed in-car video recording technology. Twenty-nine percent of the agencies surveyed said that they have no in-car video recording technology. Twenty-five percent said that they do use in-car video recording technology. Thirty-six percent stated that they have "some" of their vehicles outfitted with in-car video recording technology.[11]

### Wireless Video Streaming

The ability to transmit video from major incidents was also discussed during the aforementioned study. One of the difficulties with this technology is the ability to transmit large data streams over commercial networks. The study recommended that Congress allocate a

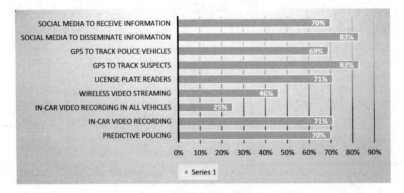

**FIGURE 2.3**   Percentages of Surveyed Agencies That Have Technologies.

*Source*: Police Executive Research Forum. (2012). *How Are Innovations in Technology Transforming Policing?* Critical Issues in Policing Series. Washington, DC: PERF.

special section of the radio network specifically for public safety agencies. This could increase the use of wireless video streaming. According to the study, 46 percent of the agencies use wireless video streaming in some form. Video streaming is used for investigations, traffic stops, officer safety, responding to calls and officer accountability. Some of the agencies surveyed also used this technology to monitor critical infrastructure areas or potential targets of terrorism. Most of the agencies stated that they intend to increase their ability to use wireless video streaming in the future.[12]

### License Plate Readers

Two-thirds of the agencies surveyed use license plate reader technology. Most of the license plate readers are affixed to patrol cars to they can scan nearby traffic hoping to find stolen vehicles as patrol officers drive around their respective patrol beats. The agencies that do not currently have license plate reader technology hope to acquire it within the next five years.[13]

### Global Positioning Systems (GPS)

Over 83 percent of the agencies use global positioning system (GPS) technology to track criminal suspects. Sixty-nine percent of the agencies use GPS technology to monitor law enforcement vehicles, although some law enforcement unions have concerns about tracking police vehicles.[14]

### Social Media

The vast majority of law enforcement agencies in the survey use social media (83 percent). Social media is used to share information with the public, receive crime tips and obtain investigative leads (criminal investigations). One of the most interesting figures is that

57 percent of the agencies have had issues with employees posting improper information or photographs on social media sites. More than half of the agencies have established policies on the use of social media.[15]

FYI, social media will also be discussed extensively in Unit 2.

## Recent Developments in Law Enforcement Technology

James Emett, communications, crime analysis, and technology supervisor for the Monrovia Police Department in California, explained how the development of communication technology has revolutionized law enforcement. "In 1975, the Monrovia Police Department bought a few portable radios that were huge and heavy. Limited range and dead spots in certain areas of the city made it difficult to communicate effectively. By the 1990s, we bought much smaller and lighter radios with a more effective communication radius. We had six radios: one for each officer on the shift. In 1993, Captain Roger Johnson, who later became chief of police, found the money to purchase a radio and charger for every officer on the department. This move greatly enhances officer safety and made individual officers responsible for the maintenance, damage or repair of the radio.

"In the 1980s, mobile dispatch terminal (MDT) systems became popular with large agencies such as the Los Angeles County Sheriff's Department and the Los Angeles Police Department. The MDT's improved communication and officer safety by reducing the amount of non-emergency radio chatter. Police officers now had the ability to receive calls for service and pertinent information while driving inside of their patrol cars. However, the system was limited because they were only able to access information from their own database. In the early 1990s, mobile dispatch computers (MDC) systems were introduced and the communication was greatly improved. The officer using the MDC in the police car could routinely access multiple data files and information sources. For example, if the officer stopped a driver for a traffic violation, they could obtain driving history and vehicle registration information from the Department of Motor Vehicles, criminal history from the Department of Justice, booking information and photographs from prior arrests within minutes. Possessing the ability to access multiple information files gave the officer additional tools to develop probable cause for a search and discover a more serious crime including false identity or lying to a peace officer."

However, one of the problems with this new technology was that officers soon became reliant on the technology and got frustrated when the MDCs were offline or not working. Nevertheless, the MDC has revolutionized modern law enforcement operations across the country.

Fast forward to the present day and consider the newest technology devices, including mobile tablets, personal data assistants, and cell phones, which basically have the same capabilities as a personal computer. This technology has improved our ability to investigate and solve crimes in the field. Retired Chief of Police Roger Johnson from the Monrovia Police

**FIGURE 2.4** Law Enforcement Mobile Data Computer Inside of a Patrol Unit.

*Source*: Courtesy of the San Bernardino County Sheriff's Department.

Department states, "In 1987, I was a detective investigating a case involving a former military member who was suspected of possessing a stolen and illegal military ordnance. My investigation revealed that the suspect had mental issues. Detective Don Lacher assisted me with the investigation. In those days, we did things the old-fashioned way. I sat at my desk and typed the search warrant on a typewriter. I drove to the courthouse and waited for my turn to meet with a judge. After the judge signed the search warrant, I drove to the police station, gathered some detectives and served the warrant. This process took hours to complete.

"At the scene, we seized a lot of evidence, including firearms, a LAWS rocket, mortar shells, hand grenades, dynamite, firearms, blasting caps and other contraband. Assisting detectives photographed the evidence with real film, taped handwritten evidence cards on every item, and someone prepared a handwritten evidence inventory. I arrested the suspect and transported him to the station for booking.

"At the police station, a detective had to run the serial numbers on the firearms to determine if they were stolen. If I was investigating the same case in 2014, the technological advances would have allowed me to process the crime scene more efficiently with less staff. Utilizing a mobile tablet or smartphone, I could have used one device to run serial numbers, photograph the evidence and barcode the evidence with reader software. All of the information would have been digitally entered in our department's record management system."

Technological advances have greatly improved the efficiency of crime scene investigation. Homicide Detective Steven Lankford of the Los Angeles County Sheriff's Department said the following: "Our homicide bureau prepares search warrants on a daily basis. Advances in smartphone technology allow us to write paperless search warrants in the field. Many times we arrive at a residence to investigate a murder. We discover the suspect might have an expectation of privacy because they lived at the residence with the victim. Under California law, we must first obtain a search warrant before we can process the scene. Any homicide detective can prepare a warrant on a PDA, laptop or smartphone, email it to the judge, obtain a signature and email back a lawful search warrant. You can imagine the amount of time we save, especially if we are investigating a case in a remote area of the county."

James Emett agrees. "For the last two decades, the push in law enforcement has been to go paperless. At the Monrovia Police Department, we are almost there. Private companies like Spillman Technologies manage our CAD (computer aided dispatch) system, which includes barcode technology for evidence and inmate tracking."

Law enforcement evidence technicians can process, catalog and store evidence more efficiently using barcode readers, which helps maintain a chain of custody for all evidence. Just like using the barcode system in grocery store chains, law enforcement barcode systems allow personnel to attach a barcode to the evidence, scan the barcode and the information is entered into a property management system. The technology also allows personnel to assign a specific area or location within the property room for storage and accountability. According to Sergeant Kasey DeCoud from the San Bernardino County Sheriff's Department, barcode technology and advances in property management systems have saved hundreds of thousands of dollars in staff time alone. San Bernardino County is the largest county in the United States and the department has sub-stations that are over four hours away from the central property room. Law enforcement personnel can easily use the barcode and property management software to enter and track evidence. This allows management personnel to monitor and track all evidence in the county. The technology is easy to use and requires very little training, which is a plus for large law enforcement agencies like San Bernardino County.

The same technology is used to identify and track inmates in our system, says James Emett. After a suspect is booked into the computerized booking system, the inmate can be tracked using a barcode on their wristband. The wristband also has a photograph of the inmate to prevent inmates from switching identities.

## Technology Spotlight—Spillman Technologies

Lance Clark, president and CEO of Spillman Technologies, has worked with and provided innovative and reliable integrated public safety technology software to law enforcement, corrections and fire departments for over 30 years.

Sarah Huizingh, marketing manager for Spillman Technologies, added that their company helps public safety professionals work safely and efficiently. Spillman is a proven leader of robust records management systems (RMS), CAD, mobile data, crime analysis and CompStat software, connecting vital department data and freeing officers to improve the quality of life in their communities. Advanced technology like Spillman's has helped police managers keep pace with information demands from the public, city or county staff and elected officials.

In the early 1990s, the Monrovia Police Department used Spillman's database technology to solve a homicide based on a tattoo and partial license plate. The technology saved hundreds of hours in staff time because the database was able to process the information quickly and timely. Even less serious events requiring data analysis can be just as important as solving serious crimes. Law enforcement managers know the importance of solving quality of life issues within a neighborhood. Spillman software enhances the abilities of law enforcement managers to address hot spots that eventually garner the interest of local elected officials.

According to James Emett, the Spillman crime-mapping feature is one of the most important tools available to law enforcement. Emett's department started to get complaints about homeless issues, drug and alcohol use, thefts, fights and other disturbances at a nearby park. Police officers worked on the issues and identified approximately seventeen individuals who were the main troublemakers. Utilizing police and community resources, the department solved the problem. However, at a future city council meeting, the chief of police needed information about the issue in order to brief the city council. Using Spillman software, the department was able to supply the chief with the required statistics, including the types of arrests, citations, law enforcement contact, and methods used to solve the problem within thirty minutes. The chief was able to successfully present the findings of the issues, explain the strategy utilized to attack the problem and the methods used to measure success. Emett explained that in the days prior to technology companies like Spillman, this process would have taken weeks to complete because numerous employees would have to hand search the data to collect the information.

This situation described above illustrates the way police managers can study crime trends and nuisance complaints to solve problems at the neighborhood level. Spillman's intelligence-led software allows law enforcement managers to make better decisions, monitor trends and view changes in crime rates. The CompStat Dashboard feature allows personnel to view crime data and spot trends without running multiple reports. Real-time data in the CompStat software provides the most accurate statistics possible. Utilizing the Pin Mapping module, the operator can visualize trends and identify strategies for reducing crimes by plotting incidents on an electronic pin map. This feature also allows the manager to see spatial relationships between incidents and suspects and, in turn, allows for easy access to records for additional information.[16]

## Chapter Summary

In conclusion, law enforcement agencies, big, medium, and small will continue to grapple with applying technology to enhance their operations, identify criminals, solve crimes and resolve related quality of life issues. Hampering these efforts is the lack of funding sources. Technology advances can be very costly and many agencies compete for the same government grants. A related issue is the training of law enforcement personnel who use the new technologies. Law enforcement agencies currently have difficulties training officers in other areas such as firearms and use-of-force tactics. Technology presents another problem. It is always changing; thus law enforcement agencies must change with it. This chapter summarized the various types of technology being used today and how the technology of the future will impact law enforcement. As illustrated by the PERF study, in-car video recording, wireless video streaming, license plate readers, global positioning systems (GPS) and social media technology are currently being used across the country. Many agencies plan on expanding these critical technology products because they benefit not only law enforcement, but also other stakeholders within the criminal justice system. Law enforcement managers must continue to evaluate and utilize technology to better provide services to the community at large. In future chapters, you will become acquainted with emerging technologies that impact the criminal justice field.

## Key Words or Terminology

| | | |
|---|---|---|
| Industrial Revolution | policing principles | Sir Robert Peel |
| police communications | CAD | smart technology |
| paperless systems | in-car video recording | social media |
| predictive policing | GPS | license plate readers |

## Discussion Questions

1. Compare and contrast how technology in the criminal justice field has specifically impacted law enforcement organizations. How has the technology helped solve problems? Has the use of technology caused problems in police organizations? If so, please provide examples.
2. What are the advantages and disadvantages of having a paperless record management system?
3. Identify strategies that can be used to help solve quality of life issues by using technology.

## Notes

1  Montagna, J. (2014). *The Industrial Revolution.* Yale-New Haven Teachers Institute. Retrieved from www.yale.edu/ynhti/curriculum/units/1981/2/81.02.06.x.html.
2  Ibid.
3  Sullivan, J. (1971). *Introduction to police science.* New York: McGraw Hill.
4  Ibid.
5  (2014). *History of police cars.* Spillman Technologies. Retrieved from www.spillman.com/history-police-cars.
6  (2012). *History of the Washington, D.C. police and fire call boxes.* The House History Man. Retrieved from www.househistoryman.blogspot.com/2012/02.
7  Wambaugh, J. (1972). *The blue night.* New York: Little Brown & Company.
8  Bellis, M. (2015). *Police technology and forensic science.* Retrieved from www.inventors.about.com/od/fstartinventions/a/forensic.htm.
9  (2012). *How are innovations in technology transforming policing?* Critical Issues in Policing Series. Washington, DC: PERF.
10  Ibid.
11  Ibid.
12  Ibid.
13  Ibid.
14  Ibid.
15  Ibid.
16  (2015). *Spillman software.* Spillman Technologies. Retrieved from www.spillman.com/products/.

# 3

# THE COURT SYSTEM

"People are stunned to hear that one company has data files on 185 million Americans."

—*Ralph Nader*

## Learning Objectives

After reading this chapter, the student will:

*   Have an understanding of the constitutional amendments that are affected by technology.
*   Define and evaluate the role of technology related to the criminal justice system and how technology can improve the overall efficiency of the court process.
*   Articulate how emerging technology can revolutionize the court process by using innovative ideas that have an impact on the judicial system and the community.

## Introduction

In this chapter, we review the role of the courts in the criminal justice system and explore the ways technology has improved efficiency and streamlined the entire process. The judicial process is complicated in that technology was not relevant when our founding fathers created the blueprint for our justice system. Technology has created significant challenges to the Fourth Amendment. In the past, the need for a search warrant on a cell phone or whether you could electronically submit a police report was not an issue. The technology did not exist. We examine the historical elements of various constitutional amendments and their effects on technology. Surveillance technology and its relationship to the court system are discussed because they have a direct impact on public safety. Finally, we also review the innovative technology related to the court system, including kiosks and virtual courtrooms.

## The Constitution and Technology

The three components of the criminal justice system include law enforcement, courts and corrections. Although the three entities operate independently, they are connected subsets that depend on each other for accomplishing justice.

The Bill of Rights, also called the first ten amendments of the U.S. Constitution, form the foundation for the courts to dispense justice, free the innocent and punish the guilty. The 1789 ratification of the Bill of Rights by the House of Representatives paved the way for the people to be protected from injustice and tyranny imposed by the recently defeated English empire. For the next 200 years, the federal and state criminal courts systems have wrestled primarily with four of the amendments in the Bill of Rights.

The Fourth Amendment protects the public from unreasonable searches and seizures. Search and seizure has been heavily litigated and contested by the courts. The court system, especially at the appellate and supreme court levels, render ever-changing case laws that restrict when law enforcement can search absent a warrant, arrest and detain suspects and seize evidence. Case law further establishes the confines of probable cause for detention, interview and interrogation and the application of constitutional safeguards to protect the rights of the accused.

The Fifth Amendment protects the accused against double jeopardy. Defendants cannot be tried for the same offense twice. Defendants are also protected from self-incrimination. They cannot be forced to give testimony against themselves. Police interrogation of suspects has become a hotbed of controversy in the criminal justice system. Law enforcement is sometimes mistrusted by the public and news of police misconduct has changed the way law enforcement preserves proof of self-incrimination during interrogations. For example, juries and judges are suspicious of confessions by defendants unless their statement is on tape or video. Without such evidence, the defense has the ability to attack the credibility of the arresting officer and establish reasonable doubt. In this day and age, very few circumstances exist for not taping a confession of a suspect. Most law enforcement agencies have interview rooms equipped with videotaping technology or their officers carry handheld recording devices.

The Sixth Amendment guarantees the accused of several vital protections during the trial process. Those include the rights to a speedy and public trial, to a trial by jury, to confront witnesses and compel witnesses to appear in court, and the right to a legal defense. The right to a speedy trial will be linked to technology and other factors later in this chapter.

The Eighth Amendment protects the accused against unreasonable bail and prohibits the rendering of cruel and unusual punishment. This amendment is the one most litigated by opponents of capital punishment. A novice or a student in the criminal justice system might ask: How does the Bill of Rights impact the relationship between law enforcement and the courts? What factors might slow the process for the accused?

### Moving Through the System

Many law enforcement agencies and district attorneys rely on the paper method to file criminal cases. Imagine you are a detective at a law enforcement agency. You arrive to work on Monday morning and discover you have three suspects in jail for separate drug offenses.

The clock is ticking. You have until Wednesday to complete your investigation and submit the cases to the district attorney or the suspects can either be released for lack of evidence or further investigation. The alternative is that the district attorney will file criminal charges. If charges are filed, the defendants will appear in front of a magistrate and be formally arraigned. At the arraignment, the defendants are either released pending trial or held on bail.

Perhaps you read the arresting officer's crime report and then conducted a preliminary drug test on the substances. Next, you arrange to send the evidence to the crime lab for final testing. If the preliminary test is positive, you have enough evidence to file charges. You review the suspect's criminal history to see if they qualify for drug diversion or you might cultivate them to become an informant. You interview the suspects to identify factors establishing the legal requirement of dominion and control. Depending on the factors of possession, you might have drug containers that could be processed for fingerprints. After conducting your investigation, you write your follow-up report. Based on the aforementioned information, you might elevate the charges to intent to distribute or transportation of a controlled substance.

When you complete all your work, you arrange to have your suspect transported to court on either Tuesday or Wednesday morning. You then drive to the courthouse and sit in line with other detectives until it is your turn to meet with a district attorney. The district attorney may ask you questions about the circumstances of each case, discuss the criminal background of the suspect and then decide on a course of action. The district attorney completes the filing paperwork and hands you the packet. You march down to the clerk's office and file the paperwork just in time for the arraignment. Each day, the same detective or court officer might find themselves repeating this process. Legal time constraints demand that those arrested take priority. The same detective still has to find the time to conduct investigations on other cases.

The experiences outlined in the scenario are typical for law enforcement organizations across the country. Felony offenses will always take center stage, but what about misdemeanors, traffic infractions, and civil cases? The court system still needs to adjudicate these minor issues. Granted, the example provided is very low-tech, so what factors have led to seeking innovative changes to improve the legal process?

In current times, the downturn in the economy has forced many public agencies, including the courts, to find practical solutions to improve efficiency and cut costs. The downturn in the economy has sent many public agencies scrambling for innovative methods to save scarce resources. The California court system is no different and has been examining how the use of technology can unclog a burdening caseload.

## Emerging Trends in the Court System

Lieutenant Jaime Alfaro from the Monrovia, California, Police Department is a recognized expert in emerging trends impacting the state court system. His Command College study entitled: "With the Decrease in California Court Resources, How Will Technology Impact the Preservation of the Sixth Amendment by 2020?" developed innovative ideas to improve court efficiency. Command College is an executive training program offered to law enforcement and is hosted by the California Commission on Peace Officer Standards and Training (POST).

Students research and write a "future study" project on a topic relevant to the field. The project is a futures study of an emerging issue, which helps the industry plan for possible scenarios that impact the topic. The students host a nominal group technique (NGT) panel of experts to identify the top emerging trends impacting the issue. The final study culminates into a journal article published by the Command College and POST. All future studies are available to police departments grappling with like issues impacting their organizations and communities.

Lieutenant Alfaro starts his article by examining the link between police departments receiving revenues from the courts in the form of traffic citations, court fines, and assessments. In California, law enforcement agencies receive a percentage of the revenues from these sources. Departments prepare their future budgets by analyzing the revenue trends from the previous years. Based on those projections, law enforcement agencies set performance goals for programs such as traffic enforcement. If the agencies are also receiving grant money from the National Traffic Safety Administration (NTSA), performance goals in the form of traffic citations, impaired driving arrests, and traffic accident reduction are directly tied to the adjudication of traffic-related offenses by the court system.[1]

Economic downfalls have a significant impact on the court system. Budget cuts are inevitable. In California, the courts are managed by the Administrative Office of the Courts (AOC). Deficient levels reported by the AOC are alarming. The first level of cuts resulted in a 24 percent reduction of staff in Los Angeles County. The state also cut $1 billion from the court budget. In 2012, the AOC closed 56 courtrooms and then merged Juvenile Traffic Court into the adult Traffic Court system. The closing caused significant delays in criminal, civil, family court and unlawful detainer cases.[2]

In 2013, the AOC closed ten courthouses, resulting in a drastic reduction of court generated revenues to law enforcement agencies. The public is suffering as well from the courthouse closings. Adjudication of divorce cases jumped from an average of five months to a year and a half. Drivers contesting a traffic citation can wait as long as fourteen months for their day in court. Homeowners wishing to evict deadbeat tenants can expect the legal process to take as long as a year that could result in them losing their rental. Lieutenant Alfaro's research concluded that the courts and law enforcement need to invest in technology to streamline justice and efficiently handle revenue return to public agencies.[3]

In 2012, the Barstow Superior Court was closed. The courthouse administered justice from the high desert communities in and around Barstow and all the way to the Nevada border. So, a violator who wished to contest the ticket and the issuing officer were required to travel to the San Bernardino County seat to appear in court. Imagine the time and monetary expense to the violator and the law enforcement agency, when you consider round trip travel time could be as long as six hours. Further imagine the scope of the issue when you consider the number of California Highway Patrol officers and San Bernardino County Sheriff deputies and the number of citations those officers issue in a month or year. The impact on drivers and law enforcement organizations is staggering considering all the factors.

## Innovative Technologies at Work

Alfaro states that the use of current technology exists to improve both efficiency and the timely administration of justice for traffic and other cases. The implementation of scanning devices for driver license and registration access is one such example of current technology. Although expensive at more than $5,000 each, the devices are currently in use by law enforcement agencies in California. Traffic violator information is downloaded into the hand-held device and electronically sent to the court. The violator leaves the stop with a ticket printed from the device. Widespread use of these devices could eliminate hand-written citations and the middleman needed to process written citations with the courts. Courts and law enforcement agencies have the ability to reduce their own staff or private contractors who process handwritten citations the old-fashioned way by adopting scanner technology. This technology replaces the paper system and is bound to be more efficient and less expensive.[4]

The Sixth Amendment or speedy trial doctrine could jeopardize the future of court fines returning to law enforcement agencies. The Alfaro study recommended that the court system evaluate the implementation of court kiosks to better service the public. Using handheld scanners that automatically upload traffic offender information to the courts would improve the court's ability to clear cases from the calendar. Kiosks have the potential to reduce overhead in the courts and improve customer service at the same time.

Currently, Los Angeles County courts contract with a third party vendor for $750,000 to extract data from traffic citations and enter them into the court computer system. California has 58 counties and the AOC spends $40 million each year to process citations by hand.[5]

Texas has already implemented kiosks to streamline their courts. In 2012, the courthouse in San Antonio, Texas, opened a kiosk to the public. According to Presiding Judge John Bull, kiosks allow the violators to talk in real-time video with a county clerk first to determine their request. Next, a judge appears on the screen and conducts the legal business. Violators can ask for a continuance if they desire a trial, conduct a probation hearing, plead guilty to a traffic offense, or request traffic school. The violator has an option to pay their fine by credit or debit card. The court provides a copy of the court order or receipt by email or by standard mail. The system cost $100,000 and has been received well by the public. No longer are offenders required to drive to the courthouse, locate or pay for parking and wait in long lines to resolve their issue. According to Judge Bull, his teenage son suggested that an application be created allowing such business to be conducted by phone, tablet, or laptop.[6]

In 2012, the San Bernardino County court system began researching the feasibility of installing court kiosks. The County of San Bernardino in California is the largest geographical county in the United States. Serving over two million people and spanning 20,000 square miles, this vast area stretches from Los Angeles and Orange County borders, east to Arizona and north to Nevada.[7]

In 2012, the San Bernardino County Court system began a program to more effectively offer technological services to their residents. Under the TURBO Program, online forms preparation services allowed customers to submit applications for civil collections, domestic violence order requests, family law issues, guardianships, small claims, and unlawful detainers (evictions) notices. No longer do customers have to wait in long lines at the courthouse for the aforementioned legal issues. The San Bernardino Court program demonstrates how courts can better manage human resources and improve overall services by the County.[8]

In September 2012, San Bernardino County installed kiosks in county structures to allow customers to tap into a variety of services. Six self-service kiosks located in three offices allow residents to conduct business with the Department of Child Services. Customers had the ability to access the kiosks to obtain general information about services, check and monitor cases already in the system, and parents could make child support payments electronically. In 2013, 4,461 customers used the kiosks to conduct legal business. Later in the year, the National Association of Child Support Services presented an achievement award to the San Bernardino County Department of Child Services for innovative services.[9]

In 2013, San Bernardino County also launched a similar program to streamline traffic and non-traffic infractions. Using the kiosk system around the county, the public can reserve a court date and avoid the long lines at the courthouse. This service allows judicial officers to move cases quickly through the justice system. Violators can also make payments for fines levied by the hearing officer at the kiosks.[10]

### The Future—Virtual Trials

The Alfaro study also makes a valid argument for the use of virtual trials. For many Americans, receiving a traffic citation is their only negative contact with law enforcement. Most of those violators admit their violation and want to avoid the embarrassment of a court appearance. Some would rather just pay the fine whereas others wish to attend traffic school. Attending traffic school is desirable to avoid increases in their vehicle insurance.[11]

Many courts around the nation currently utilize streaming video to conduct arraignments in criminal cases. Arraignment is the first legal appearance of a defendant in court. Defendants appear before a magistrate and are advised of their constitutional rights. They are formally notified of the criminal charges they are facing and bail issues are addressed. The same technology could be utilized to conduct trials for traffic and minor non-traffic offenses. Common non-traffic offenses include animal offenses, public health violations, building codes, and other minor crimes. Certainly, conveniently located kiosks could fit the bill or violators who have the technology could appear in virtual court using smart phones or tablets. Law enforcement officers could literally appear from their station or home. The judge could conduct court hearings using the same technology. Using retired magistrates to conduct these virtual hearings part-time could save money and unclog crowded court rooms. This arrangement is in the violator's best interest too. Offenders would avoid taking time off of work, the cost of transportation and parking at the courthouse and long waits in the courthouse. Paying fines, granting a future court date for a trial or other legal matters could be easily handled too.[12]

### Right to Privacy and Technology

The ability to conduct surveillance on criminals is paramount for any law enforcement agency. Surveillance is a technique that has been used for years. Common forms include video cameras, wiretapping and other forms of electronic monitoring. Wiretapping has been used extensively since 1928. Federal agents use this technology to collect evidence against individuals suspected of criminal activity. The authority to use wiretapping has been vetted by the U.S. Supreme Court. This method is effective and government agencies have started to monitor other forms of technology including emails and Internet websites. The entire process is protected by law.[13]

Recently, law enforcement agencies have started to use another form of surveillance by placing video cameras in public areas. The use of video cameras and the constant monitoring by government officials has created court battles on the proper use of technology. Many people believe that their right to privacy under the constitution has been violated. The American Civil Liberties Union stated in federal court, "The government's new surveillance programs have infiltrated most of the communications technologies we come to rely on."[14]

The Maine American Civil Liberties Union (MCLU) stated the following: "Surveillance cameras have a chilling effect on freedom of movement because people behave differently when they are under surveillance. In a free society, we have the right to be left alone unless we are hurting someone or breaking the law. All people in America are presumed innocent and law-abiding, but these surveillance cameras turn that presumption of innocence on its head into a presumption that we are all guilty."[15]

The National Security Agency (NSA) is one of the main agencies utilizing technology programs to monitor potential criminal activity. Personnel at the NSA collect millions of records from American citizens including phone data, emails, photos and Internet searches of foreign nationals overseas. The data sorting is done by computers instead of actual employees of the NSA. This ensures the privacy of our citizens. All non-relevant data is destroyed.[16] The NSA collects data from cell phones, house phones, personal computers and from technology companies including Apple, Facebook and Google. This process allows the government to monitor activity.[17]

As technology continues to evolve, the court system must balance society's right to privacy versus the needs of public safety. This controversy is apparent with the Federal Bureau of Investigation's (FBI) attempt to retrieve data from a cell phone for one of the terrorists involved in the San Bernardino (California) killings. Does a terrorist have a right to privacy? Technology companies are not willing to unlock the encryption codes that would allow law enforcement to view phone records despite having a search warrant. They state that their phone system and applications are protected. Law enforcement agencies believe the need to locate criminals and prevent potential terrorist activities from occurring trumps their privacy rights. The court system is right in the middle of this controversy and will one day decide on this complicated matter.

However, despite the controversy with surveillance programs, this type of technology has an impact on law enforcement and the court system. It helps investigators do their jobs and prevents or reduces crime in our communities. For example, a video camera surveillance system was installed in the city of Chicago in 2008. Cameras were installed at various locations throughout the city and officers monitored suspicious activity. The system was an immediate success. Serious crime declined by 17 percent and quality of life crimes declined by 46 percent. Areas without the cameras saw an increase of 151 percent.[18]

The aforementioned controversy with surveillance technology has a direct impact on the court system. The courts have to monitor technology and ensure that the constitutional rights of all citizens are protected, while allowing and trusting law enforcement personnel to do their jobs correctly. Public safety managers, specifically in law enforcement, must continue to monitor this type of technology and ensure that it is not abused. Technology has its place, but not at the risk of violating someone's constitutional rights.

## Chapter Summary

It might take years and increased funding to launch the courts into a paperless system. Across the nation, the three components of the criminal system (law enforcement, courts, and corrections) are still struggling with budget shortfalls. Crimes are still committed, traffic violators are still receiving tickets, and civil cases need to be adjudicated. The answer is to use technology effectively and to explore ways of using emerging technology to increase efficiency and at the same time satisfy the public. Public safety managers must take the lead to explore and capture emerging technologies that reduce cost and improve efficiency in their organizations.

Unless steps are taken now to unclog the courts, public safety managers will be faced with future legal challenges for Sixth Amendment violations. Defense lawyers and violators who represent themselves will use the Sixth Amendment as a shield when countering minor legal action. In reality they have nothing to lose. The losers will be law enforcement and the courts depending on fines from violators to meet their budget goals, hold violators accountable, and reduce traffic collisions by vigorous enforcement of the vehicle code. The court system must also deal with the barrage of technology innovations that will affect the privacy of all citizens. Surveillance programs have a place in law enforcement, but public safety managers must continue to monitor activities and ensure that the quest for evidence doesn't interfere with the law of the land.

## Key Words or Terminology

| | | |
|---|---|---|
| Bill of Rights | criminal justice system | law enforcement |
| courts | corrections | search and seizure |
| arrest | detention | district attorney |
| bail | magistrate | scanning devices |
| kiosks | virtual trials | evidence |
| probable cause | defense attorney | constitution |

## Discussion Questions

1. Compare and contrast how courts in your jurisdiction use current or emerging technology to improve efficiency.
2. Define and evaluate how you would reduce costs by instituting ideas mentioned in this chapter. Are there other options not discussed that could cut costs but still maintain efficiency in the courts?
3. Should fines from violators be used by law enforcement agencies? Is this a conflict of interest or a legitimate use of resources?
4. Review the use and type of surveillance technology at your local law enforcement agency. Do you see any issues with privacy and does the technology create any controversial issues within your local community?

## Notes

1 Alfaro, J. (2012). *With the decrease in California court resources, how will technology impact the preservation of the Sixth Amendment by 2020?* Sacramento, CA: California Commission on Peace Officers Standards and Training.

2 Ibid.

3 Ibid.

4 Ibid.

5 Ibid.

6 (2014, January 22). *Video kiosk tested to handle tickets, citations.* KSAT ABC 12. Retrieved from www.sanantonio/gov/courts/about/hours/kioskcourt.aspx.

7 (2014). *State and county quick facts.* Washington, DC: U.S. Census Bureau.

8 (2014). *San Bernardino courts-TURBO courts, online form reservations.* County of San Bernardino. Retrieved from www.sbcounty.gov/cao/countywire/?p=1292.

9 (2014). *Government works: Kiosks make it easy.* County of San Bernardino. Retrieved from www.sbcounty.gov/cao/countywire/?p-1292.

10 Ibid.

11 Alfaro, *With the decrease in California court resources.*

12 Ibid.

13 Carmichael, J. (2013). How surveillance has evolved in the United States. *Popular Science.* Retrieved from www.popsci.com/technology.

14 ACLU. (2014). *Rein in the surveillance state.* Retrieved from www.aclu.org/rein-surveillance-state.

15 ACLU. (2015). *MCLU supports ban on new police surveillance technology.* Retrieved from www.aclu.org/news/mclu-supports-ban-new-surveillance-technology#comment-o.

16 Dozier, K. (2013). National Security Agency: Inside the organization at center of surveillance controversy. *Huffington Post.* Retrieved from www.huffington post.com/2013/06/09/national-security-agency.

17 Ibid.

18 Harris, C. (2009). Getting an eyeful. *American City and County.* Retrieved from www.americancityandcounty.com/pubsafe/pros-cons-camera-surveillance-2000911.

# 4

# CORRECTIONS

"America is the land of the second chance—and when
the gates of the prison open, the path ahead should lead
to a better life."

—*George W. Bush*

## Learning Objectives

After reading this chapter, the student will:

- Have a basic understanding of contemporary and emerging issues in corrections.
- Explain the main trends impacting the field of corrections.
- Define the basic technology terminology used in corrections.
- Articulate the main advantages and disadvantages of using technology in corrections.
- Understand the role of a correctional manager in the evaluation of technology in a jail
  or prison.

## Introduction

In this chapter, we explore current and emerging trends in corrections. Similar to law
enforcement, correctional facilities utilize technology for a variety of reasons. This includes
the tracking of inmates on supervised release programs and within jail or prison settings.
Correctional managers will understand the importance of technology when evaluating
operational needs and preventing future litigation against a municipality, county or state
government agency. We also examine the current state of affairs in the field of corrections,
which includes prison realignment issues and prison overcrowding. A case study on prison
realignment is discussed to illustrate the way the California Department of Corrections
and Rehabilitation and local law enforcement agencies are coping with the mass transfer of
inmates to the county jails and community supervision entities.

We explain how corrections fits into the criminal justice system and how technology can be used to effectively monitor offenders in a community setting and improve the operational efficiency of a jail or prison.

## What Is Corrections?

The field of corrections is the third prong of the criminal justice system. The two main responsibilities of corrections are to incarcerate and rehabilitate offenders. At the federal level, the United States has prisons specifically for those persons convicted and imprisoned for federal violations. Throughout the nation, states maintain and control large prisons for offenders serving a lengthy amount of time. County sheriff's departments and some large metropolitan police departments house inmates in local jails.

In the United States, the main function of a sheriff is to maintain a jail system on behalf of all law enforcement agencies within the county. Many times, the sheriff's department is the largest law enforcement agency in the county. They also provide other services such as the patrol of unincorporated areas, crime scene and forensic services, specialized investigations, aviation, and special response teams.

Local police departments also house inmates for a short period of time. Typically, police departments will hold inmates that are arrested for misdemeanors and will be cited and released. If an inmate is arrested for a felony, he or she may be processed first at a local police department and then transported to a county jail for housing.

The majority of inmates in county or local jails are pre-trial, which means they are awaiting their day in court. Regardless of an inmate's status within any jail or prison,

**FIGURE 4.1** California Institution for Women (California).

*Source*: Wikimedia Commons. Retrieved from www.commons.wikimedia.org/wiki/file:californiainstitution-forwomen.jpg. Public domain.

they have certain rights based upon the state penal code or local standards. In California, county jails are guided by Title 15 of the Code of Regulations, which provides standards for housing, meals, medical, recreation, visitation, and other services.[1] County sheriffs often have policy and procedure manuals that clearly define best practices and rules that govern the correctional staff. For example, in most county jail facilities, inmates are counted several times a day, and inmates are also booked using a jail information management system (JIMS).

All of the aforementioned areas have a technology component. The jail information management system is a large database that stores pertinent information about each inmate including booking offense, court dates, demographic information, classification status and housing history. The relationship between local, state and federal correctional facilities is also important because technology links them all together. Fingerprints, photographs and charge information is captured at each level and eventually stored in federal systems like the Integrated Automated Fingerprint Identification System (IAFIS). Some states also capture DNA samples inside of their local jails and submit the sample to state or federal databases. The samples can be used to help solve cold cases when a new crime scene sample is matched against the DNA system. The concept of storing and sharing data allows other agencies to search for data when necessary because inmates (suspects) are often transitory and do not stay in the same jurisdiction. Information obtained from correctional facilities can also be used to help identify people and solve crimes.

## Current and Emerging Trends

The field of corrections is constantly changing for a variety of reasons. Before we can discuss how technology plays a role in corrections, we must review the latest trends and challenges within the corrections community. Issues like prison realignment, supervised release protocols, legislation initiatives and crime trends all play a significant part in the evaluation and implementation of technology. So what are the current and emerging trends facing the field of corrections today?

In the early 2000s, the inmate population in local, state and federal correctional facilities continued to grow at an alarming rate. Legislation like "three strikes and you are out" has helped keep inmates in custody for longer periods of time. Local and state governments have had to spend billions of dollars on new prisons or jails throughout the country. Many agencies received grant funding to build new jails or expand existing ones just to keep up with the growing inmate population.

Additionally, recent court rulings on overcrowding and the lack of medical/mental health care for inmates have taken a toll on correctional institutions. The courts imposed sanctions and essentially forced facilities to comply or face lengthy and costly legal battles. Correctional facilities were forced to remodel older facilities and add additional personnel in order to provide sufficient supervision or medical care. However, many local and state governments were also grappling with the downturn in the economy along with their counterparts in courts, law enforcement and fire services. The lack of funds made adding new personnel or undergoing capital improvement projects very difficult. Other factors driving these trends are:

- Finding innovative methods to electronically track offenders.
- Establishing remote check-in parameters for probationers.
- Providing medical care for offenders with special needs or the aging inmate population.
- Access to rehabilitation and education programs.
- Issues with classifications, especially high-risk offenders.
- Americans with Disabilities Act (ADA) compliance in correctional settings.
- Online visitation.
- Statistical or data gathering.
- Video surveillance systems.
- Inmate accountability (facility count) systems.
- Security control systems that include touchscreen monitors.

To mitigate these factors, correctional managers have utilized technology to effectively manage operations, improve efficiency and address the court sanctions. Even when faced with budget shortfalls, technology upgrades can and will save money in the long run.

However, in the last five years, some correctional facilities have observed a downward trend in inmate population. So what is driving the declining prison population and how is the decline impacting local communities and law enforcement? The U.S. Department of Justice reports that in 2012, there were nearly seven million adult offenders in local, state and federal jails. This includes those on supervised release programs. The two types of inmates in supervised release programs cited in the report were on parole or probation. Traditionally, those on parole are felons and have served time in state prisons. Probation is traditionally for offenders convicted of misdemeanors and they serve their time in county jails.[2]

In 2012, there were 6,937,600 inmates in custody in the United States. By the end of the year, that number was reduced by 51,000 inmates. This was the fourth year in a row that the inmate population decreased. In the same year, 1 in 35 adults in the United States resided in a prison or jail or some type of supervised release program. This equals 2.9 percent of the U.S. annual population.[3]

Then in 2011, the State of California was forced by federal courts to enact the Public Safety Realignment Act of 2011. This act alone pushed thousands of inmates out of prisons and jails and shortened their parole times.[4] To better understand this issue and how these trends affect technology, let's explore and review the specifics with prison realignment.

## Case Study—AB109 and the California Experience

Timeline

- 2006: Governor Arnold Schwarzenegger transferred 8,000 prison inmates to out-of-state prisons to ease overcrowding.
- 2008: A class action lawsuit is filed against the state for unconstitutional care for sick and mentally ill inmates.

- 2009: The court rules that California state prisons are overcrowded and in violation of constitutional standards for medical and mental health services.
- 2009: Governor Schwarzenegger signs into law SB678, the California Corrections Act. Ten thousand inmates are transferred to prisons in Arizona, Mississippi and Oklahoma.
- 2010: The U.S. Supreme Court rules that overcrowded conditions in the California prison system are so severe that they violate the Eighth Amendment on cruel and unusual punishment.
- 2011: Governor Jerry Brown signs into law AB109, the Criminal Justice Realignment Plan.[5]

Realignment in California became the state strategy for reducing the inmate population. The idea was designed so that felons who met certain criteria could be released back into the communities where they lived. The plan was structured to allow the felons to be supervised by county probation officers instead of state parole agents. Offenders released to community supervision programs had to remain on probation from six months to a year. The length of time was left up to each county. Los Angeles County decided that under the plan, probationers would remain on probation for twelve months.[6]

In the first year of the program, 30,000 state inmates were released to the supervision of probation departments statewide. Over 12,000 were released back into Los Angeles County alone. Another important factor in realignment was the reclassification of certain felony convictions. The reclassification of certain crimes allowed state prison inmates to serve their time in county jails as opposed to state prison. State officials believed that realignment would effectively reduce prison overcrowding, comply with the court ruling and save money.[7]

**FIGURE 4.2** Pelican Bay State Prison (California).

*Source*: Wikimedia Commons. Retrieved from www.commons.wikimedia.org/wiki/file:pelicanbaystateprison. jpg. Public domain.

Prison realignment focused on criminal sentencing, punishment and community corrections. To be eligible for the program, offenders had to be convicted of a non-violent, non-serious and non-sexual offense. Realignment also required that the offender serve their supervised release in the county where the offense occurred. The flaw in the program was that they only considered the current conviction. They did not take into consideration that inmates had prior convictions that were violent and dangerous.

Under the authority of 1170(h) of the California Penal Code, 500 crimes have been reclassified so offenders could qualify for realignment release. That left only 70 crimes on the books that require housing in state prison. Although reclassification was an advantage for inmates seeking a supervised release program, the future will dictate whether this venture actually made our communities safer or more dangerous.[8]

The California Department of Corrections and Rehabilitation (CDCR) conducted a follow-up study to determine the impact of realignment in California. The study revealed that realignment did not significantly impact recidivism rates. Sixty-two percent of pre-realignment offenders were arrested again after release from custody. By comparison, 58 percent of post-realignment offenders were arrested for new crimes. Convictions for new offenses were not much better. It was discovered that 21.3 percent of pre-realignment offenders were convicted of new offenses whereas 22.5 percent of post-realignment offenders were convicted of new crimes.[9]

Is the program cost-effective? What unanticipated consequences have occurred during realignment programs? Over $1 billion has been allocated and divided among the 58 counties in California. Most of the money went to large law enforcement and probation departments. Many medium and small law enforcement agencies received limited funds and have to deal with the negative consequences created by prison realignment.

Some experts believe that realignment works because it allows low-level offenders to be supervised near their homes or work. What is not taken into account is that most offenders in a correctional setting have severe alcohol and illegal drug dependency or addiction. Because many of these offenders commit property crimes, engage in prostitution or sell drugs to support their habits, there is little incentive to stay away from old habits and haunts.

The city of Bakersfield in California has experienced a 16 percent spike in criminal acts committed by low-level offenders who have been released back into their community. City Councilman Russell Johnson stated, "This is not a city-created problem, this is a state problem. We have to keep our officers safe." Later Mr. Johnson said, "The city is considering adding police officers to their force, but that's in jeopardy because we have all these predatory government agencies seeking to take local money."[10]

Flaws in the Los Angeles County program identified another threat to the community. Almost 2,000 low-level offenders are out of compliance, meaning they have simply disappeared and most likely are committing new offenses. In 2014, 8,298 offenders were in either jail or released on AB109 supervisions, whereas 1,844 were unaccounted for. The Los Angeles County Probation Department is trying to locate them, but their absence from supervision creates a wider threat.[11]

The city of Monrovia in California also saw a spike in crime because of AB109. According to Police Chief James Hunt, the city had an increase in residential and auto burglaries. In 2013, property crime was up 5.1 percent and violent crime was up 6.6 percent. In the first eight months of 2013, the city had a 30 percent increase in burglaries.

### *The Real Impact of the Supervised Release Program*

To illustrate the impact of AB109 on the community, Chief Hunt identified the following incidents where persons on supervised release programs committed new criminal
offenses. Teams of law enforcement officers, county probation officers and state parole
agents conducted compliance checks to make sure supervised offenders were obeying
the terms of their probation or conditions of their state parole. Over a two-week period,
compliance teams made 215 contacts with supervised offenders. They made 40 arrests
for AB109 violations, 17 arrests for parole violations, 7 arrests for sex offender violations
and 4 arrests for misdemeanor violations. They also seized 15 firearms, illegal drugs and
other drug paraphernalia. Compliance officers also witnessed an AB109 supervised person shoot into a vehicle containing two children. The suspect was arrested for attempted
murder and a handgun was recovered. While contacting a parolee at a house, the suspect fled law enforcement officers who were conducting a routine check. After a short
foot pursuit, the suspect was arrested. He was in possession of a handgun, shotgun and
cocaine. During a gang sweep, compliance officers contacted an AB109 supervised person who threw a handgun from his person. The suspect was arrested for possession of a
firearm. The investigation led to the arrest of two other gang members. These are only a
fraction of the amount of incidents law enforcement agencies are dealing with as a con-
sequence of AB109.

Prison realignment has a direct impact on technology in a variety of areas. Prison realignment has forced more inmates out into the community. Local and state agencies have utilized
new technology to monitor inmates because adding additional staffing is not cost-effective.
In order to deal with the more sophisticated inmates sent to county jail facilities, technology
has been utilized and implemented as well. Innovative technology like video surveillance
systems (VSS), jail information management systems (JIMS), biometric identification software and global positioning systems (GPS) has helped officials responsible for inmates in and
outside of a correctional facility.

## Global Positioning Technology and Corrections

Nine-year-old Jessica Lunsford was kidnapped from her bedroom in Homosassa, Florida.
John Couey, a convicted sex offender, was living in the neighborhood. He had been arrested
24 times over a 30-year period for various violations. He also failed to register as a sex
offender. Law enforcement investigators were able to locate Lunsford's body and recovered
DNA evidence inside of Couey's bedroom. DNA testing confirmed that Lunsford's DNA
was in fact in his bedroom along with Couey's DNA. Couey was arrested and confessed to
the crime. Lunsford's murder investigation led to Jessica's Law in the state of Florida. The
law became popular and spread to other states. One of the requirements of the law was the
use of electronic monitoring of sex offenders for life.[12]

In 2006, California required convicted sex offenders to wear global positioning systems
(GPS) for life. Additionally, the sex offenders could not be within 2,000 feet of a school or
park. California also changed the definition of sexually violent predatory offenders, making
more offenders eligible for the GPS requirement, thus making technology an integral part
of corrections and the supervision of inmates outside of a jail facility.[13]

Recent evidence reveals that a global positioning system (GPS) when attached to sex offenders does reduce recidivism. A National Institute of Justice (NIJ) study published in 2013 reported that sex offenders who wear GPS devices commit fewer crimes than offenders who do not. The study examined recidivism rates on sex offenders in California and discovered that sex offenders wearing devices had a significantly lower arrest rate than those on traditional supervision and not wearing the devices.[14]

The NIJ sponsored study examined 516 high-risk sex offenders paroled from prison between 2006 and 2009. One half of the group were fitted with GPS monitoring devices and placed on traditional supervision. The other group did not wear the GPS device and were also placed on traditional supervision. Parole agents from the California Department of Corrections and Rehabilitation (CDCR) supervised the 516 sex offenders. During the study, traditional supervision included regular contact visits and weekly sex offender treatment classes.

The goals of the study were to assess cost and effectiveness to reduce recidivism and evaluate the program design and implementation. Researchers surveyed 1,000 parole officers to rate GPS monitoring in general, caseload, staffing issues and the screening process for high-risk offenders. The results of the study concluded that GPS monitoring was more expensive, but offenders not wearing the device committed more crimes. Non-GPS wearing offenders had a 38 percent higher chance of returning to prison. Offenders wearing GPS devices also complied with other parole conditions compared to those who did not wear the device. The daily cost of GPS was $35.96 per day compared to $25.45 per day for traditional supervision. The increase in cost was acceptable because the efficiency and accountability was evident.[15]

## Jail Information Management Systems (JIMS) in Corrections

Efficient data management systems streamline operations, improve staff effectiveness, reduce overall costs and limit liability. Technology companies offer sophisticated jail information management systems (JIMS) for correctional facilities worldwide. Similar to other technology advances, JIMS uses state of the art technology to properly manage inmate information including:

- Demographic data
- Booking information including charges, property inventory, etc.
- Court data for pending cases
- Visitation records and schedules
- Commissary records that are used for tracking
- Classification module or matrix
- Medical information or records

JIMS provides a centralized management system for all users within the correctional setting. Most systems have one central database with multiple servers for storage. Users access the system via desktop or mobile applications anywhere within a jail facility. One benefit of a centralized JIMS is that users are trained in a consistent manner and everyone uses the same applications.

Additionally, JIMS can be integrated with other applications that are used throughout a typical jail including live scan fingerprinting devices, photo capture systems and internal administrative systems. Most technology companies work with law enforcement and adapt their technology so that they can work with other technology companies. However, some technology companies utilize proprietary systems to keep all of the technology under one company. This can create issues for public safety managers because cost is always a factor and purchasing proprietary systems is difficult because it eliminates the competitive bidding process.

## Video Surveillance Systems

Correctional facilities of all sizes are tasked with monitoring thousands of inmates. One piece of technology that helps correctional officers monitor inmates is a video surveillance system (VSS). This is often referred to as closed circuit television or CCTV. Video surveillance systems use fixed video cameras to transmit data to specific locations within each facility. In most jails, video monitors are located in specific segments or areas of concern like intake, receiving, lobby, transportation, infirmary and high-liability areas. Video surveillance assists

**FIGURE 4.3** Video Surveillance System.

*Source:* Courtesy of the San Bernardino County Sheriff's Department.

**FIGURE 4.4** Video Surveillance Camera.

*Source*: Courtesy of the San Bernardino County Sheriff's Department.

correctional officers, because it provides continuous coverage of the entire facility. There are not enough correctional personnel to keep track of all inmates. Typically, video surveillance systems are viewed by trained personnel who can closely monitor and track inmates or correctional staff. This provides an increased sense of security for everyone involved. This technology can also be used for crime prevention and criminal investigations by monitoring interaction of inmates.

Video surveillance footage is also a valuable piece of evidence. It documents use-of-force incidents, riots, weapon/narcotics smuggling and employee misconduct. It can also help reduce the amount of violence associated with inmates. Correctional managers struggle to defend a wide variety of lawsuits from inmates and eager attorneys looking to sue a municipality, county or state agency. Video surveillance systems store data for an extended period of time. This footage can be used to prove or disprove a grievance, complaint or potential lawsuit. Correctional managers should consult with their legal team to determine the specific time periods for VSS storage requirements.

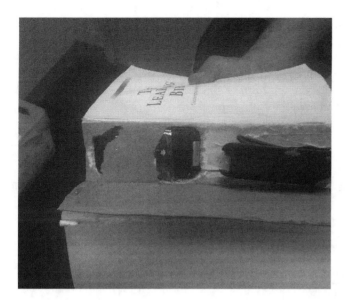

**FIGURE 4.5** This photo depicts a cell phone that was smuggled into a jail facility. Using technology, staff prevented the delivery of the cell phone to an inmate.

*Source:* Courtesy of the San Bernardino County Sheriff's Department.

There are some challenges with this type of technology. Inmates may try to tamper with video surveillance systems in an attempt to hide criminal activity. Video surveillance systems require annual maintenance contracts and ongoing training for personnel. This can be a difficult endeavor for correctional facilities. However, in the long run, the cost of maintenance and training is minimal considering the amount of money local and state governments pay out in lawsuits related to use-of-force cases, death investigations and other types of litigation. Correctional managers should understand that this type of technology is useful, but it is not meant to replace active and direct supervision of inmates by correctional officers. The best way to manage any correctional facility is to ensure that all personnel are actively engaged in their work and utilize proper supervision techniques.

Students can learn how to purchase video surveillance systems in Unit 3, "Managing Public Safety Technology."

## Security Control Systems

In recent years, many agencies have replaced old and antiquated security control systems. A security control system maintains the security of a jail or prison by coordinating locks, doors, windows and other points of entry or exit. Twenty years ago, most facilities used the latest technology to open doors throughout the facility. The security control system used a series of relays, switches and air compressors to open and close doors. The security control system was located inside housing units and was operated by correctional staff. This type of technology was the standard back then. Prior to this technology, correctional staff used keys to open and close each door, which was very time consuming and not cost effective.

Over time, the technology has continued to improve and many correctional facilities have upgraded their security control systems to integrated human machine interface (HMI) systems that use mobile or desktop computers with touch screen monitors. The new HMI systems operate with a standard desktop computer and local or wide area networks (fiber). It does not use relays, switches, and so on. If the system breaks, the software can be replaced immediately.

### Supervision Within a Correctional Facility

One of the primary responsibilities of any correctional manager is to properly identify, track and monitor inmates within a facility. As previously stated in this chapter, local, county and state agencies have a legislatively mandated duty to take care of inmates whether they are sentenced or pre-trial. This can be a significant challenge considering the amount of inmates inside of a prison or jail facility. Large prisons or jails are essentially mini cities complete with housing, medical, culinary, programs and recreational activities. The warden, captain or other high ranking person in charge of a correctional facility is tasked with this responsibility and must ensure that the inmates are properly supervised. Technology can play an important role in this area. Innovative technology products have been deployed to support correctional managers. Technology that helps identify inmates, track their movement and eventually facilitates the release of an inmate is readily available. In order to properly evaluate this type of technology, one must review the business flow of a typical prison or jail. For this purpose, we will review the operational duties of a typical county jail.

The following points represent a flow chart of a typical inmate in a county jail:

- A patrol officer or deputy sheriff arrests a suspect for a criminal charge and brings the suspect to a county jail for processing.
- Most county jails have an intake area that is used to search the suspect and facilitate the booking process.
- Patrol officers or deputy sheriffs complete a booking application that identifies the suspect, recommended criminal charges, agency specific information, etc.
- After the suspect has been searched by jail personnel, the suspect is greeted by medical personnel. The main purpose of the medical check is to ensure that the suspect can be medically housed inside the jail. Suspects with major or acute medical issues are typically sent to a local hospital for medical clearance from a physician before they are allowed inside of a county jail.
- After the suspect is medically cleared, the officer or deputy sheriff presents a booking application form to the booking officer. The booking officer enters the required information into a jail information management system (JIMS) and conducts a property inventory.

- The officer or deputy sheriff is given a copy of the booking application with a specific booking number. The officer or deputy sheriff is now free to leave the jail facility and the suspect officially becomes an "inmate" and is now the responsibility of the staff at the jail.
- The inmate is then fingerprinted and photographed based on the specific facility policy and procedures. In some states, DNA samples are captured as part of the identification process. Inmates are given an identification card or wristband that identifies them to all jail personnel. Usually the identification card or wristband has the inmate's booking number, name and photograph on it.
- After the process is complete, some inmates only remain in custody for a short period of time (cite release or posted bail).
- If an inmate is going to remain inside the jail facility for an extended period of time, they are classified based on their charge, potential for violence, gang affiliation, security level, and so on.
- After the inmate is classified, they are housed inside of a housing unit (cell, segment or dorm).
- Inside of the housing units, inmates are fed, have access to telephones, order commissary, shower, have visitation with family members and have some type of recreational activity.
- Inmates will remain inside of the housing unit until they are released, have court, have a medical appointment or have another reason to leave the area. Inmates are counted by jail personnel, usually multiple times a day.
- When the inmate's time in custody has been completed, he/she is released from the facility and back into society.

In all of the aforementioned areas, technology has a place and is relevant. Correctional managers have an incredible opportunity to utilize technology to improve efficiency and ensure the safety of staff and the inmates. Processing inmates is cumbersome and staff intensive. Technology that can be used to quickly identify, classify or track movement throughout a jail facility is essential.

## Inmate Identification Technology

Most jail facilities have live scan devices that capture inmates' fingerprints. The fingerprints are electronically sent to a regional database and eventually stored at the Federal Bureau of Investigation (FBI). Biometric technology companies have also developed specific technology that allows jail personnel to capture a simple thumbprint from an inmate for identification purposes. The thumbprint is searched against a regional fingerprint database and the identity of the inmate is returned within seconds. This type of technology can and is used at numerous parts of a jail facility. This includes intake, housing units, courtrooms and release windows.

This type of technology can be configured to work with jail information management systems and photo capture devices. It not only saves time, but it also provides an additional security measure to ensure that the inmate is not deceitful or lying about his or her identity.

Students can learn more about Biometric Technology in Unit 2.

## Inmate Classification Technology

The classification of an inmate is one of the most important parts of any jail facility. Correctional managers must ensure the safety of inmates and staff at all times. Recently the courts have ruled that jails and prisons must standardize classification protocols to ensure that inmates are not subjected to increased violence. Inmates with specific medical or mental health issues should also be identified and housed in appropriate areas within a jail or prison facility. New technology can assist jail personnel in this endeavor. Many years ago, classification officers had to print out rap sheets and other data for each inmate. They had to manually review the material and make a determination based on what they reviewed compared to the specific classification protocol of the jail facility. This took a tremendous amount of time and effort. This process was sometimes subjective and mistakes could be made.

Many prisons and jails have started to work with local universities and specialized technology companies to identify specific triggers, identifiers or indicators related to inmate populations. This also has a direct relationship to inmates being released on bail, supervised programs or their own recognizance. Several states have already adopted this new philosophy on classification standards and release inmates based on their propensity or likelihood of committing a new crime. Research and technology databases correlate inmate records (triggers, identifiers and indicators) mentioned above to properly classify an inmate and determine if they meet the criteria for release.

Technology companies offer innovative software that allows correctional personnel to simply enter a specific set of answers based on a standardized set of questions. After the information is obtained from an inmate, the computer software calculates the classification score or rating. Some systems are also integrated with the existing jail information management system and a housing location is automatically determined for each inmate. The main benefit to this technology is that after the original information is entered into the system, the classification subjectivity is eliminated and correctional managers have a "standard" based on community trends, court guidelines and department policies. If an inmate is slated to be released (supervised or own recognizance), correctional managers have some empirical data to fall back on if the inmate commits a new crime. In the end, this new classification technology is the future and will also help with jail or prison overcrowding. It is very expensive to take care of an inmate inside of a jail or prison. Local, state and federal agencies have observed a considerable reduction in inmate costs because they are no longer in custody.

## Inmate Tracking Technology

According to Captain Dana Gould of the San Bernardino County Sheriff's Department, the tracking of an inmate can be challenging, especially in large jails or prisons. Correctional personnel have a duty to monitor all inmates and ensure that they do not escape into the community. Modern jails or prisons are designed and built to eliminate inmate movement around a facility. New facilities use housing units or pods complete with outside recreation areas, showers, eating areas, barber shops, property rooms and medical offices. "The concept is simple. Keep the inmate in a specified location and bring the services to the inmate. Inmates are not allowed to wander the hallways unsupervised. This concept also ensures that inmates cannot interact with other inmates that may have a different classification."

The design and construction of self-contained housing units does help correctional personnel keep track of inmates. However, there are certain times when the inmate needs to be identified quickly and accurately. All jails and prisons have daily inmate counts. This insures that an inmate has not escaped from the facility. Inmates may need to attend court, go to the hospital or have a visit with family members. Each time the inmate moves in or out of his or her housing area, correctional staff must track the inmate's movement. This is also important for the defense of any administrative complaint or legal action. Inmate tracking technology eliminates erroneous errors including inaccurate notations by a correctional officer on a count sheet. It also ensures that the correct times are used and logs are not completed out of department policy. Inmate tracking technology can and is used for the aforementioned reasons. Technology promotes greater efficiency and ensures compliance with facility rules and regulations.

In the private sector, big shipping companies or large companies like Walmart or Target utilize technology to track and monitor products. The products can be tracked from the manufacturer to the customer via tracking software and unique identification numbers or barcodes. The product is scanned and shelved until needed.

Correctional managers can utilize the same concept when tracking inmates throughout the criminal justice system. Inmates have unique booking numbers and other biometric information. Booking numbers can be translated to a barcode and added to the inmate's wristband or identification card depending on the specific policy of the facility. Inmate wristbands and identification cards can also be color coded for classification reasons, which allows officers to quickly identify an inmate classification status. Barcodes can be scanned with handheld electronic devices manufactured by a technology company or a smart phone. Reports can be generated from the barcode technology system and used to verify inmate movement, location and verify certain activities were completed such as outside recreation or visitation.

Barcode scanning equipment can be handheld and issued to individual officers. Barcode readers can also be located at fixed points throughout a facility including housing units, transportation areas and medical offices.

## Radio Frequency Identification (RFID) Technology in Corrections

According to the article "Prisons Use RFID Systems to Track Inmates" (2008), radio frequency identification technology has been used to track inmates and prevent disturbances and misconduct. RFID technology assists correctional personnel in their daily duties. It can also be used to map incidents that may occur within the jail or prison. This is similar to a crime mapping system that is used by law enforcement agencies.[16]

In 2005, the Los Angeles County Sheriff's Department deployed a RFID system in one of their jail facilities. The initial cost of the technology was approximately $1.5 million. Over

1800 inmates were outfitted with RFID wristbands at the Pitchess Detention Facility. This facility was used as a test site to evaluate the system and the aforementioned technology. Staff was able to monitor inmate movement throughout the facility. A signal was broadcasted to a central server every two seconds. If the wristband loses contact with the inmate's skin for more than 15 seconds, an alarm sounded. The alarm also went off if an inmate was in an area that was off limits.[17] Correctional managers should always evaluate this type of technology as it may not work in all locations. Concrete walls, long distances between access points and inmates tampering with wristbands can be an issue.

## Corrections Technology—Liability

Liability is always a significant issue within any jail or prison. Jail information management systems (JIMS) provide a standardized operating protocols for jail operations, classification, fiscal, medical and housing assignments. JIMS also provides confidentiality and consistency.

Many correctional facilities are under a consent decree for various violations including excessive force, inadequate medical or mental health services, improper classification or violation of the Americans with Disabilities Act (ADA). The courts have also ruled that staff must monitor inmate–on–inmate assaults and assaults on staff.

The classification of inmates is a high priority in correctional facilities. The San Bernardino County Sheriff's Department uses a complex classification matrix and questionnaire that is part of the main jail management system. Deputies input information into the database based on responses from the inmate and other information including criminal history searches from the Department of Justice. The software application then correlates the information and identifies a specific classification and housing location. This process greatly expedites the classification process, while ensuring safety to staff and other inmates.

The medical feature of JIMS allows medical personnel to track inmate records in a confidential manner and comply with the Health Insurance Portability and Accountability Act (HIPAA). This medical feature application lists assigned physicians, appointments, medication, medical screening information and inmate charts. The main benefit is that the information is centrally located, but available to any user including medical personnel at other facilities.

Correctional technology like video surveillance systems (VSS), security control systems and inmate identification technology is essential for any jail or prison. Liability is a huge issue for public safety agencies, especially in corrections. Each year, hundreds of lawsuits are filed against local, state and federal agencies and individual personnel. The technology discussed in this chapter can and does help prevent potential lawsuits from occurring. It is up to each correctional manager to evaluate the specific issues with his or her facility and utilize technology to their advantage.

## Chapter Summary

The field of corrections is changing. Technology has revolutionized how personnel in a jail or prison effectively monitor, track and facilitate the required activities on inmates in custody. Correctional managers have to deal with extensive litigation issues. New legislation has also created new challenges. Prison advocates are actively filing federal lawsuits against jails and prisons throughout the nation. New legislation like the California Public Safety Realignment Act has forever changed the role of a warden, captain or correctional manager.

The intent of this chapter is to expose correctional personnel to technology and identify how it can assist with the aforementioned changes and challenges. Technology has a place in jails and prisons. It not only helps staff do their job, but it can also prevent inmate assaults, escapes and other high-liability actions. The ability to effectively evaluate and utilize technology in a correctional setting is paramount for all public safety managers. Perhaps the most important benefit of using technology in a jail or prison is that it provides enhanced safety for correctional personnel and inmates alike. Technology can be expensive, but the protection of those within the correctional field is worth the price.

## Key Words or Terminology

| | | |
|---|---|---|
| corrections | AB109 | ADA |
| Jessica's Law | GPS | video surveillance system |
| JIMS | AFIS | inmate |
| criminal justice system | Title 15 | integration |
| emerging trends | technology | management |
| liability | RFID | |

## Discussion Questions

1. How has prison realignment affected corrections and the criminal justice system?
2. What types of technology projects have been implemented as a result of prison realignment?
3. What role does a manager play in evaluating technology in a correctional facility?
4. How can technology help reduce potential liability in the field of corrections?

## Notes

1 (2015). *Code of Regulations Title 15: Crime prevention and corrections.* Sacramento, CA: State of California.
2 Glaze, L., and Herberman, E. (2013). *Correctional population in the U.S., 2012.* Washington, DC: U.S. Department of Justice, Bureau of Justice Statistics.
3 Ibid.
4 Lacher, D. (2014). *Contemporary issues in criminal justice management.* San Diego: Cognella Academic Publishing.
5 Ibid.
6 Ibid.
7 Ibid.
8 (2011). *Fact sheet. 2011 public safety realignment.* Sacramento, CA: California Department of Corrections and Rehabilitation.
9 Lacher, *Contemporary issues.*
10 Ibid.
11 Ibid.

12 (2007). *Couey guilty of murdering 9-year-old Jessica Lunsford.* Retrieved from www.cnn.com.2007/law/girl.slain/indez.html.

13 (2015). *Sex offender information overview.* Sacramento, CA: California Department of Corrections and Rehabilitation.

14 Bulman, P. (2013). *History of GPS monitoring policies in California.* National Institute of Justice. Washington, DC: NIJ.

15 Bulman, P. (2013). *Sex offenders monitored by GPS found to commit fewer crimes.* National Institute of Justice. Washington, DC: NIJ.

16 McKay, J. (2008). Prisons use RFID systems to track inmates. *Justice and Public Safety. Government Technology.* Retrieved from www.Givtech.com/public-safety/prisons-use-rfid-systems-to-track.htm.

17 Swedberg, C. (2005). L.A. County Jail to track inmates. *RFID Journal.* Retrieved from www.rfidjournal.com/article/view?601.

# 5

# FIRE SERVICES

"It's not a party until the fire department shows up."
—*Thom Filicia*

## Learning Objectives

After reading this chapter, the student will:

*   Understand the role of a manager in a fire department.
*   Define and evaluate common fire technology used today.
*   Discuss how advances in technology can help personnel manage fires, medical calls for service and other activities performed by fire departments.
*   Evaluate new technology and equipment used by fire departments.

## Introduction

In this chapter, we examine how technology affects fire services and their ability to manage critical incidents when necessary. The men and women working in fire departments have a very difficult job and are faced with a multitude of responsibilities. The obvious responsibility is to fight fires, provide structure protection and respond to medical emergencies. Firefighting personnel continue to utilize new forms of technology that improve efficiency, protect life and property and prevent future fires from occurring. Throughout this chapter, we discuss several different types of fire technology, including self-contained breathing apparatus (SCBA), thermal imaging cameras, fire detection software and communications technology. Managers and administrators working in fire services are no different than police or correctional managers. They must manage existing technology and evaluate new and innovative technology. The technology and equipment used by fire department personnel is critical and in many cases saves lives.

## Fire Technology

### *Thermal Imaging Technology*

Firefighters have to deal with fires, which are inherently dangerous. Fire technologies have evolved quite a bit over the years and the method of dealing with a fire has changed dramatically. Over the years, one piece of technology that has proven its usefulness in the fire industry is the thermal imaging camera. It renders thermal radiation as a visible light and the camera allows firefighters to see through different areas of smoke and darkness. "In the past 15 years or so, thermal imaging cameras have been introduced into the fire service market, allowing firefighters to virtually 'see' through smoke."[1] Sight is an important commodity for firefighters and fighting a fire inside of a structure is difficult. Smoke can deter sight and senses, which prevents firefighters from performing effectively without a thermal imaging camera.

According to the National Institute of Standards and Training (NIST), thermal imaging cameras provide first responders with valuable information that can determine the size of the fire, track its growth, locate victims or personnel and look for escape routes. The typical cost for a thermal imaging camera is $10,000.[2] This can be very expensive depending on the number of personnel in a typical fire department.

Thermal imaging cameras can also detect energy emitted through a door or wall, including energy that is reflected off of water or mirrors. The cameras detect different heat signatures. Fire rescue personnel can use this equipment because they can pick up body heat and the cameras can be used in remote places. Thermal imaging cameras can be handheld or helmet-mounted. The equipment is portable and can be shared with others.

**FIGURE 5.1** In this photograph, a firefighter uses a thermal imaging camera at a fire.

*Source*: Photo courtesy of the San Bernardino County Fire Department. Public Domain.

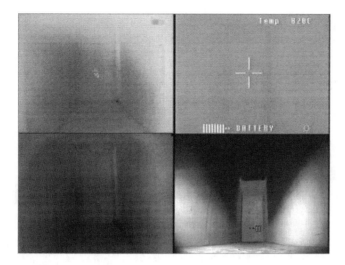

**FIGURE 5.2**  A thermal imaging camera was used to take these photos of the inside of a building
on fire.

*Source*: National Institute of Standards and Training. (2016). Electronic Safety Equipment. Retrieved on
www.nist.gov/fire/locator.cfm.

However, there are a few challenges with this equipment. The handheld equipment requires its operator to hold it, which could slow down firefighting service operations. Also,
the helmet-mounted cameras are affixed to the operator, leaving it hard to transfer to another
rescuer at the scene. This technology is also expensive and requires ongoing training for fire
personnel. Additionally, the thermal detector may become saturated due to the range of tem-
peratures, which may cause the signal to lose ratio and thermal sensitivity.[3] Despite the few
weaknesses, this equipment saves lives and has been utilized for critical incidents, trapped
victims and missing persons in dark areas. Fire personnel no longer have to search a smoke-
filled room or enter a structure that is unsafe. They can simply point the camera into the room
that needs to be searched and an image of the objects in the room appears on the screen.

## Fire Safety Technology

### Self-Contained Breathing Apparatus (SCBA)

The safety of fire personnel is paramount. Fire managers must look for ways to protect their
personnel in critical situations just like any other profession. Fire personnel are often
exposed to carcinogens and other harmful substances. The inhalation of hazardous materials
from methamphetamine laboratories can create long-term medical issues for fire personnel.
Thankfully, there is some technology that helps protect fire personnel in the aforementioned situations. The self-contained breathing apparatus (SCBA) protects fire personnel
from breathing harmful air or hazardous materials. SCBA equipment includes a bottle or
tank, breathing mask, gauges and carrying assembly.[4] This technology has continued to

improve and nearly every fire department has them available. New innovations with SCBA include the ability to detect and monitor biometric distress signals.[5]

Although this type of technology has its advantages, fire managers should be aware of potential risks when using SCBA equipment. The U.S. Fire Administration analyzed various issues with SCBAs and prepared a summary of recommendations for fire services personnel to review, analyze and implement.[6]

**TABLE 5.1** Summary of Key Issues

| Issue | Comments |
| --- | --- |
| Failure to Use | One of the most common failures of the SCBA system (i.e., SCBA + Firefighter = System) is the failure to use it. Even with the current emphasis on firefighter health and safety, and the expanding knowledge of the hazards posed by the products of combustion, some firefighters still fail to use SCBA during interior operations in smoke-filled environments, especially during salvage and overhaul. |
| Hardware Reliability | SCBA that are tested and certified according to the requirements of the NFPA 1981 (1992 and 1197 Editions) Standard on Open-Circuit Self-Contained Breathing Apparatus for Fire Fighters are extremely durable and rugged. Properly used and maintained by well-trained personnel, according to the manufacturer's recommendations, they should provide years of trouble-free service with little potential for hardware failure. |
| Catastrophic Failures | Catastrophic failures of SCBA resulting in death or injury to firefighters are very rare considering the number of routine uses by firefighters each day. Even if such a failure should occur, the fail-safe design of the SCBA may allow it to function long enough for a firefighter to escape the hazard area. |
| "Low-order" Failure | Some failures of the SCBA system do not directly result in firefighter death or injury, but may reduce efficiency and hamper fire ground operations. This type of failure is relatively common and most often attributable to operator error, physical abuse/neglect, or inadequate preventive maintenance procedures. Examples include: difficult or slow donning of SCBA due to a lack of familiarity or infrequent practice; free flowing regulators; blown O-rings during cylinder changes; and improperly connected hoses or regulators. |
| Operator Training | Many low-order failures can be prevented through proper operator training. Before entering hostile environments, firefighters must be appropriately trained in all aspects of SCBA inspection and operation. Continued drilling and practice under realistic conditions must be emphasized until complete familiarity is achieved and maintained. Complete knowledge in the use and limitations of SCBA must become second nature to all firefighters to prevent failures. |

| *Issue* | *Comments* |
|---------|------------|
| Preventive Maintenance | Regularly maintained and tested by competent, properly trained, and certified technicians using the appropriate tools, replacement parts, and testing equipment, following procedures recommended by the respective manufacturers. Fire departments should establish preventive maintenance programs for SCBA to ensure firefighter safety and compliance with applicable regulations. The 1989 edition of the NFPA 1404 Standard for a Fire Department Self-Contained Breathing Apparatus Program can be used to provide guidance for fire department preventive maintenance and training programs. |
| Upgrades | The 1992 and 1997 editions of NFPA 1981 contain realistic, updated procedures for testing and certification of SCBA. Several changes made in these editions were prompted by failure incidents mentioned in this report. Fire departments should upgrade their existing SCBA to meet the current edition of NFPA 1981, to minimize the risk of repeating past tragedies. SCBA that cannot be upgraded can be replaced with newer models. |
| Pushing the Edge of the Envelope | Despite the fact that modern, NFPA-compliant SCBA are extremely durable, the materials used in their construction have physical limitations. Firefighters and maintenance personnel must understand that SCBA are not indestructible, and that the potential exists to expose SCBA to factors in the environment that may contribute to or produce failure. |

*Source*: U.S. Fire Administration. (2001). Special Report: Self-Contained Breathing Apparatus Failures. Washington, DC: U.S. Printing Office.

All technology must be monitored for safety, efficiency and potential improvements. As illustrated by the SCBA summary, managers should ensure proper and systematic training occurs and that personnel are continually tested.

### Fire Services Communication Technology

Fire personnel are constantly looking for new ways to communicate with each other and locate potential victims at a scene. There is technology available that can assist fire personnel in this endeavor. Digital sound technology is an expanded fire alarm and smoke detector. Typical fire alarms and detectors notify people of hazards by emitting a narrow band noise. Directional sound technology utilizes multi-frequency sounds with all (low, mid and high) range signals.[7]

The human ear cannot determine the location or trajectory of a narrow band transmission. Directional sound technology allows people to follow a specific sound or noise to a safe exit. Directional sound technology also has the ability to guide people to separate exits of a building based on their current location. This technology is efficient because it decreases the amount of time it takes for a person to exit a building or residence. This technology is fairly new and can be expensive. Fire managers should evaluate potential benefits and weigh the budget impact accordingly.[8]

The use of a personal alert safety system (PASS) device is a great way to use technology to help firefighters in the field. Firefighters can get lost, overcome by smoke or unable to alert backup personnel for assistance. PASS devices sound an audible alarm so others can be guided to a specific location. It lets others know that the firefighter needs assistance. PASS devices also have motion detection technology. Some devices also incorporate thermal exposure sensors and are integrated into ground personnel accountability systems.[9]

Another form of fire communication technology is the electronic accountability system. In New York, when firefighters are in trouble and need assistance they commonly broadcast a "mayday" over the radio. When more than one firefighter radios a mayday, it becomes chaotic, and it is difficult to locate the firefighters in distress. This was prevalent during the September 11, 2001, attacks because multiple maydays were broadcasted and the chaos and

**FIGURE 5.3** Personal Alert Safety System (PASS).

*Source*: Photo courtesy of the San Bernardino County Fire Department. Public Domain.

danger to rescuers intensified as they tried to find the helpless firefighters. Since that time, the fire department has developed an accountability system that is more effective in locating distressed firefighters. To protect the firefighters, the FDNY implemented a software system known as the Electronic Fire Ground Accountability System. For every firefighter that has a radio, there is a unique seven-digit number assigned to the radio and firefighter. When the emergency button is activated or mayday call has been broadcasted, the identified fire-fighter, his/her assignment and last known location are displayed to all commanders' com-puters on- and off-scene. This allows commanders to properly account for their employees along with saving precious time in saving their lives.[10]

Fighting fires in the wilderness or large remote areas can also cause communication issues. Rugged terrain, mountains and other obstacles can cause breaks in the communication lines. Fire personnel have addressed this issue by using the same technology used in military operations. Firefighters can now utilize voice, data and video-sharing technology. This technology uses radio waves that connect the firefighter to satellites or other transmission devices. The technology can also provide the specific location of each firefighter with GPS software. The devices allow firefighters to track one another on a common digital map and mark important locations such as fire lines and water drop spot. It can also send photos or play video from a plane or drone.

This technology does have some negative aspects. Fire personnel must wear the device on the outside of their fire suit near the chest area. This could be an issue when work-ing with other fire equipment. However, the benefit for fire managers is that they can account for all fire personnel and strategically place personnel to best fight these wild land fires.[11]

## Fire Detection Technology

Fire managers can also utilize various technology products to detect and prevent small fires from expanding into larger fires. Technology companies have created software that tracks fires based on longitude and latitude. Global positioning systems (GPS) link with mobile and fixed computers, which aid fire managers with the overall management of a fire. Weather and topography can be included into the software and eventually be printed for briefings and fire assessments.

The National Aeronautics and Space Administration (NASA) has partnered with the U.S. Forest Service to help detect and fight fires. NASA's technology allows firefighters to access wildfires more quickly and utilize their resources efficiently. In 2003, wildfires con-sumed over 2.3 million acres in the United States. NASA can utilize unmanned aerial vehicles (UAV) to capture fire images from the air and transmit data within seconds. Satellites can also notify fire personnel of new fires as they travel the world. The satellites and UAVs have the ability to monitor the globe and detect hazards like forest fires.[12]

In California, the San Bernardino County Sheriff's Department uses video downlink cameras to send data to fixed or mobile sites across the largest geographical county in the United States. The video downlink cameras are attached to a fleet of helicopters and used on a daily basis. Helicopter flight officers can view activity from video monitors inside of the cockpit. This is a great benefit to the community because the helicopters routinely patrol the county and can transmit images from miles away. The video downlink system can also be used for natural disasters such as floods or earthquakes.

## Fire Training Technology

The training and safety of personnel is a very important part of any public safety manager. Technology can play a role in this endeavor. New and innovative simulators are available for fire departments across the county. The fire simulators are similar to the standard aircraft simulators used by major airlines. The simulators can help create critical situations like driving code three in a busy street, which can help prevent major accidents and liability to the department. The simulators can reinforce the importance of safe driving and mental preparation when responding to a call for service.

## Purchasing Fire Technology or Equipment

The purchase of fire technology or equipment can be difficult to say the least. Government procurement rules and the lack of funding can be challenging. Typically, police and fire departments use the majority of any discretionary funds available to a city, county or state agency. Therefore, it is imperative that public safety managers do their homework and get the best technology available and at an affordable price. Managers should always ask the following questions before purchasing public safety technology:

- How will this benefit the patient? Find out who is using the equipment or technology and evaluate the successes or failures.
- Why will this benefit the provider? The technology or equipment should also help or benefit the fire agency or EMS provider.
- Why will this benefit the system? This involves the training of personnel and the ability to monitor the new technology or equipment.
- What is the cost? This includes the original purchase, upgrades and maintenance cost.
- Who will manage the project? Minor purchases can be handled by a first-line supervisor. However, larger purchases should have a project manager or someone trained in government purchasing procedures.[13]

Unit 3 of this textbook covers the specifics on how to plan, purchase and manage public safety equipment.

## Chapter Summary

Fire managers and administrators have a variety of technology at their disposal to help fight fires and manage medical or rescue operations. Whether it is improving communications, tracking a fire or providing additional safety measures for line personnel, fire managers should strive to constantly evaluate and implement technology that improves efficiency and protects all of the stakeholders involved in a critical incident. Fire technology and equipment does come with some risk and the cost could be an issue for smaller agencies. Fire managers should look for ways to regionalize on large scale fire technology purchases and share resources when possible. This concept is not new for fire agencies as they routinely work with other agencies as part of the mutual aid process and incident command system.

## Key Words or Terminology

| | | |
|---|---|---|
| SCBA | manager | fire department |
| thermal imaging camera | NIST | communications |
| personal alert safety system (PASS) | GPS | NASA |
| unmanned aerial vehicle (UAV) | downlink | |

## Discussion Questions

1. Compare and contrast current and future fire technology and equipment in your jurisdiction. Has the technology or equipment been helpful?
2. What steps should be taken before purchasing fire technology or equipment?
3. Examine the use of simulators and other safety equipment used in fire departments. Is the use of a simulator practical for fire personnel?

## Notes

1 Jakubowski, G. (2010). *Thermal imaging cameras help firefighters see through smoke.* Retrieved from www.firefighternation.com/article/firefighting-operations/thermal-imaging-cameras-help-firefighters-see-through-smoke.
2 (2016). *Electronic safety equipment.* National Institute of Standards and Training. Retrieved from www.nist/gov/fire/technology.cfm.
3 Ibid.
4 *Self-contained breathing apparatus: Types of respirators,* n.d. University of Illinois. Retrieved from www.uic.edu/sph/glakes/confined_space/mod6/m6p5e.htm.
5 (2014). *5 most groundbreaking firefighter technologies.* Firerescue1. Retrieved from www.firerescue1.com/fire-prodcuts/personal-protective-equipment-ppe/articles/2034.
6 (2001). *Special report: Self-contained breathing apparatus failures.* U.S. Fire Administration. Washington, DC: U.S. Government Printing Office.
7 Poss, C. (2005). *Improving fire safety protection.* School Planning and Management. Retrieved from www.webspm.com/articles/2005/11/01/improving-fire-safety-protection.aspx.
8 Ibid.
9 *Electronic safety equipment,* National Institute of Standards and Training.
10 Baker, A. (2011, July 12). With new fire technology, a mayday could bring faster help. *New York Times.* Retrieved from www.nytimes.com/2011/07/13/nyregion/new-fdny-software-would-allow-faster-mayday-responses.
11 Schechter, E. (2014, September 10). Firefighters use Special Forces gear to stay connected. *Popular Mechanics.* Retrieved from www.popularmechanics.com/military/a11207/firefighters-use-special-forces-gear-to-stay-connected-17194126/.
12 Dunbar, B. (2003). *NASA creates high tech firefighting tools.* National Aeronautics and Space Administration. Retrieved from www.nasa.goc/vision/earth/everydaylife/safer_firefighting.html.
13 Potts, M. (2016). 5 questions to answer before any EMS purchase. *Fire Chief Magazine.* Retrieved from www.firechief.com/2016/03/11/5-questions-to-answer-before-any-ems-purchase/.

# UNIT 2

# Current Practices in Public Safety Organizations

Unit 2 highlights popular technology concepts, programs and equipment used in public safety today. Technology like social media, body-worn cameras, biometrics, thermal imaging cameras, fire-fighting drones and predictive policing are all part of the public safety arena. Each chapter is designed to give the reader an in-depth review of the specific technology being used today by public safety organizations. This unit also provides practical examples of technology programs and equipment that has helped transform and keep public safety organizations in tune with private sector technology.

This unit covers the following:

# 6

# SOCIAL MEDIA AND PUBLIC SAFETY

## What Is Your Role?

"Tweeting is like sending out cool telegrams to your
friends once a week."

—*Tom Hanks*

## Learning Objectives

After reading this chapter, the student will:

- Explain the historical, theoretical and practical developments of social media.
- Evaluate and interpret the role of a public safety manager as it relates to social media.
- Explain how to prepare a social media policy.
- Assess and evaluate the various constitutional issues surrounding social media and public safety.
- Assess the limitations, strengths and potentials of social media and how it can help in criminal investigations.
- Analyze how social media has changed the public safety profession.

## Introduction

In this chapter, we examine how social media has affected public safety agencies and organizations throughout the country. Social media started out as a true "social" experiment in a college and has blossomed into a force to be reckoned with. Social media has forever changed the way public safety agencies interact with the community. As technology continues to grow each and every year, it is hard to find a single person who is not using some type of social media. Millions of people each day log on to social media websites to communicate with others, post pictures or videos and express personal thoughts about everything from the latest police shooting to a funny joke. Access to social media websites is available to anyone with a computer or phone. This has created an incredible dilemma for public safety agencies. Citizens are using social media to discuss and sometimes condemn public safety personnel. People are posting video footage of crime scenes, pursuits, wildlife fires and other intoxicating events. Because public safety personnel also use social media, departments are having to quickly react and create policies and procedures to regulate when and how personnel can use social media. As a result, state and federal courts have made significant rulings that affect public safety agencies. Criminal justice managers must adopt and develop department policies and procedures that address the use of social media websites on- and off-duty.

## The Age of Social Media

Technology has a significant effect on public safety. Inventions like the bulletproof vest, semi-automatic handgun and hand-held radios have revolutionized how public safety personnel do their job each and every day. However, social media is a different type of technology. Social media transcends and integrates community norms, values and customs into public safety organizations. Social media makes the world a much smaller place because it differs from traditional media sources in several ways. Social media uses new technology and the Internet that traditional media outlets have struggled to duplicate. Social media is immediate, changes the way we have conversations with others and reaches out to different audiences. Newspapers have to be written and distributed to a residence or grocery store. Television news stations send a reporter to the scene to report the news. Social media allows news to come straight from the source in real time. The users of social media control the conversation and are usually the first ones to disseminate the information to others. When the information is on social media, other users can respond immediately with positive or negative comments. Many in society, especially the younger generation, have grown up with social media. It is part of their lives and culture. Social media has also changed how we communicate. Historically, families and friends would get together and share stories, photographs, discuss politics, the latest celebrity gossip or whatever is popular in the news. Today, the aforementioned information is commonly broadcasted via social media. Users can decide what content they want to receive and how they want to receive it. Although newspapers and television are forms of media, social media is distinct in that the forms of information are inexpensive and accessible to enable anyone that can upload or access information.

### Social Media and Public Safety

"Social media is integrated technology that allows users to generate their own content and then share that content through various connections."[1] Social media allows users to share information, including photos and personal messages with others. The most popular Internet social media websites are Facebook, Twitter, LinkedIn, Pinterest, Instagram and Myspace.[2] Millions of people utilize social media websites each year.

Users of the aforementioned websites must register under their true names, but they can also utilize a false identity, which can create issues for public safety. Social media websites allow users to stay in contact with others based on defined parameters or user preferences. Social media websites also allow users to post virtually anything on the website, including crime scene videos and other information that public safety agencies would typically keep confidential. The significance of social media is that the "user" establishes the security restrictions and only they may grant others permission to view their information. Law enforcement is no stranger to social media either. Most public safety agencies have some type of social media access or website. In 2013, the International Association of Chiefs of Police conducted a survey of law enforcement agencies across the country, representing 48 states. A total of 500 agencies participated in the survey.[3] The survey revealed that:

- 95.9% used social media in some way.
- 86.1% used social media for criminal investigations.
- 80.4% reported that social media helped solve crime in their jurisdiction.
- 73.1% stated that social media has helped them improve relations with their respective communities.

For more information on the IACP survey, visit www.IACPsocialmedia.org.

The adoption of social media by public safety has been overwhelming in a short period of time. Conduct a social media search for any public safety agency and you will get numerous hits leading you to an official website. Social media is being used by all levels of government, including municipal, county, state and federal. Social media has become the new age community policing tool for law enforcement.

Public safety managers should also become familiar with the common terminology used on the Internet. This includes blogs, feeds, forum, video/photo sharing websites, professional networks, dashboards, podcasts, location-based networks, microblogs, virtual communities,

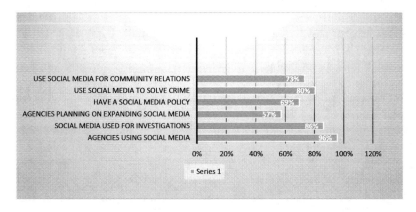

**FIGURE 6.1**  Social Media 2013 IACP Survey Results.

*Source*: International Association of Chiefs of Police. (2013). *Social Media Survey*. IACP. Alexandria, VA: Author.

wikis, and really simple syndication (RSS). A glossary of social media terminology is available at the end of this chapter.

## Constitutional Issues with Social Media

The First Amendment to the U.S. Constitution reads: "Congress shall make no law respecting an establishment of religion, or prohibiting the free exercise thereof; or abridging the freedom of speech, or of the press; or the right of the people peaceably to assemble, and to petition the Government for a redress of grievances."[4] The U.S. Supreme Court has afforded dissident political speech unparalleled constitutional protection. However, all speech is not equal under the First Amendment. The high court has identified five areas of expression that the government may legitimately restrict under certain circumstances. They include any speech that incites illegal activity and subversive speech, fighting words, obscenity and pornography, commercial speech and symbolic expression.[5] The complexities of the First Amendment are still debated today and the Internet has given rise to further debate. The Internet has led to the widespread distribution of sexually explicit materials. In an attempt to regulate this material, the federal government stepped in only to find that the U.S. Supreme Court identified First Amendment violations. "In *Ashcroft v. Free Speech Coalition*, 535 U.S. 234, 122 S. Ct. 1389, 152 L. Ed.2d 403 (2002), the Court struck down provisions of the Child Pornography Prevention Act of 1996 because they censored legally protected speech as well as unprotected speech."[6] In summary, the court held that the government's case was overbroad and violated the First Amendment. *Ashcroft v. Free Speech Coalition* is an important Supreme Court decision because it identifies cyberspace or the Internet as the location of the crime.

In 2010, the U.S. Supreme Court heard an appeal from the 9th Circuit Court of Appeals in *Quon v. Arch Wireless*. In summary, a police sergeant from the Ontario Police Department used his department-issued electronic equipment to send and receive personal text messages. He and other employees agreed to pay for any charges which exceeded the department allotment for that equipment. The chief of police ordered a study to be done to determine if the department needed to modify the contract and decide whether employees were using the department equipment for personal use. Arch Wireless, per the request of the police department, provided the recorded data of text messages to the police department. It was determined that an overwhelming amount of text messages, approximately 90 percent, were personal and contained sexual comments and communication. Sgt. Quon filed suit claiming his Fourth Amendment rights were violated. The end result was that the Supreme Court held the search of the text messages was reasonable. The comment by Justice Scalia in regards to *Quon v. Arch Wireless* and technology was interesting: "Applying the Fourth Amendment to new technologies may be difficult, but when it is necessary to decide a case, we have no choice... The times-they-are-a-changin is a feeble excuse for disregard of duty."[7]

In the United States, many officers rely on the First Amendment right to free speech and their off-duty status as protection from any job action. This reliance however is often misplaced and is likely more so in light of the U.S. Supreme Court ruling in

*Garcetti v. Ceballos,* 547 U.S. 410 (2006), which put further limits on a public employee's free speech and narrowly defines the contours of that speech.[8]

## Investigations

The use of social media in criminal investigations has become a staple in law enforcement. There are numerous examples on how law enforcement has used social media to conduct investigations. From people posting and tweeting incriminating photos and messages, to law enforcement posting "Wanted Posters" on their Facebook pages.[9]

In October of 2012, the San Francisco Giants won the Major League Baseball World Series. The city of San Francisco erupted in celebration and, unfortunately, violence. A staff photographer with the *San Francisco Chronicle* took a picture during the riots of a suspect using a metal barricade to destroy the windshield of a city bus. After the picture was printed and posted on the newspaper's website, it went viral. It was shared on social media sites and received thousands of views. People viewing the picture online quickly identified the suspect, and he was arrested.[10]

In Florida, the Broward County Sheriff's Department was dealing with a series of air conditioning thefts, and Sheriff Al Lamberti used the department's Facebook page to post the suspect and vehicle descriptions. Within two days, the sheriff's department received information that aided in the apprehension of the suspects involved in the series of thefts.[11]

Social media can also be used to incite a riot or entice others to get involved in criminal activity. On July 28, 2011, a popular Los Angeles performer sent a message out via social media inviting fans to show up at Grauman's Chinese Theater. He stated, "Let's see if the magic of social networking will work today." The crowd grew to the thousands and prompted a large response from the Los Angeles Police Department to disperse the crowd. The event resulted in the closing of Hollywood Boulevard, the arrest of two people and three damaged police cars.[12]

Criminals are going to adapt to the new policing strategies used by law enforcement personnel. Criminals will always look for ways to commit their crimes via technological advances not yet utilized by law enforcement. It is a constant game of cat and mouse. Social abuse and crimes are committed through the innovative use of technology. Due to the complexity of social media and Internet crimes, public safety experts may not always be able to explain how criminals are using technology.[13]

LexisNexis conducted a comprehensive survey that focused on the impact of social media in criminal investigations because they wanted to get a better understanding of law enforcement's use of social media, specifically the investigative process. They determined that four out of five officers use various social media platforms to assist them in their criminal investigations. Some officers used social media for community outreach, soliciting crime tips, notifying the public and for recruitment purposes. The following are common investigative uses for social media:[14]

- Identify associates affiliated with persons of interest
- Identify locations of criminal activity
- Gather photos or statements to corroborate evidence
- Identify criminal activity

- Identify persons of interest
- Identify and monitor whereabouts of persons of interest
- Soliciting tips on crimes
- Anticipating crimes that may be occurring
- Understanding criminal networks
- Use information from social media as probable cause for search warrants

## Community Interaction

Public safety managers are quickly becoming aware of the impact that social media has upon the community. Social media is entrenched in community policing and allows public safety to quickly pass on information to the community. This is especially important during natural disasters, large scale investigations or civil unrest. Public safety managers can and should utilize social media to make the public aware of problems within the community. It is an extension of neighborhood watch. Social media allows the public to interact, both publically and privately, with public safety agencies or organizations. Law enforcement agencies are increasingly posting information on crime trends as well as posting the pictures and identifying information of suspects that are wanted in connection with various crimes.

Traditionally, this type of information would be sent out to a local newspaper for distribution. The news media would decide if and when that information would be printed in the newspaper. Public safety agencies also hold press conferences to distribute information to the public. Thanks to social media, press conferences can be streamed live to the public. The public can watch them at any time because they are available on the agency's website or on the Internet.

Public safety command staff and executives should also consider using social media to promote the positive activities done by public safety personnel.

The private sector has joined forces with public safety agencies to share and pass on critical information to the public. This is accomplished through emails and text messages via the agency website. Some private vendors will work with public safety agencies to create specialized software applications that allow the public to pass on information, tips and questions anonymously.

Public safety agencies can also post videos of any type and just about any length to reach the community. Recruiting videos, recaps of community presentations and surveillance videos can be disseminated via social media. Public safety agencies can also link the video information to their specific agency website. The Sacramento Police Department uses social media for posting clips related to domestic violence and sexual assault prevention. By using social media, they direct a tailored message to their target audiences. By using social media, the messages are always available to the public.[15]

## Public Safety Conduct

Public safety personnel are held to a higher standard of conduct compared to the rest of society. They are required to wear uniforms, maintain grooming standards and uphold the laws of the land. So what happens when public safety personnel express their personal opinions about religion, politics and other forms of communication, which may reflect negatively on the department? While on duty, public safety personnel are under a microscope and must always demonstrate professionalism no matter how an event or person challenges their belief systems. Technically, off-duty personnel are free to express their personal opinions via social media. However, the off-duty personnel must be cognizant of the fact that his or her opinions may reflect back on to the department.

So does a public safety code of conduct transfer to off-duty comments on social media? Public safety agencies have department standards, which include a code of conduct. Typically, the language states that officers, firefighters or other public safety employees shall not conduct or engage in any activity that brings discredit to the department. The off-duty conduct of posting of inappropriate statements, photos or videos via social networking sites could be construed as violating the aforementioned code of conduct. One only has to watch the nightly news to hear about politically incorrect or abusive comments from public safety personnel via social media. The problem is that newer personnel are already accustomed to using social media on a regular basis. New officers have grown up with access to social networking sites and they are less inclined to see a problem with social networking even though the employer places limits on their off-duty use.[16]

In Albuquerque, New Mexico, a police officer was involved in a fatal on-duty shooting. Shortly thereafter, a local television station began researching the officer on the Internet. They discovered his publicly accessible Facebook page that listed his occupation as "Human Waste Disposal."[17] Problems like this are cropping up all over the country and law enforcement is quickly learning that social media comments need to be addressed. In 2013, a Florida safety officer was fired for a Facebook post regarding the Trayvon Martin shooting. The officer posted a disrespectful comment, which was reported to the agency. The agency later fired the officer.[18]

If a firefighter posts on a social media website that he or she is tired from working long hours, does that create a fitness-for-duty issue? What happens if an officer uses his own cell phone to take a picture of a large quantity of narcotics or marijuana? Will the photograph affect the prosecution? Can the officer's cell phone, including all other pictures, become part of the discovery phase during a trial? Under *Brady v. Maryland* (1963), the prosecution in a criminal case must disclose any evidence or information favorable to the defendant, even if it is not requested.[19] This creates a situation that makes what law enforcement officers say off-duty, under the umbrella of free speech, relevant in a criminal case.

Public safety managers must create and adopt specific policies that govern the actions and decision making of personnel who utilize various forms of social media. Crafting policies that limit an employee's speech can create some unique hurdles that must be overcome. However, public safety managers have a duty to protect the credibility of the department and ensure that the criminal justice system is not compromised because of an employee who posted some unprofessional or inappropriate material via a social media website.

## Social Media Policies and Procedures

In today's age of Internet use and social networking, criminal justice managers must develop and adopt departmental policies and procedures that address inappropriate social media postings. This includes disciplinary actions if necessary. An employee's constitutional right to free speech must also be considered when writing a department policy on social media.

The policy must spell out the circumstances that allow personnel to use social media, but they must also set limitations that deal with the conduct of personnel. Limitations placed on personnel conducting investigations will ensure that the civil rights of the people being investigated or those associated with the suspect are not violated. After the policy on social media is written, all personnel must be trained on the new policy to avoid any confusion. The policy should be taught and reinforced by the policy makers instead of being passed down to a lower rank that was not directly involved in making the policy.

The International Association of Chiefs of Police (IACP) is a great resource for the development of a social media policy. IACP has a list of examples and guidelines based on numerous interviews and contacts with other law enforcement agencies. IACP recommends that law enforcement personnel should be able to use social media sites to assist in pre-employment background checks and to reach out to the public on community projects or problems such as emergencies. Law enforcement personnel should also be able to use social media sites to gather intelligence, gather evidence and investigate crimes. Public safety agencies should always consult with their legal counsel before adopting any social media policy.[20]

When creating a policy for a department social media website link, public safety agencies should consider the following:

- Who is your audience?
- What are you hoping to get from using social media?
- What type of messages are you planning to publish?
- What other information (such as photos and videos) do you hope to publish?
- What social media sites will you use?
- Who will be in charge of maintaining your social media sites?
- How often will you post new content?
- Do you want to allow the public to post comments and feedback? If so, will you have a policy for removing offensive comments?[21]

These questions can also be addressed in your agency's social media policy. As a reminder social media can change so your social media policy needs to be flexible.

Public safety managers should also make sure that the departmental social media page is monitored and maintained. It should have the appropriate departmental contact information displayed on the page in case there are any questions. There should also be an introductory statement that clearly specifies the purpose and scope of the department's presence on the website and a link to the department's official Internet website. Employees shall abide by all copyright, trademark and service mark restrictions in posting materials and information to electronic media. These guidelines can help maintain department standards and reduce any potential liability.

## A Public Safety Manager's Perspective

Social media is not going away. Public safety managers should continue to learn about social media and use it in a positive way. The key to any form of technology is education and training. Public safety managers and executives must understand that society has

# Model Policy

| *EffectiveDate*<br>**August 2010** | | *Number* |
|---|---|---|
| *Subject*<br>**Social Media** | | |
| *Reference* | | *Special Instructions* |
| *Distribution* | *Reevaluation Date*<br>**August2011** | *No. Pages*<br>**4** |

## I. PURPOSE

The department endorses the secure use of social media to enhance communication, collaboration, and information exchange; streamline processes; and foster productivity. This policy establishes this department's position on the utility and management of social media and provides guidance on its management, administration, and oversight. This policy is not meant to address one particular form of social media, rather social media in general, as advances in technology will occur and new tools will emerge.

## II. POLICY

Social media provides a new and potentially valuable means of assisting the department and its personnel in meeting community outreach, problem-solving, investigative, crime prevention, and related objectives. This policy identifies potential uses that may be explored or expanded upon as deemed reasonable by administrative and supervisory personnel. The department also recognizes the role that these tools play in the personal lives of some department personnel. The personal use of social media can have bearing on departmental personnel in their official capacity. As such, this policy provides information of a precautionary nature as well as prohibitions on the use of social media by department personnel.

## III. DEFINITIONS

*Blog:* A self-published diary or commentary on a particular topic that may allow visitors to post responses, reactions, or comments. The term is short for "Web log."

*Page:* The specific portion of a social media website where content is displayed, and managed by an indi-

vidual or individuals with administrator rights.

*Post:* Content an individual shares on a social media site or the act of publishing content on a site.

*Profile:* Information that a user provides about himself or herself on a social networking site.

*Social Media:* A category of Internet-based resources that integrate user-generated content and user participation. This includes, but is not limited to, social networking sites (Facebook, MySpace), microblogging sites (Twitter, Nixle), photo- and video-sharing sites (Flickr, YouTube), wikis (Wikipedia), blogs, and news sites (Digg, Reddit).

*Social Networks:* Online platforms where users can create profiles, share information, and socialize with others using a range of technologies.

*Speech:* Expression or communication of thoughts or opinions in spoken words, in writing, by expressive conduct, symbolism, photographs, videotape, or related forms of communication.

*Web 2.0:* The second generation of the World Wide Web focused on shareable, user-generated content, rather than static web pages. Some use this term interchangeably with social media.

*Wiki:* Web page(s) that can be edited collaboratively.

## IV. ON-THE-JOB USE

A. Department-Sanctioned Presence
 1. Determine strategy
    a. Where possible, each social media page shall include an introductory statement that clearly specifies the purpose and scope of the agency's presence on the website.
    b. Where possible, the page(s) should link to the department's official website.
    c. Social media page(s) shall be designed for

**FIGURE 6.2** IACP Social Media Sample Policy.

*Source*: International Association of Chiefs of Police. (2011). *Social Media Model Policy*. Retrieved from www.iacpsocialmedia.org.

the target audience(s) such as youth or potential police recruits.

2. Procedures
   a. All department social media sites or pages shall be approved by the chief executive or his or her designee and shall be administered by the departmental information services section or as otherwise determined.
   b. Where possible, social media pages shall clearly indicate they are maintained by the department and shall have department contact information prominently displayed.
   c. Social media content shall adhere to applicable laws, regulations, and policies, including all information technology and records management policies.
      (1) Content is subject to public records laws. Relevant records retention schedules apply to social media content.
      (2) Content must be managed, stored, and retrieved to comply with open records laws and e-discovery laws and policies.
   d. Where possible, social media pages should state that the opinions expressed by visitors to the page(s) do not reflect the opinions of the department.
      (1) Pages shall clearly indicate that posted comments will be monitored and that the department reserves the right to remove obscenities, off-topic comments, and personal attacks.
      (2) Pages shall clearly indicate that any content posted or submitted for posting is subject to public disclosure.

3. Department-Sanctioned Use
   a. Department personnel representing the department via social media outlets shall do the following:
      (1) Conduct themselves at all times as representatives of the department and, accordingly, shall adhere to all department standards of conduct and observe conventionally accepted protocols and proper decorum.
      (2) Identify themselves as a member of the department.
      (3) Not make statements about the guilt or innocence of any suspect or arrestee, or comments concerning pending prosecutions, nor post, transmit, or otherwise disseminate confidential information, including photographs or videos, related to department training, activities, or work-related assignments without express written permission.
      (4) Not conduct political activities or private business.

   b. The use of department computers by department personnel to access social media is prohibited without authorization.
   c. Department personnel use of personally owned devices to manage the department's social media activities or in the course of official duties is prohibited without express written permission.
   d. Employees shall observe and abide by all copyright, trademark, and service mark restrictions in posting materials to electronic media.

B. Potential Uses
1. Social media is a valuable investigative tool when seeking evidence or information about
   a. missing persons;
   b. wanted persons;
   c. gang participation;
   d. crimes perpetrated online (i.e., cyberbullying, cyberstalking); and
   e. photos or videos of a crime posted by a participant or observer.
2. Social media can be used for community outreach and engagement by
   a. providing crime prevention tips;
   b. offering online-reporting opportunities;
   c. sharing crime maps and data; and
   d. soliciting tips about unsolved crimes (i.e., Crimestoppers, text-a-tip).
3. Social media can be used to make time-sensitive notifications related to
   a. road closures,
   b. special events,
   c. weather emergencies, and
   d. missing or endangered persons.
4. Persons seeking employment and volunteer positions use the Internet to search for opportunities, and social media can be a valuable recruitment mechanism.
5. This department has an obligation to include Internet-based content when conducting background investigations of job candidates.
6. Searches should be conducted by a nondecision maker. Information pertaining to protected classes shall be filtered out prior to sharing any information found online with decision makers.
7. Persons authorized to search Internet-based content should be deemed as holding a sensitive position.
8. Search methods shall not involve techniques that are a violation of existing law.
9. Vetting techniques shall be applied uniformly to all candidates.
10. Every effort must be made to validate Internet-based information considered during the hiring process.

2

FIGURE 6.2 (*Continued*)

## V. PERSONAL USE

A. Precautions and Prohibitions

Barring state law or binding employment contracts to the contrary, department personnel shall abide by the following when using social media.

1. Department personnel are free to express themselves as private citizens on social media sites to the degree that their speech does not impair working relationships of this department for which loyalty and confidentiality are important, impede the performance of duties, impair discipline and harmony among coworkers, or negatively affect the public perception of the department.

2. As public employees, department personnel are cautioned that speech on- or off-duty, made pursuant to their official duties—that is, that owes its existence to the employee's professional duties and responsibilities—is not protected speech under the First Amendment and may form the basis for discipline if deemed detrimental to the department. Department personnel should assume that their speech and related activity on social media sites will reflect upon their office and this department.

3. Department personnel shall not post, transmit, or otherwise disseminate any information to which they have access as a result of their employment without written permission from the chief executive or his or her designee.

4. For safety and security reasons, department personnel are cautioned not to disclose their employment with this department nor shall they post information pertaining to any other member of the department without their permission. As such, department personnel are cautioned not to do the following:

   a. Display department logos, uniforms, or similar identifying items on personal web pages.

   b. Post personal photographs or provide similar means of personal recognition that may cause them to be identified as a police officer of this department. Officers who are, or who may reasonably be expected to work in undercover operations, shall not post any form of visual or personal identification.

5. When using social media, department personnel should be mindful that their speech becomes part of the worldwide electronic domain. Therefore, adherence to the department's code of conduct is required in the personal use of social media. In particular, department personnel are prohibited from the following:

   a. Speech containing obscene or sexually explicit language, images, or acts and statements or other forms of speech that ridicule, malign, disparage, or otherwise express bias against any race, any religion, or any protected class of individuals.

   b. Speech involving themselves or other department personnel reflecting behavior that would reasonably be considered reckless or irresponsible.

6. Engaging in prohibited speech noted herein, may provide grounds for undermining or impeaching an officer's testimony in criminal proceedings. Department personnel thus sanctioned are subject to discipline up to and including termination of office.

7. Department personnel may not divulge information gained by reason of their authority; make any statements, speeches, appearances, and endorsements; or publish materials that could reasonably be considered to represent the views or positions of this department without express authorization.

8. Department personnel should be aware that they may be subject to civil litigation for

   a. publishing or posting false information that harms the reputation of another person, group, or organization (defamation);

   b. publishing or posting private facts and personal information about someone without their permission that has not been previously revealed to the public, is not of legitimate public concern, and would be offensive to a reasonable person;

   c. using someone else's name, likeness, or other personal attributes without that person's permission for an exploitative purpose; or

   d. publishing the creative work of another, trademarks, or certain confidential business information without the permission of the owner.

9. Department personnel should be aware that privacy settings and social media sites are constantly in flux, and they should never assume that personal information posted on such sites is protected.

10. Department personnel should expect that any information created, transmitted, downloaded, exchanged, or discussed in a public online forum may be accessed by the department at any time without prior notice.

11. Reporting violations—Any employee becoming aware of or having knowledge of a posting or of any website or web page in violation of the provision of this policy shall notify his or her supervisor immediately for follow-up action.

3

**FIGURE 6.2** (*Continued*)

**Acknowledgment**

This *Model Policy* was developed by the International Association of Chiefs of Police (IACP) Center for Social Media in conjunction with the IACP National Law Enforcement Policy Center. We are appreciative of the many policy agencies across the country who shared their existing policies.

Every effort has been made by the IACP National Law Enforcement Policy Center staff and advisory board to ensure that this model policy incorporates the most current information and contemporary professional judgment on this issue. However, law enforcement administrators should be cautioned that no "model" policy can meet all the needs of any given law enforcement agency. Each law enforcement agency operates in a unique environment of federal court rulings, state laws, local ordinances, regulations, judicial and administrative decisions and collective bargaining agreements that must be considered. In addition, the formulation of specific agency policies must take into account local political and community perspectives and customs, prerogatives and demands; often divergent law enforcement strategies and philosophies; and the impact of varied agency resource capabilities among other factors.

This project was supported by Grant No. 2006-DG-BX-K004 awarded by the Bureau of Justice Assistance, Office of Justice Programs, U.S. Department of Justice. The Assistant Attorney General, Office of Justice Programs, coordinates the activities of the following program offices and bureaus: the Bureau of Justice Assistance, the Bureau of Justice Statistics, National Institute of Justice, Office of Juvenile Justice and Delinquency Prevention, and the Office of Victims of Crime. Points of view or opinions in this document are those of the author and do not represent the official position or policies of the United States Department of Justice or the IACP.

**FIGURE 6.2** (*Continued*)

changed because of social media. Public safety managers should also share successful strategies regarding social media with other agencies.

## Social Media Glossary of Terms

Social media has its own language. Terms like *blog*, *emoticon*, and *podcast* are commonly used in our society. Therefore, it is important for public safety personnel to have a basic understanding of social media terminology or jargon. Appendix 1 lists some of the more popular social media terminology used today.

In 2012, the IACP Center for Social Media published a brief that listed the top ten things a law enforcement executive or manager should know about social media. They include:[22]

- Social media is not going away. It is here to stay.
- Social media is already being used by public safety personnel. Therefore, you should develop and adopt specific policies regarding the use of social media by your personnel.
- Before your agency uses social media, develop a list of goals and objectives. Having a comprehensive strategy will ensure that social media is used effectively.
- Ensure your agency has two-way communication with the community.
- Don't rush into the social media realm. Start small and grow your social media presence over time.
- Integrate social media tools and websites. This will ensure that your information is received by a wider audience.
- Social media should only be used to enhance your overall media strategy. Do not neglect other ways of communicating with the public.
- There is no wrong way to use social media. It depends on your agency.
- There may be a cost for using social media. Your agency must evaluate the cost of personnel and training against the benefits of enhancing community policing.
- Social media is already being used by other agencies. There is no need to create a policy from scratch. Research and learn from other agencies that are similar to your own agency.

## Chapter Summary

Social media is not just the latest trend in technology. It continues to grow at an increasing rate and will most likely continue to have more of an impact on society in the future. The younger generation has used computers and the Internet for their entire life. They are comfortable with technology like social media. As younger generations continue to grow, so will their ingenuity to create better technology than what we have today. Public safety managers must always strive to keep up with technology, specifically social media. As previously mentioned, social media has forever changed how public safety personnel perform and interact with the community. Savvy public safety managers have an opportunity to reach out to society like never before. The tools and resources are there. They just need to be identified, used properly and monitored for any potential department violations. This will ensure that public safety and the community continue to move forward in a positive direction. Public safety managers must create and adopt a social media policy for their organization. This will ensure that employees use social media for its intended purposes and not for personal reasons.

## Key Words or Terminology

| | | |
|---|---|---|
| social media | website | forum |
| blogs | RSS | virtual community |
| podcasts | policy | First Amendment |

## Discussion Questions

1. Contact a public safety agency and review their social media policy. Analyze it and list any strengths or weaknesses based on your readings in this chapter.
2. Describe a typical social media policy. What are some of the significant elements that must be part of the policy?
3. Explain and highlight any legal or case laws that could affect a social media policy.
4. Locate and identify five types of social media that can be used by a public safety agency.
5. How does leadership play a role in social media and public safety? Does social media technology require oversight from management, supervisors or line personnel?
6. Identify ten ways that social media can assist public safety agencies. (Criminal investigations, public information sharing, and so on.)

## Notes

1 (2013). *Social media fact sheet*. IACP. Alexandria, VA: International Association of Chiefs of Police.
2 (2013). *Top 15 most popular social networking sites*. EbizMBA Inc. Retrieved October 4, 2013, from www.ebixmba.com.
3 (2013). *Social media survey*. IACP. Alexandria, VA: International Association of Chiefs of Police.
4 Constitution of the United States. (n.d.). *First Amendment*. Retrieved from www.archives.gov/exhibits/charters/constitution.
5 (2002). *Ashcroft v. Free Speech Coalition*. 535 U.S. 234. Washington, DC: U.S. Supreme Court.
6 Ibid.
7 (2010). *City of Ontario vs. Quan: The Supreme Court weighs in on employee privacy expectations*. Cite 560 No. 08–1332. Washington, DC: U.S. Supreme Court.
8 Ibid.
9 (2013). *Developing a policy on the use of social media in intelligence and investigative activities: Guidance and recommendations*. Alexandria, VA: International Association of Chiefs of Police.
10 Sherbert, E. (2012). Gregory Graniss arrested on suspicion of smashing muni bus in World Series celebration. *San Francisco Weekly*. Retrieved from www.blogs.sfweekly.com.
11 Popken, B. (2011). *How a sheriff uses his 10,000 Facebook fans to solve crimes*. Retrieved from www.consumerist.com.
12 (2011). Kaskade block party turns into riot at Hollywood and Highland. *Huffington Post*. Retrieved from www.huffingtonpost.com/2011.
13 McQuade, S. (2006). Technology-enabled crime, policing and security. *The Journal of Technology Studies, vol. 32*. University of Virginia Tech. Retrieved from www.scholar.lib.vt.edu/ejournals/JOTS/v32n1/mcquade.html.
14 (2013). *Social media used in law enforcement investigations*. LexisNexis. Retrieved on July 17, 2014, from www.lexisnexis.com/government/investigations.
15 (2012). *How are innovations in technology transforming policing?* Police Executive Research Forum. Retrieved from www.policeforum.org/library.
16 Goode, E. (2011). Police lesson: Social network tools have two edges. *New York Times*. Retrieved from www.nytimes.com/2011.
17 (2011). *Social networking: The double-edged sword for cops*. Policelink. Retrieved from www.policelink.com/new/articles.
18 (2013). *Volusia beach safety officer fired on Trayvon Martin FB post*. WFTV. Retrieved from www.wftv.com/news/local.
19 (1963). *Brady v. Maryland 83*. Washington, DC: U.S. Supreme Court.
20 (2013). *Developing a policy on the use of social media in intelligence and investigative activities: Guidance and recommendations*. Alexandria, VA: International Association of Chiefs of Police.
21 Ibid.
22 (2013). *Law enforcement executives' social media top ten*. Alexandria, VA: International Association of Chiefs of Police.

# 7

# BODY-WORN CAMERA TECHNOLOGY

"The day you see a camera come into our courtroom,
it's going to roll over my dead body."

—*David Souter*

## Learning Objectives

After reading this chapter, the student will:

- Understand the role of body cameras in public safety.
- Identify the types of equipment and resources necessary to implement a body camera program.
- Assess the legal issues with body cameras including data storage, privacy concerns and Fourth Amendment issues.
- Evaluate and review department policy considerations for body cameras from a management prospective.
- Assess the advantages and disadvantages of body cameras.

## Introduction

In this chapter, we review one of the latest trends in public safety: body-worn cameras. Law enforcement officers contact the public on a daily basis and body-worn cameras can help promote legitimacy and public support for a very difficult job. The use of body-worn cameras can increase accountability and ensure that the public has confidence in law enforcement. This chapter addresses the advantages and disadvantages of using body-worn camera technology. We also review the history of body-worn cameras and various legal considerations, including privacy concerns and the improper use of video footage. Finally, this chapter includes a comprehensive list of recommendations for law enforcement personnel to review before implementing a body-worn camera program.

## Body Cameras

Law enforcement officers routinely interact with the public. One out of every five Americans has had an encounter with a police officer.[1] In 2015, Reuters conducted a poll and found that 31 percent of Americans believe that law enforcement personnel lie on a regular basis.[2] Although the vast majority of law enforcement contacts do not result in a citizen complaint or a use-of-force incident, recent high-profile incidents have raised society's conscience about the perceived conduct of law enforcement personnel. The shootings in Ferguson, Missouri, and Staten Island, New York, have reached national attention. The question always comes up. What if the police officer wore a body camera during the incident? Would this help justify the use of force or would the video be used by anti-law enforcement organizations to highlight their hatred toward law enforcement? Body-worn cameras can protect law enforcement personnel from false accusations, reduce agency liability, reduce citizen complaints and provide critical evidence in court. Unlike vehicle-mounted cameras, body-worn cameras are attached to the officer and can record more activity.[3]

Civil rights violations are not the only issue discussed in the news media. Law enforcement personnel can also break the law and disobey department policies through corruption, favoritism, discrimination and the failure to carry out their duties.[4] Periodically, police corruption and abuse of power become major issues on the public agenda.[5]

### *History of Body-Worn Cameras*

According to the National Institute of Justice, a body-worn camera is an audio and video capture device that allows law enforcement personnel to record activity or encounters with the public.[6]

Video footage from body-worn cameras provides a glimpse into a specific incident. It helps others see what law enforcement personnel are observing at the time of the incident. It also helps give some perspective about what the suspect is doing. Body-worn cameras can be placed just about anywhere on law enforcement personnel, including the uniform (usually the chest area), helmet, cap or glasses.[7]

Great Britain was the first to begin testing body-worn cameras on officers as early as 2005.[8] The initial study of body-worn cameras was done in Plymouth, England, from 2005–2006. The British police referred to the devices as *body-worn video* and wore the cameras on a headband over their left ears. The United Kingdom Home Office, which is the equivalent to the U.S. Department of Justice, reported that the use of body-worn video devices benefited law enforcement, and they recommended its continued use.[9]

The United States started to evaluate the effects of body-worn cameras around 2012. Jay Stanley writes, "Recent surveys suggest that about 25 percent of the nation's 17,000 police agencies were using them, with fully 80 percent of agencies evaluating the technology."[10] Many law enforcement agencies used some type of video surveillance technology,

**FIGURE 7.1**   Body-Worn Camera.

*Source*: Courtesy of the Monrovia Police Department.

including in-car video cameras, but there was no specific research on the overall value of this technology.

In 2012, the Rialto Police Department (California) studied the use of body-worn cameras and its relationship to citizen complaints and use-of-force incidents. The following are the highlights of the study:

- One-year study 2012–2013.
- Body-worn cameras were issued to line personnel covering 988 shifts. Some officers were not issued body-worn cameras as part of the study.
- The study revealed that the amount of use-of-force incidents was reduced by approximately 60 percent.
- Shifts *without* body-worn cameras continued to see a rise in use-of-force incidents.
- The study also revealed an 88 percent reduction in citizen complaints compared to the prior year.[11]

At the conclusion of the study, Rialto Police Chief William Farrar stated, "Whether the reduced number of complaints was because of the officers behaving better or the citizens behaving better—well, it was probably a little bit of both."[12]

Also in 2012, the Mesa Police Department (Arizona) conducted a study of body-worn cameras. The following are the highlights of the study:

- One-year pilot program designed to reduce citizen complaints and enhance criminal prosecutions.
- Fifty officers were given body-worn cameras, and another fifty officers did not receive body-worn cameras.
- The study revealed that officers without the body-worn cameras had three times as many citizen complaints compared to officers who wore the cameras.
- Use-of-force complaints were reduced by 75 percent for officers who had the body-worn cameras.[13]

The Phoenix Police Department was one of the largest agencies that completed a body-worn camera study. This study not only addressed citizen complaints and use-of-force incidents, but it also evaluated the use of body-worn cameras in domestic violence prosecutions. The following are the highlights of the summary:

- The Phoenix Police Department received a $500,000 grant from the U.S. Bureau of Justice Smart Justice Assistance Initiative.
- The study focused on one specific precinct (Maryvale).
- Maryvale had a large amount of domestic violence calls for service.
- The study revealed that prosecutors were more willing to file charges on domestic violence cases if they had body-worn camera videos as evidence.
- They also saw marked declines in citizen and use-of-force complaints.
- One interesting caveat is that despite the success of the study, some officers were still resistant to the implementation of body-worn cameras throughout the rest of the department.[14]

## Management Considerations

### Why Use Body-Worn Cameras?

Public safety managers need to identify why their agency should use body-worn cameras. Although there are many potential uses for this technology, the International Association of Chiefs of Police (IACP) identified some of the more popular reasons. They include:

### Safety

The mere presence of a body-worn camera can help deter violence against an officer. It can also help convict a person who attacks an officer.[15]

## Officer Interactions with the Public

Body-worn cameras can help protect and support the actions of law enforcement personnel during a variety of situations. They include:

- Patrol operations including calls for service (foot or vehicle patrol)
- Emergency calls for first responders
- Incidents in correctional facilities
- Critical situations like SWAT callouts[16]

## The Court Process

Body-worn camera video can be used as evidence in a court of law. Video evidence enhances the chances of a conviction and increases the amount of plea bargains. It can also help reduce the amount of time prosecutors spend on a specific case. Fifty-eight percent of prosecutors reported that body-worn camera video reduces the amount of time they spend in the courtroom.[17]

## Professionalism

The presence of body-worn cameras provides an extra layer of accountability for law enforcement agencies. It can also reduce the amount of citizen complaints for misconduct. Although some officers are reluctant to use body-worn cameras, video footage can also help protect the officer from false complaints or alleged misconduct.[18]

## Legal Obstacles

Public safety managers should consult with legal counsel before implementing a body-worn camera program. There are some federal and state restrictions that deal with video or audio recording of the public. The public has an expectation of privacy and some states require consent from involved parties before audio taping can occur. This can be an issue when recording inside a person's residence or other areas that are deemed private by the courts.[19]

Another legal factor is the possibility of a public record request from the public. The public and many citizen advocate groups like the ACLU have already submitted requests for body-worn camera footage on high-profile cases. Public safety agencies should address this issue with legal counsel and determine how and under what circumstances video footage will be released pursuant to a request.

## Purchasing Body-Worn Cameras

Before purchasing body-worn cameras, public safety managers should consider several factors including cost, budget, desired use of body-worn camera and environment.[20] There

**TABLE 7.1**  Body-Worn Camera Recommendations

| Product Selection Criteria | Description |
|---|---|
| VGA Resolution | The resolution should be at least 640 x 480 pixels |
| Frame Rate | The frame rate should be at least 25 frames per second |
| Battery Runtime | The camera should be able to record continuously for at least 3 hours on a fully charged battery |
| Data Storage | The camera's onboard storage, at the lowest video quality settings, should permit at least 3 hours of recording |
| Low-light Recording | The camera should have a low lux-rating and/or an IR illuminator for recording targets in low-light |
| Warranty | System purchase should include, at a minimum, a one year warranty |

*Source*: Sensor, Surveillance, and Biometric Technologies Center of Excellence. (2012). *A Primer on Body-Worn Cameras for Law Enforcement*: Washington, DC: National Institute of Justice.

is no perfect blueprint for a body-worn camera program in public safety; however, law enforcement personnel should address the following before any purchase:

- The type and quality of video
- Limits on recording
- Battery life
- Do you want to record at night?
- Point of view
- Do you want audio as well as video?
- How and where will the body-worn camera be placed?
- Integration with radio[21]

## Cost

Law enforcement managers should do a cost analysis of body-worn cameras before any purchase. The cost analysis should include the initial cost of the body-worn cameras (hardware and software), storage requirements, training and maintenance. The analysis should also include any staff time required to review footage and if necessary potential legal counsel fees in response to a public record request. A typical body-worn camera can cost anywhere from $800–$1,000 per unit.[22] A common mistake is to purchase only one camera for each officer. Staffing levels change over time, cameras may need maintenance and they may break during an encounter with a suspect. Therefore, law enforcement managers should consider purchasing a sufficient number of backup body-worn cameras, just in case.

## *Storage/Retention*

Another critical consideration for law enforcement managers is how and where to store video footage from body-worn cameras. Factors that must be considered include:

- What are the legal requirements to store video footage in the agency's specific jurisdiction? For example, some agencies have to comply with various state laws that define the length of storage of any video or audio evidence.[23] Most law enforcement agencies store this type of evidence at least 13 months. This ensures that the evidence is available for any civil complaint filed against the agency. Law enforcement managers should also consult with the district attorney's office and ensure that body-worn camera video footage is stored long enough to correspond with any legal proceedings. Body-worn camera videos can be used as evidence in preliminary hearings or a jury trial.
- Who will have access to the footage? Is the footage going to be available to all personnel or only available to supervisors?
- How will the video files be protected from others? Body-worn camera video footage may be controversial in nature and law enforcement managers must ensure that it is protected from hackers or unauthorized users.
- Will the body-worn camera video footage be stored on a single server or backed up on another server in a different location? Body-worn camera video footage must be stored in a secure location. Many agencies store and manage video data locally, but also have a backup storage server at another location in case of a natural disaster or event that compromises the main servers' data. Body-worn camera vendors can also offer cloud-based storage solutions at an additional cost.
- What will be your chain-of-custody policy? The integrity of the evidence is critical and must be part of any decision process on a body camera program. Time and date stamps should always be imprinted on the footage.[24]

## *Community Engagement*

Law enforcement personnel should make a concerted effort to meet with all stakeholders before implementing a body-worn camera program. This includes the public, criminal justice professionals, unions and specifically line personnel because they will be the main users of this technology. Law enforcement managers must ensure that all stakeholders are educated on the specific policies and procedures of their body-worn camera program. Open communication and transparency can also strengthen the relationship between law enforcement and the community.

Law enforcement managers should also seek out other agencies that have implemented body-worn cameras and learn how they engaged with the community.[25]

## *Privacy Concerns*

Although the public generally accepts the use of body cameras, the issue of privacy is a concern. The public wants accountability from law enforcement and body-worn cameras can help

**TABLE 7.2** Implementing a Body-Worn Camera Program: Recommendations and Lessons Learned

| Number | Lesson Learned |
| --- | --- |
| 1 | Engaging the community prior to implementing a camera program can help secure support for the program and increase the perceived legitimacy of the programs within the community |
| 2 | Agencies have found it useful to communicate with the public, local policymakers, and other stakeholders about what the cameras will be used for and how the cameras will affect them |
| 3 | Social media is an effective way to facilitate public engagement about body-worn cameras |
| 4 | Transparency about the agency's camera policies and practices, both prior to and after implementation, can help increase the public's acceptance and hold agencies accountable. Examples of transparency include posting policies on the agency's website and publically releasing video recordings of controversial incidents. |
| 5 | When presenting officers with a new technology, program, or strategy, the best approach includes efforts by agency leaders to engage officers on the topic, explain the goals and benefits of the initiative, and address any concerns the officers may have. |
| 6 | Briefings, roll calls, and meetings with union representatives are effective means to communicate with officers about the agency's body-worn camera program. |
| 7 | Creating an implementation team that includes representatives from across the agency can help strengthen program legitimacy and ease implementation. |
| 8 | Agencies have found that officers support a body-worn camera program if they view the cameras as useful tools; e.g., as a technology that helps reduce complaints and produces evidence that can be used in court or internal investigations. |
| 9 | Recruiting an internal "champion" to help inform officers about the benefits of the cameras has proven successful in addressing officers' concerns about embracing the new technology. |
| 10 | Taking an incremental approach to implementation can help make the deployment run more smoothly. This can include testing cameras during a trial period, rolling out cameras slowly, or initially assigning cameras to tech savvy officers. |
| 11 | Educating oversight bodies about the realities of using cameras can help them understand operational challenges and why there may be situations in which officers are unable to record. This can include demonstrations to judges, attorneys, and civilian review boards about how the cameras operate. |

*Source*: Miller, L., Toliver, J. and Police Executive Research Forum. (2014). Washington, DC: Office of Community Oriented Policing Services.

in this area. However, this type of technology can be intrusive and capture details that may be considered "private" by some in society. This creates a difficult challenge for law enforcement managers. The public wants law enforcement to use body-worn cameras, but they do not want their privacy violated. For example, law enforcement personnel can enter someone's home and record suspects, witnesses and victims.[26] Are officers supposed to stop recording when inside of the residence? Are they going to be thinking about the resident's legal right to privacy instead of worrying about officer safety issues? This is a difficult dilemma indeed.

Although many law enforcement agencies may not agree with some anti-police advocate groups, the American Civil Liberties Union has outlined a series of recommendations that law enforcement managers should consider when it comes to privacy. They include:

- Only uniformed law enforcement personnel should wear body-worn cameras. The public should know that the people recording an incident are in fact part of law enforcement. Obvious exceptions to the police uniform requirement include specialty units like SWAT.
- The ACLU recommends that officers notify people that they are being recorded. They also recommend that the body-worn camera have signage that indicates that they are being recorded.
- Officers should not use body-worn cameras just to obtain information protected by the First Amendment.[27]

## Body-Worn Cameras and the Criminal Justice System

Body-worn camera video footage can be an important part of any criminal investigation. In years past, law enforcement had to write a police report that describes what happened during a specific incident or call for service. The prosecutor has to evaluate if there is sufficient evidence to charge a suspect with a crime. If the suspect is charged with a crime, the prosecutor must attempt to reconstruct the event for a jury or magistrate. This can be difficult and some details can be lost during the translation process. Criminal acts are fluid and have a lot of moving parts.

Body-worn camera technology changes everything. Now stakeholders in the criminal justice system can simply push play and watch the event. A study in the United Kingdom found that body-worn camera evidence increased the likelihood of a guilty plea from a suspect. It also helped reduce the amount of paperwork an officer must prepare and in some cases helped prosecutors identify what specific crimes have occurred.[28]

## Department Policy Recommendations

A recent survey of sixty-three law enforcement agencies revealed that nearly one-third of the agencies did not have a specific policy on the use of body-worn cameras.[29] Some law enforcement managers have been reluctant to create a written policy because of the lack of guidance or best practices on using body-worn cameras.[30] In an effort to address this issue, the Police Executive Research Forum (PERF) prepared an informative study that outlines specific recommendations to law enforcement executives and managers regarding body-worn cameras. PERF recommends that the policy address the following categories:

Quick Tip: Students and law enforcement personnel are encouraged to read the entire PERF study at www.policeforum.org.

## Body-Worn Camera Usage

- Who will wear the camera? Typically, personnel who have the most public contact should use body-worn cameras. This includes patrol and traffic personnel. The policy should also indicate who *is not* required to wear a body-worn camera.
- Personally owned body-worn camera technology should not be allowed. This ensures that the chain of custody is maintained.
- Identify where the body-worn camera should be located. Chest, head, collar, etc.
- Specifically state whether officers are required to document the use of a body-worn camera during an incident. The policy should also address situations where an officer fails to activate a body-worn camera.
- The policy should state whether law enforcement personnel have to notify the public about body-worn camera recordings. Do they need consent? This is an issue when recording potential victims.
- The usage policy should address the videotaping of non–law enforcement activities including other personnel.
- The policy should identify when the use of body-worn cameras is prohibited. This includes situations where confidentially is required, locations where expectations of privacy exist and situations where certain tactics are used. For correctional personnel, the use of body-worn cameras during a strip search should not be allowed.[31]

## Download and Storage Policy

- Who will maintain the body-worn camera technology?
- The policy should include automatic audits designed to prevent unauthorized users from deleting or tampering with the video footage.
- The policy should describe how law enforcement personnel should actually download video footage? (At the end of the shift, etc.) It should also indicate how the body-worn camera video is saved in the system.
- The policy should indicate the amount of time the video will remain on the storage server based on consultations with legal counsel.
- Define the actual location of the storage server and if necessary backup servers.
- If a third-party vendor is going to store any video footage, the policy should ensure that the use and access is only allowed with permission from the law enforcement agency.[32]

## Who Can Access or Review Body-Worn Camera Video Footage?

- The policy should spell out the procedure for public record requests.
- Are law enforcement personnel allowed to view the video footage before writing a report or being interviewed by other personnel?
- How and when can supervisors review video footage? Supervisors need to have access to body-worn camera video footage to investigate complaints, ensure policies are being adhered to and identify training issues.

- The policy should also include random audits, typically from outside the officers' chain of command.
- The policy should prohibit the use of video footage for personal reasons. This includes social media sites.[33]

### Training

- All policies should have a training component. An effective body-worn camera policy should identify which law enforcement personnel needs training before using it in real life situations. The training should be ongoing.
- The training should address all applicable department policies and legal analysis of state laws on body-worn camera evidence, privacy and release to the public.
- The training policy should address how the body-worn cameras should be worn, how video footage should be labeled or downloaded properly.
- Training on using video footage in court.
- What happens if the device fails in the field (troubleshooting scenarios)?[34]

### Statistics and Evaluation of Body-Worn Camera Program

- Body camera statistics should be public and included on annual reports. Transparency is an important factor with this type of technology.
- The program should continually be evaluated to ensure law enforcement personnel are adhering to department policies.
- Is the program effective? Does the program make sense to law enforcement executives and managers?
- The evaluation should also include feedback from all stakeholders.[35]

## Chapter Summary

This chapter outlined the specific issues with body-worn cameras in law enforcement. This type of technology allows law enforcement encounters to effectively become "reality television" and, thus, law enforcement organizations have to deal with the ongoing scrutiny from the public and anti-law enforcement groups. However, this technology does have the ability to strengthen partnerships with the community and actually provide some protections to individual officers who are under investigation for misconduct or excessive force claims. It also has a tremendous effect in the judicial system because video footage can be introduced as evidence. Throughout this chapter, we reviewed numerous recommendations for law enforcement managers to consider before adopting a body-worn camera program. This technology can be tricky because it involves privacy issues, accountability and transparency. Thankfully, law enforcement does not have to venture into this area alone. Take advantage of the recommendations and incorporate them into your own body-worn camera program.

## Key Terms or Terminology

body-worn cameras     privacy     data storage
department policy     Fourth Amendment     citizen complaints

## Discussion Questions

1. What are the legal challenges law enforcement agencies face in a body-worn camera program? How can law enforcement managers overcome this issue?
2. This chapter highlighted three case studies on body-worn camera programs. Research this area and see if other agencies have had successful programs as well. Identify them by name and summarize their programs.
3. What are three of the most important factors that should be part of any body-worn camera department policy? Explain your answer and give examples as necessary.

## Notes

1 Cole, G. and Smith, C. (2011). *Criminal justice in America* (6th ed.). 5, 1311–32. Belmont, CA: Wadsworth Cengage Learning.
2 Schneider, B. (2015). *Breaking down the numbers: One third of Americans believe police lie routinely.* Reuters. Retrieved from: www.web.archive.org/web/20150116052554/www.blogs.reuters.com/great-debate/2015/01/15/one-third-of-americans-believe-police-lie-routinely/.
3 Coppola, M. (2013). The future of body-worn cameras for law enforcement. *Tech Beat Magazine.* Retrieved from: www.policeone.com/police-products/body-cameras/articles/6583291-The-future-of-body-worn-cameras-for-law-enforcement/.
4 Cole and Smith, *Criminal justice in America.*
5 Skolnick, J. and Fyfe, J. (1993). *Above the law: Police and the excessive use of force.* New York: The Free Press.
6 (2012). *A primer on body-worn cameras for law enforcement.* Sensor, Surveillance, and Biometric Technologies Center of Excellence. Washington, DC: National Institute of Justice.
7 Ibid.
8 Harris, D.A. (2010). Picture this: Body worn video devices ('head cams') as tools for ensuring Fourth Amendment compliance by police. *Texas Tech Law Review, vol. 43.* University of Pittsburgh School of Law.
9 Goodall, M. (2007). *Guidance for the police use of body-worn video devices.* United Kingdom: Police and Crime Standards Directorate.
10 Stanley, J. (2015). *Police body mounted cameras: With right policies in place, a win for all.* American Civil Liberties Union. Retrieved from: www.aclu.org/police-body-mounted-cameras-right-policies-place-win-all.
11 Miller, L., Toliver, J., and Police Executive Research Forum. (2014). *Implementing a body-worn camera program: Recommendations and lessons learned.* Washington, DC: Office of Community Oriented Policing Services.
12 Ibid.
13 Ibid.
14 Katz, C. M., et al. (2014). *Evaluating the impact of officer worn body cameras in the Phoenix Police Department.* Phoenix, AZ: Center for Violence Prevention & Community Safety, Arizona State University.
15 (2004). *The impact of video evidence on modern policing: Research and best practices from the IACP study on in-car cameras.* Alexandria, VA: International Association of Chiefs of Police.

16  Sensor, Surveillance, and Biometric Technologies Center of Excellence, *A primer on body-worn cameras.*
17  International Association of Chiefs of Police, *The impact of video evidence on modern policing.*
18  Ibid.
19  Sensor, Surveillance, and Biometric Technologies Center of Excellence, *A primer on body-worn cameras.*
20  Ibid.
21  Ibid.
22  White, M. (2014). *Police officer body worn cameras: Assessing the evidence.* Washington, DC: Office of Community Oriented Policing Services.
23  Sensor, Surveillance, and Biometric Technologies Center of Excellence, *A primer on body-worn cameras.*
24  Ibid.
25  Ibid.
26  Stanley, *Police body mounted cameras.*
27  Ibid.
28  White, *Police officer body worn cameras.*
29  Pearce, M. (2014). Growing use of body cameras raises privacy concerns. *Los Angeles Times.* Retrieved from: www.latimes.com/nation/la-na-body-cameras-20140927-story.html.
30  Miller, Toliver, and Police Executive Research Forum, *Implementing a body worn camera program.*
31  Ibid.
32  Ibid.
33  Ibid.
34  Ibid.
35  Ibid.

# 8

# BIOMETRICS AND PUBLIC SAFETY

"We are discussing no small matter, but how we ought to live."

—*Socrates*

## Learning Objectives

After reading this chapter, the student will:

- Understand the role of biometrics in public safety.
- Be able to explain the different types of biometric technology and how they are used in public safety.
- Know and understand how biometric technology can be expanded to improve efficiency and improve safety.
- Evaluate the need for innovation and expanding biometric technology.

## Introduction

In this chapter, we examine the various uses of biometric technology in public safety. Biometrics are very useful to federal, state and local law enforcement agencies because the technology can be used to help identify a subject under suspicion, involved in a crime or being booked into a jail facility. Developments in biometric technology have expanded from just fingerprints. They now include facial recognition, palm prints, iris, hand/finger geometry, voice, dynamic signature and DNA matching. The aforementioned biometric technologies are discussed in this chapter. This chapter also discusses recent uses of biometric technology in public safety and in the private sector.

## What Is Biometric Identification?

*Biometrics* is defined as the measurable biological (anatomical and physiological) or behavioral characteristics that are used for identification of an individual. The most common biometric is fingerprints. Other types include DNA, facial recognition, voice, iris and palm prints. Every human being has specific and unique characteristic that can be used for identification. Even identical twins have a different set of fingerprints.[1] The range of biometrics is as diverse and imaginative as the potential number of the body's scannable parts.

Fingerprints are the most widely used biometric tool, but other methods of identification are coming into general use, such as facial recognition, voice prints and iris scans. Additionally, some biometric characteristics are still under development. Technology companies are looking into the possibility of using blood vessels on the back of the hand and sweat pores to help identify individuals.

Biometric technology may sound simple and foolproof, but there are some significant privacy concerns that need to be addressed. Because biometric technology is used in the criminal justice system, some critics have questioned how the data is stored and whether the data is vulnerable to theft or abuse. Does biometric data have a direct link to someone's marital status, religion, health or employment status? Until these issues are addressed, privacy advocates will lead the charge to resist biometric technology claiming it is just another way for the government to keep track of its citizens. However, it is likely that national security concerns and the ability of biometrics systems to enhance the security of the United States borders will win out over privacy concerns.[2]

### *Fingerprint Identification*

Fingerprint identification is the method of identification using the impressions made by ridge formations or patterns found on the fingertips. No two people have exactly the same arrangement of ridge patterns. The ridge patterns remain unchanged throughout life. Fingerprints offer an infallible means of personal identification. Other personal characteristics may change, but fingerprints do not.[3] The National Institute of Standards and Technology (NIST) conducted a study that showed single fingerprint biometric systems had a 98.6 percent accuracy rate. The accuracy rate rose to 99.6 percent when two fingerprints were used and a 99.9 percent accuracy rate when four or more fingerprints were used. The study demonstrated that biometric fingerprint identification is nearly perfect, which is not surprising given the uniqueness of human fingerprints.[4]

Fingerprints can be recorded on a standard fingerprint card or they can be recorded digitally. The first systematic use of fingerprint identification began in the United States is 1902. The New York Civil Service Commission established the practice of fingerprinting applicants to prevent them from having better qualified personnel take their tests for them. The New York state prison system began to use fingerprints for identification in 1903. In 1904, the fingerprint system accelerated when the U.S. penitentiary at Leavenworth, Kansas, and the St. Louis, Missouri, Police Department established fingerprint bureaus. During the nineteenth century, more and more local law enforcement agencies established fingerprint bureaus. The growing need and demand by police officials for a national repository and clearinghouse for fingerprint records led to an act of Congress on

**FIGURE 8.1** Fingerprint Examiners Working at the Federal Armory During WWII.

*Source*: FBI. Retrieved from Wikimedia Commons. www.fbi/news/galleries/stock-images/jistory/fingerprint-workers-at-federal-arm. Public domain.

July 1, 1921, which established the Identification Division of the FBI. In 1992, the Identification Division was renamed as the Criminal Justice Information Services Division.[5]

### The New Age of Fingerprint Identification

Technology has made numerous advances since the early 1900s. For well over a century, fingerprinting has been the accepted and verifiable method of personal identification. Early pioneers in the forensic science field like Francis Galton and Sir Edward Richard Henry devised manual classification of fingerprinting groups so that a match could be produced in a timely manner. Fingerprint patterns are unchangeable and immutable during the course of our entire lives from gestation through death.[6] For years, most of the law enforcement agencies utilized black ink to capture fingerprints on a paper card. This traditional method worked, but was extremely time-consuming. Fingerprint cards were kept in large file cabinets and had to be classified using the Henry System.

### Live Scan Technology

Technology has evolved from antiquated ink fingerprint cards to computerized live scan fingerprint devices. Live scan fingerprint devices allow law enforcement personnel to electronically capture and submit criminal or applicant fingerprint records to local, state or federal crime

**FIGURE 8.2**  Fingerprint Unit File Room.

*Source*: Courtesy of San Bernardino County Sheriff's Department.

laboratories for comparison. A typical live scan device consists of a computer processor, monitor, fingerprint sensor and sophisticated software developed by innovative technology companies.

There are many advantages of using a live scan device:

1  Law enforcement personnel do not have to mess around with ink rollers, which are very messy and make the verification process difficult because of smears and smudges.
2  Human errors are greatly reduced because law enforcement personnel no longer have to handwrite demographic information on ink cards.
3  Live scan devices are much faster and law enforcement personnel can usually identify a suspect or inmate within minutes. With ink cards, this process could take days.
4  Live scan devices allow law enforcement managers to audit, track and obtain statistical information that can be used in executive presentations, lawsuits, and efficiency reports.

**Vendor Spotlight**

MorphoTrust is a leading U.S. provider of identify solutions to federal, state and local governments that simplify, protect and secure the lives of Americans. MorphoTrust solutions for law enforcement are based on the use of biometrics (finger, palm, face and iris) to quickly identify, book and track suspects and detainees as they move in and out of the criminal justice system.

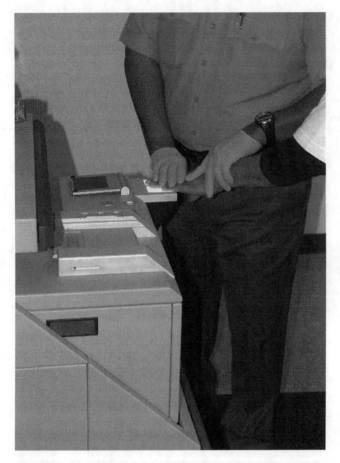

**FIGURE 8.3** MorphoTrust's TP5000 live scan device. In this photo an inmate is being finger-printed during the booking process.

*Source*: Photo courtesy of the San Bernardino County Sheriff's Department and MorphoTrust USA, Inc.

Live scan devices are an integral part of the criminal justice system and have revolu-tionized the identification and booking process for most law enforcement agencies. In most jails or prisons, live scan devices capture all ten fingers and palm prints. The benefit to capturing fingerprints and palm prints from inmates is that the fingerprint records are stored in automated fingerprint identification systems (AFIS). Fingerprint examiners compare fingerprints captured on live scan devices to fingerprint images obtained at crime scenes in hopes of identifying a potential suspect. Melissa Morrell, latent finger-print examiner for the San Bernardino County Sheriff's Department, stated "live scan technology has greatly improved my ability to identify potential suspects. The current live scan technology eliminates moisture, smears and dirt that typically hurt my ability to positively identify a potential suspect. Palm prints are especially important because crim-inals do not always leave clear fingerprints at a crime scene. However, they may touch

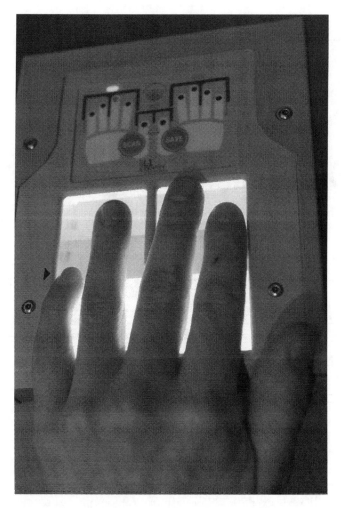

**FIGURE 8.4**  Up Close Look at Fingerprint Live Scan Device.

*Source*: Wikimedia commons. Retrieved from www.commons.wikimedia.org/wiki/file:ellsworth_fingerprint_scanner.jpg. Public Domain.

a window or other object with their palms and we can now identify them from partial palm prints."

Live scan devices also integrate with other law enforcement computer applications including jail information management systems (JIMS), photo capture systems and records management systems (RMS). This is an important factor for law enforcement managers because the integration of computer systems and databases helps improve efficiency and reduce liability.

Live scan devices can also be used for non-law enforcement purposes. Some professions require applicants to submit fingerprints to the Department of Justice pursuant to a background investigation (educators, security guards, medical personnel, and so on). This ensures

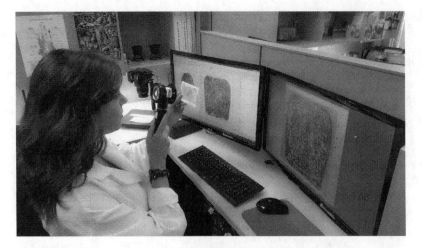

**FIGURE 8.5** Fingerprint Analyst Comparing Fingerprint Records.

*Source*: Courtesy of the San Bernardino County Sheriff's Department.

that prospective applicants are not convicted felons or have previous convictions that would prohibit them from interacting with children, carrying a firearm or handling money.

## Integrated Automatic Fingerprint Identification System (IAFIS)

The largest criminal fingerprint database in the world is the Integrated Automatic Fingerprint Identification System (IAFIS). IAFIS is maintained by the Federal Bureau of Investigation (FBI) and contains fingerprints, criminal histories, photographs, identification markings (scars and tattoos) and physical characteristics like height, weight, hair and eye color for criminal offenders. The database also includes civil fingerprint records from various professions that are required by statute to submit fingerprints to local, state or federal law enforcement agencies. IAFIS has over 70 million criminal fingerprint records and approximately 34 million civil fingerprint records. It also has over 73,000 known or suspected terrorist records. In 2009, IAFIS averaged 144,332 new submissions per day.[7] State fingerprint databases interface with the FBI making it much more effective when detectives submit unidentified fingerprints from crime scenes such as murders and other crimes. IAFIS is operational 24 hours a day, 365 days a year. It serves as the final clearing house for all public safety fingerprint and criminal history records in the United States. Many states and local public safety agencies have their own automated fingerprint identification systems (AFIS), which collect local records and submit them to the FBI's IAFIS database.

## Next Generation Identification (NGI)

Recognizing the advancements in technology and the needs of public safety personnel, the Federal Bureau of Investigation expanded on IAFIS and developed the Next Generation Identification (NGI). The new system has been developed over multiple years and has incrementally replaced IAFIS with improved functionality and capabilities. The NGI system offers the latest in biometric technology using multimodal functionality. NGI has improved its matching accuracy from 92 to 99.6 percent. It holds over 23 million photographs, millions of palm prints and supports mobile identification with rapid search capability.[8] The FBI is also working with the San Bernardino County Sheriff's Department on a "pilot" test with iris identifications. Iris identification is another way for law enforcement personnel to identify suspects similar to fingerprints. The San Bernardino County Sheriff's Department has been submitting iris records directly to the NGI system for over a year.

### What Does the Automated Fingerprint Identification System Do?

Fingerprint records are submitted to a local, state or federal automated fingerprint identification system (AFIS) for comparison. AFIS is a biometric system that uses computerized methodology to analyze digital images of individual fingerprints and compare them to a database of stored images, in search of a potential exact or partial match.[9] Although AFIS is primarily used by law enforcement agencies, there are civilian versions that are used for applicants and security purposes. It is also used for general identification and fraud prevention by the private sector.

The main benefit of AFIS is the reduction in time it takes to accurately identify a subject. AFIS uses fingerprint matching algorithms to develop a candidate list of potential subjects. This process can take several minutes depending on the type of AFIS, the quality of the fingerprint record stored in the system and the quality of the fingerprint card that is submitted by the officer. After AFIS creates the candidate list, a fingerprint examiner still has to conduct an examination of the fingerprints to make a positive identification. Many law enforcement agencies require a minimum of two independent fingerprint examiners to review the results of the identification before it is declared a match. Unlike many of the television shows that depict a fingerprint match within seconds, typical fingerprint identification can take hours or days depending on the quality of the prints.

Typical laboratories that use the automated fingerprint identification system split the workload into two sections: the ten print unit and the latent unit. The ten print unit processes fingerprints from correctional facilities. Usually the ten print unit works 24 hours a day, 7 days a week because law enforcement personnel arrest and book new prisoners during the same time period. Fingerprint examiners assigned to the ten print unit are responsible for the initial comparison, classification and input into the AFIS. Because many suspects do in fact lie to a police officer, examiners in the ten print unit are an extremely valuable resource. Ten print examiners can quickly help an officer identify the suspect based on his or her fingerprints, which helps reduce the civil liability associated with false arrests and in some cases, helps identify a suspect with a warrant for his or her arrest.

The latent unit is responsible for examining fingerprints that are received from crime scenes. This includes all fingerprints (full or partial) and palm prints. Latent fingerprint examiners are usually more experienced in fingerprint identification. Many of the fingerprints retrieved from a crime scene are partials or barely visible to the naked eye. Latent fingerprint examiners have special training and can spend days or weeks trying to identify a suspect from a partial fingerprint. According to Melissa Morrell, a latent fingerprint examiner for the San Bernardino County Sheriff's Department, new and innovative technology systems like the AFIS have helped investigators solve not only current crimes, but also prior crimes known as *cold cases*. Cold cases are criminal investigations that are still active but remain unsolved. The AFIS helps solve cold cases because it stores all fingerprint, palm print and partial prints indefinitely.

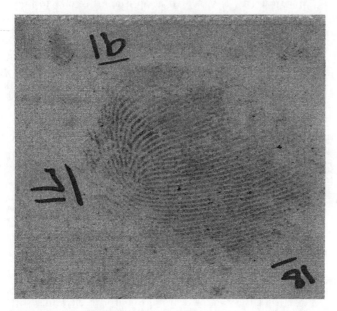

**FIGURE 8.6** Crime Scene Latent Fingerprint.

*Source*: Courtesy of the San Bernardino County Sheriff's Department.

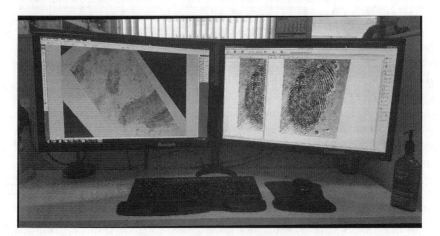

**FIGURE 8.7** Latent Fingerprint Workstation Used by Crime Laboratory Personnel to Identify Suspects.

*Source*: Courtesy of the San Bernardino County Sheriff's Department.

## Single Fingerprint Scanners

Similar to the live scan, a single finger scanner can be used to identify or verify someone's identity. The scanner is smaller than a live scan and is easy to use. It is designed to capture 1–2 fingers at a time. The most common finger used on a single finger scanner is the thumb. Single finger scanners are hard wired to a computer or wirelessly connected via a WiFi or cellular connection.

The use of single finger scanners is prevalent in correctional facilities and used for intake, booking and release windows. They can also be used for inmate counts, medical appointments or court proceedings.

Single finger scanners have become a popular piece of technology for patrol officers due to their portability and speed. Officers on patrol can use the scanners, known as *mobile identification devices*, to quickly identify a suspect within minutes.

## Mobile Biometric Identification Devices

Mobile biometric identification devices have become very popular over the last ten years. Using wireless technology, mobile biometric identification devices allow officers in the field to capture a fingerprint or photograph from a suspect and determine their identity within seconds. Mobile biometric identification devices are hand-held and use existing cell phone technology to process data including fingerprint and photograph information. Using the same fingerprint identification software used on desktop computer workstations at a local crime laboratory, technology companies have transformed the field of biometrics by allowing officers in the field to capture and submit fingerprints.

In the mid-2010s, mobile identification was in its infancy. Technology companies were experimenting with mobile technology to determine its viability to law enforcement, homeland security and the military. In California, the counties of San Bernardino and Riverside worked on a regional partnership to provide mobile biometric identification devices

 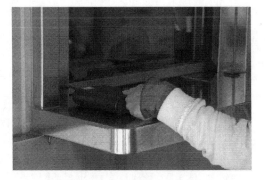

**FIGURE 8.8 AND 8.9**  Single Fingerprint Scanners Used at Intake and Release Windows in Custody Situations.

*Source*: Courtesy of the San Bernardino County Sheriff's Department.

**FIGURE 8.10**  MorphoTrust's "IBIS" Mobile Identification Device Used on Patrol.

*Source:* Photo courtesy of MorphoTrust USA Inc. and the San Bernardino County Sheriff's Department.

to local sheriff and police agencies in both counties. The first phase involved a "pilot" test of ten mobile biometric devices in each county. The devices were connected to the San Bernardino/Riverside County regional automated fingerprint identification system (AFIS), which stores over two million fingerprint records. The initial test was a success and law enforcement officers from both counties were clamoring for additional devices. Hundreds of devices were later ordered and deployed to patrol officers, detectives and coroner investigators. However, there were some technical issues with the original devices. The wireless technology at the time created connectivity issues when transmitting data. Also some of the officers complained about the battery life.

Fast forward to 2016. Technology companies have continued to support law enforcement agencies in the innovative field of mobile identification technology. New products have been released and law enforcement has benefited. One of the mobile identification devices used by law enforcement was developed by MorphoTrust. The Integrated Biometric Identification System (IBIS) uses the latest technology that allows officers to capture and wirelessly transmit forensic quality fingerprints and facial images on a handheld device. The device takes advantage of smartphone technology and allows an officer to scan a driver's license to obtain demographic information.[10]

The NEC Corporation of America has also developed the NeoScan 45 Mobile Fingerprint Capture Device. This device was designed for public safety applications in the field. It has a high degree of speed and accuracy including simultaneous two-finger capture. The device supports mobile identification, field booking and cite/release workflows inside local jails.[11]

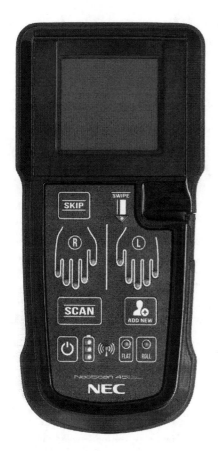

**FIGURE 8.11**   NEC's "NeoScan 45" Mobile Identification Device Used on Patrol.

*Source*: Photo courtesy of NEC Corporation of America.

## Iris and Retinal Identification

Eye scans are divided into two categories: iris and retinal. "Iris scans digitally process, record and compare the light and dark patterns in the iris's flecks and rings, something akin to a human bar code."[12] Iris identification is a new technology and has been around since the early 1990s. The iris is actually a muscle inside the eye that regulates the size of the pupil, which controls the amount of light that enters the eye. Essentially, the iris is developed during the prenatal period and an individual's irises become unique, which are used for identification purposes. There is some research that indicates that this technique is more accurate than a fingerprint and can be employed at a distance so that the person being scanned is unaware.

Retinal scans are more intrusive and require close-up scanning of the pupil. Retinal scans use the blood vessels at the back of the eye in order to determine the individual's unique pattern.

Law enforcement agencies must use high-quality cameras that have some type of illumination to capture an iris or retinal scan. Today's technology uses infrared light to illuminate the eye without causing any damage to the subject. After the iris is photographed, the image is processed using a complex mathematical formula and is compared to other images in the database.[13] Many law enforcement agencies across the country are starting to use this new technology in correctional facilities and in the field. The Jefferson County Sheriff's Department in Colorado uses an iris identification system inside their jail. The system has reduced the amount of time it takes to identify inmates when moving in and out of the jail.[14]

## Facial Recognition

Facial recognition software analyzes facial features or patterns to identify a person. Facial recognition can be accomplished from both photographs and videotapes using specialized software manufactured by various biometric companies. Complex software scans the face and creates enough information to search against a larger database. Facial recognition software uses 3D sensors to capture information about the face and characteristics, including the eye socket, chin, and nose. It can also analyze a person's skin texture by calculating specific lines, patterns and spots, then putting the information into a mathematical formula which is used for comparison.[15] The advantage of facial recognition is that it can be used from a distance and does not require contact. Facial recognition can also be used for security control and surveillance investigations.

## Palm Print Identification

Palm print identification uses many of the same characteristics that are used in typical fingerprint identification. This includes ridge flow, ridge characteristics and ridge structure. Palm prints also have the same uniqueness as fingerprints and have been used as a form of identification for over 100 years.[16] In the early 2000s, several states established palm print databases and started to collect data from local agencies. The California Department of Justice collected its first digital palm prints record in 2004 with the implementation of the California Automated Palm Print System (CAPPS). The San Bernardino and Riverside County Sheriff's Departments already had a local automated palm print database and sent the first digital palm print to CAPPS as part of a cooperative agreement with DOJ. Several months later, other law enforcement agencies established their own palm print databases and started to send records to CAPPS. Fingerprint examiners now have the ability to search a larger state database for palm prints, which has increased the overall hit rate. In the end, more suspects were positively identified because of palm print identifications.

## Hand/Finger Geometry

Hand geometry is a type of biometric technology that reads the outline or shadow of a hand. It does not actually analyze the handprint. Hand geometry is commonly used for

**FIGURE 8.12**   Crime Scene Palm Print Card.

*Source*: Courtesy of the San Bernardino County Sheriff's Department.

access purposes in buildings. Public safety agencies often implement hand geometry that includes a pin number and hand scan for identification or access control. Unfortunately, hand geometry is not the most accurate type of biometrics because hand shapes can be similar in size.[17]

## Voice Recognition

Voice or speaker recognition is another type of biometric technology that can be used by public safety agencies. Voice recognition analyzes an individual's voice tract and behavioral characteristics. Voice recognition is commonly used by public safety because of the availability of samples via telephones or other recording devices. However, voice recognition is vulnerable because of background and channel noises based on the specific technology that is used to capture the voice sample. Voice recognition is not the same as speech recognition. Speech recognition uses words as they are spoken, not the specific pitch or tone.[18]

## Dynamic Signature

Another type of biometric technology is dynamic signature recognition. This type of technology captures and analyzes the anatomic and behavioral characteristics. This includes the direction, stroke, pressure and shape of the individual's signature. After the data is captured, it is compared to existing data on file in order to make a match. The first signature recognition system was developed in 1965. The technology has continued to evolve and now includes complex algorithms that can incorporate a learning function that will explain the natural changes that occur in a signature over time.[19]

Dynamic signature recognition should not be confused with electronic signature capture devices that are used in commercial stores during the checkout process. Electronic signatures can be forged. Dynamic characteristics are difficult to replicate because they are unique to the style of the individual.[20]

## DNA Matching

DNA matching is a form of biometric technology and has continued to evolve over the last twenty years. DNA has become a common way for law enforcement agencies to identify criminals based on a number of sources including blood, hair, fibers, saliva, semen or any other source that has DNA. DNA is sensitive and needs to be collected properly. Similar to the automated fingerprint identification system (AFIS), DNA profiles are kept in the Combined DNA Index System or CODIS. CODIS is a national DNA database that is maintained by the Federal Bureau of Investigation. CODIS was established in 1990 as part of a pilot project.[21] Participating states collect samples from criminal offenders during the booking process. The DNA samples are sent to the CODIS repository. When crime scene evidence is obtained, investigators can search DNA found at the scene against the profiles inside of CODIS.

There are two types of DNA: nuclear and mitochondrial. Nuclear DNA is inside of the nucleus of a specific cell. It can be found in blood, semen, bone, cigarette butts, clothing, weapons, bottles, etc. Mitochondrial DNA is found in the mitochondrial part of a cell. It is normally extracted from evidence like hair, bone and teeth. DNA has proven to be a useful tool in public safety because criminals often leave their DNA at a crime scene. The processing of DNA evidence is time consuming and expensive. Many local law enforcement agencies utilize regional or state crime laboratories to process DNA evidence. The main benefit of DNA is that it has been accepted in court. According to the FBI, the chance of two different people having the same DNA profile is less than one out of 100 billion.[22]

One of the more interesting and innovative DNA technologies is the portable DNA analyzer developed by one of the largest technology companies in the world. NEC Corporation is a leading provider of innovative IT, network and communications products and solutions for service carriers. NEC's portable DNA analyzer is the world's first fully integrated portable DNA analyzer that helps speed up criminal investigations. The device is light enough to be carried to crime scenes and integrates all four steps of the DNA analysis process, which include the DNA extraction, polymerase chain reaction (PCR), electrophoresis and STR analysis. The entire process takes less than 60 seconds.[23] This type of innovative technology is a blessing for public safety managers because DNA analysis is now the norm in crime scene investigations, and DNA is one of the most reliable ways to help identify a suspect.

**FIGURE 8.13** NEC's portable DNA analyzer. This device can help speed up criminal investigations and aid crime prevention efforts. It integrates all four steps of the DNA analysis process.

*Source*: Photo courtesy of the NEC Corporation.

## Other Uses for Biometric Technology

Fingerprint recognition could also be used as a safety feature for weapons. Firearms can be configured to only fire a projectile by an authorized user via a fingerprint scanner. This technology will prevent accidental discharges, gun theft and illegal access by children. The U.S. military has weapons that only their personnel can fire by putting a ring with their biometric information on their hand. The firearm will only fire when the ring is in the correct position. The military is also testing the same technology with "smart" rifles. Government and law enforcement agencies have requested demonstrations of the potentially game changing technology.[24] This type of technology can reduce liability and improve safety, which is an important part of any public safety manager's job.

Biometric technology has become easier to use and less expensive over the last few years. The technology has evolved, making the devices more portable and accurate. It is also compatible with many other devices including laptops and cell phones. Newer cell phones have an optional fingerprint login sensor to prevent anyone from accessing data and information on the user's cell phone. Biometric scanners can also be used on desktop computers to ensure privacy and prevent the unauthorized release of confidential data. For example, law enforcement agencies have access to criminal and highly sensitive database information. If a password is compromised, the data can be released without permission. The use of a biometric fingerprint scanner can prevent this from occurring. Law enforcement managers should look into the aforementioned uses of biometric technology keeping in mind that a strong department policy and legal review should be addressed before implementation.

## Chapter Summary

What makes biometric technology unique is that we have billions of people around the world, but everyone has a specific characteristic or way to be identified. Biometrics use characteristics and biological traits as a measurement to verify personal identity. It can also be used to prevent unauthorized access to a building, computer or cell phone. Biometric technology encompasses measurable biological and behavioral characteristics in human identification including irises, DNA, voice pattern analysis, fingerprints, palm prints and facial recognition. Biometric technology is utilized by law enforcement to solve crimes and share intelligence on suspects. Biometric information is stored in databases like the automated fingerprint identification system (AFIS) and the Combined DNA Index System or CODIS. Law enforcement managers should always ensure that the data inside of these systems are accurate and complete. They should also share the data with other law enforcement agencies in the hopes of catching criminals that cross state lines.

"Propelled by cheaper and better software and hardware, as well as enhancing security and eliminating pesky passwords, biometrics, many people believe, will become increasingly popular during the next few years."[25] Many people will forget things like passwords and PIN codes. However, biometric features are permanent and hard to forget. The future of policing depends on creative technology that does not violate one's legal rights. Although biometric technology does help public safety personnel, it can have a controversial side. Public safety managers should continue using biometric technology, but they must also ensure our right for privacy. This type of data cannot be compromised and managers have a duty to ensure the data is used for official purposes only.

## Key Words or Terminology

| | | |
|---|---|---|
| fingerprint | AFIS | facial recognition |
| mobile identification | iris | wireless technology |
| privacy | scanner | live scan |
| biometrics | FBI | management |
| law enforcement | corrections | technology |

## Discussion Questions

1. Research and identify your nearest automated fingerprint identification database. Which agency manages the data and information? How many biometric records do they have?

2. Identify a local law enforcement agency that uses innovative biometric technology like mobile identification, facial recognition or palm print technology. Identify and discuss any of their success stories or if applicable any problems with the technology. Does it work as advertised?

3. Review and explain the various types of biometric technology and how they apply to public safety. Do you see any additional uses of this type of technology in your personal life?

4. Explain how technology in the private sector transforms the public sector. Is technology leading law enforcement too far? Does this type of technology violate our personal right to privacy?

## Notes

1 (2015). *Fingerprints and other biometrics.* Federal Bureau of Investigation. Retrieved from www.fbi. gov/about-us/cjis/fingerpints_biometrics.

2 Boggo, T. (2007, April 18). *Privacy issues surrounding biometric technology.* Retrieved from www. articlesfactory.com/articles/computers/privacy-issues-surrounding-biometric-tec.

3 Federal Bureau of Investigation, *Fingerprints and other biometrics.*

4 Ibid.

5 Martinez, S. (2013, June 19). *Statement before the House Committee on Oversight and Government Reform.* Retrieved from www.fbi.gov/news/testimony/overview-of-biometrics-efforts.

6 (2016). *Fingerprint patterns.* Fingerprinting.com. Retrieved from www.fingerprinting.com/ fingerprint-patterns.php.

7 (2015). *Integrated automated fingerprint identification system.* Federal Bureau of Investigation. Retrieved from www.fbi.gov/about-us/cjis/fingerprints_biometrics/iafis.

8 (2015). *Next generation identification.* Federal Bureau of Investigation. Retrieved from www.fbi.gov/ about-us/cjis/fingerprints_biometrics/ngi.

9 *AFIS,* n.d. Retrieved from www.dictionary.com/browse/afis.

10 (2016). *IBIS mobile identification system.* MorphoTrust. Retrieved www.morphotrust.com/ identitysolutions/forlawenforcement/officer360/mobileID3.

11 (2015). *NeoScan 45 mobile fingerprint capture device.* NEC Corporation of America. Retrieved www. necam.com/biometrics/doc/cfm?t=NeoScan.

12 (2006). *Iris recognition.* National Science and Technology Council. Retrieved from www.biometrics. gov/documents/irisrec.pdf.

13 Ibid.

14 (2006). The eyes have it. *Tech Beat.* National Law Enforcement and Corrections Technology Center. National Institute of Justice. Washington, DC: Government Printing Office.

15 (2015). *Facial recognition.* National Science and Technology Council. Retrieved from www. biometrics.gov/documents/facerec.pdf.

16 (2015). *Palm prints.* National Science and Technology Council. Retrieved from www.biometrics. gov/documents/palmprintsrec.pdf.

17 (2015). *Hand geometry.* National Science and Technology Council. Retrieved from www.biometrics. gov/documents/handgeometryrec.pdf.

18 (2015). *Voice recognition.* National Science and Technology Council. Retrieved from www. biometrics.gov/documents/voicerec.pdf.

19 (2015). *Dynamic signature.* National Science and Technology Council. Retrieved from www. biometrics.gov/documents/dynamicsignaturerec.pdf.

20 Ibid.

21 (2015). *Combined DNA index system.* Federal Bureau of Investigation. Retrieved from www.fbi.gov/ about-us/lab/biometric-analysis/codis/codis_brochure.

22  Ibid.
23  (2015). *Portable DNA analyzer*. NEC Corporation. Retrieved from www.nec.com/en/global/solutions/biometrics/prodcuts/portable_dna_analyzer.html.
24  McGarry, B. (2014, January 15). *U.S. Military begins testing "smart" rifles*. Retrieved from www.defensetech.org/2014/01/15u-s-military-begins-testing-smart-rifles/.
25  Edwards, J. (2001, February 1). *Biometric technologies: Fingerprint recognition, retina scans and facial recognition*. Retrieved from www.cio.com/article/2441829/servers/biometric-technologies-fingerprint-recognition-retina-scans-and-facial-recognition.html.

# 9

# USE-OF-FORCE TECHNOLOGY

"No one knew what Rodney King had done
beforehand to be stopped. No one realized that he was
a parolee and that he was violating his parole. No one
knew any of those things. All they saw was this grainy
film and police officers hitting him over the head."

*—Daryl Gates*

## Learning Objectives

After reading this chapter, the student will:

- Identify and evaluate the common types of less-lethal technology used by law enforcement personnel.
- Assess the controversy with less-lethal weapons and how they affect law enforcement organizations.
- Evaluate the need for alternatives like less-lethal weapons in law enforcement.
- Understand the role of a police manager when dealing with use-of-force technology.
- Explore the basic fundamentals of an effective department policy and training program for less-lethal technology.

## Introduction

In this chapter, we examine how use-of-force technology has changed law enforcement's approach to dealing with suspects in a patrol or custodial setting. Less-lethal weapons like Tasers, pepper spray or beanbag rounds can be found in most law enforcement agencies. This technology has greatly improved an officer's ability to deal with a combative subject without resorting to a higher level of force. As a result, the amount of injuries to officers and suspects has decreased when less–lethal force is utilized. There is some controversy from various community groups who feel that less–lethal technology can be abused, but in the end, less–lethal technology does its job when used properly. This chapter offers specific recommendations to public safety managers that deal with use-of-force issues in their own jurisdictions. We also explore department policy and effective training programs for less–lethal technology.

## Use of Force in Law Enforcement

One of the biggest concerns for police managers is the amount or type of force used by law enforcement personnel when dealing with a suspect or inmate. Most law enforcement agencies have specific policies that guide law enforcement officers on the parameters of use-of-force tactics and the various court decisions that apply to use-of-force situations. Police officers receive extensive training in the police academy and in-service training seminars. They participate in scenario training that provides real-time examples of how and when to use force. The majority of all contacts with suspects are resolved without the need to use force. Only 15–20 percent of arrests involve a use of force.[1] However, there are times when force must be applied for the safety of the officer, suspect or nearby citizens. In an effort to minimize the potential for injuries, less–lethal technology has been developed and is used routinely in the criminal justice system.

The concept of less–lethal weaponry is not new. Law enforcement has long operated with what is called a "continuum of force." It provides guidance to officers when selecting the type of weaponry to use in a variety of situations. The continuum normally begins with asking a subject to respond to voice commands. If the subject does not respond, the continuum may elevate to the next level of force, which in many cases is pepper spray.[2] If the subject is displaying a firearm, lethal force may be used. Law enforcement has long recognized that a wide and dangerous gap exists in the range of tools available to them. The only tools traditionally available (baton or gun) may be either too weak or too strong in response to some situations. This fact became clear after the U.S. Supreme Court ruled in *Tennessee v. Garner* that the use of deadly force to apprehend apparently unarmed, nonviolent fleeing felons was an unreasonable seizure under the Fourth Amendment.[3]

## The Need for Less-Lethal Technology

The demand for less–lethal weapons can be traced to the rise of television in the early 1960s. Television coverage allowed everyday Americans to witness controversial tactics used to deal with the civil rights and anti–war movement. Prior to less–lethal technologies, police officers had few options for riot control or civil disturbances. Common tactics used by police included a wall of officers with batons slowly advancing toward a crowd or officers on horseback trained to deal with crowd control. Some agencies used shotguns loaded with lower powered cartridges or "salt shells" that would ricochet off of the ground. A few police departments in larger cities had integrated fire control systems and were able to use high-pressure fire hoses to disperse a crowd. Trained dogs were also commonly used to scare and disperse rioters and apprehend individuals.[4]

The arrest of Rodney King in Los Angeles hampered law enforcement agencies and caused them to rethink the use of traditional police tools such as batons and other blunt force weapons. America is an ever increasingly violent society and the public demands the law enforcement community react swiftly and firmly to a problem. At the same time, law enforcement is under intense scrutiny from the media, trial lawyers' associations, the American Civil Liberties Union (ACLU) and other citizens armed with video cameras.

Today's rapid advancement in media and telecommunications technology allow people to record and publicize images or video footage of officers engaging in potentially excessive force situations. Authorities are aware of how images of violence play out publicly. In 1997, a joint report from the Pentagon and the U.S. Justice Department warned: "A further consideration that affects how the military and law enforcement apply force is the greater presence of members of the media or other civilians who are observing, if not recording, the situation. Even the lawful application of force can be misrepresented to or misunderstood by the public. More than ever, the police and the military must be highly discreet when applying force."[5]

The pressure to add new, less-lethal weapons to police arsenals increased in the 1980s. Edwin Meese, who was U.S. Attorney General at the time, called a conference to address the need for alternatives to deadly force. As a result of this conference, the National Institute of Justice established a less-lethal technology program. Through this program, the National Institute of Justice sought out technology that provided new, less-lethal options for law enforcement and corrections professionals, which would enable them to reduce the number of deaths and injuries to suspects.[6]

The National Institute of Justice, which is part of the U.S. Department of Justice, conducted research and found that advances in less-lethal technology offer the promise of more control over resistive suspects with fewer serious injuries. The study determined that law enforcement agencies that deployed pepper spray and conducted energy devices (CED) had an advantage because both types of weapons can prevent or minimize physical altercations that can lead to injury. Pepper spray and CEDs did cause pain, but they were less likely to result in death or serious harm.[7]

The study also combined and evaluated the use-of-force data from several law enforcement agencies including the Miami-Dade Police Department, the Seattle Police Department and the Richmond County Sheriff's Department. Overall, more than 24,000 use-of-force incidents were evaluated, which allowed researchers the ability to determine which circumstances affected injury rates. The study revealed that use-of-force encounters that involved the hands, feet, or fists had an increased chance of injury to the officer or suspect. However, the use of pepper spray or conducted energy device decreased the likelihood of injuries.[8]

## Less-Lethal Weapons

Less-lethal weapons were developed to provide law enforcement, corrections and military personnel with an alternative to lethal force. Less-lethal weapons are designed to temporarily incapacitate, confuse, delay or restrain a suspect in a variety of situations. They are used primarily in law enforcement and correctional scenarios including cell extractions, suicide preventions, civil disobedience riots, prison disturbances and hostage rescues. There are seven types of less-lethal devices. They include:

- Chemicals (pepper spray, tear gas, etc.)
- Conducted energy devices (Taser, stun gun or stun belts)
- Directed energy devices (radiated energy to achieve same effect as blunt force)
- Distraction (laser dazzler, bright lights and noise)
- Vehicle-stopping technology (equipment used to disable vehicles)
- Barriers (nets, foams and physical barriers)
- Blunt force (projectiles like beanbags)[9]

## Pepper Spray

One of the first widely used less-lethal technologies utilized by law enforcement agencies was pepper spray. In 1989, the Firearms Training Unit (FTU) of the FBI Academy in Quantico, Virginia, completed three years of intensive research on Oleoresin Capsicum (OC). The FBI later authorized the use of OC (pepper spray) for its special agents and SWAT teams. The FBI was attracted to the OC pepper spray results to control unruly subjects without having to resort to physical violence or use deadly force. The use of pepper spray in law enforcement agencies started to increase in the early 1990s. More than 3,000 law enforcement agencies, driven by the FBI endorsement of pepper spray as a safe crowd deterrent, started to use it in their arsenal.[10] Although the use of pepper spray allowed an officer to subdue an offender or someone resisting arrest, it does have some negative effects. Officers have to use it close range, which could lead to the officer being assaulted and attacked. Another negative effect of pepper spray is that pepper spray could contaminate the officer or his partners and make it difficult to complete the job at hand.

## Beanbag Rounds

Impact projectile weapons are designed to deliver non-penetrating contact energy from a safer distance than a police baton.[11] One such type of weapon, which has been in use for about 30 years, is the beanbag round.[12] *Beanbags* refer to square, rectangular or circular fabric bags that contain lead shot. The round is intended to flatten on impact, hitting face on, and to spread its energy over a large area. When manufactured, the beanbags are rolled into a 12-gauge shotgun shell. After leaving the muzzle, the beanbags unroll and rotate into the flat orientation to strike the target broadside. The lead shot acts like a fluid medium that distributes its kinetic energy over the surface contact area. The beanbag collapses and delivers a solid blow. The impact is comparable to being struck with a baseball traveling at 95 miles per hour or being punched by a professional boxer.[13]

If the beanbag round hits before it is completely unfurled or on an edge-on orientation, the full force of the impact is distributed over a smaller area, usually causing more damage.

**FIGURE 9.1**   Officer Using Pepper Spray.

*Source*: Wikimedia Commons. Retrieved from www.commons.wikimedia.org/wiki/file:102_naziaufmarsch_
24.3.2012_frankfurt_oder... Public domain.

Square beanbag rounds have been in use for many years and have been extensively tested for safety under the prescribed use conditions.[14] The head, throat and face are not considered acceptable targets because the bags will almost certainly cause serious injury, if not death. The beanbags must deliver a blow sufficient to produce pain and induce compliance from uncooperative and aggressive suspects, so the torso was once considered the most appropriate target for the bags.[15]

However, because of the potential for causing damage to the chest by blunt trauma, the recommended point of aim is the center of the body or the belly button area. Unfortunately, because of their shape, beanbag rounds are wildly inaccurate and have been known to veer off-course and strike individuals elsewhere on the body, causing serious injuries. Improving on the square beanbags, researchers have developed sock rounds. These rounds are designed

**FIGURE 9.2** Officer Holding a Beanbag Shotgun.

*Source*: Wikimedia Commons. Retrieved from www.commons.wikimedia.org/wiki/file:beanbag_shotgun.jpg, www.flickr.com/photos/2010observers/4354268939/in/photostream/.

to have no edges or corners that could lead to penetration and tend to have a tail to aid stabilization in flight. Sock rounds as well as the beanbag rounds are typically launched from a pump–action shotgun or a single round tear gas gun. The type of clothing worn by the suspect will affect the effectiveness of the rounds, as well as the point of aim and distance traveled.

## The Taser

Out of all the less-lethal technologies mentioned so far, none has had such a big impact or come with as much controversy as the electronic control device, more commonly known as the Taser. Developed in the 1960s by NASA scientist John Cover, the Taser is the embodiment of science fiction becoming science fact. It differs from other stun guns and electroshock weapons in that it could be fired and deployed at a distance. The weapon was directly influenced by the popular "Tom Swift" science fiction stories, namely "Tom Swift and His Electric Rifle." The word "Taser" in fact is an acronym for Thomas A. Swift's Electronic Rifle.[16]

The first model, invented by Cover, used gun powder to launch electrified darts. Because of this, it was classified as a firearm and did not see widespread use in law enforcement. In the early 1990s, Tom Smith and Rick Smith approached Cover, looking to develop a means to reduce deaths resulting from violent confrontations. They created the Air Taser, a weapon that fired darts using air rather than gun powder, shedding its firearm classification. The new deployment method allowed it to stand on its own as a less-lethal intermediate weapon. A newer, more effective and versatile device was soon developed and the law enforcement community began to see the potential benefits of the device. By 1999, law enforcement agencies across the country began to purchase the weapons for their officers. As it began to see widespread use among police agencies, the Taser was quickly heralded as a revolutionary new way to protect both officers and suspects.[17] When used correctly and appropriately, the Taser can prevent serious injury to the suspect and police officers.

The advanced Taser X26 was developed by Taser International. It uses an 18- to 26-watt electrical signal that overrides the central nervous system to directly control the skeletal muscles. The X26 is shaped like a standard duty pistol, which makes it easy to use. The Taser

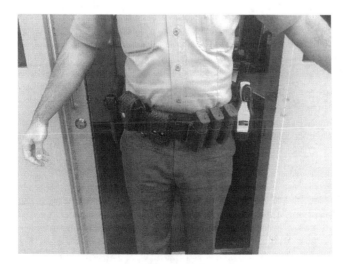

**FIGURE 9.3** Deputy Sheriff Wearing Standard Duty Belt That Includes a Firearm, Taser, Extra Ammunition, Tape Recorder and Baton.

*Source*: Courtesy of the San Bernardino County Sheriff's Department.

is a conducted energy device that fires a cartridge with two small probes or darts that are connected to the weapon by a high-voltage insulated wire. When the probes contact the target, they transmit a very short duration, high-energy, and electrical pulse along the wires to overwhelm the sensory nervous system, which stuns the target. One interesting aspect of the X26 is that it has a microprocessor. There is an onboard memory card that records the dates and times of the most recent times the unit has been fired. The X26 has a Windows XP/7/Vista compatible data port that allows the data to be downloaded to a computer using a special adapter cable.[18]

This feature enables law enforcement managers to monitor usage patterns and could help protect officers from excessive force allegations. The advanced X26 Taser uses air cartridges containing compressed nitrogen as a propellant to expel the two barbed probes. According to Taser International, the optimum range for the X26 Taser is 12 to 18 feet. The probes of the X26 Taser do not have to penetrate the skin or cause injury to work. The electrical signals of the Taser can penetrate over two inches of clothing, including leather jackets. Another benefit of the Taser is that officers on an arrest team can physically restrain a subject while the probes are "hot" without any fear of the charge being transferred.[19]

Tasers commonly used in law enforcement have a range of about 12–18 feet. This has created a "capability gap" where the officer could not use a Taser and was hesitant to use a gun, but the assailant could still throw something deadly. The Extended Range Electronic Projectile (XREP) is a self-contained version of a traditional Taser is the answer. Firearm manufacturer Mossberg and Taser International combined forces to make the Taser X-12 LLS (less-lethal shotgun). The X-12 LLS has Radial Ammunition Key technology to prevent it from accepting real 12-guage shotgun rounds that could accidentally be placed in the weapon during high-stress situations.[20] The XREP cartridge, as described by the Taser International website, is a "self-contained, wireless projectile that delivers the same neuro-muscular incapacitation bio-effect as the handheld Taser, but up to 100 feet."[21]

Tasers and the XREP have unique benefits, but both operate on the same basic principle of interfering with human's electrical communication signals. Every human needs electricity to survive and function. Most importantly to conducted energy devices, electrical signals are used in the body to send communications between the brain and muscles. These weapons do not operate on sheer power alone, but instead they mimic the electrical signals between the brain and muscles and interrupt them.[22]

## Management Concerns with Less-Lethal Technology

Allegations of intentional abuse, potential injuries and community mistrust can affect a manager's decision to use less-lethal technology like Tasers, beanbag rounds or even pepper spray. In some cases, police officers may rely on less-lethal technology too much and become complacent. Inadequate training and the lack of a department policy may contribute to the aforementioned factors. Some law enforcement agencies are rethinking the use of less-lethal technology because of unwanted media attention, legal challenges and recent reports that they might actually be dangerous.

## Are Tasers Safe?

There has been some research that indicates that electronic devices like Tasers are safe when applied properly. According to Taser International (2013), Taser applications are safer than high school sports.[23] In the 2005–2006 school year, there were approximately 7.2 million high school athletes. During the year, two million students were injured, 50,000 students visited the doctor's office and 30,000 students were hospitalized.[24] Therefore, 28 percent of high school athletes were injured during one academic school year. By comparison, 99.75 percent of assailants or suspects that were subjected to a Taser suffered only minor to no injuries. *Minor* injuries are defined as small scratches or bruises.[25] The University of California, San Diego also conducted a study and found that there are no lasting effects on healthy suspects shocked with a Taser.[26]

## Less-Lethal Technology Controversy

When discussing less-lethal technology there are differing opinions. Law enforcement personnel argue that less-lethal technology is a humane alternative to a more violent means used to effect an arrest. Opponents of less-lethal technology argue that police officers can potentially exert greater power over its subjects. The negative view towards less-lethal technology by various environment, socialist and anarchist groups is not surprising, given the fact that protesters associated with these groups have most often been the target of less-lethal weapons.

According to the human rights organization Amnesty International, more than 500 people have died in the United States after having been exposed to a Taser or other electronic control device since 2001. However, few of the so-called Taser-related deaths have been directly attributed to the effects of the devices themselves and instead are the result of specific officer and subject factors.[27]

## Use of Less-Lethal Technology by Civilians

Police managers must also understand that some less-lethal technology is available to the public, including criminals. Tasers can be purchased via the Internet because the transactions are not tracked or monitored. Pepper spray can be purchased at your local department store for as little as ten dollars. Criminals understand the stopping power of less-lethal weapons and are using them in their criminal activity and against law enforcement personnel.

For example, on April 6, 2013, the Prince William Police Department reported that a 24-year-old man was robbed by three men inside of his residence in Daly City. The suspects used an electronic device on the victim.[28] On March 30, 2013, four men pepper-sprayed employees at the Food City grocery market in Yuma, Arizona, as they tried to flee from the store after shoplifting.[29] These are just a few examples of criminals using less-lethal weapons to commit crimes. Criminals have figured out that by using less-lethal weapons instead of a firearm, they are less likely to receive longer prison sentences if convicted.

## Department Policy on Less-Lethal Technology

Less-lethal devices like Tasers, beanbag shotguns and pepper spray are rapidly overtaking other force alternatives. Although less-lethal devices can reduce the probability of injuries, their widespread use can raise some concerns for misuse. Law enforcement managers should always ensure that the department has specific policies that address less-lethal applications. They should also ensure that officers are properly trained and that use-of-force encounters involving less-lethal technology are monitored and officers are held accountable for misconduct.[30]

The department policy should clearly indicate when and under what conditions less-lethal weapons can be used. This will mitigate the potential for injuries and resulting department liability. When less-lethal weapons were originally deployed, some police departments did not have sufficent department policy to address the aforementioned areas. In Seattle, Washington, officers used a Taser on a pregnant woman because she refused to sign a citation.[31] After the incident, there was community outrage over the incident because the woman was pregnant. Although the officers were cleared of using excessive force, the department changed its policy and now discourages the use of Tasers on pregnant women.

A clearly defined department policy ensures that use-of-force applications are only used to protect law enforcement personnel, suspects, inmates or bystanders. The department policy should include the various factors that an officer should use to evaluate the level of resistance by the suspect. This includes:

- Type of weapon used by suspect
- Age of suspect
- Physical characteristics or size of the suspect
- Gender
- Physical disability or health concerns
- Immediate surroundings during the incident including flammable liquids, risks or other hazards

Regardless of the encounter or type of force used, officers should always ensure that medical treatment is available, if necessary. This is especially important if the suspect shows any signs of distress.

An effective department policy should also address officer accountability during a use-of-force situation. Law enforcement managers and supervisors should continually monitor and evaluate use-of-force situations involving less-lethal technology. When personnel are caught misusing or overusing less-lethal weapons, public safety managers must make sure the problems are identified and corrected. This can be accomplished with additional training or progressive discipline. It is important that public safety managers handle misconduct swiftly because these situations pose a great risk of liability to the department and continued issues can damage the public's trust of public safety organizations.

## *Training with Less-Lethal Technology*

Public safety agencies should always have intensive training requirements for any personnel carrying or using less-lethal technology. Most states require that public safety personnel receive initial and ongoing training in force options, which includes less-lethal weaponry.

The California Peace Officer Standards and Training (POST) regulate law enforcement training for peace officers. Officers are required to not only receive classroom and scenario training, but they also must display proficiency in the selected force option. For example, deputies assigned to the San Bernardino County Sheriff's Department qualify with less-lethal weapons several times each year. This ensures that department policy is addressed on a regular basis and deputies can show their proficiency in the required application of less-lethal weapons like the beanbag shotgun, pepper spray or Taser.

Public safety managers should ensure personnel receive not only classroom training, but also situational training. This type of training ensures that officers explore the various scenarios that one may face on patrol or inside of a jail. Training scenarios should include difficult situations that make the officer evaluate the circumstances before utilizing less-lethal force. Typical scenarios include the following:

- Need to use less-lethal force versus other force options. Can the officer handle the situation by simply talking to the suspect and gaining cooperation?
- Situations where the application of less-lethal force may not be practical. For example, a training scenario could have the suspect standing on the ledge of a rooftop. What are the ramifications if the officer deployed his or her Taser and the suspect fell to the ground?
- Training scenarios should also address situations where officers can become too reliant on less-lethal technology. Does the distance between the officer and the suspect make a difference? Can the officer upgrade or downgrade the type of force based on the suspects' actions?
- Scenarios where the officer is not physically able to use less-lethal force. Assume the officer was involved in a lengthy foot pursuit. Could the officer effectively use a beanbag shotgun while out of breath?

Classroom training should include the following:

- Nomenclature and safe use of any less-lethal device that is provided by the department. This includes proper maintenance and cleaning if applicable.
- Officers should be required to demonstrate sufficient justification for the use of force before, during and after the situation. What was their state of mind during the incident? When should the use of force stop? This may include instruction from legal counsel.
- Officer should also receive training on the proper documentation of a use-of-force incident. If an officer or supervisor cannot properly document use-of-force incidents, there may be an issue with civil litigation or even criminal prosecution.

Officers should also be taught how to properly carry or store less-lethal weapons. For example, Tasers are very similar to a firearm. It is carried on their duty belt usually on the opposite side of the duty weapon. What happens if the officer accidently grabs their duty weapon instead of their Taser in a confrontation with a suspect? Generally, officers are trained not to look down when they reach for one of their force options. They keep their eyes on the threat in front of them and draw their weapon without looking. Obviously, there can be some major repercussions if an officer uses the wrong force option. If the situation calls for lethal force and the officer grabs their Taser instead, it could present harm to the officer. If the officer grabs and discharges their firearm instead of their Taser, the repercussions can be very serious.

On January 1, 2009, Northern California Bay Area Transit Authority (BART) officer Johannes Mehserle "accidentally" discharged his firearm instead of his Taser into the back of a suspect. The suspect later died from his injuries. Officer Mehserle resigned his position when a charge for murder was filed against him.[32] The incident drew a lot of media attention, in part because the whole incident was captured on several cell phone cameras. It is because of this that the impact of technology on law enforcement was shown two different ways in the same incident. Videos taken at the scene were disseminated to the media and put on the Internet where they had millions of viewers. Training became an issue in this situaton because Officer Mehserle always practiced drawing his duty weapon ever since he graduated from the academy. However, he only drew his Taser a few times during training and only three times while on duty. The important factor to consider is police officers need to practice drawing their Tasers just as much as they do their duty weapons.[33]

Mehserle was later found guilty of involuntary manslaughter and was sentenced to two years in prison. Although Mehserle has dealt with his legal issues, the worry of these types of issues coming up in the future always looms for public safety managers. This incident caused many departments to reevaluate their policies on when an officer can use a Taser. Policies on training and how to carry a Taser were also evaluated. Although incidents like this don't happen very often, the legal implications of something like this happening are serious enough for it to be a legitimate concern.[34]

## Chapter Summary

Today wide assortments of less-lethal weapons have found their place in law enforcement agencies' armories. Less-lethal technologies have given law enforcement officers an alternative to using other physical force options that potentially are more dangerous to officers and suspects alike. Public safety managers should strive to provide law enforcement and correctional officers with the necessary equipment that protects them and the public; thus, reducing the possibility of injury, death or civil liability.

Although there has been some controversy with less-lethal technology, if used properly, less-lethal technology can reduce injuries and even save lives. Less-lethal weapons have proven to be effective when it comes to subduing suspects, during civil disturbances or even in the prevention of a suicidal subject. Not only do less-lethal weapons save lives, but they ultimately strengthen community relations with law enforcement and preserve their image. Law enforcement managers must do their best to ensure that less lethal weapons are not misused. This includes proper training programs, effective, clearly defined department policy and proactive monitoring of use-of-force applications. Less-lethal weapons are a very important tool for law enforcement and the benefits from using them far outweigh the cons.

## Key Words or Terminology

less-lethal

use of force

training

conducted energy devices

beanbag

controversy

case law

pepper spray

Taser

department policy

NIJ

## Discussion Questions

1. Contact the nearest law enforcement agency and ask them for their use-of-force policy. Does it include information about less-lethal technology? If so, describe the elements.
2. Research *Tennessee v. Garner* and describe how it applies to use of force and less-lethal options used by law enforcement personnel.
3. How important is a department policy and training program to a public safety agency? Explain the various components of a good policy and training program.
4. Discuss the various controversial issues with less-lethal technology. Are the concerns valid?

## Notes

1 Bulman, P. (2010). Police use of force: The impact of less-lethal weapons and tactics. *National Institute of Justice Journal*, issue no. 267. Retrieved from: www.ncjrs.gov/pdffiles1/nij/233280.pdf.
2 Pearson, C. (2003). *Less-lethal weapons*. Retrieved from: www.nleta.com/articles/lesslethal weapons.html.
3 Ibid.
4 (2013). *Non-lethal weapon*. Wikipedia, the free encyclopedia. Retrieved from www.en.wikipedia.org/wiki/Non-Lethal_weapon.
5 Khalek, R. (2011). *6 creepy new weapons the police and military use to subdue unarmed people*. AlterNet. Retrieved 5/8/2015 from www.alternet.org/story/151864/6-creepy-new-weapons-the-people-and-military-use-to-subdue-unarmed-people.
6 Hart, S.V. (2002). *Less-than-lethal weapons*. Retrieved from www.nij.gov/about/speeches/past-directors/aviation.htm.
7 Bulman, *Police use of force*.
8 Ibid.
9 (2015). *Types of less-lethal devices*. U.S. Department of Justice. Retrieved from www.nij.gov/topics/technology/less-lethal/pages/types.aspx.
10 (2010). *History of pepper spray*. The History of Pepper Spray: An Informational Website Dedicated to the History of Pepper Spray. Retrieved 5/08/2015 from www.historyofpeppersray.com/.
11 Ijames, S. (2002). Less lethal. *Law and Order Magazine*. Retrieved from www.hendonpub.com/resources/article_archive/results/details?id=3124.
12 (2002). Beanbags as an effective alternative. *Law and Order Magazine*. Retrieved from www.hendonpub.com/resources/article_archive/results/details?id=3124.
13 (2000). Portable, less lethal alternatives. *Law and Order Magazine*. Retrieved from www.hendonpub.com/resources/article_archive/results/details?id=3124.
14 *Law and Order Magazine*. Beanbags as an effective alternative.
15 Ibid.
16 Roufa, T. (2012). *Electronic control devices: Shocking developments in police technology*. About.com. Retrieved 4/24/2015 from www.criminologycareers.about.com/od/Career_Trends/a/Electronic-Control-Devices-Shocking-Developments-In-Police-Technology.htm.
17 Ibid.

18  Nielsen, E. (2004, October). Taser International X26. *Law and Order Magazine*, 52(10).
19  Ibid.
20  (2008). *Mossberg & Tasers X-12*. Tactical-life.com. Retrieved April, 22, 2015, from www.tactical-life.com/guns-and-weapons/mossberg-tasers-x12.
21  Khalek, *6 creepy new weapons*.
22  (2013). *Research & safety*. Taser International. Retrieved from www.taser.com/research-safety/science-and-medical.
23  Ibid.
24  Weisenberger, L. (2010). *Putting a stop to sport injuries*. American Academy of Orthopedic Surgeons. Retrieved from www.aaos.org/AAOSNow/2010/May/youraaos/youraaos8/?ssopc=1.
25  Czech, T. (2009). Taser fatalities studied. *York Daily Record*. Retrieved from www.ydr.com/ci_11756300.
26  Khalek, *6 creepy new weapons*.
27  Roufa, *Electronic control devices*.
28  Leon, R. (2013). *Man Tased, restrained and robbed by three men in Dale City*. Patch.com. Retrieved 3/1/15 from www.dalecity.patch.com/articles/police-dale-city-man-tased-restrained-robbed-by-three-men.
29  Gilbert, J. (2013). *Charges filed against three who allegedly used pepper spray in shoplift attempt*. Yumasun.com. Retrieved 7/15/2015 from www.yumasun.com/news/yuma-86481-garcia-pepper.html.
30  Bulman, *Police use of force*.
31  (2005, June). Police use a Taser on a pregnant woman. *Police Department Disciplinary Bulletin, 13*(6), 5. Northeast Publishing Group.
32  Griffith, D. (2010). *Lessons learned from the Mehserle trial*. Retrieved from www.policemag.com/channel/patrol/articles/2010/08/lessons-learned-from-the-mehs.
33  Ibid.
34  Ibid.

# 10
# PREDICTIVE POLICING

"Anywhere, anytime ordinary people are given the chance to choose, the choice is the same: freedom, not tyranny; democracy, not dictatorship; the rule of law, not the rule of the secret police."

—*Tony Blair*

## Learning Objectives

After reading this chapter, the student will:

- Understand the concepts of predictive policing and how it affects the criminal justice system.
- Evaluate the need for predictive policing technology.
- Analyze and explain how public safety managers can utilize this type of technology and how it can improve operational efficiency.
- Differentiate between traditional crime analysis and predictive policing.

## Introduction

In this chapter, we examine how predictive policing, data mining and predictive analysis support the overall mission of law enforcement. This technology builds upon the existing models of crime analysis and crime mapping. Modern police managers have adopted predictive policing because traditional crime methods are limited and because predictive policing can be more effective with the advent of new technology throughout society. Predictive policing uses technology to determine deployment patterns and identify measureable factors to address crime trends. This chapter also discusses various success stories from law enforcement agencies and gives police managers the necessary background on the topic before purchasing this innovative technology.

## What Is Predictive Policing?

Predictive policing is the gathering of crime data from several different sources, analyzing the data and then using the results to anticipate, prevent and respond more effectively to future crime.[1] Predictive policing represents stepping even further back to see more of the big picture. It assumes that crime is part of a larger pattern of criminal, economic and social issues, so it incorporates more data related to these issues into its predictions.[2] Predictive policing is designed to anticipate the location of future crime hot spots before they emerge, putting the police in position ahead of the crime so they can effectively disrupt the crime before it occurs.[3]

Predictive policing holds great potential for maximizing the effectiveness of limited resources that law enforcement agencies have available to them and it has attracted a great deal of attention from law enforcement executives. In 2012, two hundred police departments in the United States were surveyed and seventy percent of the respondents reported that they planned to use or increase the use of predictive policing programs in the next five years.[4]

Predictive policing is at the cutting edge of law enforcement technology. It combines the technology of data mining and predictive analytics with criminology and seeks to prevent crime by deploying police to various locations before a crime is committed. It represents the future as law enforcement managers struggle to remain effective with fewer resources. Predictive policing holds too much potential to be ignored. Law enforcement managers have to find a way to implement predictive policing and continually be open to technological developments. As technology advances, it provides great opportunities for law enforcement to become more effective, even as overall available resources become scarcer. At the same time, agency managers must always remain mindful of the many challenges that technology presents. One of the greatest challenges of adopting new technologies like predictive policing is doing so without losing the trust of the public. Many communities are already leery of law enforcement, and they are concerned about giving the police any form of technology that could potentially be used to profile individuals or invade the privacy of the public.

### The Private Sector

The business community has used data analysis to predict market conditions and trends to help develop marketing strategies. Large retailers like Walmart understand the importance of anticipating and predicting what customers will purchase. For example, if the store anticipates a large weather storm approaching, the store may shift its supply chain to stock up on specific merchandise like duct tape, bottled water or Pop Tarts. These items can be shipped prior to events like a hurricane or other natural disasters. This is an example of risk-based deployment.[5]

**TABLE 10.1**   Predictive Policing Myths

| | |
|---|---|
| 1 | Can a computer predict the future? The answer is no. Computers simplify a search for patterns or trends. Extrapolations from the past make predictions only as good as the information entered into the database |
| 2 | The computer does everything for law enforcement. False. Some predictive policing solutions are comprehensive, but humans still must collect important data, analyze it and interpret the results. |
| 3 | Predictive policing solutions must be expensive and high-powered. False. There are many inexpensive models out there that can support predictive policing methods. Increases in predictive power can sometimes show diminishing results. |
| 4 | Predictive policing will lead to major crime reductions. False. Predictive policing solutions only give "predictions." It still requires law enforcement personnel to take action in order to reduce crime. |

*Source*: Newcombe, T. (2014) Predictive Policing: The Promise and Perils. Retrieved from www.governing.com/templates/gov_print_article?id=276204191.

Risk-based deployment also applies to law enforcement organizations. For example, the U.S. Department of Justice reported that in 2003, law enforcement agencies deployed police resources in areas that routinely have "shots fired" calls on New Year's Eve. As a result, police departments reported a 47 percent reduction of random gunfire complaints. The amount of law enforcement resources was also reduced as opposed to previous years, therefore saving law enforcement agencies an estimated $15,000 savings in personnel costs alone for an 8-hour time period.[6]

Predictive analytics software does everything from guessing what books or music are likely to interest a customer, which consumers are likely to be interested in changing to a new credit card and what medical services will be needed by individual policyholders in the future.[7] Predictive policing is essentially predictive analytics software applied to criminology.

## Traditional Crime Analysis versus Predictive Policing

Law enforcement personnel have used statistical data and geospatial analysis to predict or forecast crime for many years. Technology has become increasingly sophisticated and predictive policing solutions have increased law enforcement's ability to forecast crime. Some people argue that crime is too random because it involves humans. However, a growing body of evidence indicates that technology can identify patterns or trends.[8]

Traditional crime analysis has represented law enforcement's effort to step back from individual crimes and see the bigger picture in order to make informed decisions about how to allocate resources that will have the greatest impact on crime. Police presence in crime hot spots is known to reduce criminal activity, so traditional crime analysis identified existing or emerging hot spots, and managers targeted them with police resources in order to disrupt crime.[9] However, criminal activity is dynamic, so traditional crime analysis is always a step or two behind the crime trends.

Predictive policing represents stepping even further back to see still more of the big picture; it assumes that crime is part of a larger pattern of criminal, economic and social issues. It incorporates more data related to these issues into its predictions.[10] Predictive policing is designed to anticipate the location of future crime hot spots before they emerge, putting the police in position ahead of the crime, so they can effectively disrupt the crime before it occurs.[11]

Law enforcement agencies rely heavily on reporting what has already happened. Annual crime reports, monthly crime summary reports and year to date reports all focus on criminal events that have happened in the past. Predictive policing helps law enforcement agencies see what may happen in the future, as opposed to only seeing what has already happened. This vision allows agencies to effectively deploy resources in front of the crime, therefore possibly changing the outcomes.[12] Predictive policing makes law enforcement less reactive. "The predictive vision moves law enforcement from focusing on what happened to focusing on what will happen and how to effectively deploy resources in front of crime, thereby changing outcomes," writes Los Angeles Police Chief Charlie Beck.[13]

## CompStat

CompStat is short for *computer statistics* and uses a computer-based program that utilizes four specific standards. They include intelligence, tactics, rapid deployment and regular follow-up. The main purpose of CompStat is to provide intelligence in the following areas:

- Crime and arrest statistics
- Calls for service
- Citizen complaints

This data is analyzed and used to create crime maps or reports that help investigators, supervisors and managers identify criminal behavior. When the specific behavior has been identified, law enforcement personnel can determine what tactics will be used to reduce or eliminate criminal activity. The rapid deployment of tactics is critical and increases the chances of solving criminal issues within the community. Law enforcement personnel should also ensure regular and timely follow-up to verify that the tactics are working and if necessary make adjustments.[14] CompStat requires ongoing and regular meetings to ensure success and accountability. The meetings will also give police managers the opportunity to identify what is working and facilitate future operations.

The New York Police Department was one of the early users of CompStat technology. They started using CompStat to reduce crime based on behavior patterns that were identified by computer generated data. CompStat was a concept used by a New York Transit Police Officer named Jack Maple. In the late 1980s, Maple started to chart all of the violent crime in the New York subway system on large maps. In 1990, Chief William Bratton became the chief of the New York City Transit Police Department and was impressed with Maple's maps. The department adopted Maple's maps and strategies. In 1994, Bratton became the chief of the New York City Police Department and appointed Maple as a deputy police commissioner. Maple's concept was termed as the "maps of the future," which was later transformed into the CompStat program used today.[15]

## PredPol

PredPol uses three data points (past type, place and time of crime) and a unique algorithm to help identify criminal behavior patterns. Their software provides law enforcement personnel with potential locations and times of criminal activity. PredPol software provides small areas, 500-feet–by–500-feet boxes on maps, to law enforcement personnel on every shift.[16]

PredPol produces daily hot-spot reports for each beat. The reports consist of a beat map with approximately half-block–sized red boxes, which represent the predicted hot spots. Beat officers spend available discretionary time in the hot spots. Agencies using PredPol typically leave it to the discretion of the beat officer how to patrol the hot spots. PredPol emphasizes that the program is an aid and not a replacement for police experience and intuition.[17] PredPol claims that if the officers spend 5 to 15 percent of their shifts inside those boxes, they will stop more crime than they would by relying on their experience and intuition alone.[18]

Dr. George Mohler and Dr. Jeff Brantingham, founders of PredPol, developed the predictive policing software using concepts similar to those used to help identify earthquakes and aftershocks. Dr. Mohler proposed that the same processes used for predicting aftershocks could be adapted to crime modeling. They refined and validated their algorithms against historical crime data in Los Angeles. Although PredPol's algorithm is a trade secret, the company emphasizes that the algorithm uses only location, time and type of previously reported crimes.[19]

## Incorporating More Data into Predictive Policing

Although PredPol software uses only location, time and type of crime in its algorithms, other researchers have added additional types of data to their predictive algorithms in hopes of improving the overall success of predictive policing models. This includes geographic and demographic data and even data from social network posts.[20] The additional data may help identify new patterns that would not be apparent or identifiable to a human crime analyst.

Law enforcement agencies collect vast amounts of data based on crime reporting, calls for service, traffic stops and field interviews. Researchers and police departments have experimented with using predictive policing with other types of existing data that may be connected to some of the underlying drivers of criminal behavior. One such effort is Blue CRUSH (Crime Reduction Utilizing Statistical History), a partnership between the Memphis Police Department and the University of Memphis. "The campaign is credited with helping to slash the numbers of major property and violent offenses by 26 percent citywide since the initiative was launched in 2006. Car break-ins, muggings and murders have plunged by 40 percent."[21]

## Predictive Policing at Work

### Richmond, Virginia

Every New Year's Eve, the city of Richmond, Virginia, would see increases in random gunfire. Local police started to gather intelligence and data specific to the gunfire. They were able to anticipate the time, location and nature of possible incidents. Random gunfire complaints were reduced.[22]

### Arlington, Texas

Police personnel used data on residential burglaries to identify specific "hot spots" and then compare the data to areas that had various code violations. They found that there was a relationship between the physical decay of the area and the amount of burglaries. Police then developed a strategy to help identify these "fragile neighborhoods." The police and other city departments now work together to help prevent crime.[23]

### Santa Cruz Police Department

The Santa Cruz Police Department uses PredPol technology that focuses on burglaries, vehicle thefts and violent crimes. The predictive policing model uses five years of data and identifies specific hot spots within the city. The information is disseminated to patrol personnel and officers increased patrol in the identified areas. Over a six-month period, burglaries declined by 19 percent and officers made over two dozen arrests.[24]

### Los Angeles Police Department

The Los Angeles Police Department also used predictive policing methods in their city. Los Angeles is a much larger city with more complex patrol needs than Santa Cruz. LAPD decided to use PredPol technology as an experiment in their Foothill Division. Officers were given hot spot maps on some days and traditional maps on other days. Officers were unaware of who generated the maps. As a result, the amount of burglaries declined by 12 percent. After realizing the benefits, the Los Angeles Police Department deployed the same predictive policing model to other divisions. Each division saw decreases in crime.[25]

Several other law enforcement agencies have implemented predictive policing programs. Time Magazine named predictive policing as one of the top 50 best inventions for 2011.[26]

## Potential Issues with Predictive Policing

### *Legal Challenges*

As law enforcement agencies struggle to catch up with and utilize technological advances, legal protections in the form of statutory and department policies lag behind as well. Concerns have been raised that with predictive policing, as in any statistical analysis, outcomes can be tipped just by the collection and handling of the data. So far, there is no real oversight for these programs.[27] Critics have also expressed concerns that the areas highlighted by predictive policing software may exaggerate a neighborhood's dangers in the minds of inexperienced officers, putting them on edge and at odds with residents.[28]

Predictive policing is too new to make any definitive conclusions about the merits of this type of technology. Growing interest in this technology and increased publicity will eventually create some constitutional arguments in the future. For years, law enforcement officers have utilized a variety of prediction techniques to help solve crime. Officers serving a search warrant are essentially predicting that a crime is being committed or contraband can be found at a specific location. Investigative detentions are predictions that a person is committing or about to commit a crime. Probable cause, activity in high crime areas and reasonable suspicion are all based on the probability that criminal activity will occur. Because predictive policing does have an impact on the Fourth Amendment's reasonable suspicion analysis, the courts will have to ensure that this technology meets the reasonable standard of reliability and accuracy.[29]

It stands to reason that ensuring the validity, reliability and accuracy of predictive policing data and algorithms is critical for ensuring the delivery fair and impartial law enforcement services. Doubts about the validity of predictive policing programs will undermine the credibility of the actions taken by the police employing the programs in the eyes of the community.

## Training Concerns

The lack of training or knowledge about predictive policing is another potential issue. Law enforcement officers who do not have a good understanding of predictive policing models and how they work may misuse the data or dismiss the concept completely. Failure to understand and interpret the data can complicate matters and lead to frustration for line personnel.

## Predictive Policing and Community Oriented Policing

Concerns over predictive policing make it critical that it is part of an overall community oriented policing strategy. If law enforcement agencies want to gain community support for predictive policing, complete transparency is a critical first step. Law enforcement personnel must engage their communities, listen to their concerns and be open to suggestions for mitigating bias in both the data inputs into the predictive policing program and the ways in which the data outputs are employed by the police. "Police agencies must develop policies and procedures for using the data and ensure that communities fully trust it is being put to use honestly, fairly and in the public's best interest."[30]

Law enforcement agencies can also increase the legitimacy and acceptance of predictive policing with the community by using it as a problem-solving tool instead of exclusively as an enforcement tool. Police agencies should use predictive policing not just to identify the at-risk areas, but also to identify the underlying issues and attempt to address them through community engagement. Enforcement should be part of an overall problem-solving strategy that is decided in conjunction with the stakeholders.

## *Overcoming Challenges with Predictive Policing Technology*

The negative feedback about predictive policing is centered on two main issues: the reliability of the data used for the predictions and the privacy concerns for the public. Law enforcement agencies must keep this information in mind when they use predictive policing models. Gaining and maintaining the public trust is essential for all law enforcement agencies.[31] Law enforcement agencies using predictive policing models should ensure that the data and resulting information is transparent and constitutional.[32] Agencies must be able to explain how they came up with the data, how it was used and how they came up with the predictions. Users must ensure that the data is clean, reliable and valid. They must also have processes in place to assess and reassess their efforts and outcomes.[33] The use of peer validation that is commonly used in the academic world will help validate the data for court purposes. Law enforcement agencies should also have a specific department policy that deals with this type of technology.

The issue of privacy is another concern. Law enforcement agencies should strive to collaborate with all stakeholders including the public, privacy groups and criminal justice professionals. The community must have confidence in law enforcement and this technology. Police managers should work to alleviate any privacy concerns from the outset of any predictive policing program.[34]

## Chapter Summary

Predictive policing is a relatively new technology that provides public safety managers with another resource to help advance the efficiency and effectiveness of law enforcement. Predictive policing models can help law enforcement managers and executives reduce crime without sacrificing public safety. However, if predictive policing is going to be part of a successful policing strategy, law enforcement agencies must have support and trust from the community. Predictive policing has the potential to jeopardize the public trust in law enforcement and further degrade the already strained relationship between the police and traditionally marginalized communities if it is not implemented correctly.

Law enforcement agencies must partner and be transparent with the community. This includes educating the public about the program, what data it uses, what type of predictions it makes and how the police will utilize the information. Predictive policing does not replace community policing. It is just another technology tool that can help law enforcement deal with crime and quality of life issues. The future of programs like predictive policing is only limited by technology, available funding and the imagination of all stakeholders.

## Key Words or Terminology

| | | |
|---|---|---|
| predictive policing | technology | algorithm |
| criminology | crime analysis | risk-based deployment |
| CompStat | PredPol | |

## Discussion Questions

1. Identify and discuss the myths surrounding predictive policing. What strategies should you employ to deal with these myths?

2. Analyze the differences between traditional crime analysis and predictive policing. What are the major differences and should both types be used in the criminal justice system?

3. As a member of a law enforcement agency or as a member of the public, explain how predictive policing would help reduce crime in your area. What are the first steps to establishing an effective program?

4. Seek out nearby law enforcement agencies and determine if they have predictive policing programs. Are they productive? How do they measure the success of their programs?

## Notes

1  Pearsall, B. (2009). Predictive policing: The future of law enforcement. *National Institute of Justice*, 16–19.

2  Vhalos J. (2012). The department of pre-crime. *Scientific American*, 306(1), 62–67.

3  Mohler, G.O., et al, (2015). Randomized controlled field trials of predicted policing. *Journal of the American Statisical Association*, 110(512), 1399–1411.

4  Huet, E., & Kahneman, D. (2015). Server and protect. *Forbes*, 195(3), 46–47.

5  Pearsall, Beth. (2010). Predictive policing: The future of law enforcement? *National Institute of Justice, Journal*, no. 266. Retrieved from www.nij.gov/journals/266/predictive.htm.

6  Beck, C. (2009, November 8). Predictive policing: What can we learn from WalMart and Amazon about fighting crime in a recession? *Police Chief Magazine*. Retrieved from www.policechiefmagazine.org/magazine/index.cfm?fuseaaction=print_display&articl.

7  Vhalos, *The department of pre-crime.*

8  Newcombe, T. (2014). *Predictive policing: The promise and perils.* Retrieved from: www.governing.com/templates/gov_print_article?id=276204191.

9  Mohler et al., *Randomized controlled field trials of predicted policing.*

10  Vhalos, *The department of pre-crime.*

11  Ibid.

12  Beck, *Predictive policing.*

13  Pearsall, *Predictive policing: The future of law enforcement?*

14  Godown, J. (2009, August). The CompStat process: Four principles for managing crime reduction. *The Police Chief*, LXXVI (no.8). Retrieved from www.policechiefmagazine.org/.

15  Dussault, R. (1999). *Jack Maple: Betting on intelligence.* Retrieved from www.govtech.com/magazines/gt/jack-maple-betting-on-intelligence.html.

16  *How PredPol works*, n.d. PredPol. Retrieved from www.predpol.com/how-predpol-works/.

17  Greengard, S. (2012). Policing the future. *Communications of the ACM*, 55(3),19–21.

18  Huet & Kahneman, *Server and protect.*

19  Ibid.

20  Camacho-Collados, M., & Liberatore, F. (2015). A decision support system for predictive police patrolling. *Decision Support Systems*, 75, 25–37.

21  Vhalos, *The department of pre-crime.*

22  Pearsall, *Predictive policing: The future of law enforcement?*

23  Ibid.

24  Friend, Z. (2013). Predictive policing: Using technology to reduce crime. *FBI Law Enforcement Bulletin*, 82(4), 1–4.

25 Ibid.

26 Ibid.

27 Gordon, L.A. (2013). Predictive policing may help bag burglars, but it may also be a constitutional problem. *ABA Journal*, 99(9), 1.

28 Huet & Kahneman, *Server and protect.*

29 Ferguson, A. (2012). *Predictive policing and reasonable suspicion.* Retrieved from www.law.emory.edu/elj/_documents/volumes/62/2/articles/ferguson.pdf.

30 Greengard, *Policing the future.*

31 Pearsall, *Predictive policing: The future of law enforcement?*

32 Vhalos, *The department of pre-crime.*

33 Ferguson, *Predictive policing and reasonable suspicion.*

34 Pearsall, *Predictive policing: The future of law enforcement?*

# 11

# AVIATION TECHNOLOGY

"When once you have tasted flight, you will forever walk
the earth with your eyes turned skyward, for there you
have been, and there you will always long to return."

—*Leonardo Da Vinci*

## Learning Objectives

After reading this chapter, the student will:

* Be able to define an unmanned aircraft vehicle (UAV) and how they affect public
  safety.
* Evaluate the need and purpose of aviation technology in public safety.
* Explore the various controversy with UAV technology including privacy issues.
* Be able to explain the different types of UAVs commonly used in public safety, the
  military and in the private sector.
* Examine other aviation technology and equipment used in public safety including heli-
  copters and fixed-wing aircraft.

## Introduction

In this chapter, we examine the various types of aviation technology used in public safety.
This includes an in-depth analysis of unmanned aircraft vehicles (UAVs), also known as
drones. The use of drones in public safety is one of the biggest challenges for public safety
agencies. The use of drones can be controversial, but with proper oversight they can be
one of the more effective uses of technology in public safety. Drones can be a force multiplier and save public safety agencies money compared to traditional aviation assets like

helicopters or fixed-wing aircraft. This technology has been used in the military for years, and just recently the Federal Aviation Administration (FAA) allowed public safety to experiment and use them in real-life situations. Throughout this chapter, we focus on the specific laws with drone technology, and on management considerations and discuss what should be included in a department policy for drones. Additionally, we review the latest helicopter technology used today, including navigation systems, downlink cameras and infrared imaging systems.

## Aviation Technology

Public safety has used aviation technology for many years. Fire departments use helicopters and fixed-wing aircraft to fight fires across the country. Law enforcement uses helicopters on patrol assisting officers on the ground. Helicopters are routinely used in vehicle pursuits, which are sometimes captured on local and national news stations. Aviation assets are also used by both fire and law enforcement agencies in search and rescue operations. The technology used by helicopter and fixed-wing aircraft personnel has dramatically changed over the years as well. According to Sergeant Al Daniel, of the San Bernardino County Sheriff's Department, "the technology used in the aviation field can help save lives. Our helicopters are equipped with external hoists so we can extract an injured victim within minutes. The remoteness of our county is a challenge and our ability to get a victim to a nearby hospital in a timely manner is paramount. Our helicopters also have complex navigation and accident avoidance systems to keep us safe in the air. Law enforcement helicopters also use infrared imaging systems to search for suspects at night."

**FIGURE 11.1**  In this photo, San Bernardino County Sheriff's Department Aviation Division is performing a hoist rescue 150 feet above the ground.

*Source*: Photo courtesy of Skip Robinson.

However, helicopters and fixed-wing aircraft can be expensive and most public safety agencies cannot afford them. Smaller agencies typically reach out to larger agencies for these services or they regionalize with other agencies to share the costs associated with aviation services. Nobody underestimates the need and value of helicopter and fixed-wing aircraft in public safety, but what does the future have in store for aviation technology and equipment? Updated surveillance systems are in high demand in law enforcement. Criminals understand that law enforcement agencies use helicopters and fixed-wing aircraft for surveillance missions. Global positioning systems (GPS) are also used, but criminals have found ways to avoid this type of technology. Public safety, specifically law enforcement, has started to evaluate and use new aviation technology that has become available in recent years.

## Unmanned Aircraft Vehicles (Drones)

One piece of aviation technology that has become popular in public safety is the drone or unmanned aircraft vehicle (UAV). A drone or unmanned aircraft vehicle is an aerial vehicle designed to be used without a human pilot onboard. UAVs can be remotely controlled or completely automated.[1]

### History of UAV Technology

Unmanned aircraft vehicles have been around for many years. The concept of using this type of technology dates back to the mid-1800s. During the Civil War, Union and Confederate troops used hot-air balloons in military missions. They were also used in the Spanish–American War when they filled balloons with makeshift bombs. This allowed

**FIGURE 11.2**   In this photo, a member of the military is deploying a drone in Iraq.

*Source*: Wikimedia. Retrieved from www.commons.wikimedia.org/wiki/file:RQ-11_raven_1.jpg. Photo in public domain.

military forces to attack their enemies without the risk of losing soldiers. The U.S. military later added cameras to kites, which provided the first use of aerial photographs. Drones were also used in World War I and World War II. In World War II, Germany used drones with missiles that could be maneuvered by radio technology. The United States and Russia also used drone technology to control the path of rockets in the 1950s. As technology progressed, drone technology was used during the Vietnam War. Drones were used in over 3,500 missions. The country of Israel also used drones in the Gaza Strip during various wars with neighboring countries. The drones could be launched from specific locations, some over 115 miles away.[2]

The United States increased the use of drones after the terrorist attacks in New York City on September 11, 2001. The Pentagon wanted to make at least one third of the United States Air Force unmanned aircraft vehicles or drones. Drones have evolved and are currently weaponized, which allows military forces to destroy targets without the risk of losing pilots or expensive airplanes.[3] In 2007, the United States deployed over 700 drones in Iraq. Because drones fly in higher altitudes, they usually cannot be seen from the ground. They are also very small and maneuverable. This means drone surveillance often occurs without the knowledge of the individual being monitored.[4]

The use of UAV technology in the military has paved the way for their use in public safety. The technology is readily available and public safety agencies just needed permission from the federal government to implement them in domestic functions. In 2012, President Obama admitted that the United States was using drone technology to track terrorists in the Middle East.[5] The success of the drone program led many public safety agencies wondering if the same technology could be utilized to track suspects or use in natural disaster situations. Many law enforcement agencies are actively testing and using unmanned aircraft vehicles or drones. They are exploring the advantages and disadvantages with this technology. Although the testing period continues, many in the community are wondering about the impact of privacy because drones can effectively spy on the public with limited oversight.

## Strengths

Public safety managers and personnel must evaluate the strengths and weaknesses of UAV technology and determine if it would benefit their agency. Below is a summary of the main strengths and weaknesses that should be taken into consideration before purchasing UAV technology.

UAVs are:

- Less expensive compared to traditional helicopters or fixed-wing aircraft. Smaller agencies can afford to purchase a UAV.
- Small enough to fly in specific areas with little or no risk to the public.
- Can be used in search and rescue missions.
- Because UAVs do not carry personnel the risk of injury or death of the flight crew is reduced.
- Search large areas with sensor and high-definition technology.

- They come in a variety of sizes, which may benefit public safety agencies.
- They can be deployed from just about any location. They do not need a runway for take-off or landing. They can also be transported by vehicle.
- They are quiet and covert, which is helpful during surveillance operations.

### Weaknesses

- Inability to transport personnel or large payloads.
- The technology used in UAVs could be compromised or hacked.
- Although they can assist in search and rescue operations, UAVs cannot communicate with victims or perform hoist operations.
- They are limited in technology because of their inability to fly with heavy equipment.
- UAVs are not fast and more susceptible to attacks from people on the ground.
- Require FAA oversight and approval.

### UAVs versus Traditional Aircraft

Public safety personnel have a variety of aviation resources available depending on the type of mission. Domestic public safety UAVs are divided into two categories: surveillance and less-lethal. The majority of the UAVs are used for surveillance purposes. Surveillance UAVs allow public safety personnel to scan large areas and record suspicious activity. Less-lethal UAVs are being introduced to law enforcement agencies due to their ability to carry non-lethal weapons like Tasers, chemical agents and beanbag rounds.[6] The less-lethal weapons could be used for crowd control and other missions where it is dangerous for line officers to engage directly with a suspect.

Although the drone is the most popular type of UAV technology, there are other types of aircraft that can be used by public safety agencies. Some are unmanned and others have a flight crew. They include the following:

### Powered Parachutes

A powered parachute is a tandem two-seat aircraft that has a parachute as a wing. The parachute is attached to a cart with an open cockpit. The parachute is attached to the cart by a series of cables, which are used to help steer the aircraft. The aircraft can be flown by both occupants because it has dual controls. They can be deployed from just about anywhere without the need for a runway. The normal speed for a powered parachute is about 30 miles per hour. Powered parachutes cost anywhere from $15,000 to $30,000. They can provide public safety personnel with a 270-degree view of a crime scene, fire or other incident. One disadvantage is that the aircraft cannot fly in bad weather or strong winds.[7]

### Fixed-Wing Aircraft

Public safety also uses traditional fixed-wing aircraft or small planes. The San Bernardino County Sheriff's Department is the largest county in the United States, covering over

**FIGURE 11.3**  Powered Parachute Flying in a Field.

*Source*: Wikimedia. Retrieved from www.commons.wikimedia.org/wiki/file:powered-parachute-flying.jpg. Photograph in public domain.

20,000 square miles. Mitch Datillo, a lieutenant with the San Bernardino County Sheriff's Aviation Division, stated that they use fixed-wing aircraft for search and rescue operations, fire recognizance and personnel transport, including inmates. "During the attacks of September 11, 2001, the FAA grounded all aircraft until they could evaluate any potential threats against the country. Because our department has several fixed-wing aircraft, we were asked to transport a high ranking member of the federal government back to Washington, D.C. We also use fixed-wing aircraft for narcotic related cases. It would be impossible to track suspects around our county without this type of asset," said Datillo. Fixed-wing aircraft cost anywhere from $60,000 to $300,000 and have an increased range of speed. Fixed-wing aircraft can fly in inclement weather and carry a larger payload. They are easily available and commonly used throughout public safety. The problems with small aircraft are reduced visibility, increased training requirements and expense.[8]

## Gyroplanes

A gyroplane is similar to a helicopter because the rotor blades are on top of the aircraft. However, the engine is located in the rear of the aircraft in order to provide forward thrust. Another difference is that the rotor blades spin as a result of airflow, not engine power. This is also known as autorotation. Gyroplanes cost anywhere from $60,000 to $100,000 and do not require a runway. They can essentially take off vertically and have enhanced visibility. Gyroplanes can fly at low speeds and can be used for surveillances. However, there is a lack of standards from the Federal Aviation Administration, which makes them a difficult sell to public safety agencies.[9]

**FIGURE 11.4** U.S. Customs and Border Protection Fixed-Wing Aircraft with Surveillance Radar.

*Source*: Wikimedia. Retrieved from www.commons.wikimedia.org/wiki/file:cbp_C-12_on_patrol.jpg. Photograph in public domain.

### Small Unmanned Aircraft

A small unmanned aircraft typically weighs less than 25 pounds and is flown by pre-programmed technology or manual controller. They usually have cameras that downlink to monitors on the ground. They can be very useful in time-sensitive situations like a hostage situation. In order to operate one of these aircrafts, public safety agencies must get permission from the FAA. Small unmanned aircrafts cost anywhere from $40,000 to $125,000 each. They are portable and can be launched anywhere. Some problems with small unmanned aircrafts include limited camera technology, no long-term periods of flight (40 minutes or less) and they cannot be flown in protected airspace.[10]

### Aerostats

Aerostats are similar to weather balloons. They can be deployed immediately and have radio or camera equipment onboard. They can be deployed for up to 72 hours because the balloon is filled with helium. Aerostats are commonly launched with radio repeater technology and act as radio towers during disasters or in areas with little or no radio service. The cost of an aerostat is anywhere from $5,000 to $500,000. There are some limitations with aerostats. They are difficult to launch and recover. There are fewer regulatory issues for aerostats because they are anchored to the ground.[11]

### Helicopters

Helicopters are routinely used in public safety missions. Fire departments use helicopters to drop water on a fire, provide surveillance and transport fire personnel. They can also be used for medical transport purposes. Law enforcement uses helicopters for police missions including the transport of personnel and the pursuit of suspects on foot or in a vehicle. Helicopters also provide an aerial view of a crime scene, crime in progress, and so on. They are a force multiplier and can greatly assist law enforcement officers on the ground because they can observe the entire scene. They are commonly used for burglaries, robberies and grand theft auto calls. The helicopter can carry large payloads including high-tech equipment and personnel. However, helicopters can be expensive to operate. Typical law enforcement helicopter range from $500,000 to over $5,000,000 depending on the type and equipment installed. Helicopters require increased maintenance, which can make the hourly cost more expensive compared to other aircrafts discussed in this chapter. Although they can be expensive, the helicopter is the most widely used type of aircraft in public safety. They provide numerous advantages and in most cases they can save lives, which makes the cost worthwhile.

**FIGURE 11.5** San Bernardino County Sheriff's Patrol Helicopter.

*Source*: Photo courtesy of Skip Robinson.

**FIGURE 11.6** Sheriff's Rescue Helicopter Helping a Victim Stranded in a Flood.

*Source*: Photo courtesy of the San Bernardino County Sheriff's Department.

**FIGURE 11.7**   Sheriff's UH–1H Helicopter Dropping Water on a Fire.

*Source*: Photo courtesy of Skip Robinson.

### Who Is Using UAVs?

Over 600 agencies in the United States have permission from the FAA to use UAVs. UAVs are being used by law enforcement, border patrol, fire services and military.[12] Some agencies have been actively using UAVs since they were first approved for use by the FAA. Other agencies are still testing the technology and evaluating whether they should continue to use UAVs in the future. Regardless, UAV technology is here to stay. The following are examples of agencies using or testing this technology today:

In Virginia, the Nelson County Sheriff's Department was involved in a standoff with a local rancher on a 3,000-acre farm. Numerous allied agencies were called in to assist including the state highway patrol, SWAT team, emergency medical personnel and law enforcement from neighboring counties. Law enforcement officials hoped to resolve the situation without injuries. Sheriff Kelly Kanke wanted to use all of the resources available, so he requested a Predator B aircraft drone from the U.S. Customs and Border agency. This aircraft can stay in the air for up to 18 hours and was equipped with high-tech surveillance equipment including radar, infrared sensors and high-definition video. The Predator B drone circled overhead, helped law enforcement pinpoint three suspects and verified that they were unarmed. The suspects were later arrested without incident. This was one of the first known arrests with the assistance of a UAV.[13]

In British Columbia, the Royal Canadian Mounted Police (RCMP) are using drones to assist analysts investigating crash sites. The drone allows them to hover overhead and take photos or video. The images are then sent to officers on the ground, which allow them to reconstruct the accidents. The drone flies at a lower altitude and can provide better photographs.[14]

The Montgomery County Sheriff's Office (Texas) is testing the Shadow Hawk drone. It was purchased for $300,000 with a Federal Homeland Security grant. The Shadow Hawk has the ability to provide surveillance for narcotic cases, traffic congestion, pursuits and high-risk SWAT deployments. The Shadow Hawk also has a low audible signature, which allows it to follow suspects undetected. The Shadow Hawk is remotely operated by a pilot using a controller system, which looks like a laptop with a game controller connected. If the connection from the pilot and the drone is severed, the drone automatically initiates an automated emergency landing in order to prevent a crash or injury.[15]

The Los Angeles County Sheriff's Department is testing the SkySeer autonomous drone for surveillance and reconnaissance.[16] This drone is small and only weighs about five pounds. It is also hand launched. The SkySeer flies along a predetermined path set by the operator and has a range of about two miles.[17] The benefit to this type of UAV is that it is inexpensive and can provide surveillance in large areas like a forest or rural area.

Other agencies using UAVs include the Ogden Police Department (Utah). In 2011, they purchased a surveillance blimp to deter new crimes from occurring. The Houston Police Department (Texas) is evaluating drone technology when issuing traffic tickets.[18]

So what does the public think about UAV technology? Eighty percent of Americans support the use of unmanned aircraft vehicles in search and rescue missions. The majority also support the use of UAVs in the apprehension of suspects and the protection of the border. Coincidentally, a poll conducted by the Associated Press revealed that people were more concerned about privacy with their social media accounts.[19]

## Aviation Laws

The Federal Aviation Administration governs the use of UAVs or drones. UAVs are subject to the same rules as any other aircraft in the skies.[20] Before UAVs could be used by public safety, they had to be approved by the FAA and Congress. On February 14, 2012, President Obama signed H.R. 658, also known as the FAA Modernization and Reform Act. The following is a summary of the applicable laws that deal with UAVs.[21]

### Title III—Safety: Subtitle B—Unmanned Aircraft Systems

### Section 332

Requires the Secretary to develop a plan to accelerate safely the integration by September 30, 2015, of civil unmanned aircraft systems (UAS, or drones) into the national airspace system.

Requires the FAA Administrator to establish a pilot program to integrate drones into the national airspace system at six test ranges meeting specified criteria. Directs the Secretary to develop a plan to designate permanent areas in the Arctic where small drones may operate 24 hours per day for research and commercial purposes.

### Section 333

Requires the Secretary to determine if certain drones may operate safely in the national airspace system before completion of the plan.

## Section 334

Requires the Secretary to:
(1) issue guidance regarding the operation of public drones to expedite the issuance of a certificate of authorization process, and for other specified reasons; and (2) enter into agreements with appropriate government agencies to simplify the process for issuing certificates of waiver or authorization to operate public drones in such system. Requires the FAA Administrator to develop and implement, by December 31, 2015, operational and certification requirements for the operation of public drones in the national airspace system.

## Section 335

Directs the FAA Administrator to carry out all safety studies necessary to support the integration of drones into the national airspace system.

## Section 336

Prohibits the FAA Administrator from promulgating rules or regulations on model aircraft flown strictly for hobby or recreational purposes and meeting certain other criteria.[22]

UAVs or manned aircraft are not allowed in restricted airspace without permission. Examples included Washington, D.C., military bases, sporting events and theme parks. The FAA often issues temporary flight restrictions (TFR) to ensure unauthorized aircraft does not fly in the aforementioned areas.[23]

Many states have proposed or adopted laws that regulate UAVs. In California, the state legislature approved AB1327, which mandates that government agencies notify the public if they intend on using a drone. It also requires that the drone-collected data is destroyed within one year. AB1327 also prohibits drones from carrying any type of weapon.[24]

## Unmanned Aircraft Vehicle (UAV) Policies and Recommendations

After the Federal Aviation Administration authorized the use of UAVs or drones, public safety officials sought out guidelines or policy recommendations to help navigate the use of this technology. The International Association of Chiefs of Police (IACP) developed an executive report that identifies the recommended guidelines for any agency wanting to use drones. The report highlights five key areas: definitions, community engagement, system requirements, operational procedures and image retention.[25] The recommended guidelines are listed below:

### Definitions

- Model Aircraft—A remote controlled aircraft used by hobbyists, which is manufactured and operated for the purposes of sport recreation and/or competition.
- Unmanned Aircraft—An aircraft that is intended to navigate in the air without a pilot. Unmanned aircrafts are also called remote piloted aircrafts or drones.

- UA Flight Crew Member—A pilot, observer or other person assigned duties for a UA for the purpose of a flight.
- Unmanned Aircraft Pilot—The person exercising control over an unmanned aircraft during flight.[26]

## Community Engagement

1 Law enforcement agencies desiring to use UA should first determine how they will use this technology, including the costs and benefits to be gained.
2 The agency should then engage their community early in the planning process, including their governing body and civil liberties advocates.
3 The agency should assure the community that it values the protections provided citizens by the U.S. Constitution. Further, that the agency will operate the aircraft in full compliance with the mandates of the Constitution, federal, state and local laws governing search and seizure.
4 The community should be provided an opportunity to review and comment on agency procedures as they are being drafted. Where appropriate, recommendations should be considered for adoption in the policy.
5 As with the community, the news media should be brought into the process early on its development.[27]

## System Requirements

- The UA should have the ability to capture flight time by individual flights over a period of time. The ability to reset the flight time counter should be restricted to a supervisor or administrator.
- The aircraft itself should be painted in a high-visibility paint scheme. This will facilitate line-of-sight control by the aircraft pilot and allow persons on the ground to monitor the location of the aircraft. This recommendation recognizes that in some cases where officer safety is a concern, such as a high-risk warrant service, high visibility may not be optimal. However, most situations of this type are conducted covertly and at night. Further, given the ability to observe a large area from an aerial vantage point, it may not be necessary to fly the aircraft directly over the target location.
- Equipping the aircraft with weapons of any type is strongly discouraged; given the current state of the technology, the ability to effectively deploy weapons from a small UA is doubtful. Further, public acceptance of airborne use of force is likewise doubtful and could result in unnecessary community resistance to the program.
- The use of model aircraft, modified with cameras or other sensors, is discouraged due to concerns over reliability and safety.[28]

## Operational Procedures

- UA operations require a certificate of authorization (COA) from the Federal Aviation Administration (FAA). A law enforcement agency contemplating the use of UA should contact the FAA early in the planning process to determine the requirement for obtaining a COA.

- The UA will only be operated by personnel who have been trained and certified in the operation of the system. All agency personnel with UA responsibilities, including command officers, will be provided training in the policies and procedures governing their use.
- All flights will be approved by a supervisor and must be for a legitimate public safety mission, training or demonstration purposes.
- All flights will be documented on a form designed for that purpose and all flight time shall be accounted for on the form. The reason for the flight and name of the supervisor approving will also be documented.
- An authorized supervisor/administrator will audit flight documentation at regular intervals. The results of the audit will be documented. Any changes to the flight time counter will be documented.
- Unauthorized use of a UA will result in strict accountability.
- Except for those instances where officer safety could be jeopardized, the agency should consider using a "reverse 911" telephone system to alert those living and working in the vicinity of aircraft operations.
- Where there are specific and articulable grounds to believe that the UA will collect evidence of criminal wrongdoing and if the UA will intrude upon reasonable expectations of privacy, the agency will secure a search warrant prior to conducting the flight.[29]

### Image Retention

- Unless required as evidence of a crime, as part of an ongoing investigation for training or required by law, images captured by UA should not be retained by the agency.
- Unless exempt by law, retained images should be open for public inspection.[30]

## UAV Technology Can Be Controversial

There is no doubt that the use of UAVs or drones is controversial. Public safety is already scrutinized for a variety of reasons, but invasion of one's privacy is an issue that public safety personnel must address before using this type of technology.

The American Civil Liberties Union (ACLU) has stated that rules must be in place before UAVs are used. In order to regulate their use, the ACLU has recommended the following safeguards for the use of police drones:

- Drones should be deployed by law enforcement only with a warrant, during an emergency or when there are specific and articulable grounds to believe that the drone will collect evidence relating to a specific criminal act.
- Agencies should limit the retention of images captured by police drones only when there is reasonable suspicion that they contain evidence of a crime or are relevant to an ongoing investigation or trial.
- Public representatives, not police departments, should adopt drone usage policies. The policies should be clear, written and open to the public.

- Agencies should have open audits and proper oversight to prevent misuse of police drones.
- The use of drones equipped with lethal or non-lethal weapons is discouraged.[31]

The ACLU makes some good points on this issue of UAVs. Public safety agencies need to understand the concerns of advocate groups and the community. Public safety agencies in general can respond to these concerns by setting a foundation of policies as recommended by the IACP's report. In addition, engaging the public early in the planning process will help alleviate the concerns the community may have. The police helicopter was once a concern of the public with the similar privacy issues. The use of UAVs can become an effective tool for public safety agencies.

## Public Safety Management Considerations

### Cost

Public safety managers should evaluate the cost of aviation technology or equipment based on the needs of the agency. If the agency covers large geographical areas, then the purchase of a helicopter or fixed-wing aircraft makes perfect sense. However, some agencies may only want a UAV for SWAT callouts or crime scene investigations. The cost benefit associated with aviation technology, specifically UAVs and their potential ability to replace traditional police aircraft, is something many public safety agencies are considering.

Costs associated with maintaining and operating law enforcement helicopters make the adoption of UAVs and their associated cost savings an enticing option to public safety agencies. There are many costs associated with operating a helicopter. They include the purchase or rent of an aircraft hangar, fuel, maintenance, personnel and training expenses. A typical public safety helicopter can cost $4,000,000. Daily operational costs range from $300–$1500 depending on the type of mission. By comparison, the cost of a UAV or drone can range from $15,000 to $300,000 depending on the type of aircraft or mission. Operating costs are much lower because there is no need for a highly trained aircraft pilot or flight crew. UAVs offer an amazing potential in cost savings.

### Safety

Public safety managers must also consider the safety issues that come with this type of technology. Pilots around the country have reported an increase in near-collisions or encounters with UAVs or drones. During the time period of June 2014 to December 2014, there were 25 episodes where small UAVs almost crashed into larger aircraft. The reports came from pilots and airport controllers and usually occurred during takeoffs and landings at busy airports.[32] In 2013, an Air Force drone plummeted to the ground and landed on a Florida highway. Later that year, a New York City man was hit in the head with a model helicopter.[33] Despite all of the near misses with larger aircraft and the injuries sustained by people hit with a UAV, the FAA continues to be pressured to open the air space for new users of UAVs like real estate agents, delivery firms, farmers and photographers.[34]

In 2015, the Federal Aviation Administration put out a press release that discussed safety concerns when UAVs interfered with manned helicopters fighting wildland fires. The FAA stated, "If you fly, we can't." The FAA stated that anyone who endangers a manned aircraft such as a helicopter or fixed-wing aircraft could be liable for a fine ranging from $1,000 to $25,000. The FAA provided guidance to law enforcement because they are often the first responders and in the best position to deter, detect, investigate and take action on anyone violating FAA rules and regulations.[35]

## Law Enforcement Response to Safety Issues

In January 2105, the FAA provided guidance to law enforcement agencies describing the options for legal enforcement against unauthorized or unsafe users of UAV technology. Six recommendations were identified. They include:

- Law enforcement should identify potential witnesses to any violation involving UAVs. This includes initial interviews about what they observed at the scene. FAA investigators will re-interview involved parties at a later date.
- Identify the operator or pilot of the UAV. They should determine the purpose of the flight (hobby or commercial) and if the UAV is present, obtain the registration number.
- Officers should process the scene, which includes the taking of pictures or video if possible. Lighting, weather conditions, damage or injuries and the number of people near the actual use of the UAV is important to the investigation. Landmarks, maps or diagrams should also be identified and preserved.
- Identify sensitive location, events or activities. Law enforcement officers should become familiar with any temporary flight restrictions (TFR). This will be important information if a UAV is sighted inside of the TFR.
- Law enforcement officers should immediately notify FAA officials at one of the Regional Operation Centers (ROC).
- Law enforcement officers should also make every attempt to identify and collect any pertinent evidence. This includes any public or private security systems that can provide visual evidence of UAV operations. Examples include photographs or video from private citizens, news media or commercial operators.[36]

## Should I Buy a UAV?

Should public safety managers purchase an unmanned aircraft vehicle or drone for their agency? It depends on several factors that must be considered before any purchase of technology. Examples include:

- What does it cost?
- What are the training considerations?
- What are the ongoing maintenance issues?
- How will the technology help the agency's operation?
- What is the true effect of the technology? Officer safety or more efficient?[37]

The aforementioned questions must be addressed before the purchase of a UAV or drone. The advantages and disadvantages of this type of technology have already been discussed. However, does every public safety agency in the United States need their own personal UAV? Probably not. In fact, it may be more cost effective to regionalize the purchase and share the resource. Public safety managers have to decide if this type of purchase is a "must have" or simply "nice to have." UAVs are dangerous and require extensive planning, training and oversight. Most agencies will not have the staffing and expertise to manage this type of technology. Another consideration is that the process of obtaining a UAV is difficult. Public safety agencies must obtain a certificate of waiver or authorization (COA) from the Federal Aviation Administration. This process is complicated and time-consuming.[38]

## Other Aviation Technology

Throughout this chapter, we discussed manned and unmanned aircraft systems. There are other types of aviation technology or equipment that are used today to help public safety personnel do their jobs. Let's review some of the innovative technology used in helicopters and other aircraft.

### Downlink Cameras

Downlink camera systems allow public safety agencies to share real-time video feeds to ground personnel during critical incidents like fires, natural disasters or police activity. Downlink camera systems include a specialized antenna that is typically mounted underneath the aircraft. The antenna is connected to an onboard camera system which is operated by a flight officer. The flight officer uses the camera to focus on a suspect, vehicle, fire or other type of object. The downlink antenna then transmits the video data to ground control centers. The ground control centers can be mobile or fixed locations depending on the situation. Command staff personnel can immediately view real-time video and make important decisions based on information provided by the downlink system. The concept of downlink cameras has been around for many years. The news media has used downlink camera systems for many years. They are commonly used in vehicle pursuits. However, the cost to use downlink systems prohibited public safety agencies from adopting the technology until the late 2010s. Many public safety agencies have used grant funds to purchase downlink technology and have regionalized with other agencies. Captain Dale Gregory, Commander of the San Bernardino County Sheriff's Aviation Division, stated that his department was able to purchase helicopter downlink cameras with funding from the Urban Area Security Initiative (UASI). This type of funding is available on a regional basis and benefits the citizens of San Bernardino County.

### Infrared Cameras

Infrared imaging camera systems are commonly used by helicopter personnel to track and identify suspects on the ground. Using high-powered cameras, high-definition monitors and

**FIGURE 11.8**   This photo shows a downlink antenna on the bottom left of the helicopter. On the bottom right is a high-powered infrared camera.

*Source*: Photograph courtesy of Skip Robinson.

hand controllers, flight crews in public safety can quickly locate a suspect on the ground or a vehicle involved in a pursuit on a local freeway. This type of technology is so sophisticated that it works at night using thermal imaging technology. It can pick up body heat, which can help officers locate a suspect hiding in the bushes or in a nearby field.

## Navigation Systems

Navigation systems have been around for many years. They are installed in newer model vehicles and have basically eliminated the need for paper maps. In the aviation field, advanced navigation systems are available to help aircraft crews locate addresses or specific locations

**FIGURE 11.9**  Photograph of Hiker Stranded on Mountain Ledge Taken with an Infrared Image Camera.

*Source*: Photograph courtesy of the San Bernardino County Sheriff's Department.

**FIGURE 11.10**  Sheriff's helicopter crew flying at night using the latest navigation equipment. On the left side you can see the in-flight map directing the crew to a call for service.

*Source*: Photograph courtesy of the San Bernardino County Sheriff's Department.

within seconds. The navigation systems used in public safety helicopters or fixed-wing aircrafts have many other features not offered in your vehicle navigation system. The crew inside of the aircraft can type in an address and the navigation system will chart a course for the aircraft to fly. It gives the specific latitude and longitude, along with estimated time of arrival. The system will also identify any specific hazards including ground wires (telephone or electrical), landmarks, airspace restrictions, altitude and the speed of aircraft.

## Chapter Summary

Aviation technology has continued to evolve and public safety agencies are the beneficiaries. The private sector and the military have led the way with new technology like unmanned aircraft vehicles (drones), downlink cameras and enhanced navigation systems. Drones are an effective resource for public safety agencies when fighting fires, conducting surveillance and other law enforcement operations. The widespread adoption of UAVs for domestic use is only a matter of time and public safety personnel should continue to evaluate the benefits of this important technology.

Understandably, there are both supporters and opponents of UAV technology. The community is skeptical and wants assurances that public safety will not misuse this technology. UAV technology has the ability to peer into the personal privacy of our society. Public safety agencies should draft specific policies that clearly identify the purpose and scope of UAV technology. Managers of UAV technology should also understand the legal and safety implications of UAVs and ensure that they are used for lawful purposes.

## Key Words or Terminology

| | | |
|---|---|---|
| drone | unmanned aircraft vehicle | downlink camera |
| navigation | surveillance | aviation law |
| Federal Aviation Administration | | |

## Discussion Questions

1. What steps can law enforcement officers do when confronted with an unauthorized use of an unmanned aircraft vehicle or drone?
2. Identify the various factors that public safety managers should consider before implementing and purchasing a UAV or drone.
3. Conduct research in your local area or state and identify any current uses of UAV technology. Give examples. What are your thoughts about the incidents?
4. What is a certificate of authorization? Explain how the Federal Aviation Administration provides oversight on issues with UAV technology.
5. How should public safety personnel deal with the controversy over drones?

## Notes

1 *Domestic unmanned aerial vehicles (UAVs) and drones,* n.d. Electronic Privacy Information Center. Retrieved from www.epic.org/privacy/drones/.
2 Hastings, M. (2012, April 16). The rise of the killer drones: How America goes to war in secret. *Rolling Stone Magazine.* Retrieved from www.rollingstone.com/politics/news/the-rise-of-the-killer-drones-how-america-goes-to-war-in-secret-20120416.
3 Ibid.
4 Electronic Privacy Information Center, *Domestic unmanned aerial vehicles (UAVs) and drones.*
5 (2012, January 31). *Drones: What are they and how do they work?* BBC News. Retrieved from www.bbc.com/news/world-south-asia-10713898.
6 Greenwald, G. (2013, March). Domestic drones and their unique dangers. *The Guardian.* Retrieved from www.theguardian.com/commentisfree/2013/mar/29/domestic-drones-unique-dangers.

7 *Types of lower cost aircraft.* National Institute of Justice. U.S. Department of Justice. Retrieved from www.nij/gov/topics/law-enforcment/operations/aviation/pages/types-of-aircrafts.aspx.

8 Ibid.

9 Ibid.

10 Ibid.

11 Ibid.

12 Bond, M. (2015, August 10). Drones a benefit for law enforcement, but raise concerns. *The Philadelphia Inquirer.* Retrieved from www.governing.com/templates/gov_print/article?id=32186221.

13 Wylie, D. (2012, May). *Unmanned aerial system for SWAT.* PoliceOne.com. Retrieved from www.policeone.com/airborne-maritime/articles/5483918-Unmanned-aerial-systems-for-SWAT/.

14 (2011, August). *Police consider $30k drone to take over helicopter work.* PoliceOne.com. Retrieved from www.policeone.com/police-products/accident-reconstruction/articles/4302314-Police-consider-30k-drone-to-take-over-helicopter-work/.

15 Dean, S. (2011, October 31). *New Texas police drone could carry weapons.* Officer.com. Retrieved from www.officer.com/news/10444041/new-texas-police-drone-could-carry-weapons.

16 Koebler, J. (2013, March 21). Law enforcement blindsided by public 'panic' over drone privacy. *US News.* Retrieved from www.usnews.com/news/articles/2013/03/21/law-enforcement-blindsided-by-public-panic-over-drone-privacy.

17 (2013, March 19). *SkySeer UAV (unmanned aerial vehicle).* Octatron. Retrieved from www.octatron.com/prodSkySeer.php.

18 Stanley, J., & Crump, C. (2011, December 1). *Protecting privacy from aerial surveillance: Recommendations for government use of drone aircraft.* Retrieved from www.aclu.org/files/assets/protectingprivacyfromaerialsurveillance.pdf.

19 Davis, B. (2013, June). Unmanned aircraft systems: All of the boxes checked, but challenges remain. *The Police Chief,* vol. LXXX, no.6. Alexandria, VA.

20 Huerta, M. (2015, December). Drones and law enforcement. *The Police Chief,* vol. VXXXII, no.12. Alexandria, VA.

21 (2013). *H.R. 658 (112th): FAA Modernization and Reform Act of 2012.* Library of Congress. Govtrack.us. Retrieved from www.govtrack.us/congress/bills/112/hr658.

22 Ibid.

23 Huerta, *Drones and law enforcement.*

24 Heaton, B. (2014). *California legislature passes law to regulate drones.* Government Technology. Retrieved from www.governing.com/templates/gov_print_article?id=273072891.

25 (2012, Aug.). *Recommended guidelines for the use of unmanned aircraft.* International Association of Chiefs of Police. Retrieved from www.theiacp.org/portals/0/pdfs/iacp_uaguidelines.pdf.

26 Ibid.

27 Ibid.

28 Ibid.

29 Ibid.

30 Ibid.

31 Stanley, J. (2015). Police chiefs issue recommendations on drones: A look at how they measure up. *American Civil Liberties Union.* Retrieved from www.aclu.org/blog/police-chiefs-issue-recommendations-drones-look-how-they-measure.

32 Whitlock, C. (2014, November 26). Near-collisions between drones, airliners surge, new FAA reports show. *The Washington Post.* Retrieved from www.washingtonpost.com/world/national-security/near-collisions-between-drones.

33 Hastings, *The rise of the killer drones.*

34 Whitlock, *Near-collisions between drones, airliners surge.*

35 (2015). *FAA: Wildfires and drones don't mix.* Federal Aviation Administration. Retrieved from www.faa.gov/news/press_releaases/news_story.cfm?newsid=19234.

36 (2015). *Law enforcement guidance for suspected unauthorized UAS operations.* Federal Aviation Administration. Retrieved from www.faa.gov/uas/regulation_policies/media/faa-uas-po-lea-guidance.pdf.

37 Davis, *Unmanned aircraft systems.*

38 Ibid.

# UNIT 3

# Managing Public Safety Technology

Congratulations! You have finally been promoted to supervisor or manager. You are very excited about your new position and eager to learn. Most public safety agencies do a tremendous job training and preparing new supervisors or managers in law enforcement, fire services, corrections or the criminal justice system. However, very few public safety agencies offer or provide any sort of training in "managing technology." Unfortunately, many supervisors or managers are often tasked with the basic management of existing technology or the development of new technology projects. Public safety managers are even tasked with working through the incredible maze of the procurement process, requests for proposals (RFP), vendor selection and budget analysis. Unit 3 summarizes the various steps or phases in the technology management process. Unit 3 is designed to teach a new supervisor or manager the basics of managing technology, including funding sources, project approval, needs analysis and planning. After the technology project has been approved, funded and designed, managers still have to purchase, implement and maintain the technology. This is no easy task.

This unit covers the following:

- Chapter 12—So You Want to Manage Technology?
- Chapter 13—The Budget Process and Learning How to Fund Your Project
- Chapter 14—Developing the Technology Project
- Chapter 15—Do You Really Need This Technology?
- Chapter 16—Creating a Project Plan
- Chapter 17—How to Acquire Technology
- Chapter 18—Installation, Maintenance and Closure of Your Project... The Final Steps

# 12

# SO YOU WANT TO MANAGE TECHNOLOGY?

"Individual commitment to a group effort—that is what
makes a team work, a company work, a society work,
a civilization work."

—*Vince Lombardi*

## Learning Objectives

After reading this chapter, the student will:

- Have a working knowledge of the technology management process.
- Be able to discuss and interpret the difference between technology management and leadership.
- Define the basic terminology used by technology professionals.
- Articulate the main advantages and disadvantages of public safety technology.
- Have a working knowledge of the seven facts one should know about technology projects.
- Understand why technology projects succeed or fail.

## Introduction

In this chapter, you learn about technology and why technology is important to public safety managers. We discuss the important roles of each stakeholder within the entire process, and we discuss the lessons learned by successful public safety managers. The good thing about technology management is that you are not the first person to do it. There are many ways to manage a project and this chapter covers the fundamental concepts so that you have a basic understanding of the process.

## Technology Management

*Technology management* is a set of management disciplines that allow organizations to manage their technological fundamentals to create competitive advantage. The role of the technology management is to understand the value of certain technology in each organization. The continuous development of technology is very important to any public safety organization provided that the user (police officer, firefighter, and so on) benefits from the specific technology. It doesn't do any good to purchase a piece of equipment if no one is going to use it.

Technology management involves a great deal of integrated planning and design. The Association of Technology and Applied Engineering defines technology management as the field concerned with the supervision of personnel across the technical spectrum and a wide variety of complex technological systems.[1] Technology programs typically include instruction in production and operations management, project management, computer applications, quality control, safety and health issues, statistics and general management principles.[2] Generally, technology projects are often referred to as *information technology* or *IT*.

The management of technology requires substantial leadership skills and abilities. Leadership is a part of management. "To be a manager is to bring about, to accomplish, to have charge of, responsibility for, to conduct. Leading, on the other hand, is influencing, guiding in direction, course, action, opinion."[3] Leaders have a vision. Managers have schedules and focus on the job at hand. An effective public safety manager must demonstrate both leadership and management skills in order to manage a technology project. Some of the most important characteristics related to project management are:

- Effective communication skills—Both verbal and written.
- Ability to listen effectively—This is very important with the stakeholders.
- Ability to coordinate with others—Both inside and outside of the department or agency.
- Decision making skills—The ability to say "no" when necessary.
- Motivation skills—The ability to get the project and the team on track when necessary.
- Technical ability—You don't have to be an expert, but a good manager takes the time to understand the basics.
- Be accountable for the project—You are the manager. If the project stalls or fails, take responsibility and do not blame someone on your team. You should also give credit to those who do a good job. Managing a technology project is not about YOU. It is about the process and the overall result.
- Empowerment—Trusting others to do their job is essential. You cannot be everywhere, all the time.

Remember, "If you're a competent manager, you're getting the most out of your resources. If you're a competent leader, you are pointing their energy in the right direction."[4]

## Overview of Public Safety Technology Management

Managing technology or IT is a double edged sword for most public safety agencies. Like any other profession, public safety has welcomed and utilized technology for many years. Technology has many advantages and disadvantages. They include:

### *Advantages*

Technology allows public safety agencies to share information and communicate effectively. Computer databases like computer aided dispatch (CAD) provide police officers with critical information including the type of call, victim information, suspect discretion or direction of travel and numerous other details that the officer needs to be efficient and safe. Computer systems like the National Criminal Information Center (NCIC) provide information on criminal offenders across the nation including those with outstanding warrants. Law enforcement agencies are able to share this information across state lines within minutes.[5]

Technology also improves the overall efficiency of public safety operations. As technology evolves, information can be obtained quickly and accurately. In the 1970s and 1980s, law enforcement personnel had to request information via a car radio system. In the late 1980s, law enforcement patrol cars were outfitted with computers. This allowed officers to receive information quickly.

Data collection and distribution is also improved with technology. Public safety agencies are required to maintain and provide statistical information to elected officials, state or federal oversight agencies and the public at large. Personnel are able to quickly access large databases including record management systems (RMS) to locate and print off police reports for the public. Prior to this technology, personnel had to hand search large file cabinets, which was very time-consuming. Today, police reports can be located in a database and printed or emailed within minutes.

Technology also has a significant effect on safety. Technology advancements like the hand-held radio or handie-talkie (HT), medical defibrillators and mobile biometric identification devices have actually saved lives. Hand-held radios can communicate via wireless networks, which gives an officer the increased ability to maneuver, chase suspects and relay important information to others. Fire and paramedic personnel utilize a variety of medical instruments including defibrillators, portable communication devices and electrocardiograms (EKGs) to diagnose or treat injuries and communicate with hospital personnel on a real-time basis. Mobile biometric identification devices provide an officer with real-time information on suspects in a patrol setting. Suspects frequently lie to a peace officer and may be considered armed and dangerous. By utilizing mobile biometric identification technology, an officer can quickly identify a dangerous suspect, which provides an increased sense of safety for the officer.

Technology can also save money. Although some technology projects are quite expensive in the short-term, one of the greatest benefits of technology is that it can replace a human being. For example, consider how long it takes a fingerprint examiner to hand search one million fingerprint records for a latent fingerprint crime scene comparison. The search could take days or weeks depending on the quality of the fingerprints and skill level of the fingerprint examiner. However, by using specialized fingerprint software and the automated fingerprint identification system (AFIS), the same fingerprint examiner could conduct hundreds of searches each day. Managers of forensic laboratories could reduce some staffing (fingerprint examiners) because technology has streamlined the process.

## Disadvantages

The startup and ongoing expenses can be a deal breaker for some public safety agencies. Public safety agencies typically have a limited amount of money to fund technology projects, especially if the project is something new to the department. Law enforcement managers routinely plan on replacing outdated technology or equipment based on its life span. This includes patrol cars, weapons or standard computer workstations. However, what about new innovative projects like body-worn cameras, unmanned drones or helicopter downlink camera systems? New technology can be very expensive, so it is imperative that public safety managers do their homework and determine if the financial investment is worth it and it benefits the taxpayers.

Some technology is difficult to implement or maintain. This is always a major concern with larger agencies. New technology often requires extensive training and instruction. How do you train 5,000 officers? This can be quite a challenge for a police manager or supervisor. The public safety profession is not alone when it comes to the difficulties of implementing technology. The private sector also has difficulty trying to get the public to use new technology. People do not like change or even the thought of using new technology. Technology can be scary for some staff, so managers should take that into consideration when implementing new technology. Maintaining technology can also be challenging. Monitoring service and maintenance contracts is a full-time job in some agencies. The ongoing cost of maintaining equipment is often a discussion topic during the budget preparation period with department heads and elected officials.

Technology can also provide a false sense of security. In the 1980s, many law enforcement agencies placed mobile dispatch computers (MDCs) in each police car. The computers provided the officer with the ability to retrieve information using computer aided dispatch (CAD) software. However, law enforcement managers started to get some complaints about officer safety because calls for service were no longer aired over the radio system. The dispatcher simply sent the call information to the officer in the car via the MDC. This presented some safety issues for the officers. Backup officers and supervisors did not know where their partner officers were located and what type of a call they were handling. Modern law enforcement training dictates that when an officer is handling a call for service in a high crime area that nearby officers start toward that location just in case something happens. Over time, law enforcement agencies were able to make the necessary changes in MDC policies and now high priority calls are usually broadcasted over the radio for officer safety reasons.

## So Why Learn About Technology?

An informed and educated public safety manager is better able to not only manage technology, but is also more apt to utilize technology in an effective way. Public safety agencies spend thousands of dollars each year training personnel on use-of-force options, fire suppression or inmate management tactics. However, when was the last time public safety personnel had a class on how to purchase a video surveillance system? Public safety managers must have a basic understanding of technology in order for the project to be successful. One only has to read the local newspaper to find a story about how the public is upset at local politicians because money was spent on a project, only to see it fail because of poor management.

The ability to manage a technology project is critical in any public safety organization. One only has to look at history to see how a "mismanaged" technology project can create havoc and waste millions of dollars of taxpayer funds. For example, in September 2013, representatives from the state of Oregon gathered to test President Obama's Affordable Care Act website.[6] Sadly, the website crashed, which denied thousands of citizens the opportunity to obtain healthcare online. An investigation into the apparent mismanagement revealed the following:

- Staff working on the project did not manage the budget properly.
- State officials entered into a contract with no fixed price. This reduced the state's ability to hold the contractors accountable.
- State officials did not hire an expert in information technology. They decided to oversee the project themselves despite the fact that they lacked the expertise to do so.
- According to the *Oregonian* (2013), the state of Oregon handed over the developmental responsibility for the website to a large computer company out of California. Oregon paid the company over $90 million and received substandard software codes, repeated broken promises and one of the least functional sites in the country.[7]

To be fair, the aforementioned computer company was not entirely at fault. The deadline to create the insurance exchange was very quick. The federal government kept making changes to the specific requirements, which delayed production. The exchange also had to interact with other parties.[8]

Technology can also help managers and supervisors train, give direction to subordinates and deploy resources. One of the most important responsibilities for a supervisor or manager is the training of personnel. Distance learning or video conference training programs that utilize simulated classroom activities can be sent to all employees and everyone should receive the latest information on department policies, case laws or officer safety information.

Police managers can also use specialized software that analyzes data to determine where crimes are being committed and deploy resources as necessary. For example, if a supervisor notices that a specific area or beat is having a lot of grand theft autos, he or she can use geospatial information systems (GIS) to pinpoint the exact times and locations of the crimes.[9] Additional personnel or investigators can use this information for surveillances and hopefully capture any future suspects. Fire department managers can use GIS software to track and monitor the direction and severity of fires. In San Bernardino County, sheriff and fire personnel collaborate on fire suppression by using a helicopter downlink system. The helicopter downlink system is a specialized camera system that is attached to the bottom of the helicopter. The camera captures real-time video footage of a fire as the helicopter flies overhead. Ground command personnel can view the video footage from their fire trucks or mobile command centers.

Finally, the public expects and demands that public safety managers understand and utilize technology in the performance of their jobs. The general public watches television and is surrounded with innovative technology and equipment. The public expects public safety agencies to use the same type of equipment to solve crime, save lives and protect property.

## What Is Your Role in Technology?

Public safety agency personnel are usually divided into three categories: line staff, supervisors and managers. Technology affects all three categories and is essential to their core function.

- Line staff *use* the technology. They utilize the technology on a daily basis and are paramount to the overall success of any technology project. In order to gain support from the line staff, technology must be easy to use. Not every cop on the beat has extensive technical background. If the piece of equipment is too difficult to use, more than likely the officer will not use it. The equipment must also have a purpose. Does the equipment help an officer solve crime, locate stolen vehicles (ALPS) or process inmates inside of a correctional facility? Public safety personnel can easily see the importance of the aforementioned technology; thus this type of technology will most likely be successful and used by the line staff on a regular basis.
- Supervisors *use* and *provide* oversight of technology. Supervisors must understand and support technology. If the supervisor does not support the technology, his or her subordinates will generally do the same thing. The supervisor should also ensure that the technology is used properly to prevent any errors or misconduct. Supervisors can also use technology to train employees when necessary. Finally, because supervisors are usually in the field, they can use technology to analyze and plan activities. The use of crime analysis is a perfect example. As previously mentioned in this chapter, supervisors can deploy personnel to high crime areas based on crime trends or patterns.
- Managers (sworn or civilian) are the decision makers for the technology project. They are tasked with the overall responsibility to evaluate the cost of the technology versus the benefits and must ensure that the taxpayer's money is spent wisely. Managers must be able to justify the expense of any technology project or procurement when asked by the public. Managers can also use technology in the strategic planning process (data collection). Managers are also responsible for seeking out new technology. Department heads or managers often collaborate with other agency representatives and have the ability to regionalize and share the expense of technology.

## Technology Terminology

One of the scariest parts about managing a technology project is understanding some of the common terminology used during the overall process. The good thing is that managers do not have to be the expert in this area. However, they should have a basic understanding of any terminology used in the technology project. Throughout this chapter and the rest of

Unit 3, you will be exposed to specific terminology related to funding, planning, acquiring technology and implementing technology. The following are some fundamental terms used in the overall management process:

*Public safety agency management strategy*—A comprehensive plan for using technology that addresses the needs of the agency.
*Technology infrastructure*—The base or foundation for the delivery of technology to support the agency's programs or operational needs.
*Applications*—Software that is designed and purchased that benefits the agency's overall operational needs.
*Architecture*—Guidelines or blueprints that the agency, department or organization follows when designing, acquiring or implementing technology.
*Equipment*—Specific platforms or hardware used by the agency.
*Funding*—Current and projected funding sources that have been identified for the purchase of technology.
*Policy*—The specific rules or protocols that govern the specific agency.
*Procedures*—Defined steps for designing, planning, implementing, operating, maintaining and using technology; also known as *processes*.
*Software*—Computerized operating systems that enable users to operate and control application systems.[10]

*For a complete list of information technology terminology, review Appendix 2 at the end of this book.*

## Seven Facts You Should Know About Technology Projects

In 2002, the U.S. Department of Justice, Office of Community Oriented Policing Services entered into a cooperative agreement with SEARCH Group Incorporated to publish a comprehensive report that outlines how to plan, purchase and manage technology.[11] Their report identified *seven key facts* that one should know before attempting to manage a technology project.

The complete report can be located at the following: *The Law Enforcement Tech Guide: How to Plan, Purchase and Manage Technology (Successfully!) A Guide for Executives, Managers and Technologists*. Washington, DC: U.S. Department of Justice, Office of Community Policing Services.

### Fact #1 "Implementing Technology Is Difficult"[12]

In 1994, the Standish Group studied over 8,000 public and private technology projects. The study revealed that many agencies went over budget, lost functions and software features and had their projects cancelled before completion.[13]

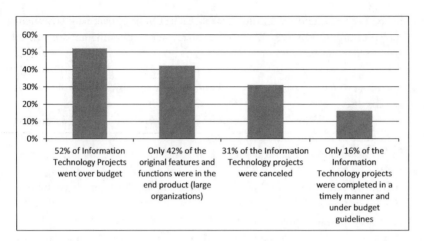

**FIGURE 12.1** Study on Information Technology.

*Source*: SEARCH Group Incorporated, Harris, K. & Romesburg, W. (2002). *Law Enforcement Tech Guide: How to Plan, Purchase and Manage Technology (Successfully!) A Guide for Executives, Managers and Technologists,* Washington, DC: U.S. Department of Justice, Office of Community Oriented Policing Services.

Technology projects can be difficult to manage.

- Some projects are so large that they cover multiple years or budget cycles.
- Technology projects have multiple lines of authority or require approvals outside of the law enforcement agency's change of command.
- Some projects need to be completed quickly based on the needs of the agency.[14]

Technology can be challenging and the details do matter. Public safety personnel should be aware that there are specific indicators that let you know that the project may be in jeopardy. They include:

- Some stakeholders fail to understand how technology can help law enforcement agencies meet their essential business goals or mission.
- All stakeholders are not involved in the technology process. (Planning, purchasing, and so on.)
- Best practices are not followed in the planning and implementation of the project.
- Budget and funding streams are too restrictive or fail to include funding for ongoing expenses.
- Just because the technology is available, it doesn't mean it will work for all public safety agencies.[15]

## Fact #2 "Planning and Installing IT Is Different Than Other Projects"[16]

Purchasing technology equipment is significantly different compared to other types of purchases (furniture, clothing, and so on). Public safety agencies often just trust the technology vendor and assume the vendor knows what they are doing. However, what happens when the technology equipment is not exactly what is advertised by the vendor? Compare this to the purchase of a desk or table for your office. If the desk or table has flaws or does not look like the catalog picture, the mistake will not affect how many criminals are apprehended, help identify a suspect in a dark alley or protect an officer on patrol.[17]

"Information technology, on the other hand, often radically changes the way an agency does business—and it should! It can help officers better identify and deal with suspects, make dispatchers more effective, aid analysts in identifying crime patterns and detectives in solving cases. If chosen hastily, however, technology can jeopardize mission-critical public safety activities, and/or hamper users and management, so its potential benefits may never be realized. Furthermore, because IT impacts mission-critical activities, its implementation causes major changes and most folks are reluctant when it comes to accepting change. So, although a desk may be criticized for not having enough writing space or drawers, these issues will not readily cause the department to throw away the desk and waste a great deal of taxpayer dollars. Dissatisfied users of an information systems downfall and demise, despite large investments of time and money."[18]

## Fact #3 "IT Planning and Implementation Is Not a One-Time Activity"[19]

It doesn't take a rocket scientist to know that technology changes so quickly that when you purchase a laptop at a local electronics store, by the time you get home, there is a new and better version available. Changes in hardware and software are continuous. This doesn't mean that public safety agencies should never purchase or acquire technology. It does mean that managers should always plan to replace and reinvest in newer technology when applicable.

Many managers often forget that technology is not a onetime event. Proper planning must be done to ensure that the piece of technology is maintained on an ongoing basis.[20]

## Fact #4 "IT Must Support the Strategic Business Mission Goals and Objectives of the Law Enforcement Agency"[21]

In order to have a successful technology project, public safety agencies should have strategic plans that emphasize the organization's mission, goals or objectives. The project must have the support of a public safety department head, chief or sheriff. A department's strategic plan should emphasize the use of technology and how it will serve the core mission of the department.[22] For example, many public safety agencies have vision statements. The San Bernardino County Sheriff's Department has a specific section in their vision statement that reads "we will relentlessly investigate criminal acts and arrest those guilty of violating the law, while building positive relationships with those we serve."[23] So how does technology or information technology play a part in the aforementioned vision statement? Innovative technology like automated license plate readers or mobile biometric identification systems can greatly enhance law enforcement's ability to locate and arrest criminals. Social media technology can assist the department's ability to pass on critical information to the public and also receive feedback from residents within the community.

## Fact #5 "Successful Projects Require Strong Management"[24]

Technology projects are deemed successful if they are completed on time, within budget and meet the overall goals and objectives of the department or agency. The project must also have strong project management. However, a project manager does not have to be a technical person.[25] A good leader knows the importance of being surrounded by experts in the field. People commonly judge the overall success of any politician based on his or her accomplishments. It is true that the politician is the figurehead, but in reality he or she probably has an abundance of advisors, consultants and subject matter experts to make sure decisions are made accurately and with wisdom. In the end, effective project management is an important and critical part of any technology project.[26]

## Fact #6 "All Projects Require a Plan"[27]

"The project plan forms the basis for all management efforts associated with the project."[28] A good plan identifies the user needs and priorities and considers what technology is available. The plan is also referred to as a "roadmap" for the agency or department. It keeps all of the stakeholders focused on the task at hand and ensures that the project runs smoothly. The plan should also address any future needs of the department.[29] Remember Fact #3, this process is not a one-time activity. Finally, the plan should be in writing. This is very important for long-term projects because people come and go in public safety. People are often transferred or promoted before the project is finished and having the plan in writing will help bring about a successful completion.

## Fact #7 "Successful IT Implementation Can Happen"[30]

Managing a technology can be daunting, but it can be done. Like any other task, it will take time and effort on your part. The good thing is that you have a variety of resources at your disposal. First, you can use this book as a guide or reference when faced with any issues that

**TABLE 12.1** Seven Facts You Should Know About Technology

1 Implementing information technology is difficult
2 Planning and installing information technology is different than other projects
3 Information planning and implementation is not a one-time activity
4 Information must support the strategic business mission, goals and objectives of the law enforcement agency
5 Successful projects require strong project management
6 All projects require a plan
7 Successful information technology implementation can happen!

*Source*: SEARCH Group Incorporated, Harris, K. & Romesburg, W. (2002). *Law Enforcement Tech Guide: How to Plan, Purchase and Manage Technology (Successfully!) A Guide for Executives, Managers and Technologists,* Washington, DC: U.S. Department of Justice, Office of Community Oriented Policing Services.

may come up during the management of the project.[31] Second, there is usually someone in your organization or nearby department that has probably been through the process. Public safety agencies have a strong history of cooperation and teamwork. It is perfectly acceptable to contact and learn from other agencies. In fact, it may be best to wait for another agency to implement a new piece of technology. Let them work out all the bugs and fix the issues *before* you purchase anything.

## Chapter Summary

Public safety agencies and organizations have a multitude of technology available to them. This includes record management systems (RMS), computer aided dispatch (CAD), less-lethal tactical equipment, biometrics, aviation technology, just to name a few. Public safety personnel have many options and opportunities to improve their own department. However, as you have learned already, the management of technology is not easy to do. There is a set process that must be followed. This is especially important when many public safety agencies are struggling to find funding sources. This chapter is the first of seven chapters in Unit 3 that focus on your role as a public safety manager. There are many decisions that will need to be made by you and your agency when it comes to technology. Regardless of the type of technology, the process of managing technology must be vetted, scrutinized, transparent and cost effective. As a public safety manager, your leadership skills will be tested. The mere fact that you will be dealing with personnel outside of your department will sometimes be difficult. However, after reading, interpreting and analyzing the next few chapters, you *will* have a better understanding on how to manage technology. So are you ready for the next chapter? Let's jump right in and start the process.

## Key Words or Terminology

| | | |
|---|---|---|
| technology management | information technology | NCIC |
| management strategy | technology infrastructure | equipment |
| hardware and software | | |

## Discussion Questions

1. Why is the management of technology such an important part of public safety?
2. Identify the advantages and disadvantages of technology in public safety.
3. In this chapter, we discussed the problems associated with the roll out of the Affordable Care Act website. Research a public safety agency (could be your own) and see if they had similar issues with technology. Describe them.
4. This chapter highlighted the "seven facts you should know about technology." Evaluate the seven facts and see how they relate to a previous, current or future project that you have been involved in. Are there any areas that stand out?
5. Identify at least five key leadership traits that you must have in order to manage a technology project.

## Notes

1 (2009). *Definitions.* Association of Technology, Management and Applied Engineering. Retrieved from www.atmae.site–ym.com.

2 Ibid.

3 Bennis, W. & Nanus, B. (1985). *Leaders.* New York: Harper & Bros.

4 Wisenhand, P. & Ferguson, F. (1996). *The managing of police organizations.* Upper Saddle River, NJ: Prentice Hall.

5 (2014). *National Crime Information Center.* Washington, DC: U.S. Department of Justice..

6 Budnick, N. (2013). Oregon health exchange technology troubles run deep due to mismanagement, early decisions. *The Oregonian.* Retrieved from www.oregonlive.com/health/index.ssf/2013/12/oregon_health_exchange_technol.html.

7 Ibid.

8 Ibid.

9 (2014). *Geospatial information systems (GIS).* Sacramento, CA: California Department of Technology.

10 Ibid.

11 SEARCH Group Incorporated, Harris, K. & Romesburg, W. (2002). *Law enforcement tech guide: How to plan, purchase and manage technology (successfully!) A guide for executives, managers and technologists.* Washington, DC: U.S. Department of Justice, Office of Community Oriented Policing Services.

12 Ibid.

13 Ibid.

14 Ibid.

15 Ibid.

16 Ibid.

17 Ibid.

18 Ibid.

19 Ibid.

20 Ibid.

21 Ibid.

22 Ibid.

23 (2014). *Vision statement.* San Bernardino, CA: San Bernardino County Sheriff's Department.

24 Harris & Romesburg, *Law enforcement tech guide.*

25 Ibid.

26 Ibid.

27 Ibid.

28 California Department of Technology, *Geospatial information systems (GIS).*

29 Harris & Romesburg, *Law enforcement tech guide.*

30 Ibid.

31 Ibid.

# 13

# THE BUDGET PROCESS AND LEARNING HOW TO FUND YOUR PROJECT

"The way to get started is to stop talking and start doing."
—*Walt Disney*

## Learning Objectives

After reading this chapter, the student will:

*   Understand the basic concepts of budget preparation and oversight.
*   Be able to explain the different types of budgets and how they apply to your agency or organization.
*   Understand the importance of a budget and how funding is established in a municipality, county or state agency.
*   Know and understand the basic elements of the grant writing process.
*   Learn the role of a public safety manager in the budget process.

## Introduction

In this chapter, we discuss the parameters and formats of a budget. Additionally, we review the grant writing process, which, if prepared correctly, can be a vital component of your project. It is no secret that funding will play an important part of your technology project. Public safety agencies are not like the private sector, where a company can raise capital to invest in technology. Large companies like Apple or Microsoft have billions of dollars for the research and development of new products. Public safety agencies are sometimes at the mercy of whatever technology is available. Technology or information technology (IT) companies try to develop equipment based on feedback from public safety personnel or from the military. Speaking of the military, many of the technology systems used by public safety organizations were originally developed for military applications. The United States government has the money and resources to develop technology that can eventually be used in public safety. One obvious example is the unmanned drone. The drone was developed for military use and is now being tested and used by public safety agencies.

Despite the type of technology or system that is needed by a public safety agency, the lack of funding is a common reason why organizations do not invest or have adequate technology. In order to manage technology successfully, one must have a basic understanding of the budget process. Many law enforcement, fire or correctional safety managers have a minimal understanding of the budget process.

## What Is a Budget?

A *budget* is the amount of money available for spending that is based on a plan for how it will be spent.[1] For public safety purposes, a budget is a statement of the financial position of an administration for a definite period of time based on estimates of expenditures during the period and proposals for financing them.[2] Essentially, the budget is a legal document that serves as the government's financial plan. The budget is also a reflection of the organization's policy and procedures. For example, if the city council supports public safety, they will usually ensure that public safety is given priority status when it comes to information technology projects. This is an important element of managing a technology project because the governing agencies must support your project financially.

Because public safety agencies are funded with tax dollars, the budget is a mechanism to show how the money is spent. This gives the public the ability to review and ask questions about your project if necessary. Public safety managers should always be prepared to justify the need for funding on any technology project. If by chance, public safety is not the priority, you may need to find additional revenue sources like a grant, which will be covered later in this chapter. Regardless of the type of funding source, a budget is a necessary requirement for any public safety project.

Government agencies, which include local, state and federal public safety agencies, will normally divide the budget into two areas: short-term and long-term. A short-term budget is a one-year budget, which can be a calendar year (January to December) or a fiscal year (July 1 to June 31). A long-term budget is usually three-to-five years in length. Short- and long-term budgets allow the decision makers the ability to plan for increased or decreased revenue sources over a period of time. For example, the city manager or chief operating officer will need to approve your technology project and give a recommendation about the funding source to the city council or board of supervisors. Common review sources include property or sales taxes. Many technology projects cover multiple budget cycles, so it is important to have the funding source approved on a long-term basis.

## Budget Overview

Budgeting is a process, and it involves the following:

- Analyze and determine future needs
- Maximize available resources

- Predict expected income
- Develop an allocation plan (the budget)
- Provide resources for emergencies

To say that the budget process is political is an understatement. Public safety agencies are governed by elected officials, who have specific agendas and priorities. Political preferences are often expressed in the appropriation process of a budget. Additionally, budgets are affected by local, state and federal mandates. Mandates are an official order to do something or the power to act that the voters give to their elected leaders.[3] Unfortunately, government agencies or even the voters often mandate a specific program or function, but fail to adequately fund the mandate. This can create a problem for public safety managers. For example, what happens if the state mandates that all public safety agencies will electronically send fingerprint records to a state repository by 2020? Local jurisdictions are now faced with the responsibility of ensuring that the mandate is fulfilled, usually with little or no funding from the state agency that issued the mandate. The most important part of any budget is the enactment. It reveals in financial terms what the priorities are for the elected officials.

## Types of Budgets

There are generally two types of budgets: operational and capital. The operational budget usually covers a twelve-month period or one fiscal year. The operational budget includes annual salaries, benefits, consumables, general supplies, and so on. A capital budget is used for long-term projects or expenditures, which are spread out over a number of years. A good example of a capital budget is the replacement of a records management system or computer aided dispatch. These projects require extensive planning, design, testing and training, which are accomplished over several years. Department heads allocate funding for these types of projects in capital accounts. A capital budget is also used for new building projects like a new police station or jail.

When the capital budget for a specific project is established and authorized, the cost to maintain a project is included in the operational budget.

## Budget Cycle

Each budget has four steps;

1 Preparation of the budget
2 Review and approval of the budget
3 Execution of the budget
4 Audit of the budget

### Preparation

The preparation of a budget is critical. It includes a vast amount of research including the current and projected costs for services. It includes a review of past budgets to see what items can be excluded from the proposed budget and a complete analysis of projected revenue sources. The budget preparation process takes place several months before the renewal of the next fiscal budget. Specific dates are generated during the budget preparation process, including requests for additional funding from various departments including public safety. As a manager, this is the time and place to make a pitch for funding your technology project. For example, if you need $100,000 for a new camera system at the station, you will need to have some background information on the project, which includes several quotes from vendors. It doesn't have to be exact, but you should at least include some estimates so it can be included into the budget process. Sometimes public safety managers will be required to meet with his or her chief, sheriff, or warden to discuss the project in advance. The head of the department may decide to prioritize each project before submitting it to financial personnel responsible for the final budget.

## Review and Approval

Each public safety agency is governed by an elected official(s) within a specific jurisdiction. This includes a city council, board of supervisors, fire protection commissioners or various state legislators. Elected officials will often have several budget meetings to discuss the elements of the budget and ask questions of any staff member or department head. As a public safety manager, you may be required to attend a budget meeting and give additional information or answer any questions. The elected officials will then prioritize each part of the budget, including your request for funding and tentatively approve the budget. This is usually where the budget cuts occur. The formal budget is then presented in a public meeting, which allows the general public the opportunity to comment on the budget and make any recommendations. After the governing representatives have approved the budget, it is final.

## Execution of the Budget

When the final budget is approved, each department head or elected official is given his or her budget amounts. Budgets cannot be overspent without authorization from the governing representatives. The budget execution phase is also known as the "action" phase because this is where the funds are spent to achieve a specific goal or objective. The budget should be reviewed and adjusted on a regular basis. Budgets are usually broken down into specific categories. Each category has a specific fund amount, but the fund amount can be reallocated as long as the overall amount does not increase. For example, if you have $40,000 in one item (special department expenses) and you need $5,000 in maintenance, you can transfer funds with approval from your financial personnel.

It is also common during hard economic times or at the end of a budget cycle to "freeze" the budget or a specific part of the budget. Throughout the year, the folks responsible for the budget (auditor, finance, and so on) will make recommendations to the elected board to conserve funds based on projected revenue shortfalls. On occasion, your department budget could be cut. This could be a drastic event for your technology project, so you should also plan for this contingency.

All budget expenditures have some type of internal controls to make sure purchases and spending are within the city, county or state guidelines. Public safety agencies have very strict rules on the procurement of services and equipment, which are discussed later in this book.

### Audit

The audit is the final part or phase of the budget process. Audits are usually conducted by an independent or outside party each year. Government agencies are audited by certified public accountants (CPA) from financial companies that are experienced in government operations. The CPA reviews and examines all financial records, including any documents associated with your technology project. The CPA looks for waste, fraud or abuse of the procedures approved by your agency or state/federal laws. The audit process also examines the procurement process you used. Was the bidding process fair? He or she also reviews the math computations listed in your individual project for accuracy.

## Budget Formats

There are several different types of budget formats used by government agencies. It is critical that all public safety managers understand the specifics, goals and objectives of each format.

### Line Item Budget

The line item budget is the oldest and simplest type of budget. Line item budgets are widely used by government agencies for a variety of reasons. Line item budgets focus on how much money is spent rather than the activity or outcomes. This type of budget format is easy to construct, administer and understand. Each item or line within the budget is assigned an object code (salaries, maintenance, travel, and so on). Public safety managers can easily make changes to the budget using this format. Line item budgets are also common for public safety technology projects. Managers can reduce or increase line items as necessary to meet the goals of the project.

Line item budgets do have some disadvantages. Long-range planning is neglected because the line item budget is designed for shorter time lines. Additionally, this type of budget is not tied to performance or efficiency issues. Finally, because line item budgets are widely used by public safety agencies, annual budgets are often copied into the next year. This can create a problem because the prior year may include a one-time purchase of technology. The one-time purchase amount does not need to be included into future year budgets.

**TABLE 13.1**  San Bernardino County CAL-ID Line Item Budget

*San Bernardino CAL-ID Local AFIS (SDA)*

*Budget Report For Fiscal Year 2005/2006*

| Object | | Budget | Expended | % |
|---|---|---|---|---|
| 2025 | Clothing | $400 | $0 | |
| 2034 | Communications | $17,000 | $14,707 | |
| 2062 | 800 MHZ | $0 | $324 | |
| 2075 | Memberships | $3,000 | $1,300 | |
| 2130 | Non-Inventory Equipment | $45,000 | $7,884 | |
| 2135 | Special Departmental Expenses | $10,000 | $42,265 | |
| 2140 | Training | $15,000 | $3,175 | |
| 2304 | Non-Central Stores | $5,000 | $30,698 | |
| 2305 | General Office | $20,000 | $20,349 | |
| 2310 | Postage | $500 | $1,553 | |
| 2323 | Printing Services | $500 | $150 | |
| 2340 | Shredding | $3,000 | $476 | |
| 2420 | Distance DP Equipment | $1,000 | $0 | |
| 2445 | Data Proc (OMS) | $13,700 | $0 | |
| 2450 | OMS System Development | $1,000 | $0 | |
| 2840 | Medical Supplies | $100 | $66 | |
| 2855 | Maintenance | $3,00,000 | $1,58,243 | |
| 2860 | Auto Repair (Outside) | $4,000 | $2,395 | |
| 2870 | Structure Maintenance | $2,000 | $0 | |
| 2920 | Mileage | $500 | $0 | |
| 2930 | County Garage | $3,000 | $735 | |
| 2935 | Other Travel | $5,000 | $14,734 | |
| 2945 | Air Travel | $3,000 | $3,857 | |
| | Total Services and Supplies | $4,52,700 | $3,02,911 | 66.90% |
| 4040 | Equipment | $3,00,000 | $2,80,453 | 93.50% |
| 4050 | Vehicle Purchase | $11,000 | $0 | 0.00% |
| 5012 | Rent/lease | $1,39,088 | $77,378 | 55.6 |
| 5045 | Salary and Benefits | $28,29,318 | $10,82,441 | 38.30% |
| | **FY2005/2006 TOTAL** | **$37,32,106** | **$17,43,183** | **46.70%** |

**19.9% UNDER BUDGET**

Target Budget      66.60%
100/12 = 8.33 per month

*(Continued)*

*San Bernardino CAL-ID Local AFIS (SDA)*

*Budget Report For Fiscal Year 2004/2005 – (January YTD)*

| Object | | Budget | Expended | % |
|---|---|---|---|---|
| 2025 | Clothing | $400 | $0 | |
| 2034 | Communications | $16,200 | $5,760 | |
| 2062 | 800 MHZ | $0 | $0 | |
| 2075 | Memberships | $3,000 | $1,180 | |
| 2130 | Non-Inventory Equipment | $20,000 | $22,691 | |
| 2135 | Special Departmental Expenses | $8,000 | $5,286 | |
| 2140 | Training | $12,000 | $5,141 | |
| 2304 | Non-Central Stores | $5,000 | $4,454 | |
| 2305 | General Office | $20,000 | $12,403 | |
| 2310 | Postage | $500 | $1,566 | |
| 2323 | Printing Services | $500 | $98 | |
| 2340 | Shredding | $3,000 | $330 | |
| 2410 | Data Processing (OMS) | $13,700 | $481 | |
| 2420 | Distance DP Equipment | $1,000 | $0 | |
| 2445 | Professional Services | $65,000 | $0 | |
| 2450 | OMS System Development | $1,000 | $0 | |
| 2840 | Medical Supplies | $0 | $123 | |
| 2855 | Maintenance | $3,00,000 | $83,046 | |
| 2860 | Auto Repair (Outside) | $4,000 | $1,233 | |
| 2870 | Structure Maintenance | $2,000 | $0 | |
| 2905 | Rent/Lease | $1,35,200 | $1,35,200 | |
| 2920 | Mileage | $500 | $0 | |
| 2930 | County Garage | $3,000 | $509 | |
| 2935 | Other Travel | $3,200 | $8,176 | |
| 2945 | Air Travel | $3,000 | $2,224 | |
| | Total Services and Supplies | $6,20,200 | $2,89,901 | 46.70% |
| 4040 | Equipment | $4,40,000 | $3,80,000★ | |
| 4050 | Vehicle Purchase | $10,215 | $10,215 | |
| 5012 | Rent/lease | $1,49,236 | $89,160★★ | |
| 5045 | Salary and Benefits | $23,69,557 | $7,68,986 | 32.40% |
| | **FY2004/2005 TOTAL** | **$35,89,208** | **$15,38,262** | **42.80%** |

**15.5% UNDER BUDGET**

Target Budget
100/12 = 8.33 per month
7 × 8.33 = 58.3%

*Source*: Rose, J. (2005). San Bernardino CAL-ID Local AFIS (SDA) Budget. San Bernardino, CA: Author.
★ Purchase of Identix Palm Live Scan Machines via Regional NKA budget
★★ Lease amount for Cal-ID building in FY2003/2004

### Program Budget

Program budgets are basically a series of mini-budgets, which show the specific activities that each department performs. For example, the traffic division could have a program budget for driving under the influence (DUI) enforcement, commercial enforcement or traffic education. Each is a different program and would have a separate budget.[4]

### Performance-Based Budget

A performance-based budget is very similar to a program budget. However, a performance-based budget includes one new component: performance.[5] Expenditures are based on specific activities and their costs. Performance-based budgets use benchmarks to compare programs or activities (dates, times and goals, and so on). A good example is a budget used for a gang team. The budget would use criteria or statistics to determine if the program has reduced gang activity or violence. Performance-based budgeting provides spending data that the city, county or state can examine at the end of the year to identify the amount of service produced by the department or program.[6] The biggest disadvantage of performance-based budgeting is that it takes a considerable amount of time to gather data and other statistical information. The identification of measureable performance goals is also difficult to achieve. Did the crime rate go down because the city added more officers or did it drop because of changes in the demographics and economic conditions within the community?

### Zero-Based Budgeting

Zero-based budgeting requires all departments to defend their programs or activities at the end of the year. Regardless of any prior funding, department heads must show how increased personnel or equipment would improve a specific program or activity. If the item cannot be justified, it is cut from the budget. Each item is scrutinized by the final decision makers. Do you really need three clerks this year or could you manage with two?

A zero-based budget can detect an inflated budget, and it increases communication and coordination within the organization. The major drawback to zero-based budgeting is that it is very time-consuming and staff-intensive. Financial personnel and department managers also require specialized training, which is difficult to justify when there are other budget formats available.

## How to Write a Grant

In order to effectively manage a technology project, public safety managers should have a basic understanding on how to write a grant. Why, you ask? Funding for technology is difficult to obtain from local and state agencies. Salary and benefits (staffing) make up the majority of any public safety budget and there is very little discretionary funding available for technology projects. Savvy public safety managers seek out alternative sources of funding, and the most popular source is a grant. Writing a grant can be challenging and very few public safety agencies provide any formal training in this area. Large agencies can afford to hire a grant writer or manager, but smaller agencies must rely on someone within the management ranks to be the resident "expert" on grants. Public safety agencies can obtain and utilize grant funding for a variety of areas or disciplines. State and federal agencies offer numerous grant opportunities for staffing, technology, school safety, fire suppression and corrections. In the next few pages, public safety managers will learn about the basics in grant writing. However, every jurisdiction is different, so make sure you consult with legal counsel and appropriate finance department before attempting to write a grant.

## What Is a Grant?

A *grant* is an award of financial assistance from a governmental agency, corporation or individual person to a recipient to carry out a specified project or program.[7] A *grant proposal* is a formal document that describes why the funds are needed, what the funds will be used for and how the funds will be managed.

## Types of Grants

There are several types of grants used by public safety agencies. Some of the more popular types of grants are categorical, formula, block and private.[8] Grants are given to individual agencies, not to one person. When researching and eventually writing a grant, public safety managers must understand the differences in each grant.

- Categorical—Specific and well defined area of interest.
- Formula—Funds are allocated according to a set of criteria (Population, unemployment, crime rate).
- Block—Funds are given to states in "blocks" and the states decide how to spend the money. This includes the distribution of funds to local agencies.
- Private—Also known as a *foundation grant*. Awarded by a private family (trust) or corporate groups for a specific need.

Public safety managers may also obtain funding via congressional earmarks, also known as *pork*. If a technology project is significant enough, public safety agencies can request funding via their congressional representatives. If the congressional representative determines that the funding would benefit his or her constituents, they will try to include the funding request into federal appropriation bills. In 2004, the Counties of San Bernardino and Riverside, both in California, requested $3.6 million to purchase mobile biometric identification devices. Sheriffs in both counties cosponsored the request and worked with various local congressional representatives to obtain funding for the project. The project was funded and the mobile biometric identification project has been hugely successful and benefited numerous local law enforcement agencies in both counties.[9] The process of appropriations is very political because the most powerful politicians in the U.S. Congress manage trillions of dollars in the federal budget. Appropriations for local projects have been drastically reduced in recent years, but they still may be available.

Another source of funding is a state or federal contract. Many times, state or federal agencies need to work with local jurisdictions to manage large scale projects or programs. State or federal agencies will enter into "contracts" with local public safety agencies to provide a service or support collaborative efforts that benefit everyone involved. Contracts are usually awarded to the lowest bidder. State or federal contracts usually expire after a specific time period, but can be extended indefinitely. A good example of a federal and local partnership is the housing of federal inmates in county prisons. Due to prison overcrowding, the federal government has entered into contracts with county jails to house federal inmates. Local counties are paid a set fee for housing, medical and transportation costs.

## Grant Writing Recommendations

The following are recommendations that should be considered if you decide to write a public safety grant:[10]

- Grant writing is very political.
- The majority of writing a grant is the *research!* It takes work to locate and write a grant.
- READ THE GRANT INSTRUCTIONS.
- Pay attention to grant due dates and times.
- Outline your proposal before submitting it online.
- Do not use any public safety jargon unless it is specific to the grant. The grantor most likely is not familiar with public safety terminology.
- Be compelling when writing a grant. Use human interest stories whenever possible. If you are applying for school safety funds, mention how the funds will possibly help prevent another Columbine tragedy.
- Don't exaggerate. Stick to the facts. Nobody wants to read a novel of material. Remember that the grantor reads thousands of grants each year.
- Simplify your grant when possible. The length of the proposal will not affect the outcome.
- Revise, edit and then clarify (have other people review your work before submission).
- Stay involved in the process. Staying in contact with the grantor can be beneficial in the long run. Always be professional.
- Try to use key words or phrases when writing the grant, such as *interoperability, regionalization, partnership, homeland security, prevention, school safety,* and *this project will save tax-payer funds in the long run.*[10]

## Basic Grant Information

There are many websites for public safety grants. Grants.gov is "a storefront web portal used to collect data (forms and reports) for federal grant-making agencies."[11] Individual agencies must register with the website to gain access to grant information. The process is very simple and only has to be done once.

Each public agency is issued a data universal numbering system number (DUNS). The DUNS number is issued by Dun and Bradstreet, which is a company that provides marketing research, credit reports, industry statistics and telemarketing reports. The DUNS number is unique and has nine digits. The DUNS number identifies a specific agency or group. If you work for a county that contracts with a local city for police or fire services, remember that the city may also have a DUNS number. Make sure you use the correct DUNS number when submitting a grant.[12]

The primary registrant database for the federal government is the Central Contractor Registration (CCR). CCR collects, validates and stores data from grant users and vendors. The DUNS and CCR numbers take several days to obtain, so plan ahead.[13]

## Basic Grant Format

Most grants require or have a similar type of format. This keeps the process consistent and fair for all grantees. A typical grant has the following categories:

- Cover letter or introduction
- Abstract or executive summary
- Problem statement (needs assessment)
- Goals and objectives
- Plan of operation
- Evaluation plan
- Sustainability plan
- Budget plan

> For your review, excerpts from an actual grant are located in Appendix 3 at the end of this book. The grant was used to procure hand-held mobile biometric identification devices by the San Bernardino County Sheriff's Department and the Riverside County Sheriff's Department.

## Cover Letter (Introduction)

The cover letter is used to introduce your agency to the grantor. Keep in mind that there are thousands of public safety agencies in the United States. This is your opportunity to give a brief background about your agency and assure the grantor that you have support from your chief, sheriff, and so on. The cover letter should also state what you are asking for and how much you need. The cover letter should be signed by an elected official, chief or sheriff. Some grants allow electronic signatures; however, the final grant requires approval from the city council, board of supervisors, and so on. If allowed by the grantor, try to use department letterhead and address the letter to the person named on the grant announcement.

## Executive Summary

The executive summary, also known as an *abstract*, is used to identify the key points of the proposal. The intent of the executive summary is to invite the reader (grantor) to read further. This is where the grant writing must convince the grantor that the proposal is important and that the funds are desperately needed. The executive summary should also state the need for the specific piece of technology or program and what is expected from it. For example, if your agency is requesting grant funds for a records management system (RMS), you should explain how the RMS is going to streamline efficiency, save money or track data. This is an opportunity to use some of the key words or phrases mentioned in the grant writing secrets section—phrases like *fight crime, reduce DNA backlog, decrease the time it takes for officers to respond to emergency calls,* or *protect life and property* are persuasive.

   The executive summary should explain why your agency deserves the grant. This is a competitive process, so take the time to explain why your agency deserves the funds and not some other agency. Also explain what your agency will do with the funds and how much the project or piece of technology will cost.

   Finally, thank the reader (grantor) for considering your request. The executive summary should be no more than one-to-two pages in length.

## Problem Statement

The problem statement is also known as a *needs assessment*. The problem statement will address the specific needs of the department or organization. Keep in mind that the grantor must agree that there is a specific need or they will not fund the project. The problem statement should focus on the people that your agency serves, not just the organization. The problem statement should also match your agency's mission or value statement. It doesn't hurt to quote the actual mission statement to show your commitment to the project.

   When writing a problem statement, always remember to keep it simple, concise and to the point. If possible, use any statistical data to support your agreement. The use of crime rates, trends, fire safety data, recidivism rates and response times are all excellent examples of statistical data that can be mentioned in the problem statement.

   As previously mentioned, try to use heartfelt or humanistic stories if possible. If your agency is requesting grant funding for a portable traffic speed indicator, you should discuss the amount of traffic accidents that have occurred in the specific location. If there have been any fatalities as a result of excess speed along the roadway, make sure to mention how the portable traffic speed indicator will hopefully prevent future fatalities. Another trick is to attach any press releases or comments from public officials, politicians or family members. Having a quote from the mayor shows support for the project and having a heartfelt comment from a mother that lost her child in a traffic accident will show emotion and hopefully entice the grantor to pick your agency.

   Finally, provide a sense of urgency. Explain why the grant funding is critical to your agency or organization. Also make sure to list what your agency or organization has done to address the problem. Did the department already increase traffic enforcement in the specific area of concern?

## Goals and Objectives

The goals and objectives section of the grant is critical because it spells out the specific accomplishments that the grant funding provides. Typically, this section includes various results or outcomes related to the technology project. All of the goals and objectives must relate back to the original problem statement. It is important to use key words like *decrease, deliver, establish, improve, produce,* and so on. The aforementioned words are used to describe a result or outcome. For example, if one of the goals of the project is to improve the efficiency of the jail booking process, then state "the grant funds will be used to purchase single fingerprint biometric scanners, which will decrease the amount of time it takes to book a prisoner into a local jail. This will allow the officer to spend more time on patrol handling important calls for service and protecting the public."

Remember that "goals" are not objectives. An objective is a step toward accomplishing the goal. Objectives are precise, concrete and can be measured. The goals and objectives section should also identify the target audience and must be capable of being accomplished within the grant period. For example, "patrol officers will begin to utilize mobile biometric identification devices in a patrol setting by December 2020." Always allow plenty of time to write the goals and objectives and the ways the agency will measure them.

## Plan of Operation

The plan of operation section explains how the process or program will work. How will the agency use the piece of technology? How will it be managed and staffed? Will the agency or organization handle the project in-house or outsource it? The plan of operation will also include a basic timetable of events to illustrate that the department, agency or organization has a specific plan. The timetable should include major milestones including how and when the technology will be acquired, purchased, evaluated and maintained. It should also describe how public safety personnel will be trained. The plan of operation should provide some detailed information to the grantor about all aspects of the project, program or piece of technology.

The evaluation plan is exactly as it sounds. What is your agency's plan on evaluating the project, process or piece of equipment? Were the goals and objectives achieved? Grantees must be honest and critical with the results. It doesn't matter what the project encompasses, public safety agencies can always improve. In this section, the prospective grantee lists the type of evaluation tool that will be used.

- Data analysis—Crime statistics, response times, lack of citizen complaints, fiscal data or officer safety
- Personal observation—Project manager or vendor observations
- Feedback from stakeholders—Written (survey) or verbal feedback
- A combination of all three

## Sustainability Plan

Most grantors will want to know that the project will continue on a long-term basis. In this section, the grantee will explain the agency's plans to continue with the project or program after the grant expires. Does the agency have plans and adequate funding to continue with the project? This is your opportunity to finish the story and provide a "sequel" to the original proposal. Always try to show support from department heads, the public and elected officials.

## Budget Plan

The budget plan is probably the hardest part of the grant process, but do not be intimidated. Unless you are experienced in budget management, you will need help from the finance department. The budget plan has two sections: a narrative that describes the elements of the budget and budget analysis that is detailed on some type of spreadsheet. The budget plan includes direct and indirect costs. Direct costs include personnel, travel, equipment and supplies. Indirect costs include facilities, insurance and utilities.

Personnel costs should include full salary and benefits, overtime and any future raises if applicable. Grants have specific instructions for personnel, so it is very important that this section is completed accurately.

Travel expenses are heavily scrutinized so make sure they are explained in detail and are well justified. You will also need to explain the agency's per diem policy. Try to be realistic. Does your agency really need to send two officers to Japan just to see how the software is developed?

Explain all equipment costs in detail. How does the purchase of equipment address the problem statement? Does your agency or department already have this equipment? Actual quotes from vendors can be very helpful if asked for details from the grantor.

Finally, the budget should never drive the proposal. Do not ask for a luxury vehicle when a simple economy vehicle will do. Always document the funds that the department or agency will contribute toward the project. This demonstrates commitment to the project. If matching funds are a requirement for the grant, explain how and where the department will provide the matching funds.

## Grant Process Review

To review the grant process:

- Research and timing are two keys to a successful proposal and receipt of funds.
- Take your time and ask for help.
- Follow the aforementioned basic format.
- Utilize elected officials for support of the technology project.

## Chapter Summary

As you have seen, the budget process isn't easy. There are many factors involved in the budget process. However, the good news is that the budget process is standardized. Public safety managers should be familiar with and have a complete understanding of the various rules, regulations and laws within your agency or organization. Government agencies have a fiduciary duty to maintain and protect the taxpayers' dollars. More than likely, your agency or organization has a team or division that is responsible for the overall budget process.

The grant process can sometimes be overwhelming. It takes practice and you will need some help writing your first grant. Similar to the aforementioned budget process, grant writing is usually standardized. The format, rules and regulations are straightforward and usually included in the grant notification letter or website. Public safety managers are already accustomed to using government documents (police reports, incident command forms, and so on), so writing a grant shouldn't be too difficult. Just remember the basic format for grants and fill in the blanks!

This chapter also covered some of the information that public safety managers will need to know in order to be successful on the job. There are numerous websites available that can also be of assistance when preparing a budget or looking for new funding sources.

## Key Words or Terminology

| | | |
|---|---|---|
| budget | grants | DUNS number |
| appropriations | mandate | budget cycle |

## Discussion Questions

1. Research the public safety budget process in your jurisdiction. Ascertain and evaluate the types of budgets used in the specific agency. How are they administered? What types of services do they provide?
2. Describe the grant writing process. Think of a piece of technology, program or project for which you would like to write a grant using the information listed in this chapter. Using the sample grant in Appendix 3, write an executive summary for the grant.
3. Explain the importance of an audit in the budget process.
4. Locate and identify seven grant writing secrets. Describe why they are important and how they may also apply to public safety.
5. How does leadership play a role in the budget process? What areas will require supervision and management oversight?

## Notes

1 (2014). *Glossary of budget terms.* Sacramento, CA: California Department of Finance.
2 Ibid.
3 (2014). *Finance glossary of accounting and budgeting terms.* Sacramento, CA: California Department of Finance.
4 Ibid.
5 Ibid.
6 Ibid.
7 *Grants 101,* n.d. National Institute of Justice. Office of Justice Programs. Retrieved from www.ojp. gov/grants101/overview.
8 Ibid.
9 Rose, J. (2004). *San Bernardino & Riverside County COPS technology grant application.* San Bernardino, CA.
10 National Institute of Justice, *Grants 101.*
11 Ibid.
12 *Apply for grant opportunities,* n.d. U.S. Department of Health and Human Services. Retrieved from www.grants.gov/web/grants.
13 National Institute of Justice, *Grants 101.*

# 14

# DEVELOPING THE TECHNOLOGY PROJECT

"Technology is dominated by two types of people: those who understand what they do not manage and those who manage what they do not understand."

—*Archibald Putt*

## Learning Objectives

After reading this chapter, the student will:

- Understand the role of a public safety manager in a technology project.
- Explain the role of a project manager.
- Assess the limitations, strengths and potential of a technology project and how it can benefit a public safety agency.
- Explain the importance of obtaining support for a technology project.
- Evaluate the use of an outside consultant in a technology project.

## Introduction

The good thing about project management is that there is a specific structure or method that can be used for just about any project. Regardless of the type of technology you wish to purchase and implement in your agency or organization, effective project management requires patience, understanding and sometimes a little bit of luck. There are numerous articles available in the media that discuss project management principles and ways to be a successful project manager. The common theme in project management is to start with a general foundation and build the project from there. A general contractor building a home doesn't just show up at the property and start installing fixtures or plumbing. They first build the house from the ground up, which includes making some specific decisions about the construction project. Who is in charge? Who will approve the architectural plans? Does the general contractor hire outside help? All of these questions need to be answered before he or she starts to work on the house. More importantly, the entire process is codified into some type of a document. The document can be called the *scope of work*, *foundation* or *work plan*. The important part is that the document answers the aforementioned questions. When that information has been clarified, the project can move forward.

In this chapter, we discuss and highlight the initial steps of managing a technology project. Keep in mind that we have not conducted a needs analysis or created a project plan yet. This chapter just deals with an analysis of who will manage the project and how that will be accomplished.

## Building Organizational Support

Organizational support is critical in any successful project. If the command staff does not support the project, then most likely it will fail. Public safety managers must understand that the chief, warden or sheriff is ultimately responsible for the project, regardless of whether or not they are intimately involved in the process. The first step is to identify who will serve as the sponsor for the project. Typically, this person must be a supervisor or manager with decision making authority.[1] Most public safety agencies have personnel at the commander level and they have the authority to make decisions about budget and personnel. The project manager must make every effort to stay in constant communication and give frequent updates to those in command staff positions.

### *Identify the Stakeholders*

The basic concept of community policing is to involve all stakeholders and come up with solutions that address quality of life issues and solve crime. A stakeholder is anyone who is engaged in the activity or project whose interests are affected by the project completion.[2] This includes personnel from public safety, the public, media, and businesses. Public safety managers must apply the same logic and philosophy used in community policing. Depending on the type of technology project, the identification of any stakeholders is essential. For example, if your agency wanted to install a large-scale video surveillance camera system across the city, it makes sense to reach out and contact the various business leaders, allied government agencies (public works, parks, and so on), local politicians and of course the public. One or more of the stakeholders may have an issue with your project, so it is important to have them on board in the beginning. The stakeholders will help you identify any major weaknesses with the project and will be there to support you when necessary.

### *So Who Is in Charge of the Project?*

Determining who is in charge of the project can be difficult, but it must be done *before* the project progresses. Typically, a member of the department is designated as the *project manager*. This person can be a line officer or someone with rank. It really depends on the type of project. The San Bernardino County Sheriff's Department has a division called

CAL–ID. Personnel assigned to the CAL–ID division are responsible for the biometric projects throughout the county. This includes fingerprints, facial recognition, IRIS identification, palm prints and DNA. The division is managed by a sheriff's lieutenant, who has the authority from the sheriff to make significant decisions regarding the budget process, procurement, implementation of technology and forensic investigations. The lieutenant also acts as the project manager on all technology projects at CAL–ID, which includes the development and implementation of mobile biometric identification devices, the purchase of and upgrades to the automated fingerprint identification system and the assessment of any emerging technology that can be used by the region.

Some projects require a different type of decision maker. Global or large scale projects often have steering committees. A *steering committee* is generally comprised of high-level managers within the department or agency. They have the authority and can assign subordinate staff or resources to the project as needed. A steering committee can help provide guidance for your project. They will oversee your progress, deliverables, and so on.[3] The second type of committee is a *user group*. They are made up of technical experts or line staff that most likely are the end users of the technology. Public safety managers should make every attempt to have representatives from any end-user on this committee. If your department is going to replace the computer aided dispatch (CAD) system, it would make sense to have personnel from IT, dispatch and patrol assigned to the user group committee. The goal of the user group is to identify specific workflow and operational issues with the project. This includes any software or technical solutions.[4] The user group will report their findings to the project manager or steering committee, if applicable.

### Do You Need Help with the Project?

Public safety personnel spend countless hours training and learning about their craft. Whether it is fire suppression, crime fighting or managing a prison riot, public safety personnel are clearly the experts. However, if the project is outside of your capabilities, it may make sense to get some outside assistance.[5] The use of an outside expert may include the use of a consultant, sub-contractor or hiring an entire company to manage the project. To emphasize this point, if your agency or organization wants to upgrade the software in your jail information management system (JIMS), do you really have anyone experienced enough to accomplish this task? It may be wise to hire an expert if your project involves data integration, network infrastructure changes or major changes to the overall public safety operation. Additionally, your project may require changes in existing technology systems that are proprietary in nature, which means only the company that created the system can modify it.

Outsourcing or hiring a consultant has many advantages. They include:

- The project timeline is reduced.
- The outside company is contractually obligated to complete the project. Can you guarantee that someone from your department will be around to finish the job? They could be transferred, promoted or even retire from the department.
- A consultant has years of experience in the field of technology and can help save your agency or organization time and money in the long run.

However, outsourcing is not cheap. Public safety managers need to weigh the overall value of outsourcing or hiring a consultant based on the specific budget for the project. Additionally, you must ensure that the motives of the consultant are the same as yours. Do not let the consultant expand your project, just so they can continue with the consulting contract. Make sure you have done your homework by checking out any references and develop very precise contract language that defines the purpose, scope and budget for the outside company or consultant.[6]

## Identification of a Project Manager

The project manager is a critical component of any technology project. It doesn't matter if the project manager is from within your agency or organization or if they are hired from the outside. The success of the project depends on the project manager. A project manager has many responsibilities including:

- Manage the entire project, which includes planning or scheduling of activities.
- Coordinate with anyone involved with the project. This includes any stakeholders, sub-contractors, other vendors, etc.
- Act as the single point of contact.
- Display leadership and make decisions when necessary.
- Ensure the project goals and objectives are followed.
- Report as necessary to any command staff or committee that has the overall responsibility for the project.[7]

## Create an Executive Summary

The final step in this chapter is to codify or create a written document that can be used throughout the project. The document is often called an *executive summary*. The executive summary should include the following:

**Background of the project**—This includes an analysis of current technology and operational systems within your organization and any stakeholders. Include any basic facts or information about your department, agency or organization.

**Title of project**—The title can be something simple as "video surveillance system for ABC police department." Don't get crazy with names and titles at this point.

**Scope of the project**—The scope of project at this point is only a preliminary list of objectives or goals. It should summarize and describe the project and include the stakeholders, decision makers, project manager (if applicable). "The scope clearly identifies the boundaries of the project."[8] A detailed scope of work will be created later on in the project.

**General information about the project**—This includes any agency specific rules, procedures or guidelines that are used for technology projects. Include any constraints, including time, budget and personnel.

**TABLE 14.1** Establish the Project Scope

| | |
|---|---|
| Who | Describe what the users want. Do they want functions, speed, etc. |
| What | Identify what you are trying to accomplish. |
| How | Identify how the specific requirements will be met. (Quality control) |
| Why | Explain the value of the project to your organization. |
| When | Identify when the project should be completed and list any constraints to the timeline. |

*Source*: SEARCH Group Incorporated. Harris, Kelly J., & Romesburg, William H. (2002). *Law Enforcement Tech Guide: How to Plan, Purchase and Manage Technology (Successfully!). A Guide for Executives, Managers and Technologists*. Washington, DC: U.S. Department of Justice, Office of Community Oriented Policing Services.

**Preliminary budget**—Be sure to include any estimated costs associated with your project.

**Timeline or schedule for the project**—Because the project is still in its infancy, the actual project schedule will not be available. However, at this point it is okay to give some time estimates as to the "flow" of the project.

**Marketing plan**—Wait a minute, I am a cop, not a marketing director or salesman! Relax; a marketing plan is used in this process to help highlight the significance of the project. Otherwise why should we move forward? A good marketing plan will put into context why this project should be a priority for your organization. The marketing plan will also be helpful when justifying the project and the cost to your governing or approval authority (city council, board of supervisors, and so on).

After the executive summary has been crafted, the official sponsor of the project needs to approve it before moving forward. The executive summary will also be used later in the process when we discuss the development of an actual technology project work plan.

## Chapter Summary

Hopefully, you are getting an idea about the process of managing a technology project. Keep in mind that this is one of several components or phases. This chapter established the basic foundation of the project. As a public safety manager, you will have to make a conscious effort to build support for the project. This will require leadership and the ability to work with others who may or may not be under your chain of command. This chapter also discussed the importance of having a project manager. The project manager must demonstrate leadership throughout the entire process in order for the project to be successful. The development of an executive summary is another critical part of the process. The executive summary will act as an abbreviated synopsis of the project and can be used to brief department heads and elected officials about your project.

**San Bernardino County Sheriff's Department**     **Riverside County Sheriff's Department**
**San Bernardino, California**                                  **Riverside, California**
**Gary Penrod, Sheriff-Coroner**                          **Bob Doyle, Sheriff-Coroner**

### Regional Fingerprint Identification Project

**Request Continued Funding:**                                    **Cost:** $4.3 million

### Background:

The need to identify criminals and threats to national safety has always been a priority within the criminal justice system. The ability to share information is one of the ways in which to reach this goal. In 1985, the counties of Riverside and San Bernardino embarked on a joint venture to create a regional identification system designed to be shared by all law enforcement agencies in the 27,360 square mile jurisdiction (with a combined population of over 3,250,000). Under the California Identification System (CAL-ID) umbrella, we developed a regional Automated Fingerprint Identification System (AFIS) and participate in the State of California Cal-Photo program. The system as it operates today, provides fingerprint, photo and DNA services to all public safety agencies including local police departments, district attorney, school districts, coroner and Sheriffs' Departments in Riverside and San Bernardino counties. It is also available to other state and federal law enforcement agencies that utilize these services on a routine basis.

The tragic events of September 11th once again brought to the forefront our need to properly identify suspected terrorists and other criminals. It caused the country to rethink its permeable borders, the anonymity granted in large cities, and vastness of the geography that enables anyone to virtually disappear. How often were some of these persons of interest checked by local police agencies through routine checks? How often do known, wanted individuals come in contact with local police agencies and give false identifications?

The ability to prevent foreign and domestic terrorism is extremely difficult and solutions are varied; however, a proactive approach is preferable to a reactive one. The Department of Homeland Security has recognized this need and has recently instituted biometric techniques to better document travelers to the United States at all ports of entry; policy analysts have given the highest priority to look-out systems that can identify suspicion persons. Although the first line of defense lies with the Department of State, the ability to continue to verify identities and query individuals is paramount, especially as new intelligence becomes available.

One solution is to enable competent intelligence gathering networks to provide information to decision-making bodies and to share this intelligence amongst them. However, the lack of interoperability of intelligence systems across law enforcement agencies and jurisdictions is a huge obstacle. This obstacle is well known by those operating on the other side of law enforcement and they too realize that interagency communication is only as effective as its weakest link. To combat not only terrorism but

**FIGURE 14.1**  Executive Summary: Regional Fingerprint Identification Project.

*Source*: Rose, J. (2005). Regional Fingerprint Identification Project: San Bernardino County Sheriff's Department & Riverside County Sheriff's Department. San Bernardino, CA: Author. (Some information has been deleted for confidentiality reasons.)

also other threats to public security and quality of life, it is necessary to further integrate intelligence systems throughout our criminal justice system. One deficiency identified is the inability of a police officer to properly identify a person of interest in the field. The counties of Riverside and San Bernardino have worked collaboratively to address this need in the Inland Empire.

**Proposal:**

This collaborative project has the ability to address not only Homeland Security concerns, but also the increasing threats to officer safety, and the administrative dangers of prison overcrowding. This comprehensive integrative project will expand on the successful CAL-ID system, by enabling the immediate verification of identification of a subject who cannot prove his or her identity or to verify the positive identification of a prisoner prior to release. The proposed program's technology utilizes the most current and reliable equipment available and  will enable the sharing of intelligence amongst all law enforcement agencies in Riverside and San Bernardino Counties. This information will further enhance the information available to all other law enforcement agencies that access the system.

 The monies would fund a collaborative project that would enable officers in the field to fingerprint suspects using handheld Mobile Identification Devices (MID) that transmit information via cellular communication to a regional server capable of handling multiple data requests. This server would then return a photograph and descriptors from CAL-ID mugshot databases of the top three closest matches using a point scale system. The MID device will also conduct a search of a regional mug shot database using facial recognition software. This will allow the officer in the field to immediately and positively identify the individual. If the 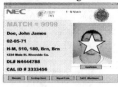 suspect is positively identified, a screen replicator linked to a mobile data computer would allow the information to download into subsequently required forms. This process not only increases officer safety and reduces the loss of a wanted person through the suspect's deceit; it has the added benefit of increasing public safety by putting the officer back on patrol more quickly by reducing the amount of paperwork and time it takes to properly book a prisoner. Additionally, the ease of recording information increases intelligence and accuracy of the information gathered. Because of the success of the Riverside and San Bernardino County's CAL-ID project, other jurisdictions are beginning to replicate the model.

The Department of Justice has historically been reluctant to take the next logical step of making their AFIS database available to remote access due to encryption and other security issues. Riverside and San Bernardino counties provide the perfect opportunity to pilot test such a program and have been recently approved to serve as the beta site, which

**FIGURE 14.1** *(Continued)*

will capitalize on the availability of technology necessary in our fluid and transient environment. The diversity of the bi-county service area is perfect for the replicability of this project: the area encompasses five climactic zones, rural and urban areas, and more than 27,360 square miles.

As we work toward the future, a key to our continued success will be interoperability through the purchase of advanced technology to provide immediate identification solutions to law enforcement agencies in the field. Given the nature of our current environment and the critical urgency of real-time identification needs for Homeland Security, additional funding will be necessary to equip our officers with the tools necessary to accomplish the mission set before them.

**Budget:**
The project budget includes the following:

| Item | Cost |
|---|---|
| Automated Fingerprint Identification System for mobile and fixed identification (including advanced matchers) | $1 million |
| Regional Photo Server / Facial Recognition Systems | $1 million |
| Integrated data system (RMS/CNI/JIMS/CAD/CII) that integrates with multiple agencies and allows for expansion | $300 thousand |
| Product development/research/pilot programs | $500 thousand |
| Mobile identification equipment/devices (handheld devices, unit computer, software development and upgrades, fixed terminal hardware/software | $1.5 million |
| **Total** | **4.3 million** |

The original project budget was $8,600,000. $2,000,000 has been earmarked for this project from a Department of Justice COPS Technology Grant, which was awarded in 2006.

The San Bernardino/Riverside Regional CAL-ID program has invested approximately $2,300,000 towards this project. All personnel costs are also covered by our Regional CAL-ID program.

This is a request for continued funding total ... **4.3 million**

**Contact:**
Jeff Rose, Lieutenant
Cal-ID Project Manager
San Bernardino County Sheriff's Dept.
Office: (909) XXX-XXX
Cell:   (951) XXX-XXXX
E-mail:

**Contact:**
Randy E. Throne, Deputy Chief
Legislative Director
Riverside County Sheriff's Department
Desk: (951) XXX-XXXX
Cell:   (951)XXX-XXXX
E-mail:

**FIGURE 14.1** *(Continued)*

## Key Words or Terminology

| | | |
|---|---|---|
| project manager | stakeholder | steering committee |
| user group | consultant | marketing plan |
| executive summary | | |

## Discussion Questions

1. Research a public safety agency in your jurisdiction and find out who has the authority to approve a technology project. Explain how the process occurs.
2. Research and review any technology projects that have been completed by a public safety agency or department. Analyze and interpret the process and paperwork associated with the project.
3. Identify a piece of technology, program or project that you would like to manage. Using the concepts in this chapter, put together a sample executive summary. When the executive summary is complete, have someone read it and see if they would consider approving it if they were your supervisor, manager or executive.

## Notes

1 SEARCH Group Incorporated, Harris, Kelly J., and Romesburg, William H. (2002). *Law enforcement tech guide: How to plan, purchase and manage technology (successfully!). A guide for executives, managers and technologists.* Washington, DC: U.S. Department of Justice, Office of Community Oriented Policing Services.
2 SEARCH Group Incorporated, Kraus, Benjamin R. (2011). *The "accidental" project manager.* Washington, DC: U.S. Department of Justice, Office of Community Oriented Policing Services.
3 Harris and Romesburg, *Law enforcement tech guide.*
4 Ibid.
5 (2001). *A guide for applying information technology in law enforcement.* Washington, DC: National Law Enforcement and Corrections Technology Center.
6 Harris and Romesburg, *Law enforcement tech guide.*
7 Ibid.
8 Ibid.

# 15

# DO YOU REALLY NEED THIS TECHNOLOGY?

"If we continue to develop our technology without
wisdom or prudence, our servant may prove to be our
executioner."

—*Omar Bradley*

## Learning Objectives

After reading this chapter, the student will:

- Define the needs analysis process and articulate the importance of completing the process before moving on to the planning stage.
- Create current and future process project management maps.
- Assess the current technology environment within an organization or department and develop a list of strengths and weaknesses.
- Understand the role of supervision and management in technology projects.
- Evaluate the use of a consultant or outside expert in a technology project.

## Introduction

In this chapter, we review the step-by-step process of a needs analysis for a technology project. This is one of the most important steps in managing a technology project. A project manager has to determine exactly what type of technology, equipment or program is needed by a public safety agency. At this point, the project manager determines whether this technology is "nice to have" or "critical to the agency." We go through each step carefully and use specific examples to help illustrate the needs analysis process. This chapter highlights the following steps:

- Assessing your own operational processes.
- Creating a process map or outline that defines your current operational systems, configuration and networks.

- Analyzing your current process map to determine where and how you can improve the overall efficiency of the operation or streamline the process.
- Developing a new or proposed process map that illustrates the new equipment, systems or elements that will improve your current system.
- Creating a list of general system requirements for your project.[1]

## Why Do We Need a Needs Analysis?

A *needs analysis* is a comprehensive process that helps you identify current operational policies, procedures, infrastructure, software and hardware.[2] It analyzes the operation from the standpoint of every stakeholder. The needs analysis process strives to ask questions about the project and to determine whether the venture is worthwhile. For example, if a jail manager wants to replace the jail information management system (JIMS), he would first need to understand how JIMS affects correctional officers or inmates. What are the core functions of JIMS? Are there any specific policies and guidelines that dictate the parameters of the jail information management system? Do they need to be replaced or revised as well? The needs analysis should review all manual and automated systems, including current databases and networks. The analysis should also review the layout between each system, security issues or requirements.

The needs analysis should review every part of the process and determine what parts are critical and what parts can be improved. The needs analysis helps public safety agencies identify and implement a new technology solution that is cost effective and improves the overall efficiency of the operation.

### Feasibility Study

Some public safety agencies require a feasibility study before moving forward with a technology project. The scope of the study must analyze the nature, complexity, risk, expected cost and use of the proposed project or piece of technology. The study must provide the necessary information to assure the public safety agency's department head or authorized elected officials that the proposed project meets the needs of the agency or organization.[3] The study helps those in a public office make informed decisions on whether to spend taxpayer dollars on a project.

### Assessing Your Own Operation

The first step is a needs analysis is to review your own operation. Public safety managers must define the following:

- All manual and automated systems
- Any internal and external networks
- Databases used by your department or other agencies

- Transactional volume
- Relationships and configurations between any of your systems[4]

This process may be accomplished by yourself, a group of people (stakeholders) or an outside technical consultant. It really depends on the type of process that you are going to review and evaluate. For example, let's review the standard call for service at a local police department:

1  An officer responds to a nearby business in reference to a commercial burglary.
2  The officer completes the burglary report and turns it in for review. The report is either handwritten or typed.
3  The report is reviewed by a supervisor.
4  The report is then entered into some type of tracking system by a records clerk.
5  The report information (demographics, date, time, method of operation, and so on) is entered into the computer system for statistical tracking or as a requirement by the Department of Justice.
6  The police report is filed in a file cabinet or electronic database.

By reviewing the aforementioned six steps, a public safety manager can assess and evaluate any areas that could be improved. This also helps identify who is doing the work, why it is being done in a certain way, where the work is being accomplished and what is being accomplished.[5] It also puts the process in writing. Sometimes it is difficult to evaluate and assess a process when the information is presented in paragraph form. The use of pictures, charts or graphs can be extremely helpful in this process.

## Create a Process Map

The private sector often uses organizational maps or charts to illustrate how a specific product is made. A good example is the assembly line process used in the automobile industry. The assembly line is constructed in such a way, that a manager can easily determine where, if any, weaknesses occur. The assembly line process can be portrayed in a diagram, flow chart or picture.

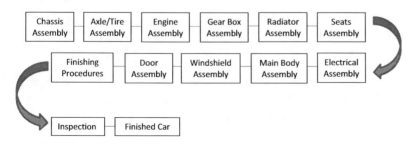

**FIGURE 15.1**  Vehicle Production Flow Chart.

Okay, that is great in the private sector, but what about in public safety? Let's develop a map that describes the standard booking process at a local jail. The premise of our map is to determine whether a jail should revise the booking process and purchase biometric single finger scanners for the jail.

The following is the current inmate booking process used at a typical jail in the United States:

1  A patrol officer arrests a suspect for burglary and transports him to a county jail for processing. The officer does not know who the suspect is because he has no positive form of identification.
2  Inside of the jail, the officer searches the suspect and turns him over to jail personnel.
3  The officer completes a booking application, probable cause form and any other forms required by the jail (manually, either typed or handwritten).
4  The suspect is screened by a medical professional.
5  The officer waits for jail personnel to enter the suspect's information into a jail information management system (JIMS). The information is manually (typed) entered into the system. Up to now the suspect still has not been "positively" identified.
6  Jail personnel fingerprint the suspect using ink cards or by an electronic live scan device. The suspect's information has to be typed into the system or handwritten on a fingerprint card. The fingerprints are submitted to the department of justice or other agency for identification purposes. The identification process may take several hours or even days depending on the process.
7  The suspect has his picture taken by a photo-capture device. Again, his information has to be manually input into the photo system. The photographs are then sent to a regional or state depository. Still no positive identification on the suspect!
8  The suspect is classified and housed inside of a cell awaiting bail or a court hearing.
9  The suspect is finally identified via his fingerprints.

Okay, now let's review the operational process at the jail:

•  The aforementioned process is extremely time-consuming. At every part of the process, someone had to handwrite or type the suspect's information into a system. The manual entry of data takes time and is unnecessary. It also promotes mistakes because the data can be misinterpreted or entered incorrectly.
•  The suspect was not positively identified until the very end of the process. This is an obvious officer safety issue for all personnel including the officer on patrol.
•  It took multiple personnel to process the suspect.
•  Due to the amount of time it took to process the suspect, the jail manager becomes frustrated because of overcrowding in the intake area of the jail. The jail manager wishes that the process could be quicker and more efficient.

Now that we have reviewed the current booking process, can you identify any areas that could be improved? As a public safety manager, this is where you use a needs analysis to evaluate any available technology and incorporate it into the current process. A possible solution would be to purchase single finger biometric scanners for the jail and perhaps for the patrol officer. If the officer on patrol utilized a mobile identification biometric device, he or she could have positively identified the suspect immediately. This assumes that the suspect had previously been arrested and is in the system. A jail manager could also have the single-finger biometric scanners installed in the intake area, fingerprint/photo capture area and other locations inside of the jail, including the release window. Single-finger biometric scanners are currently available and being used in large jails across the country. This would allow jail personnel to eliminate the need to retype the suspect's demographic information at every stage of the process. The information is entered only once, which decreases the possibility of incorrect data entry. Another benefit is that the suspect would be identified at the beginning of the encounter, not at the end. This ensures that your personnel are safe. Finally, could the purchase of this type of technology actually improve your operation and perhaps reduce the amount of personnel needed to complete the task? This is the benefit from using the needs analysis exercise. Now let's look at the entire process by putting the process into a picture, graph or chart.

Figure 15.2 describes the booking process in a typical county jail. You will see that it includes single-finger biometric scanners at intake, photo capture and release portions of the process. It also includes a mobile biometric identification scanner for use in the field by patrol personnel. The exhibit can be used by public safety managers to not only review

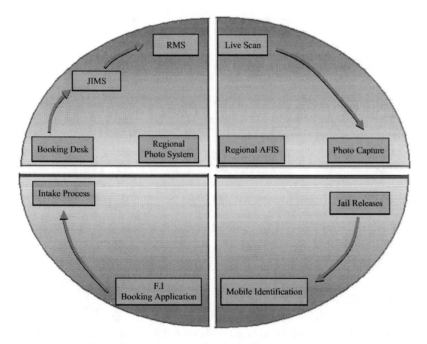

**FIGURE 15.2** Chart Illustrating a Booking Process.

*Source*: Rose, J. (2004). San Bernardino CAL-ID RAN Board Presentation. San Bernardino County Sheriff's Department: Author.

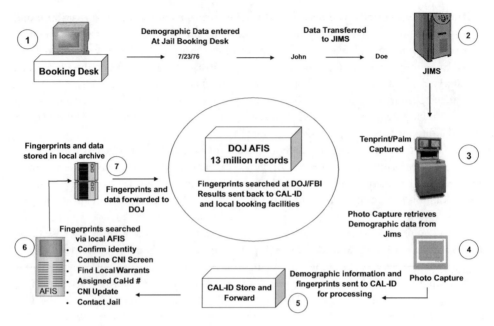

**FIGURE 15.3**   Detailed Booking Process.

*Source*: Rose, J. (2004). San Bernardino CAL-ID RAN Board Presentation. San Bernardino County Sheriff's Department: Author.

current operations and processes, but it can also be used to help "market" the idea or concept to a department head or other governing official.

Figure 15.3 is a more detailed version of a typical booking process. Specifically, it helps identify how fingerprints and booking information is captured and electronically sent to local, state or federal automated fingerprint identification systems (AFIS). Figure 15.3 will help a public safety manager assess the process and determine where things could be improved or replaced. The difference between Figure 15.2 and Figure 15.3 is the detail extracted from the process. Figure 15.3 also is numbered so the reader can clearly understand and follow the process.

## Analyze Your Process Map

Now that you have reviewed your current processes and created a process map, it is time to break the process into more detail. This allows you to review a specific process and ask questions that may require the use of stakeholders or outside experts. If your goal is to increase the speed of a computerized system, you do not need to know the make and manufacturer of a processor or network switch. However, someone will need to know this information, so the use of technical experts will be an important part of this process. Generally, you or someone else who is assigned as the project manager will meet with the stakeholders and technical experts on several occasions. The benefit of meeting with the stakeholders is that you will gain support for the project early in the process. Take the time to listen to their ideas and suggestions.

During the meetings, the group will review current configurations, infrastructure, information systems and agency policies and procedures.[6] The group should also review any warranties, proprietary or interface issues. Remember that some technology vendors do not like to share their products or systems with others. It does no good to purchase a new piece of technology that is incompatible with the other parts of your system. The group should also compare this information to other agencies that may have new or more modern equipment.[7] The project manager will formulate and document any changes or solutions to the problems discussed by the group. This includes the following:

- Any strengths or weaknesses with the current technology. Is the system easy to use? Does the system break down often? Does the system produce the necessary data you require?
- Any obstacles to the project. Is cost an issue? Identify any training issues.
- How can the current process be improved? Will the new system be faster, web-based, connect to other systems and cost-effective?

## Create a Proposed Process Map

Now that you have reviewed the current technology used by your agency or organization, it is time to draft a conceptual drawing or map of what you would like to have. The new process map will include any general system requirements. General system requirements include:

- Number of people using the system or technology
- Number of workstations or notebooks
- Type of hardware and software to be used
- Location of all equipment[8]

The general system requirements can be broken down into subcategories, depending on the type of project. For example, if you are purchasing an automated fingerprint identification system (AFIS), you may want to include information on specialized equipment, interaction with other software programs (internal or external) and speed or volume transactional data. If you want the system to process a fingerprint transaction in a certain time period, you will need to include some specific information about the size (bandwidth) and amount of fingerprints that the current system handles. Once again, this part of the process requires the help from technical experts and stakeholders. For example, if you decided to purchase the single-finger biometric scanners that we discussed earlier in the chapter, how many do you need? Where would you put them? Does the software work with your existing jail information management system?

The proposed process map and corresponding information helps put the new system into context and identify the new components. The proposed system requirements may also include any transaction volumes and growth expectations. This information can be used as a guide for the rest of the project and will definitely be part of the actual project plan, which is covered in Chapter 16.

## Should You Hire Someone to Complete the Technology Project?

The decision to hire someone to complete your technology project varies depending on the type of project. Larger agencies usually have some technical personnel that can help install or manage small projects. However, if your project is large or encompasses multiple computer systems or databases, it may be beneficial to hire an expert. A big factor to consider is the overall cost of the project. Hiring an expert may save money in the long run because you do have some recourse if the vendor does not complete the project as advertised. For example, if you decide to have one of your employees manage a project, create a customized program or maintain a piece of technology, what happens when they leave? Do you have anyone else on the department with that amount of expertise to handle this type of project? Some agencies like to build their own systems because they can customize it and hopefully save money. However, that is not always the case. For example, the California Department of Motor Vehicles designed and built a driver's license and registration project with a projected cost of $26 million. The project did not work or benefit the DMV and was canceled after spending over $45 million.[9]

Most private companies are in the business to make money and want your business. They usually think long term and want to be your technology provider for years to come. As a public safety manager, this can give you some reassurance that the project will be successful. However, it is important to make sure that the vendor can deliver on what they promise. Always ensure that your contract has some type of performance bond or penalty if the vendor fails to perform. Remember one of the favorite words of a technology company is *change order*. A change order means that you did not do your homework and the company is going to charge you for some part of the project. This is very evident when a public safety agency asks for something that is "customized." It may be better to purchase something off of the shelf and save money. Just remember that every project is different and that you should evaluate each of them based on your organizational goals, requirements and policies.

## Chapter Summary

The introduction of any new technology in your agency will require substantial research and effort on your part. Public safety managers have a duty to evaluate technology and its use within the organization. The needs analysis process is comprehensive and may seem tedious at first. However, this process allows you, the public safety manager, the opportunity to determine if the technology is worthwhile and if your department or organization should move forward with the project. You have a duty to manage taxpayer funds in an honest and effective manner. Even if you decide not to move forward with a particular project, the needs analysis exercise will give you and your department an inside look at the various operational processes. This may allow you to make any necessary changes such as policy or procedure changes. An effective leader within any organization consistently reviews, inspects and monitors the operation to ensure it is running efficiently.

Now that you have completed the needs analysis process, it is time to move on to the planning process in Chapter 16.

## Key Words or Terminology

process map                          feasibility study              needs analysis
general system requirements          change order

## Discussion Questions

1.  Identify an operational system at a local public safety agency. Create a process map for the system that details the relationship from the beginning stage to the end stage. This can be something as simple as reviewing a report writing system or a review of the incident command system.
2.  Analyze the aforementioned system and determine how and where improvements can be made to the system or operation. Research and determine if there is technology available that could improve the operational system. Did the process map help you understand the process?
3.  Review a public safety agency's policy on a feasibility study. Are they required before any purchases can be made?
4.  Identify and highlight any leadership traits that were discussed in this chapter.
5.  Using the operational system that you identified in Question #1, write a "needs analysis" and justify why you should be allowed to purchase the technology.

## Notes

1  (2001). *A guide for applying information technology in law enforcement.* Washington, DC: National Law Enforcement and Corrections Technology Center.
2  Ibid.
3  (2014). *SAM- information technology, feasibility study scope.* Sacramento, CA: California Department of Technology.
4  SEARCH Group Incorporated, Harris, Kelly J., and Romesburg, William H. (2002). *Law Enforcement Tech Guide: How to Plan, Purchase and Manage Technology (Successfully!). A Guide for Executives, Managers and Technologists.* Washington, DC: U.S. Department of Justice, Office of Community Oriented Policing Services.
5  Ibid.
6  See note #1.
7  See note #1.
8  See note #4.
9  See note #4.

# 16

# CREATING A PROJECT PLAN

"If you fail to plan, plan on failing."

—*Anonymous*

## Learning Objectives

After reading this chapter, the student will:

- Understand the importance of having a comprehensive project plan.
- Clearly identify the various components of a project plan.
- Understand the concept of project methodology.
- Evaluate and interpret the role of a public safety manager in the project planning process.

## Introduction

Creating a comprehensive project plan is a critical part of the overall technology management process. Without a project plan, the vendor or in-house technology personnel will not know how to build or design your technology project. Think about building a house. Would you start building without some sort of architectural plans that have been reviewed by the city planner or code enforcement? Of course not! The creation of a project plan, like many other chapters in Unit 3, is a process. Depending on the type of project, you need to identify the specific details and include information in several key areas, including the project scope, schedule (timeline), cost estimation (budget), risk management issues, quality assurance and communication platform. This chapter summarizes each area and gives you enough information to draft your own plan. We also discuss the fundamental leadership components that public safety managers must utilize when drafting a project plan.

## Project Methodology

Project methodology serves several purposes. It ensures that the technology project, service or program is delivered on time and within the project budget. More importantly, sound project management ensures that the customer (user) is happy with the outcome. The methodology used in project management includes the creation of several plans that adequately address the following:

- Overall management—Executive sponsor, project manager, etc.
- Scope of the project—Lists the specific deliverables and functions.
- Schedule or timeline—Includes dates and times of the project milestones and activities.
- Cost analysis (budget)—Contains details on the estimated and final procurement cost of the project. It also includes information on how the technology will be purchased.
- Installation and maintenance plan—Defines how the project will be maintained and continue after the initial project is completed. It also describes how the technology will be installed or implemented.
- Risk management—Identifies any risks associated with the project, including change orders and performance bonds, etc.
- Communication structure—Point of contact, how information is disseminated, etc.
- Quality assurance plan—Identifies who and how the project will be evaluated for completeness and accuracy.
- Closure of project—Outlines the final stages of the project including the project sign-off documentation.[1]

As a public safety manager, you will have some challenges during the project. Whether the project manager is you or a person you assigned, you must always ensure that there is a comprehensive plan that focuses on the basics: scope, schedule, cost and quality.

## *What Is a Project Plan?*

A *project plan* is a comprehensive document that focuses on all parts of the project. The plan lists the various details that are necessary to produce and implement a product or system. In Chapter 14, we focused on building the global foundation of the project. A product plan refines that concept into a series of deliverables that explains what will be accomplished. It also summarizes who will be doing the work and how it will be accomplished.

There are five things that a manager of a technology project should know. They include:

- The project plan will change and evolve over time. Expect to have several revisions, but it is important to maintain one master document that is used by everyone involved in the project.
- The planning process is creative and is based on the type of technology that is available.
- Project planning is not always definitive. On occasion, the plan may change based on the risk and analysis phases of the project.

- The project plan must be used. It doesn't do any good to prepare a plan and then deviate from it. Public safety managers must always ensure that the plan is adhered to, but also ensure that the plan is reviewed and modified if necessary based on the needs of the agency or organization.
- The planning process should be systematic and well structured. Although planning is an important part of the overall process, it should not dominate the amount of time that is dedicated to the project. Develop a schedule and stick with it.[2]

## Project Scope

The project scope is basically the "nuts and bolts" of the project. It includes a list of deliverables, functions and systems that will be used or designed by agency personnel or an outside vendor. The scope identifies all of the work that is required in order to complete the project successfully. The scope is specific in nature and will include a list of needed hardware, software, training needs, etc. The scope breaks down the information that was identified in the initial proposal or concept for your project.[3] For example, if the main goal of the project is to "give an officer the ability to identify a suspect in the field," the project scope will refine the goal to "officers in the field will be able to quickly identify a suspect in the field by using a hand-held mobile biometric identification system." The scope can even have subcategories that refine the process even further. For example, "the mobile biometric identification devices must have a turnaround response time of less than 30 seconds." Instead of saying, "the users will have improved access to data," the project scope should state, "The users will have the ability to create crime analysis documents sheets or print booking applications."

**TABLE 16.1**  SMART Planning Process

| Specific | The planning must be specific and have some structure. |
|---|---|
| | Example: The officer must have the ability to quickly identify a suspect in the field or the video surveillance system must store video at 15 frames per second. |
| Measurable | There must be a way to measure the activity or product. |
| | Example: The AFIS must process a ten print card within one minute or the mobile identification hand-held unit must have a response within 45 seconds. |
| Achievable | The program, equipment or activity must be achievable. |
| | Example: Is it possible to obtain AFIS responses as indicated above? If not, then you will need more data to ensure the project is viable. |
| Relevant | Is the technology relevant to your agency's mission statement or goals? |
| | Example: The processing of latent fingerprints in a timely manner is directly related to law enforcement's mission statement of apprehending criminals. |
| Time-Based | There must be a clear and realistic timeframe for the technology project. |
| | Example: If the technology has not been developed yet, then your timeframe needs to be adjusted or you can wait for the technology to develop on its own and then purchase it. |

### Schedule or Timeline

After you have completed the project scope that outlines all of the deliverables, you will need to develop a schedule or timeline for the project. A project schedule includes the estimated dates or times for the following basic information:

- Start and end of the project
- Kick-off meeting
- Time estimates for each phase of the project
- Procurement information
- Equipment delivery
- Field or bench test information
- Submittal information (statement of values, shop drawings, product data)
- Installation of products
- Training
- Acceptance of product
- Other information based on the type of project

The aforementioned items are just samples of what can be included in the project schedule. It really depends on the type of project and the needs of the agency or organization. If the project is simple and doesn't involve software development or in-depth design, then the project schedule can be modified to include the basic elements of procurement, delivery, installation, testing and approval. If the project is extensive and requires specific deliverables or activities, the schedule should reflect each area of concern. For example, a specific part of a deliverable could read like this:

- Create a software application for the mobile identification system based on the criteria listed in the request for proposal (RFP)
- Submit a rough draft of the software to the agency by June 1, 2005
- Submit an edited version to the agency by December 1, 2005
- Submit a final version to the agency by March 1, 2006

Public safety managers or project managers should utilize historical data and other background information to determine fair timelines and deliverables. The schedule should also be in chronological order from the beginning to the end of the project. When developing a schedule, it is important to utilize some type of spreadsheet or worksheet. There are many types of schedule templates available to public safety agencies. In most cases, a simple Microsoft Excel sheet will do the trick.

### Cost Analysis (Budget)

Every project plan should include information about the estimated cost of the project. Public safety agencies do not have extensive amounts of revenue and must plan for technology purchases in advance. Usually large scale projects will be part of the city, county or state capital

**TABLE 16.2** Technology Server Upgrade Schedule

*ABC Sheriff's Department*

| Task | Duration | Start | End |
|---|---|---|---|
| Equipment Order and delivery | 15 days | 05-07-2003 | 15-07-2003 |
| Hardware set-up | 2 days | 20-07-2003 | 21-07-2003 |
| **System Design/Review for Development** | 51 days | 01-05-2003 | 20-06-2003 |
| System Specification Review | 26 days | 01-05-2003 | 26-05-2003 |
| **System Build** | 341 days | 01-05-2003 | 06-05-2004 |
| System Development | 61 days | 19-06-2003 | 18-08-2003 |
| System Environment Build | 3 days | 20-09-2003 | 22-09-2003 |
| Set Up Support | 89 days | 21-08-2003 | 17-11-2003 |
| Software Release | 0 days | 15-12-2003 | 15-12-2003 |
| Testing at Factory | 0 days | 27-12-2003 | 27-12-2003 |
| User Guide Development | 12 days | 15-01-2004 | 26-01-2004 |
| Shipping and On-Site Delivery | 5 days | 05-02-2004 | 09-02-2004 |
| On-Site Testing | 28 days | 12-02-2004 | 11-03-2004 |
| Training | 12 days | 12-03-2004 | 23-03-2004 |
| **Acceptance Test** | 2 days | 26-03-2004 | 28-03-2004 |
| Switchover to New Servers | 3 days | 28-03-2004 | 30-03-2004 |
| Conversion | 0 days | 01-05-2004 | 01-05-2004 |

improvement budget. Small projects can be funded from individual operational budgets. The ability to estimate the cost of a technology project varies depending on the type of technology. You need to determine what type of technology is available and whether the technology is specific to your agency. You can reach out to nearby agencies or organizations to establish a cost estimate if they have installed a similar system. Formal cost estimates have to come from a vendor. Vendors are used to giving public safety agencies quotations on technology products via the request for quotation (RFQ) process. The RFQ is non-binding and gives public safety agencies an estimated cost for the technology.[4] Chapter 17 discusses many other ways that you can receive cost estimates and procure technology products. At the end of the process, you also need to determine and identify any other costs that should be part of your cost proposal. Typically, the following cost estimates are included in technology projects:

- **Initial costs** include anything that is purchased before and during the project (hardware, software, consulting, etc.).
- **Ongoing costs** occur after the project has been completed. Ongoing costs are typically used for maintenance or training programs. Ongoing maintenance costs for hardware are typically 10 percent of the initial purchase price and 12.5 percent of the initial software purchase price.[5]

Failure to include estimated ongoing costs in the budget increases the chances that your project will fail over the long term. For example, your agency spends $1.5 million dollars on a photo capture system in the jail. Most vendors include a one-year warranty on the system. In year two, the system goes down and you do not have any funds in the budget to repair it. Now you have to ask for additional funds from your governing authority, which can be cumbersome and embarrassing. Some elected officials will question the purchase and ask why the ongoing costs were not part of the original cost estimate. An effective manager always plans for the future and includes ongoing costs into the project plan.

- **Contingency costs** should always be part of the project plan. During the procurement process (Chapter 17), vendors submit an estimated bid for your project. They estimate the cost based on what they know about your project, your department or agency. After the vendor is awarded the project, there will be things that need to be changed from the original proposal. The changes can be vendor or customer initiated. Another reason for a contingency is that the cost of technology changes daily. The price of materials and labor will vary based on global demands and labor contracts. Most technology projects will have a 10–15 percent contingency amount added to the original budget proposal.[6]

Public safety agencies often receive special government discounts on technology equipment. The General Services Administration (GSA) is an independent government agency that allows local, state and federal agencies to purchase technology at a reduced or discounted rate. GSA screens and pre-authorizes each vendor's product before they are listed

**TABLE 16.3**  Expanded Budget for Regional Fingerprint Identification Project

| Initial Costs | Total |
|---|---|
| Mobile-ID Software | $3,500,000 |
| Mobile-ID Devices with Accessories (300) | $15,000,000 |
| Mobile-ID Server/Rack | $1,550,000 |
| Training Books and Supplies | $25,000 |
| Contingency | $20,000 |
| **Total** | **$20,500,000** |
| *Ongoing Costs* | |
| Cellular Service Accounts (Includes first year) | $2,250,000 |
| Annual Maintenance | $2,400,000 |
| Software Licenses (ID Units and Server) | $1,500,000 |
| **Total** | **$6,150,000** |
| *Personnel* | |
| Project Manager | $128,000 |
| Systems Support Analyst | $75,520 |
| Clerical Staff | $41,000 |
| **Total** | **$1,16,648** |

on the available technology list.[7] Many states have similar programs available for public safety agencies. The main benefit of the aforementioned federal and state programs is that the technology vendors cannot overcharge your agency or organization for products and waste our precious tax dollars.

> Students can get more information about the General Services Administration (GSA) by visiting their website at www.gsa.gov.

## Installation and Maintenance

Your project plan should contain information on the installation process or protocol based on the type of project being managed. The plan identifies how the technology will be delivered, installed and tested by your agency or organization. The installation plan should follow the aforementioned schedule or timeline. Maintenance information should also be identified and included in this section. Do you want the vendor to maintain the technology or will someone within your agency or organization handle this part? Remember, a major key to the overall success of any project is to keep the technology working properly. Otherwise, public safety personnel will disregard the technology and it will most likely sit on the shelf.

## Risk Management

Every technology project should have some type of risk assessment or management plan. A risk management plan will help mitigate any potential pitfalls or problems with your project. Public safety managers should work with the stakeholders of the project and prepare a list of any potential risks to the project. The stakeholders and the project manager should then evaluate the list and determine which ones will add additional time or may affect the quality of the project. Some common risks for technology projects include: loss of funding from an agency, the vendor goes out of business or personnel changes.[8] Public safety managers should always anticipate the risks and have suitable plans for dealing with them if necessary. One way to avoid a potential risk is to have the vendor provide a performance bond for the project. If the project is not completed as advertised, your agency can obtain reimbursement of funds from the bond or insurance company. Another way to avoid risk is to have the vendor prove their ability to perform before signing a contract. Many vendors are willing to let a public safety agency "pilot test" a product for free. The pilot test allows the public safety agency to evaluate the product and make any recommendations to the vendor. The vendor actually benefits from the process because they can then make any modifications to the product based on your recommendations.

For example, in 2006, the San Bernardino County Sheriff's Department wanted to upgrade their automated fingerprint identification system (AFIS). The upgrade had an estimated cost of over $2 million. Prior to executing the contract, the county asked the vendor to demonstrate the product and its functionality in a "live" situation. The vendor agreed and set up a sample AFIS with duplicate fingerprints from the existing AFIS. County fingerprint examiners then tested the new system, which included a review of the quality of the fingerprints, transaction volumes and response times. The company's AFIS worked as advertised and the county purchased the upgraded system. The county was able to success-fully mitigate the risk by doing a simple "pilot test."[9]

## Communication

The project plan must also have some type of communication protocol. A communication plan typically includes information about the main point of contact for your department and the vendor. It addresses how each party should be contacted and how each stakeholder will be part of the process. The plan identifies which issues can be handled via electronic means or in person.

> Quick Tip—Always remember to keep a written copy of anything promised to you by a salesperson. During the planning process, you may discuss part of the project and verbally agree to a specific function or deliverable with a salesperson. Have them put it in writing and save that information. If the agreement is not in writing, the vendor may not provide the function or deliverable without charging you addi-tional fees. Remember, any discussion about performance or price should always be in writing!

## Quality Assurance

Information on quality control should also be part of the project plan. Quality assurance (QA) protects the agency or organization from defective products, improper programing or anything else that was not delivered by the vendor. The project plan should identify who will evaluate the technology after it is designed, delivered and implemented. The end user is commonly used to test and evaluate the product or system. The quality control plan should also be part of the overall schedule to ensure that the process is not forgotten.

## Closure of Project

The final part of the project plan is to have information about the final closure of the project. The closure plan identifies any steps that are required by the vendor or the agency. It also includes language that states the project has been completed as described by the contract and that the project is now under the management of the agency or organization. The closure plan requires that the project manager and the vendor thoroughly discuss and review all aspects of the project and agree that each component or issue has been addressed.

This process is similar to the process of purchasing a house. Before a buyer accepts the house from the seller, they typically walk through the house and identify anything that needs to be fixed. When the buyer is satisfied with the house, the seller is no longer responsible. On major technology projects, the vendor and county usually have some sort of formal documentation that establishes the closure of the project.

> Quick Tip—After the project has been completed, it is a good idea to meet with the stakeholders and evaluate the entire process. Be critical and come up with any recommendations or changes that need to be made before the next project.

## Final Thoughts about the Planning Process

The planning associated with a technology project shouldn't be a difficult activity. Public safety managers routinely plan a variety of activities including patrol operations, personnel scheduling, and budgets. As a leader within your organization, your ability to plan effectively is essential and critical to the overall success of the mission. Planning a technology project is equally critical because a failed project can dramatically affect the organization in a negative way. Technology projects and the terminology used during the project can be daunting, but a true leader does not shy away from things that they are not comfortable with. An effective leader engages and learns about the project. President John F. Kennedy once said, "It is time for a new generation of leadership to cope with new problems and new opportunities. For there is a new world to be won." Technology is the future and the new generation of leaders must embrace technology in order to be successful.

## Chapter Summary

The planning of a technology project involves a variety of steps and a comprehensive plan is critical to the overall success of the project. As previously mentioned, one cannot build a house without a set of plans or drawings. Planning provides guidance and keeps the project on track and hopefully under budget. Let's review some of the key components of a project plan. The plan should include information on:

- Scope
- Schedule
- Cost analysis (budget)
- Installation and maintenance
- Risk management
- Communication
- Quality assurance
- Closure of project

Depending on the type and complexity of the project, you may want to hire a consultant or technical expert to help prepare the project plan. By following the steps outlined in this chapter, you are now ready to move on to Chapter 17, "How to Acquire Technology."

## Key Words or Terminology

| | | |
|---|---|---|
| project methodology | project plan | project scope |
| planning | schedules | cost analysis |
| initial cost | ongoing cost | contingency cost |
| risk management | quality control | vendor |

## Discussion Questions

1. Identify three situations in your current assignment, profession or current career path where planning played an important part of the experience. Use the planning techniques listed in this chapter and see if your prior situations would have been different.
2. Identify at least three supervisory or management traits that are imbedded in the technology planning process. Why are they important?
3. Research a nearby public safety agency and identify at least two technology projects that have been implemented in the last five years. Outline how their project was structured and identify any strengths or weaknesses with the project.
4. Prepare a sample project plan that includes all of the steps or categories listed in this chapter.

## Notes

1 (2014). *Project management methodology reference manual,* p. 16. Sacramento, CA: California Department of Technology.
2 SEARCH Group Incorporated, Harris, Kelly J., and Romesburg, William H. (2002). *Law Enforcement Tech Guide: How to Plan, Purchase and Manage Technology (Successfully!). A Guide for Executives, Managers and Technologists.* Washington, DC: U.S. Department of Justice, Office of Community Oriented Policing Services.
3 California Department of Technology, *Project management methodology reference manual.*
4 (2001). *A guide for applying information technology in law enforcement.* Washington, DC: National Law Enforcement and Corrections Technology Center.
5 Harris and Romesburg, *Law enforcement tech guide.*
6 Ibid.
7 (2014). *Cooperative purchasing guidelines.* Washington, DC: United States General Services Administration.
8 Harris and Romesburg, *Law enforcement tech guide.*
9 (2004). *Board of supervisor's agreement 03-255 A-2, AFIS upgrade.* San Bernardino, CA: County of San Bernardino.

# 17

# HOW TO ACQUIRE TECHNOLOGY

"Those parts of the system you can hit with a hammer are called hardware; the program instructions that you can only swear at are called software."

—*Anonymous*

## Learning Objectives

After reading this chapter, the student will:

*   Understand the basic concepts of the procurement and solicitation process.
*   Be able to explain the different types of solicitations used by public safety agencies. This includes the request for proposal (RFP).
*   Know how and why leadership is essential in the procurement process.
*   Understand the importance of knowing the various rules, regulations and laws pertaining to the procurement and solicitation process.

## Introduction

One of the most difficult and sometimes frustrating parts about managing a technology project is determining how an organization or agency will actually "obtain" technology hardware or software. There are many rules, policies and even laws that deal with the procurement process. The difficulty is attributed to the fact that public safety agencies must relinquish the responsibilities of the project to someone outside of your chain of command. Public safety agencies or organizations have specific personnel that are responsible for the acquiring technology. They are usually assigned to the finance department or auditor-controller division. There are many rules that must be adhered to as a condition of being part of a government agency. Agencies have a great deal of discretion when creating policies and procedures on evaluating technology proposals or projects. "Nevertheless, requirements should be well defined and the process should always be thoroughly followed."[1]

In this chapter, we deal with the basics of procurement for public safety organizations. We also include an example of an actual request for proposal (RFP) used to purchase a security control system at a local jail facility.

## Procurement Basics

*Procurement* is defined as "a structured method for determining the required hardware, software and services needed to fulfill the project goals and objectives."[2] The process of procurement allows public safety agencies the opportunity to seek out new technology, purchase technology and maintain technology within the guidelines of the aforementioned rules and guidelines. Your procurement protocol, guidelines or procedures must be detailed and accurate.[3] Many vendors are experts in their respective fields, but they can only bid or send a public safety agency a quote based on what is listed in your procurement statement or description.

The actual procurement process is actually a very simple process. Think about your own agency and how much technology or other goods are purchased every year. Public safety agencies purchase vehicles, fuel, safety equipment, office supplies and technology equipment, just to name a few. All of these items were purchased and obtained by following the procurement process.

The first part of the process is understanding the basic rules for purchasing. Public safety agencies have strict rules on who and how to purchase goods and services. State and federal laws dictate the majority of the procurement process; however, local public safety agencies have some latitude on adopting policies and procedures for obtaining goods and services. For example, a city manager may have the authority to approve the purchase of goods, provided it doesn't exceed a certain dollar amount. Other agencies may require city council approval for any purchase regardless of the cost. As a public safety manager, it is your responsibility to learn the basic rules of procurement within your own agency. This information can be obtained from your finance or purchasing department. The information includes the various requirements for advertisement, contact with vendors, product demonstrations, proposal guidelines and who has the authority to sign a contract. Managers should always consult with legal counsel, department heads and finance (purchasing) personnel before entering into any negotiations with a prospective vendor.

## Elements of the Solicitation Process

### Advertisement

Depending on the type of procurement, public safety agencies are required to do some type of public advertisement when soliciting for goods and services, including technology equipment.

The advertisement process ensures that vendors have equal access to public safety agency procurement opportunities. Vendor competition is an essential factor in achieving this objective and promotes efficiency and effectiveness in procurement, discourages monopoly situations and avoids favoritism. A balance needs to be achieved when deciding on how many vendors should be asked to participate in the procurement process. If there are too many vendors, the process becomes time-consuming for both the vendor and the public safety agency. If there are too few vendors, then there is no competition.[4]

There are many variations to this general type of notice requirement, including the number of times the notice must be published, the number of newspapers it must be advertised in, the target circulation of those newspapers and the number of days prior to receipt of bids it must be published. The contents of the notice itself are frequently mandated as well: e.g., it must include a general description of the items to be purchased, must state the location at which bid forms and specifications may be obtained and must state the time and place for opening bids. Advertising for goods and services is usually done through various market networks including trade associations, commercial procurement listing services and established mailing lists.[5]

One of the main goals of advertising a technology solicitation is to maximize competition. With that as your goal, the following may be of assistance:

- Decide on which type of media (newspaper, Internet or other method) that has the broadest readership in the business community.
- Advertisements are expensive. Try to negotiate with newspapers or web services to advertise your project as a public service to the community. They might advertise for free or at a reduced cost.
- Most government agencies have a link on their website that displays solicitations for public safety organizations and other city/county departments. The information is public and can be viewed by anyone. It usually includes a "frequently asked questions" tab for prospective vendors.
- Most government agencies utilize their website for procurement purposes. The use of "hard copy" solicitations is done on occasion and depends on the specific public safety agency.
- If you have scheduled a pre-bid conference, this will be one of the first pieces of information upon which the vendors will act. Remember, what you want to gain from this advertisement are responses from potential bidders to your upcoming procurement and their interest in receiving the solicitation you plan to issue.

Vendors do incur costs in the preparation and submission of their proposals. Every effort should be made to ensure that each vendor has a clear understanding of the process and has an equal opportunity to bid on the project. The decision on how to procure varies between each public safety agency. Standard rules of public procurement apply independently, based on the type of procurement (goods, works or services). The rules protect each organization or agency from claims of corruption or misconduct. If an organization or agency fails to abide by their policy on advertising or the solicitation process, vendors can protest the final award to the city council, board of supervisors or other elected body.

"A bid protest occurs when one or more vendors object to an element of the procurement process, usually caused by the agency's failure to follow the selection process outlined in the bid document. When a bid protest occurs, the vendor's attorney files a legal notification with the City or County, notifying them of the protest. The City or County will ordinarily suspend the procurement until such time that the matter has been fully resolved (which usually requires several months). Therefore, playing by the rules is absolutely imperative."[6]

## Pre-Bid Conference or Job Walk

A pre-bid conference or job walk is used in more complex technology projects. This gives the prospective vendor or bidder an opportunity to discuss any complicated specifications and requirements before the solicitation is submitted to your agency or organization. This is also an open forum for the potential bidders to ask questions or address any ambiguities in the solicitation documents that may require clarification. Notice of the pre-bid conference or job walk should be included in the original solicitation. The solicitation should identify a specific format for questions that are submitted prior to or after the pre-bid conference or job walk. Encourage vendors to submit questions in advance if possible. Any questions or comments discussed during the pre-bid conference or job walk should be documented and provided in writing (online) to all vendors bidding on the project.

There should be some type of agenda for the pre-bid conference or job walk. The agenda should identify the appropriate staff members present and the activities to be covered. The project manager or assistant should have a sign-in sheet for all attendees. Copies of the sign-in sheet should be emailed to each of the vendors or published online if required. The list is often used by other vendors to determine who else is bidding on the project.

The project manager should clarify that any remarks, comments or explanations at the pre-bid conference or job walk are not official unless they are specifically identified in a written amendment and furnished to all vendors. The pre-bid conference or job walk is not designed to recap or cover all of the elements in the original solicitation for services or goods. The solicitation must stand alone as a contractual document.

The main benefit of the pre-bid conference or job walk is to identify any special provisions or areas not clearly identified in your scope of work. It is very helpful to have any technical experts in attendance to answer any questions that may come up.

A job walk also allows the prospective vendors or bidders an opportunity to see firsthand the location or area where the equipment will be installed. For example, a correctional facility may want to have a job walk with vendors and bidders when replacing a jail management computer system or video surveillance cameras. The vendors or bidders will want to see where the devices will be installed and have the opportunity to document or photograph (if allowed) critical areas of concern that they will need to evaluate when preparing their final bid.

When the pre-bid conference or job walk is completed, the project manager may need to issue a solicitation amendment. The amendment will identify any questions or issues raised by the vendors. Try to answer each question accurately to avoid any future conflicts with the solicitation process. Remember to publish (online) or send a written copy to all vendors that clearly identifies any questions or issues discussed during the pre-bid conference or job walk.

Project managers should make every effort to accommodate requests for job walks. Many vendors travel for long distances at their own cost and they will want to accomplish multiple tasks during their trip. Depending on the type of project, your agency or organization may want to make the pre-bid conference or job walk mandatory. You need to consult with your legal counsel or finance department for guidance.

### Standard Solicitation Elements

Your solicitation for a proposal from a vendor identifies the procurement, the agency and the contact person(s). It contains simple, clear instructions for preparing an offer, often including a checklist of the items in the offer. It clearly states the time and specifications for submitting the offer and any time constraints relative to the project.[7] Government agencies are required to have and use standard solicitation guidelines for all procurements. Some complex procurements, where the specification or scope of work is more extensive, the solicitation process can take several months or even years to complete. However, most solicitations for bids are done within a 1- to 3-month time period and are very simple to complete. The most expeditious procurements often result from the inclusion of a complete contract in the solicitation. When this is incorporated in the offer, no further terms have to be discussed or executed when the agency accepts the offer.

It is important not to include any unnecessary requirements and keep the solicitation as simple as possible. Large or complex solicitation packages discourage some potential vendors from bidding on a project.[8] However, public safety agencies commonly utilize information technology that is highly complex and extensive, so there are vendors that specialize in this area that are accustomed to complicated solicitations.

Regardless of the solicitation method used, there are certain common elements that will be present in a solicitation issued under either the competitive bidding or competitive proposal method of procurement. Many government agencies have developed procurement forms that detail what is included as "boilerplate" in the solicitation process and include the common elements of any solicitation method that is used. Regardless of which method you use (or any variation of them), the common elements include:[9]

- A form that acts as the official solicitation document. The form is signed by the bidder or proposer and acts as the offer which, if accepted by the contracting officer or buyer, results in a binding contract. Although it is typically a single page, it is not unusual for the acceptance document (the contract) to be a separate form. The form typically identifies:

  ◦ A solicitation number for reference
  ◦ Agency contact person to answer any questions
  ◦ Summary of any pre-bid or job walk conferences (date and time)
  ◦ The date, time and manner the bids or proposals are to be received (electronic)
  ◦ Complete description of documents needed for proposal
  ◦ Space for the price (offer) to be included
  ◦ Space where amendments to the solicitation can be acknowledged

- ○ Space where the firm can be identified
- ○ Space for the firm official to sign and date the bid or proposal[10]

- If the form is multi-purpose and also acts as the contract, it will typically have space for the contract number, contract amount, line items awarded (if applicable), and a place for the contracting officer to sign and date the contract.
- If the instructions are lengthy, and because of the many certification forms typically required, it is becoming more common to provide a separate checklist of all the documents or other submissions required in a responsive offer.
- Information that clearly identifies the following information:

  - ○ Type of business (individual, partnership, sole proprietorship, etc.)
  - ○ Vendor qualifications and experience
  - ○ Pricing information or cost basis
  - ○ References

- Any information that identifies the solicitation instructions and conditions. This typically includes instructions relating to: offer preparation, instructions relating to acknowledging amendments to the solicitation, rules relating to late submissions, modifications and withdrawals of offers, instructions as to how the contract will be awarded, bid/proposal protest procedures, the ability of agency to cancel the solicitation and a discussion on how inconsistencies between provisions of the solicitation are to be resolved.
- Any special contract requirements or provisions relating to this particular solicitation and contract that are not addressed elsewhere in the solicitation. This includes bonding requirements, insurance requirements, any special permits or licenses required, what will the public safety agency provide to the vendor or contractor, liquidated damages, warranties, indemnity provisions, etc.
- Standard legal terminology or general provisions. This includes forms for construction services, architectural and engineering services, information services, technical services, consultants and service contracts. This is where you include information on the following; termination for default and convenience, inspections, federal, state and local taxes, differing site conditions, excusable delay, handling of any disputes, governing laws, indemnification, pricing of adjustments, examination of any records or documents and payment terms. Your legal counsel needs to review this information and approve it before submitting it to the city council or county board of supervisors for approval.
- Any statement of work (scope of work) that describes what it is that you are buying. This information varies from project to project, but it will be used to measure satisfactory performance of the contractor or vendor. Did they perform or supply the services or equipment as promised?

There is no such thing as a perfect or all-encompassing solicitation. The aforementioned items are some of the common elements in a solicitation document that are typically used. Each public safety agency will have specific guidelines on how the solicitation is packaged, submitted and eventually evaluated. The bottom line is that you want to create a document that will get you through the solicitation and contract award process with little or no controversy.[11] This ensures that your project is on-time and within or under budget.

## Types of Solicitations

There are several mechanisms to obtain goods or information from a vendor. They include:

### Request for Qualifications (RFQ)

A *request for qualifications (RFQ)* is used to determine if there are any bidders available for a specific project. It establishes and determines if a vendor meets the minimum qualifications to perform the work required for the project. The RFQ does not require a cost proposal or any specific details. RFQs are not competitive in nature, but they often lead to formal request for proposal (RFP). The RFQ should always be reviewed by legal counsel and finance personnel before advertisement.[12]

A request for qualifications should have the following information:

- **Introduction**—Describe your agency, objectives and brief background of your project. This section also includes any specific terms, conditions or provisions.
- **Scope of services requested**—Include specific information about your project, including a historical review, current issues and purpose of the solicitation. Does your agency require a certain type of technology format or compatibility with existing technology? Describe the minimum qualifications that will be required for your project. Have the vendors describe their qualifications in detail.
- **Schedule of events**—List any specific timelines or events relative to this project.
- **Written qualification submission guidelines**—List the basic submission requirements used by your agency. How many pages, how will the RFQ be submitted (paper or online), and specific headings that are required for your project.
- **Evaluation criteria**—Describe the evaluation criteria for this project. Include information about the process and how it will be scored. It is helpful to list the specific scoring range for each category listed on the evaluation form.
- **Selection and notification information**—Describe what happens after a vendor is selected. How will they be notified? Typically, all vendors that submitted the RFQ will be notified in writing.

### Request for Information (RFI)

A *request for information (RFI)* is used during the planning phase to identify information about vendor products, requirements, specifications and purchase options. Pricing information is not necessarily part of an RFI, but it can be added if necessary. The RFI should also state that the award of any contract will not automatically follow. Public safety agencies can utilize an RFI to determine if a certain type of technology even exists or is available to the public sector. The RFI is not a proposal; it is just a statement of facts from a vendor.

A request for information should have the following information:

- **Introduction**—Describe your agency, objectives and brief background of your project.
- **Purpose of RFI**—Describe what you are asking for. Are you looking for a specific piece of technology, jail management software, biometric devices, etc. Perhaps you are looking for information on possible cost-effective methods for the delivery of services in your department. Ask the vendor to give product information, samples, or references if applicable. It is also acceptable to obtain some generic pricing information and delivery estimates.
- **Written submission guidelines**—List the basic submission requirements used by your agency. How many pages, how will the RFI be submitted (paper or online), and specific headings that are required for your project.
- **Contact information and general information**—List any department contact information, specific legal definitions pursuant to your agency's guidelines on solicitations.

## Request for Proposal (RFP)

A *request for proposal (RFP)* is a formal solicitation document used by government agencies to obtain goods and services. In this case, the vendor is required to make an actual "proposal" to your agency based on the criteria listed in the RFP. The format of an RFP is usually standard or "boilerplate." Some project managers have trouble writing the specific technology requirements or scope, so the use of experts or a consultant is recommended. The RFP is a complete package that includes pricing, schedules and all of the details about your project. At the conclusion of the RFP process, one vendor will be selected. The public safety agency will then enter into negotiations with the vendor and a contract will be drafted. The RFP package should always be reviewed by legal counsel and finance personnel.

A request for proposal should have the following information:

- **Introduction**—This section describes the purpose of the RFP, the term of the agreement, minimum proposer requirements, pre-bid conference or job walk information, correspondence or vendor questions information and the submission deadlines.
- **Scope of services requested**—This section includes a complete background on the project, description of the project, scope of work, general information, project schedule and any alternates or options. This section includes the "nuts and bolts" of your project and should be very detailed and specific.
- **Schedule of events**—List any specific timelines or events relative to this project.
- **Proposal conditions**—This section describes any contingencies, incurred costs, negotiations, improper influence, final authority, modifications and the evaluation process.
- **Proposal submission guidelines**—List the basic submission requirements used by your agency. This includes the proposal presentation and format.
- **Proposal evaluation and award criteria**—This section includes information on how the proposal will be reviewed or evaluated. It also describes the evaluation

committee and criteria. This section also covers the negotiation and award of contract terms.

- **Selection and notification information**—Describe what happens after a vendor is selected. How will they be notified? Typically, all vendors that submitted the RFP will be notified in writing.
- **Any other attachments**—This section typically has a proposal checklist, sample contract, sample payment and performance bond information and any additional terms and conditions.

> Because the RFP is the most widely used solicitation document used by public safety agencies, an actual RFP proposal is included in Appendix 4 at the end of this book. The RFP was used for an integrated security system upgrade at a local jail facility.

## Invitation to Bid (ITB)

An invitation to bid requires a vendor to submit a proposal solely based on the specific requirements of the public safety agency. There is no negotiation and the award usually goes to the lowest bidder. The ITB process is not used on a regular basis.

## Procurement Types

### Purchase Order

A *purchase order* is a document that authorizes the purchase and delivery of a service or goods. The purchase order acts as a "contract" between the buyer (public safety agency) and the seller (vendor). The purchase order defines all quantities, product descriptions, payment terms and other terms or conditions. The purchase order is one of the most common procurement types used by government agencies.

### Non-Competitive or Sole-Source Bidding

During certain circumstances, government agencies do not have to abide by the competitive bidding process. Non-competitive bidding, also known as "sole-source," is done when the public safety agency has demonstrated to the approval authority (city council, board of supervisors, and so on) that they can only purchase goods or services from one vendor. Reasons for sole source procurement include: the vendor has the proprietary right to service or maintain the equipment, there are no other vendors capable of fully meeting the requirements of the project and other vendors provided poor performance or did not have suitable parts for the job. For example, many public safety agencies have customized software programs like computer aided dispatch (CAD) or a record management system (RMS), which is proprietary in nature and only the vendor can maintain the system or make any changes to the software program. Sole-source procurement is applicable because no other vendors have the ability or right to make changes to another vendor's system or software. However, the use of a sole-source or non-competitive procurement should only be done as a last resort. Government agencies should make every attempt to be transparent and allow vendors to bid on a specific project or piece of technology.

### Blanket Purchase Order

A blanket purchase order is a term contract or agreement between a government agency and a specific vendor. A blanket purchase order is issued to support an existing contract that has been previously negotiated. The blanket purchase order should be used under the following conditions:

- Repetitive purchases, specified services or categories of items from the same supplier, which are ordered and paid in a predictable manner during a certain time period, which is usually one fiscal year.
- The government agency orders materials or maintenance supplies that require several shipments during the fiscal year.
- Enable the agency to obtain more favorable pricing through volume commitments (fuel).
- Generally, a blanket purchase order is for one fiscal year; however, it can be extended for multiple years in certain circumstances with approval from the city council or board of supervisors. Public safety agencies commonly use blanket purchase orders for fuel (auto and aviation), automobile repair services, safety equipment and office supplies.

### Common Procurement Terminology

### Product Demonstrations

Product demonstrations are a beneficial way for project managers to solicit information on technology projects, but they can be used to ensure that the vendor can actually "deliver as advertised." Public safety personnel, specifically law enforcement, are by nature skeptical when dealing with others. Trust is an important part of the procurement process. When in doubt, ask the vendor to demonstrate their project in person or perhaps ask them to provide the piece of technology for a "pilot" test. This should be done at no cost to your agency.

### Competitive Bidding

Competitive bidding for service or products ensures that the public safety organizations obtain a fair price for goods or services. Competitive bidding promotes competition among the vendors. Typically, a public safety agency will require a minimum of three competitive bids for products or services. If all of the bids are equal (quality of equipment or services), then the agency should select the lowest bidder. However, if the lowest bidder does not provide the best service or equipment for the public safety agency, they can select another bidder, no matter the cost.

## Evaluation and Negotiation Process

### Evaluation Process

After you have successfully prepared the RFP and received responses from the vendors, you need to complete some type of an evaluation to determine who will win the bid on your project. The evaluation criteria should be very specific, measurable and always *in writing*. This helps ensure that your agency or organization does not receive any protests or complaints from a vendor. The evaluation criteria should be based upon the information listed in the RFP. For example, if the RFP requires a timeline, work plan or list of products, then the evaluation should also have some type of criteria to evaluate that information. Did the vendor submit a timeline? Was the work plan thorough and did it meet your goals and objectives listed in the RFP?

After the evaluation criterion has been established, you will need to review all of the proposals and remove any ones that are considered "non-responsive." A non-responsive bid is one that fails to address all of the requirements listed in the RFP. Some examples are: failure to complete all sections of the proposal, failure to submit any required documents (insurance bond, licenses, and so on), the proposal does not match your required schedule or timeline or the bidder is clearly unqualified to perform the work.

After the non-responsive proposals have been eliminated, you need to assemble an evaluation team. Generally, it is recommended that more than one person review an RFP. The evaluators should include any stakeholders in the project. For example, if the project involves a wireless or local area network, then someone from your technical services division should participate in the process. If the project involves dispatch operations, then someone from dispatch should be on the evaluation team.

It is important that the evaluation team take the necessary time to properly evaluate each proposal. Public safety managers should not rush this process because you want the best and most qualified vendor for the project. The project manager should meet with the evaluation team and thoroughly describe the project and objectives listed in the RFP. Provide each participant with the list of rules for the evaluation process. Your finance or purchasing department should have a list of rules or procedures for reviewing RFPs. The main rules are discussed during the process and the RFP evaluation forms cannot be removed from the evaluation site.[13] The project manager should then distribute the evaluation forms and discuss each area in detail. He or she should highlight the key areas that are important to your agency or organization. The forms should include each area or category that is being reviewed and if necessary any points that can be awarded.

After the participants have been properly briefed on the process, they should evaluate the RFPs independently. After all of the RFPs have been reviewed and evaluated, you can meet with them as a group. If your agency or organization allows it, you may discuss the RFPs as a group. This will vary by jurisdiction. Keep in mind that the process is supposed to be fair and impartial. Do not let one evaluator try to persuade another evaluator to change their scores. After all of the RFPs have been scored, a bidders list is established. The bidders list is then submitted to the purchasing authority for processing.

Some RFPs split the review process into two sections: technical and cost. If that is the case, the evaluation team should review the technical section first. When the evaluation

**TABLE 17.1** Sample RFP Evaluation

**AGENCY: ABC SHERIFF'S DEPARTMENT**
**PROPOSAL EVALUATION WORKSHEET**
**Sample RFP for the Purchase of "Widgets"**

PROPOSER_____ RATER #_____

## A. TECHNICAL REVIEW – 100 POINTS – MAXIMUM NUMBER OF POINTS LISTED FOR EACH SECTION

| | *MAX. POINTS* | *SCORE AWARDED* |
|---|---|---|
| 1. **FIRM QUALIFICATIONS** | 5 | |
| • Clearly demonstrated that they are fully qualified to perform the required work as listed in the RFP (2) | | |
| • Has required certification and licenses (1) | | |
| • Years in business (2) | | |
| COMMENTS | | |
| | | |
| 2. **FIRM EXPERIENCE** | 10 | |
| • Prior experience (Widgets) with public safety and/or governmental agencies (8) | | |
| • Prior (Widgets) with the ABC Sheriff's Department (2) | | |
| COMMENTS | | |
| | | |
| 3. **PROPOSED PROJECT STAFF** | 5 | |
| • Identified and provided resumes for the specific personnel that will be working on this project (engineer, project manager, etc.) This includes all parts of the project (Widgets). (3) | | |
| • Identified the entire project team including an organizational chart that clearly shows the organization of the team & the hierarchy of members. (2) | | |
| COMMENTS | | |
| | | |
| 4. **REFERENCES** | 10 | |
| • Governmental Agencies (2) | | |
| • Completed projects on time (3) | | |
| • Overall satisfaction with project (5) | | |
| COMMENTS | | |

*(Continued)*

5.    **PROJECT WORK PLAN**                                                     35
- Complete and detailed summary of the management and work plan for this project. (5)
- Proposal included specific product data, quantities, samples and specifications for the following:
  Widget software (3)
  Widget Hardware (1)
  Sequence of Operations (7)
  System Diagrams/site drawings (1)
- Proposer articulates that the proposed software/hardware is non-proprietary. Can software be serviced or re-programmed by county personnel or other third party company? Can software/hardware be purchased at local third party company? (5)
- Proposed schedule for completion and acceptance identified the following:
  Schedule plan is satisfactory (7)
- Warranty information (2)
- Detailed training plan (2)
- Maintenance information including a local presence to ABC County and 24/7 help line (2)

COMMENTS

6.    **EXPERIENCE WITH SIMILAR PROJECTS**                            25
- Demonstrated prior experience with Widget programming development (15)
- Clearly identified prior experience Widget software (4)
- Clearly demonstrated prior experience and ability to integrate all of the proposed systems as listed in RFP. (6)

COMMENTS

7.    **DEMONSTRATED UNDERSTANDING OF RFP**                      10
- Proposer clearly understood the intent of the RFP and the needs of the department
- No unnecessary downtime (2)
- Proposer makes County a priority regarding design, programming and development of software. Installation of equipment is scheduled in a reasonable amount of time (2)
- Complied with requirements listed in RFP (4)

|  | MAX. POINTS | SCORE AWARDED |
|---|---|---|

- Written and verbal proposal was comprehensive, professional and organized. Proposer answered questions appropriately and addressed any concerns from the evaluation panel (2)

COMMENTS

| Totals |  |  |
|---|---|---|
|  | 100 |  |

team has identified the top three finalists based on their technical proposals, the cost or fee proposals should be reviewed. The evaluation team should review each fee proposal carefully. Keep in mind that the cheapest proposal does not necessarily mean it is the best proposal.

> At the conclusion of the evaluation process, it is important to keep all of the evaluation criteria forms, scoring sheets and other information used to generate the final bidders list.

## Negotiations with a Vendor

When the top finalist has been selected, your agency or organization will enter into negotiations with the vendor. Depending on the agency or organization, a department head, purchasing agent or project manager will handle the negotiations with the vendor. Negotiating successfully takes skill and practice. Always keep in mind that the vendor is in the business to make money as well, so try to be fair and professional. You want the vendor to stay in business over the long term so they can support your project. However, as a public safety manager, it is your responsibility to make sure the final price for the technology project is fair and does not waste any tax dollars.

A good negotiator does the following:

- Does the appropriate amount of research when reviewing fee proposals. What areas of the fee proposal seem high? Is it cheaper to have someone within your agency or organization complete part of project instead of paying the vendor to do it? Vendors will commonly increase the price of maintenance programs or items that can be purchased by your agency. Always ask for a price reduction.
- Define your goals prior to the negotiation.
- Only deal with vendor representatives that are allowed and authorized to make concessions and decisions on the final contract.

- Silence can be a good tool in negotiations. Vendors will sometimes fear that you have lost interest and will pick someone else.
- Compromise is okay. Just make sure you can live with any concessions.
- Do not display any unprofessional demeanor. Remember, you are a public safety manager and represent your department.

If you and the vendor cannot agree on a price, move on to the vendor who scored second on your list. Each agency has specific rules on negotiations. Always consult with legal counsel and finance personnel when dealing with negotiations.

## Contract Award

The final step in the procurement and solicitation process is to issue the award to the winning bidder. The RFP or other type of solicitation should clearly identify the process and type of contract that may be awarded to the winning bidder. Typically, the vendors RFP proposal becomes part of the actual contract. A payment schedule is identified and agreed upon by both parties.[14] Always stagger the payment amounts to the vendor based on the importance of your project. Never give the vendor a significant amount of money upfront. An important part of this process is to require the vendor to supply a payment or performance bond. A bond protects your agency from default or incomplete work. There is a cost for a payment or performance bond, so make sure you include information in the actual RFP. Most vendors will work with your agency or organization.

The final component to this process is to have the final award or contract approved by the governing authority, which is usually the city council or board of supervisors. Typically, an agenda item is developed by you or another department head. The agenda item details the RFP process and how the vendor was selected. It also includes the actual contract between the vendor and your agency or organization. When the governing authority has approved the agenda item, you have "acquired the technology."

## Chapter Summary

The process of developing a solicitation and acquiring technology can be cumbersome at first. However, remember that there is always someone out there that can help you in this process. Some key things to remember from this chapter include:

- Identify your goals and objectives. This should help identify what you are looking for and how you intend on purchasing it.
- How do you intend on buying the product? What type of solicitation will you use? RFP, invitation to bid or a simple purchase order?
- Take your time and utilize other experts with your organization.
- Don't get frustrated with the process. You have to rely on other people to get this part of the project completed.
- Managing a technology project requires leadership. As a public safety manager, you must take charge of the project and ensure that the rules for procurement are followed at all times.

Now it is time to move on to the final chapter in Unit 3, "Installation, Maintenance and Closure of Your Project... The Final Steps."

## Key Words or Terminology

| | | |
|---|---|---|
| request for information | request for qualification | request for proposal |
| procurement | bid protest | sole-source |
| blanket purchase order | contract award | performance bond |

## Discussion Questions

1. Research your local public safety agency and review their procurement policy. Who is responsible for preparing procurement documents? Who is the governing authority at the agency?
2. Describe the basic elements of the solicitation process. List the main differences and explain which ones are more commonly used in public safety.
3. Identify at least five key areas of the overall procurement process that require leadership and oversight by a public safety manager. What difficulties do you foresee during the aforementioned process? How will you address these issues?
4. Identify a piece of equipment or technology program that you would like to purchase. What type of procurement process would you use? Are you going to use the RFP process or sole source?

## Notes

1 SEARCH Group Incorporated, Harris, Kelly J., and Romesburg, William H. (2002). *Law Enforcement Tech Guide: How to Plan, Purchase and Manage Technology (Successfully!). A Guide for Executives, Managers and Technologists.* Washington, DC: U.S. Department of Justice, Office of Community Oriented Policing Services.
2 SEARCH Group Incorporated, Kraus, Benjamin R. (2011). *The "accidental" project manager.* Washington, DC: U.S. Department of Justice, Office of Community Oriented Policing Services.
3 Harris and Romesburg, *Law enforcement tech guide.*
4 *Methods of solicitation and selection,* n.d. Federal Transit Authority. Retrieved from www.fta.dot.gov/12831_6187.html.
5 Ibid.
6 Harris and Romesburg, *Law enforcement tech guide.*
7 Federal Transit Authority, *Methods of solicitation and selection.*
8 Ibid.
9 Ibid.
10 Ibid.
11 Ibid.
12 Harris and Romesburg, *Law enforcement tech guide.*
13 (2001). *A guide for applying information technology in law enforcement.* National Law Enforcement and Corrections Technology Center. Washington, DC: U.S. Department of Justice, Office of Justice Systems.
14 Ibid.

# 18

## INSTALLATION, MAINTENANCE AND CLOSURE OF YOUR PROJECT... THE FINAL STEPS

"Never let a computer know you are in a hurry."
—*Anonymous*

### Learning Objectives

After reading this chapter, the student will:

- Have a working knowledge of the final steps of the technology management process.
- Be able to discuss the importance of having a detailed quality assurance plan.
- Define the basic terminology used by technology professionals.
- Articulate the benefits of having a comprehensive training program.
- Understand the role of supervision and management in technology projects.

### Introduction

Chapter 18 is the final chapter in Unit 3. In this chapter, we review the final steps of project management, which are installation, maintenance and closure of the project. Up to this point, you have received instruction on how to prepare a comprehensive plan that details how the project will commence. Now it is time to actually complete the work. This chapter highlights the various parts of the installation or implementation plan, which is essentially the template for the entire project. After the technology product or system has been installed, it needs to be tested. This is part of the quality assurance process that was briefly described in prior chapters. The project manager must ensure that the product or piece of technology works as advertised by the vendor before closing out the project. The final part of the process is to ensure that the project is maintained by either in-house technicians or by having a maintenance contract with the vendor. This chapter also focuses on the management and leadership skills that are necessary to finally complete a technology project.

## Installation Plan

The installation part of any technology project is the most exciting phase in the entire process. Public safety managers have spent countless hours developing the project, planning for everything and obtaining funding for the project. Now is the time to deliver. Sadly, this part can also be the most frustrating part of the process. What happens if the technology doesn't work or if the project is delayed? How do you explain why the project went over budget? The installation plan will hopefully minimize any lingering doubts about the process and why it is important to follow all of the steps outlined in Unit 3 precisely.

The *installation plan*, also known as the *implementation plan*, essentially describes how the technology will be delivered, installed and tested by your agency or organization. It also establishes how each deliverable of the project will be monitored. The installation plan should follow the schedule outlined in the project plan. The schedule should be discussed in detail with the vendor who will be installing the technology. Your job as a public safety manager or project manager is to hold the vendor accountable based on the aforementioned schedule.

The installation plan includes information about the project including the location of any equipment or products that will be used during the installation process. Vendors should provide any specific information concerning their needs when installing a product. This includes space considerations, electrical requirements, air conditioning, and so on. The plan should also address any specific concerns on behalf of your agency or organization.[1] This includes any security concerns, background requirements, system shutdown protocols and other issues that may affect your operation. For example, if your project requires a vendor to install a video surveillance system inside of a local jail, the installation plan will identify how the vendor and any sub-contractor will enter the facility. The background security information should clearly state the agency rules on what can be brought into the facility and what will happen if there is a violation. Jails are protected environments, so it is vital that vendors be told up front that they cannot bring in contraband like cell phones, narcotics, alcohol, weapons or anything else that is illegal to bring into a jail facility.

Another consideration that needs to be addressed in the installation plan is personnel. Who from your agency or organization will be on-site with the vendor? As previously mentioned, a jail facility must be secured, so your plan may require sworn or non-sworn personnel to escort the vendor inside the facility. If the technology is being installed in a police department, the vendor will need to be let into secure parts of the building and may require an escort. Regardless of the type of project, it is very important to identify and list any specific rules and regulations of your agency or organization in the plan.

The installation plan should also clearly describe the who, what, where, when and why surrounding the project. This is especially important because the project now includes a new member—the vendor.[2] The installation plan follows the information listed in the project plan in detail and focuses on the deliverables. As things are being installed, it is a good idea to frequently meet with the vendor and stakeholders. This helps avoid any miscommunication during the installation process.

Finally, the installation plan should address the work and payment schedules also known as a statement of values. During the installation phase of the project, vendors require payment for services rendered. Often times, the project is divided into specific parts that

**TABLE 18.1** Sample Implementation Plan

| *Implementation Overview (Plan)* | | |
| --- | --- | --- |
| Contractors approach will be to design, configure and build the "fingerprint system" for the ABC Sheriff's department. This will allow time to test and import the necessary components for the system. | | |
| *Existing Components* | *Upgrade Features* | *Comments* |
| AFIS | New matching system | Hardware, OS, applications |
| Archive | Storage expansion | Keep current DAS |
| CAPPS (new purchase) | New hardware and integrated applications | SB=7 and RC=5 |
| Fingerprint Controller | Linux SC Server | Attached storage will be replaced. |

**TABLE 18.2** Sample Payment Schedule

| ABC Sheriff's Department Sample Payment Plan | | |
| --- | --- | --- |
| *Payment Terms* | | |
| Upon acceptance of order | $736,000 | 20% |
| Upon completion and approval from customer on engineering design | $552,000 | 15% |
| Upon delivery and acceptance of equipment from customer | $1,472,000 | 40% |
| Upon installation of equipment | $552,000 | 15% |
| Final testing and approval from customer | $368,000 | 10% |
| Totals | $3,680,000 | 100% |

allow vendors to be paid when specific milestones are accomplished. For example, if the technology project requires some type of software development or design, the vendor could ask for payment when the software is sufficiently tested and approved by the public safety agency. Other milestones that will trigger a payment include the delivery of equipment or the completion of a certain percentage of the project.

## Quality Assurance Plan

A *quality assurance plan* ensures that the vendor's equipment or product works according to the specific details listed in the project plan and, if applicable, the request for proposal guidelines. The quality assurance plan addresses each deliverable and ensures that they are reliable and perform as advertised. Acceptance testing should be done in phases or when specific parts of the project are completed. Usually this information is spelled out in the request for proposal and project plan. A typical quality assurance test requires the vendor to fully demonstrate the product or technology to the agency or organization.[3] If the technology is complicated, it is important to have technical experts or the end users from your agency or organization verify the validity of the test. In other words, you wouldn't purchase a vehicle without test driving it.[4] A quality assurance test makes the vendor prove that the product actually works.

After the agency or organization has tested and approved the technology, the vendor will require payment. If the technology doesn't work properly based on the specifics, it is important to withhold any payment to the vendor. Typically, this process is addressed in the statement of values or payment plan.

## Training

One of the biggest mistakes in any technology project is underestimating the importance of training. The use of technology can be difficult to comprehend and a public safety manager's ability to adequately train personnel is paramount. Public safety agencies typically do

**TABLE 18.3**  Sample Quality Assurance or Acceptance Test

---

*Acceptance Test*

---

The Acceptance Test shall be conducted within thirty (30) days after the contractor (vendor) has certified that the system is working as described in the contract. Customer will begin to conduct acceptance testing which includes the following:

- Testing of system accuracy rates.
- Testing of throughput rates.

The "fingerprint system" shall be accepted on the date that the "fingerprint system" performs at the accuracy and throughput rates specified below:

*Accuracy*

- The "fingerprint system" must achieve 98% accuracy when testing fifty (50) subjects. Accuracy is defined as the location of the subject being found in the top three of the candidate list.
- The "fingerprint system" must achieve 90% accuracy with a one finger search.
- The test will be conducted in the field (night and day), under existing conditions.

*Throughput*

- 50 fingerprint inquiries within one hour will be completed within 60 seconds.
- 50 latent inquiries will be completed within one hour (over a 24-hour period).
- 600 Mobile ID 1:N inquiries will be completed within 60 seconds (over a 24-hour period).

*Functionality Test*

At the workstation, the following functions were demonstrated:

| Function | Y/N | Date |
|---|---|---|
| Browse Functions | | |
| Job Control Functions | | |
| Workstation Functions | | |
| Database Functions | | |

a great job of providing training in the core aspects of the job. Law enforcement officers receive extensive training in use-of-force tactics, firearms, community policing and patrol operations. Fire personnel routinely train and practice fire suppression tactics. Correctional personnel receive substantial training in cell extractions, state or federal laws and jail operations. Think about your own agency or organization and how the training programs are delivered. Are they done in person? Is the training presented by lecture or by practical scenarios? Perhaps the training was presented using the "train the trainer" method. As you think about your own training programs, examine how prior technology projects were received by your personnel.

After you have reviewed your current training practices, establish a training plan for the new technology that you plan on implementing into your agency or organization. Public safety officers do not like change and technology can be scary for some of your personnel. Some of your personnel will be resistant to your new technology. There are a few tips that can help you train members of your agency or organization. They include:

- Incorporate the department values, mission and value statement into the training program.
- Highlight the importance and success stories surrounding the technology. Perhaps an agency has adopted the technology and it improved officer safety or improved operational efficiency.
- Clearly identify the need for the training. Nobody wants to spend time training on something that they don't understand.
- Ensure the top management of the agency or organization attends the training program and endorses it.
- Use technology to enhance the training program. The use of media (video, Power-Point, etc.) is extremely valuable in the training process.
- Require each person to demonstrate their understanding of the technology.

These are just a few of the methods that can be used to help you stress the importance of using the technology. Above all else, ensure that the training component of the plan includes a process for ongoing training. Ongoing training is essential if your technology project is going to be successful. If public safety personnel lose interest or forget how to use the technology, it will sit on the shelf and not be utilized.

## *Maintenance*

"Technology projects fail when a system is implemented, then neglected."[5] It is very important that your plan includes information that describes how the technology will be maintained. Most vendors will offer maintenance programs with their technology equipment or product. The cost for maintenance can vary depending on the type of technology. Your plan should identify if your agency plans on maintaining the equipment or if you are going to have the vendor handle the maintenance. Larger agencies or organizations can usually handle the basic maintenance or troubleshoot a problem that may occur; however, software or problems involving proprietary information need to be fixed by the vendor. *Proprietary* means that the vendor is the only one who can fix or make modifications to the technology product. This also includes any future system upgrades.

There are several types of maintenance plans offered by vendors. The most common are telephone support or on-site service.[6] If your technology project is not complex, the telephone option may work the best. However, if the technology is complicated or involves a safety issue, the maintenance plan should include on-site service with a response time that is acceptable to your agency. A safety issue is something that your agency can not go without or endangers your personnel or the public. Examples include security controls inside of a jail facility, radio system, generators that control power to your facility, and so on.

### Closure of the Project

The closure of the project doesn't mean you accept the technology and walk away. The closure of the project formally finalizes the project or activities and delivers it to your agency or organization.[7] The closure process is ongoing and requires several steps. The goal of any project is to complete it and receive customer acceptance. Elements that are listed in the project plan (deliverables) help identify whether the project is successful or not. When the project has been completed, the public safety manager or project manager should do the following:

- Prepare a final report that summarizes the project process (good or bad) and reassures management that the technology has met the project goals and objectives.
- Ensure that all members of the project team are comfortable and accept the technology before the final payment has been made to the vendor.
- Ensure that all documentation for the project has been collected from the vendor. This includes any product data information, training guides, warranty information, system drawings, test results, etc. One of the most important documents to obtain from the vendor is any developed software. You will need a copy of their source code and programming information. If by chance the vendor goes out of business, you will not be able to upgrade or maintain the software without it. If the vendor will not provide the software source code, have them place it in escrow with a condition that it will be turned over to your agency if they go out of business.[8]
- A complete list and location of any technology that has been installed. This information will be very helpful if you or the project manager is no longer with the agency or organization.

Finally, public safety managers should meet with all of the stakeholders and obtain constructive feedback about the project. The entire process should be evaluated and a list of suggestions should be written down and used during the next project. The technology should also be evaluated on an ongoing basis to ensure it continues to perform and function as required.

> Quick Tip—At the conclusion of the project, place all of the written materials associated with the project (RFP, entire project plan, warranties, and so on) into a binder or save them on a disc. The information can and will be used by future public safety managers or project managers. This ensures that the project continues into the future.

## Final Thoughts about Managing a Technology Project

Managing a technology project is a process. It takes time and effort on your part. This chapter and the rest of Unit 3 were designed to give you, a public safety manager, a complete overview of the management process. Technology can be complicated, but you do have help. There are many experts available that can provide consulting services on large scale projects. If you are unsure about a certain part of the process, simply review Unit 3 or ask another expert for help. As public safety manager, your leadership and management skills are essential. You are expected to provide guidance when necessary, motivate all stakeholders, ensure that the project is cost effective and more importantly ensure that the technology project provides some type of benefit to the agency, organization and the public at large. Unit 3 is not just about technology, it is about leadership. Leaders of the future will embrace technology and everything it has to offer the public safety profession. Your job as a leader is to seek out technology and see how it can help your operation and support the mission and values of your agency or organization. Winston Churchill once said, "Responsibility is the price of greatness." Will your technology project rise to the level of greatness?

## Chapter Summary

This chapter focused on the final parts of the technology project: installation, quality control and the closure of the project. Let's review the final steps:

- The installation plan describes how the technology will be delivered, installed and tested.
- The quality assurance plan ensures that the product works and functions as specified in the project plan or RFP.
- Training is an important part of the overall project and helps ensure that the technology is received properly and used by agency personnel in an effective way.
- The technology project will not succeed unless there is some type of maintenance plan. The plan should address how and who will maintain the technology.
- The final step is the closure of the project. Although the project itself is over, the process will continue with ongoing assessments and evaluations.
- Remember as a leader, it is your responsibility to manage any project and ensure that it is successful.
- Leaders should also seek out new technology and support the agency or organizational mission statement regarding the use of technology.

## Key Words or Terminology

| | | |
|---|---|---|
| closure of project | implementation | quality assurance |
| acceptance testing | leadership | management |

## Discussion Questions

1. Identify the final steps of the technology management process and explain why they are important to the overall process.
2. Throughout Unit 3, you were asked to identify or select a piece of technology, program or equipment. Now it's time to finish the project by preparing a sample installation, maintenance, quality assurance, training and closure plan.
3. Identify at least three supervisory or management traits that are imbedded in the final stages of the technology management process.
4. Research and locate a public safety technology project that has failed. Did it have a quality assurance, training or installation plan? If you were in charge of the project, what would you have done?

## Notes

1 (2001). *A guide for applying information technology in law enforcement.* National Law Enforcement and Corrections Technology Center. Washington, DC: Office of Justice Programs, National Institute of Justice.
2 SEARCH Group Incorporated, Harris, Kelly J., and Romesburg, William H. (2002). *Law Enforcement Tech Guide: How to Plan, Purchase and Manage Technology (Successfully!). A Guide for Executives, Managers and Technologists.* Washington, DC: U.S. Department of Justice, Office of Community Oriented Policing Services.
3 (2014). *Project management methodology reference manual,* p. 16. Sacramento, CA: California Department of Technology.
4 Harris and Romesburg, *Law enforcement tech guide.*
5 Ibid.
6 National Law Enforcement and Corrections Technology Center, *A guide for applying information technology in law enforcement.*
7 Ibid.
8 Ibid.

# UNIT 4

# Emerging Trends in Public Safety Technology

Unit 4 provides a glimpse of the future of technology in public safety, with an emphasis on the criminal justice system. New technology innovation will continue to play a crucial role for public safety managers. Equipping public safety personnel with the latest technology is vital because criminals are consistently using innovative technology to commit crimes against society. Students will review the latest technology concepts and ideas that will hopefully benefit future public safety organizations and the communities that they serve each and every day. This unit also includes several research papers written by command-level professionals in public safety. The papers seek to determine the future of public safety and how technology will inspire, transform and revolutionize their respective professions.

This unit covers the following:

- Chapter 19—The Future of Public Safety Technology
- Chapter 20—Case Studies of Public Safety Technology

# 19

# THE FUTURE OF PUBLIC SAFETY TECHNOLOGY

"Some men see things as they are, and ask why? I dream
of things that never were, and ask why not?"
—*Robert F. Kennedy*

## Learning Objectives

After reading this chapter, the student will:

- Evaluate and assess the new trends in public safety technology.
- Assess and explore the various types of technology used today.
- Understand the importance of planning for the future by incorporating technology into strategic plans.
- Examine the various recommendations of President Obama's Twenty-First Century of Policing Report.

## Introduction

In this chapter, students explore the future of technology and how it relates to the public safety field. "The evolution of technology directly affects the way the criminal justice system operates at fundamental levels. The adoption and implementation of public safety technology also directly shapes the police and practices of the justice system."[1] So what is the future of technology? One only has to watch television or surf the Internet to see some of the innovative technology being discussed around the world. For example, will there be a time when police officers use cloaking technology to conduct surveillance on drug dealers? Could the courtroom of the future use augmented-reality technology? These are just a few of the possibilities being considered by public safety agencies around the country.

This chapter is designed to give you a glimpse of the innovative technologies being used or evaluated by public safety agencies across the country.

## Future Trends

Public safety has fundamentally changed over the last few years. Think about how your own personnel technology has changed. Flip or brick cell phones have developed into "smart" phones that are basically mini-computers. If you used a desktop computer in the early 2000s, you are probably using a smaller notebook or laptop today. The private sector dictates the technology field and public safety must pay attention and adapt to the technology standards as best they can. Obviously, the cost of technology is a barrier for most public safety agencies, but public safety managers must be creative and use technology whenever possible.

In 2014, the Police Executive Research Forum prepared a report called the *Future Trends of Policing*. PERF surveyed approximately 200 law enforcement agencies from all over the United States to identify the biggest trends and challenges facing law enforcement. The report emphasized the use of technology and stressed the importance of using tech savvy officers to bridge the gap with older officers that have not embraced technology.[2]

**TABLE 19.1** Future Trends in Policing

| Strategy | Currently Use | Implement or Increase in Next 2–5 Years | Eliminate or Decrease in Next 2–5 Years |
|---|---|---|---|
| Community policing | 93.7% | 31.7% | 2.6% |
| CompStat | 66.1% | 30.2% | 7.9% |
| Problem-oriented policing | 88.9% | 34.9% | 1.6% |
| Hot Spot Policing | 79.9% | 41.3% | 2.6% |
| Directed police patrols/ focused deterrence | 92.1% | 35.4% | 2.1% |
| Targeted known offenders | 79.3% | 47.3% | 2.1% |
| Targeted specific problem addresses/locations | 91.5% | 39.2% | 1.1% |
| Information/Intelligence-led policing | 72.7% | 54.0% | 1.6% |
| Predictive policing | 38.2% | 70.4% | 2.2% |
| Crime prevention programs | 90.5% | 29.6% | 4.2% |
| Violence prevention programs | 69.5% | 37.4% | 3.2% |
| Real-time crime center | 18.0% | 54.6% | 6.0% |
| Regional fusion center | 65.6% | 36.0% | 2.7% |
| Intelligence databases | 76.5% | 44.4% | 0.0% |
| Crime mapping | 86.2% | 40.4% | 0.0% |
| Crime analysis | 85.1% | 45.7% | 0.0% |
| Regional task forces | 80.4% | 31.7% | 5.3% |

*Source*: Police Executive Research Forum. (2014). *Future Trends in Policing*. Washington, DC: Office of Community Oriented Policing Services.

**TABLE 19.2**   Innovative Technology Used in Crime Fighting Strategies

| Technology | # | % |
|---|---|---|
| Social media/Outreach | 31 | 26.3 |
| Cameras/CCTV | 30 | 25.4 |
| Mapping/Hot Spots/GPS | 25 | 21.2 |
| License Plate Readers | 22 | 18.6 |
| RMS/Shared Database/Intranet | 20 | 16.9 |
| In-Car Computer/Tablet | 19 | 16.1 |
| Analysis | 14 | 11.9 |
| Computer Forensics | 10 | 8.5 |
| In-Car Camera | 8 | 6.8 |
| Automated/E-Ticket Device | 8 | 6.8 |
| Online Crime reporting | 7 | 5.9 |
| ShotSpotter | 6 | 5.1 |
| CompStat | 6 | 5.1 |
| Cell Phone Tracking | 6 | 5.1 |
| Text-a-Tip | 5 | 4.2 |
| Inter-Agency Data Sharing | 3 | 2.5 |
| Mobile/Electronic Fingerprinting | 3 | 2.5 |
| Ballistics Partnership | 2 | 1.7 |
| Patrol Vehicle Locator | 2 | 1.7 |
| Other | 33 | 28.0 |

*Source*: Police Executive Research Forum. (2014). *Future Trends in Policing*. Washington, DC: Office of Community Oriented Policing Services.

Law enforcement agencies are using technology to fight and prevent crime, interact with the community and keep officers safe in the field. Table 19.2 lists information from the PERF report about the use of technology in law enforcement.

Throughout this book, we have discussed different types of technology used in public safety including biometrics, thermal imaging cameras, social media and body-worn cameras So what other types of technology are being used today or at least being considered by public safety agencies across the country? Let's review a few of the more popular ones.

## Next Generation 911 Dispatch Technology

Public safety is seeing a big shift on how people communicate. Text messaging and other forms of social media have dramatically changed how public safety personnel handle calls for service. For over forty years, the 911 telephone system has served the needs of the public. However, the current system has been stretched to its limits and cannot keep up with the demands of public safety. The majority of the call centers in the United States use analog technology, which is inherently limited. The next wave of dispatch technology is called *Next Generation 911*. Next Generation 911 is an Internet protocol (IP) system that allows public safety agencies to send or receive digital information instead of analog. This includes pictures, text messages and video.[3] This is an important factor considering that the majority of callers use wireless technology like cell phones.

The goal of the Next Generation 911 system is to standardize the nation's 911 systems and create centralized databases that interconnect with public safety agencies.[4] The main benefits of the Next Generation 911 system are:

- Dispatch operators can receive information from a variety of sources including text messages, images and video data.
- Callers can contact dispatch via 911 from just about any networked device.
- Public safety answering points (PSAPs) can easily transfer emergency calls to other agencies.[5]

### Nationwide Public Safety Broadband Network

For many years, public safety agencies have been working with state and federal agencies to secure a nationwide interoperable network. In 2012, President Obama signed H.R. 3630 into law. Part of this law includes funding and authority to implement a nationwide public safety broadband network. The network will provide much needed interoperability for public safety personnel during an emergency situation like a terrorist act or natural disaster. Broadband technology allows agencies to access video images and communicate at high-speeds. This legislation secured a part of the radio spectrum called *D Block*, which can be only used for public safety first responders. The *D Block* is a 10 megahertz section of the radio spectrum, which will be added to the existing 10 megahertz section that is already established for public safety agencies. That gives public safety agencies a total of 20 megahertz of dedicated network infrastructure.[6]

### Cloaking Technology

Imagine a time when law enforcement officers could essentially walk up to a suspect selling narcotics and not be discovered. Taking a cue from the military, law enforcement personnel are evaluating the possibility of using cloaking technology. *Cloaking* is defined as "the selective bending of electromagnetic waves, microwaves in this case, around an object to make it seem invisible."[7] Officers could use cloaking technology for undercover operations or other high-risk situations. Cloaking technology can also be used to hide equipment like patrol cars and airplanes.

### Augmented Reality Implementation

An emerging piece of technology that could change the criminal justice system is called *augmented reality*. This technology provides real-time examination of enhanced real-world physical environment using computer-generated virtual information. Augmented reality uses interactive computer-based technology that overlays virtual images into real-world experiences.[8]

An example of this technology is the virtual overlays on headgear that relay information to the user. The news media uses one of the oldest forms of augmented reality technology during the weather report. Newscasters superimpose images, video and animations onto a blank green or blue map. This allows the user to show more dynamic real-time information. The user can also incorporate gestures or smart devices into the presentation.[9]

Augmented reality could be used in a number of public safety applications including patrol, corrections, courts and fire services. It could also be used in training programs, patrol operations or even high-risk situations. Another interesting use of this technology would be in a courtroom setting. It could project the images and audio of people who are not present in the courtroom.[10] People could testify from other locations using a holographic real-time representation of their virtual presence. Obviously, this technology would be controversial and needs to be vetted by the criminal justice system. Augmented reality would challenge the meaning of being "physically present" in court. Because defendants have the right to see their accusers in person, this technology would need to be evaluated and will most likely be litigated in the judicial system.

## Real-Time Crime Centers

Many law enforcement agencies have implemented real-time crime centers as an extension of a typical intelligence unit. These facilities combine specific data to help law enforcement personnel solve crime and protect officers in the field. Important data like booking information, photograph, and warrant information can be generated quickly and shared with personnel and other agencies.[11] During major incidents, law enforcement agencies can use real-time crime centers to examine and track social media sites for information that could be helpful to officers in the field. This can help protect officers and assist in criminal investigations. The real-time crime centers also use satellite imaging and mapping technology to provide a real-time assessment of resources throughout the city, county or state jurisdiction.[12]

## Cybercrime

One of the most difficult crimes to investigate is cybercrime. Although cybercrime is not necessarily a technology tool used by law enforcement, the crimes themselves are deeply rooted in technology. Law enforcement's ability to investigate cybercrime is significantly hampered by jurisdictional issues, lack of Internet investigative skills by officers and the fact that many prosecutors have difficulty prosecuting cases because the parties involved may not live in their respective jurisdictions. The Police Executive Research Forum conducted a study on cybercrime and identified several specific points to consider when dealing with this type of crime.[13] They include:

- This type of crime is underreported by the public.
- The total losses from cybercrime exceeded the total losses from bank robberies in 2011.
- Cybercrime uses technology to trick victims into revealing their password or other identifying information. Because many members of the community are not well versed in technology, the criminals have found ways to obtain bank information and, thus, steal from innocent people.

- Some law enforcement agencies have been slow to address cybercrime.
- Law enforcement agencies should help victims with cybercrime issues and ensure the crimes are reported to the Internet Crime Complaint Center.
- Police officers should at least have a basic understanding of cybercrime investigative techniques.
- Finding officers that have the ability and desire to work cybercrime investigations has been challenging. The private sector often attracts the most skilled employees that have the needed cybercrime expertise because they can afford to pay them more money. Law enforcement officials should know that there are specialized training programs available from various state and federal agencies (FBI, Secret Service, etc.).
- Law enforcement officials are encouraged to partner or regionalize with other agencies.[14]

## Geographic Information System

"A geographic information system (GIS) combines layers of information about a place to give you a better understanding of the place."[15] GIS gives public safety personnel the ability to assess environmental damage and detect crime patterns. It also provides emergency management personnel valuable information like parcel locations, transportation infrastructure, location of any critical areas like hazardous materials or vulnerable areas and other data that is necessary in the protection of a city, county or state.[16] GIS has several specific benefits including:

- Reduction in loss of life because GIS can help management personnel plan and understand where emergency events could occur.
- Public safety personnel can receive the best available information when responding to dangerous situations. This helps personnel make appropriate decisions under difficult and stressful situations.
- Helps cities or counties recover from emergencies quickly.[17]

For example, fire departments can use geographic information systems to obtain fire hazard areas, size of a wildfire, elevation of terrain and locations of any natural resource that must be protected. Fire managers can use this information when planning and deploying resources to a large scale event like a wildfire.[18]

## Mobile Technology Trends

Mobile technology continues to evolve and is a cornerstone in public safety, specifically law enforcement. Let's review a few of the latest trends in mobile technology in law enforcement.

### Hyper-Networked Patrol Cars and Personnel

Mobile technology has certainly changed over the last few years. Traditional law enforcement protocols required patrol officers to request information from dispatchers over the radio. Future patrol personnel will use their patrol car as a "single access point" for device connectivity and to access information without the need for using dispatch. The use of hot spots will allow officers to connect to a variety of communication platforms. The patrol car will become their office and make law enforcement more efficient.[19]

## Adaptive Computing Devices

Another growing trend is allowing officers to use a single portable device for computing. The device can consolidate several communication platforms that can be carried and used in the field, station or other locations.[20] This concept gives the officer the ability to have law enforcement applications like booking information, record checks, photographs and police reports all in one device, which makes their job more efficient.

## Body-Worn Wearable Technology Devices

The private sector has already experimented with wearable technology like Google Glass and equipment that assesses environmental sensory information. Public safety can expand on this technology by using heads-up display units that provide officers with an added sense of situational awareness.[21] Think about the movies *Robocop* or *Iron Man*. Cognitive data and other information can be displayed to public safety personnel via the heads-up display unit. The wearable technology could constantly assess the immediate areas surrounding public safety personnel and provide information like traffic conditions, potential threats from suspects and hazardous situations. Fire personnel could use this technology to receive critical information like floor plans, fire exits and other environmental factors when fighting a fire.

## Predictive User Experiences and Eye-Tracking

This technology examines your user preferences and experiences to predict what information you will likely use in the future. Eye-tracking monitors your eye movements to determine user input. The combination of these technologies could have a place in public safety. For example, this technology could dispatch an officer to a call for service based on reading your text messages, emails or calendar. Predictive user technology would scan your calendar and learn that you are planning to eat lunch with another officer at a specific time and location. The technology would alert dispatch of your future plans and they could dispatch you a call near that location. The eye-tracking technology would monitor your eyes and know when you have read messages from dispatch. This technology could make law enforcement more efficient.[22]

## Listening and Awareness Technology

There is technology available that can monitor social media conversations. It can also determine the location of people using social media. This technology could be combined with another technology called sentiment analysis. The combined technology will allow public safety personnel to learn and assess an individual's emotions or reactions to the material posted online. The private sector already uses this technology to understand the habits of their customers. If public safety agencies used this information, they would have a better understanding of their communities.[23]

## Community Policing and Technology

As a public safety manager, you must work with city or county elected officials and department heads to ensure the overall vision, mission and goals are achieved. The public and other non-public safety city/county employees are just as dedicated and want the best for their respective jurisdictions. They want to see their city/county evolve and use innovative technology to address quality of life issues outside of the normal police or fire realm.

If a public safety agency wants to install a citywide video surveillance system, it makes sense to include city or county personnel in the project. Maybe they were already planning on increasing the communication infrastructure for the city or county. Regardless, effective public safety managers should take every opportunity to work with city or county personnel when implementing technology. This ensures consistency, saves time and makes the city or county more efficient. It is also an important step in community policing. There are a few strategies that can help public safety managers in this area. They include:

- Conduct an operational assessment of the city or county. Identify how the city or county operates. Examine any strengths or weaknesses. This will be helpful when addressing any technology needs for the city or county.
- Assess the technology used in the city or county. Evaluate existing systems that may have an effect on public safety. This includes traffic controls, safety equipment, communication portals, etc.
- Determine the capacity for city or county operations including public safety (Fire, EMS and law enforcement). Identify areas that have excess capacity and can be shared with other communities or public safety agencies. If the city or county is lacking in capacity, identify what is needed to address the issue.
- Use technology to your advantage. Leverage all data available and incorporate technology into all activities within the city or county.
- Help city or county officials implement preventive programs that address all issues within the community. Educational training on fire and crime prevention is essential.
- Partner with other agencies whenever possible. Regionalization is the future because smaller agencies simply cannot afford to go it alone. Technology projects are a great opportunity to regionalize and share the cost with other cities or counties.[24]

## Recommendations

In December 2014, President Obama signed an Executive Order that established the President's Task Force on Twenty-First Century Policing. The purpose of the task force was to examine and provide recommendations to the President on how law enforcement can work with the community to strengthen public trust, foster strong relationships and reduce crime.[25]

In May 2015, the final report was released to the public. It contains six pillars that address the aforementioned areas of concern. One of the pillars discussed technology and illustrated how technology plays an important part in any law enforcement strategic plan for the future. The final report provides law enforcement managers with several action items and recommendations specific to technology.[26] They are listed below:

### Recommendation #1

The U.S. Department of Justice and the National Institute of Justice should work with law enforcement to establish national standards for the research and development of technology. Compatibility and interoperability are a necessity.

Action items for this recommendation include the following:

- The federal government needs to develop and deliver training that helps law enforcement personnel learn, acquire and implement technology.
- The national standards should address the privacy concerns in accordance with the Constitution.
- Law enforcement should use smart technology that prevents the tampering or manipulation of evidence.[27]

### Recommendation #2

The implementation of law enforcement technology should consider local needs and national standards.

Action items for this recommendation include the following:

- Law enforcement should work with and collaborate with the community when developing new policies that deal with technology.
- Law enforcement should utilize an assessment tool that gauges the effectiveness of new technology. It should include input from all stakeholders.
- Law enforcement should use new technology to better serve people with special needs or disabilities.[28]

### Recommendation #3

The U.S. Department of Justice should develop best practices that deal with the acquisition, use, retention, and dissemination of auditory, visual and biometric data used by law enforcement.

Action items for this recommendation include the following:

- The U.S. Department of Justice and law enforcement agencies should consult with various civil rights groups concerning any constitutional issues that could become an issue with new technology.

- The U.S. Department of Justice should create the appropriate toolkit that will provide law enforcement agencies with a one-stop clearinghouse for information and resources.
- Law enforcement should review and consider the Bureau of Justice Assistance's body-worn camera toolkit when implementing body-worn cameras.[29]

## Recommendation #4

Federal, state, local and tribal legislative bodies should be encouraged to update public record laws.[30]

## Recommendation #5

Law enforcement agencies should create and use model policies for technology-based community engagement that increases trust and access.[31]

## Recommendation #6

The federal government should support the development of less-lethal technology.
    Action items for this recommendation include the following:
    Relevant agencies should study the development and use of less-lethal technology and its impact on the community.[32]

## Recommendation #7

The federal government should help develop and build a segregated radio spectrum and increase the bandwidth used by public safety agencies.[33]

## Chapter Summary

This chapter highlighted the importance of planning for the future. Technology will always continue to evolve and public safety agencies must continue to research and evaluate new technology. This will ensure that public safety agencies are efficient, well protected and have the necessary tools to get the job done. Public safety managers are encouraged to work with others and share resources, ideas and concepts. The recommendations by President Obama's Twenty-First Century Policing task force should not be taken lightly. They emphasize the future of public safety, specifically law enforcement. This information should be shared throughout your agency, city/county and to the public. Finally, it should be very obvious that many of the technologies discussed in this chapter and the rest of the textbook did not happen overnight. Somebody had to visualize the concept or identify the need for advanced technology in public safety. That is where you come in. It doesn't matter if you are a public safety manager, supervisor, line staff or even a criminal justice student. It is up to you to seek out technology and find a way to incorporate it into public safety. Leadership is about risk-taking and making change when appropriate. So what are you waiting for?
    Never forget to take care of each other, and be safe!

## Key Words or Terminology

cloaking

Next Generation 911

cybercrime

augmented reality

broadband

future technology

real-time crime centers

## Discussion Questions

1. Identify at least two types of technology that you believe will continue to grow in the next ten years. Explain how and in what context.
2. Research other futuristic public safety technology not identified in this chapter. List examples and explain how they help or hurt public safety.
3. How does leadership play a role in the exploration of technology in public safety? What is your role?

## Notes

1 Holt, T. (2013). *Technology and the criminal justice system*. Retrieved from www.oxfordbibliographies. com/view/document/obo-9780195396607/obo-9780195396607-0173.xml.

2 (2014). *Future trends in policing*. Police Executive Research Forum. Washington, DC: Office of Community Oriented Policing Services.

3 (2015). *Next Generation 911: Research overview*. Washington, DC: U.S. Department of Transportation, Research and Innovative Technology Administration.

4 Ibid.

5 Police Executive Research Forum, *Future trends in policing*.

6 (2012). *Nationwide public safety broadband network*. U.S. Department of Homeland Security. Washington, DC: U.S. Department of Homeland Security, Office of Emergency Communications.

7 Brown, K. (2012). *Fiction to fact. How science fiction inspires future scientists to push boundaries of the known, into the unknown*. Retrieved from www.prezi.com/f3vg9m1k250b/fiction-to-fact/.

8 Furht, B. (2011). *Handbook of augmented reality*. New York: Springer-Verlag.

9 Lawler, S. (2010). CNN uses augmented reality, iPads to cover midterm election results. *EnGadget. com*. Retrieved from www.engadget.com/2010/11/02/cnn-uses-augmented-reality-ipads-to-cover-midterm-election-resu/.

10 Lederer, D. (2005). Technology-augmented courtrooms: Progress amid few complications or the problematic interrelationship between court and counsel. *William and Mary Law School Facility Publications*, no. 56. Retrieved from www.scholarship.law.wm.edu/facpubs/56.

11 Newcombe, T. (2014). *Forecasting the future for technology and policing*. Retrieved from www.govtech. com/public-safety/forecasting-the-future-for-technology-and-policing.html.

12 Police Executive Research Forum, *Future trends in policing*.

13 Ibid.

14 Ibid.

15 *Mapping the future of public safety*, n.d. ESRI GIS Software. Retrieved from www.esri.com/library/ brochures/pdfs/public-safety.pdf.

16 Ibid.

17 Ibid.

18 Ibid.

19 Haisler, D. (2014). Top 10 mobile trends for law enforcement. *Government Technology*. Retrieved from www.govtech.com/public-safety/GT-Top-10-Mobile-Trends-for-Law-Enforcement.html.

20 Ibid.

21 Ibid.

22 Ibid.

23  Ibid.

24  Nevins, E. (2015). Public safety and the city of the future. *Management Issues.* Retrieved from www.management-issues.com/opinion/7033/public-safety-and-the-city-of-the-future/.

25  (2014). *Executive order—Establishment of the President's Task Force on Twenty-First Century Policing.* The White House, Office of the Press Secretary. Retrieved from www.whitehouse.gov/the-press-office-2014/12/18/executive-order-establishment-pr.

26  (2015). *Final report of the President's Task Force on Twenty-First Century Policing.* President's Task Force on 21st Century Policing. Washington, DC: Office of Community Oriented Policing Services.

27  Ibid.

28  Ibid.

29  Ibid.

30  Ibid.

31  Ibid.

32  Ibid.

33  Ibid.

# 20

# CASE STUDIES OF PUBLIC SAFETY TECHNOLOGY

"At every crossing on the road, each progressive spirit is opposed by a thousand appointed to guard the gates of the past."

—*Maurice Maeterlinck*

## Learning Objectives

After reading this chapter, the student will:

*   Compare and contrast the various uses of technology in public safety.
*   Evaluate the future of technology and how it can help or hurt public safety.
*   Illustrate the importance of innovative technology and how public safety managers must continue to evaluate technology that can help improve efficiency, promote community policing and improve the safety of all public safety stakeholders.

## Introduction

In this chapter, we review an assortment of research papers prepared by public safety managers and experts in the field. The papers highlight the importance of being a "futuristic" thinker and finding ways to improve public safety operations. They consolidate trends, data and evaluate the possibilities of technology in the future. The research topics in this chapter include mobile biometric identification technology, innovative booking procedures, technology designed to monitor stress and physiological systems of police officers, videoconference police reporting systems and police pursuit technology.

## The Future of Technology

The following research papers were written by graduates of the California Commission on Peace Officer Standards and Training (POST) Command College Program. POST sets the minimum standards for all peace officers in the state of California. Command College is an 18-month program designed to prepare law enforcement leaders of today for the challenges of the future. Each graduate prepares a "futures study project" on a specific emerging issue related to public safety. The research papers in this chapter focus on possible scenarios that would be helpful in strategic policing for public safety organizations. However, they do not attempt to predict the future.[1] "The views and conclusions expressed in the Command College Futures Project and journal article are those of the author, and are not necessarily those of the CA Commission on Peace Officer Standards and Training (POST)."[2]

Public safety personnel and students are encouraged to visit the POST Command College website. The website has an online library that contains numerous academic research papers prepared by leaders in law enforcement. For additional information, visit www.post.ca.gov/command-college.aspx.[3]

---

### Case Study 1
### Listen to Your Body

*By Neil Gallucci, Carlsbad Police Department*

The police recruit arrives early for the first day of academy training. He is proud to have successfully made it through the arduous hiring process, but nervous about academy training. His heart is pumping as uniformed training officers arrive and begin to yell at the recruits. The adrenalin dump occurs as a uniformed training officer turns his attention towards the recruit. The yelling increases and the recruit cannot understand why his heart is pumping so hard. He seems to have developed tunnel vision and clumsily follows orders, but cannot seem to perform at optimum ability.

All law enforcement officers have witnessed this scene and understand the rationale behind sensory overload techniques. If you cannot learn to perform in the controlled environment, success on the streets is doubtful. Law enforcement training concentrates on developing skills, which can be performed under pressure. After all, performing learned skills during times of stress can be the difference between life and death for law enforcement officers. But, can the human body be better prepared to perform motor skills? This article will discuss the benefits of including biofeedback in law enforcement tactical training.

The goal of training is to instruct or condition the learner to some manner of behavior or performance; to make proficient through special instruction or drill (Webster's Dictionary, 1996). Law enforcement training paradigm mirrors this definition. Law enforcement officers are put through special instruction and vocation specific drills from day one of a police academy. Officers continue training for perishable and tactical skills throughout their careers. These repetitive training sessions, which often lack feedback, become an exercise in updating personnel files, rather than preparing officers for optimum performance. Many occupations require initial training to obtain needed knowledge and skills. Continued professional education is also common in many occupations such as cosmetology and practicing attorneys. However, there are very few professions that regularly expose people to dangerous situations, which trigger the 'fight or flight' response from the autonomic nervous system (specifically the sympathetic nervous system).

Unlike a stressful courtroom encounter for a lawyer, the officer on the street has to act immediately to mitigate life or death situations. Teaching or training the human body to recognize sympathetic nervous system stress responses and effectively function during these responses could increase law enforcement and civilian survivability during tactical law enforcement operations. Like it or not, law enforcement officers are required to make life and death decisions; cognitive awareness of nervous system response and meaningful preparation are the key to favorable outcomes. Hesitation or lack of preparation is catastrophic, 'The god of war hates those who hesitate' (Euripides: Heraclidae, 425 B.C.).

## Background: Nervous System Responses

The human nervous system is a myriad of cells that send electrochemical signals, which coordinate the body's response to stimulus (Andreassi, 2000). Nervous system responses are both voluntary and involuntary; controlling everything from movement to digestion. Training for law enforcement primarily deals with controlling voluntary human response. It is what can be seen and therefore trained to a level of competency. But, what can't be seen are the involuntary nervous system responses. The irony is that the unseen or involuntary responses have a large impact on the voluntary or visible responses to stimulus. Including training on how to effectively deal with involuntary response could greatly increase the seen or voluntary response. This thesis has been tested effectively in elite athletes competing on a global level in the Olympic Games. In fact, Olympic athletes have attributed their success to understanding and training their involuntary nervous system response (Harkness, 2009).

Humans have nervous systems that are wired for extreme responses to perceived threats. If a threat is perceived hormones are released which increase blood flow, heart rate, and respiration. These sympathetic nervous system responses are automatic; in other words the physiological effects will occur (Gorman, 2005). Because stress response (fight or flight) is a known human reaction to threats, law enforcement should include stress response regulation in tactical training. This training should take into account that not all stress is bad; controlled stress response can increase performance. According to public safety wellness instructor Kathleen Vonk, controlled stress response is a human survival mechanism. She writes that "In one of the most comprehensive definitions, McGrath (1970) defines stress as the interaction between three elements: perceived demand, perceived ability to cope, and the perception of the importance of being able to cope with the demand. This definition encompasses not only an officer's own skill and confidence to the task at hand, but also the relative importance of handling the challenge successfully" (Vonk, 2009, p. 86).

*(Continued)*

## Tactical Training: Individual Officer Stress Response

One of the primary goals of tactical law enforcement training is to establish instinctive responses to stimulus (for the purposes of this article the term 'tactical' is used to discuss the problems and issues encountered in the approach to or actual combat; Webster's Dictionary, 2013). These responses include muscle memory (drawing a firearm) and preconditioned cognitive responses (utilizing cover if fired upon). The problem with these preconditioned responses is that current training paradigm does not consider individual stress responses. The law enforcement profession is made up of individual humans. We all have sympathetic nervous systems, which will respond to threats (meeting a bear on a trail while hiking). But, not every officer's reaction will be the same to threatening stimulus in tactical field situations. Human variables such as job tenure, rate of exposure, and personal history are factors (Vonk, 2008).

Sports psychologist Penny Werthner used biofeedback to train the 2010 Canadian Olympic ski team. The biofeedback training taught the athletes to understand how their bodies reacted to stress and how to effectively regulate the stress response, managing Olympic level stress to obtain optimum performance was the goal (Starkman, 2009). Olympic athlete Abinav Bindra used biofeedback to train for his gold medal victory in shooting. He felt understanding his body's stress response and how to regulate the response would be critical to his performance. Abinav's trainer, Sports Psychologist Timothy Harkness, came to the conclusion that biofeedback training taught the athlete to prepare for the application of the skill, not to execute the skill (2009).

Understanding the human stress response and the ability to cope with stress is only partially considered in modern law enforcement tactical training. Reality-based training is conducted to prepare officers for tactical encounters; however current paradigm relies heavily on habituation. In other words, repeated exposure to stimulus to reduce stress reaction and elicit a desired outcome. This scenario-based training is extremely useful because it includes psychomotor coordination, the need for intuitive decision making, and can reinforce a survival mindset (Lynch, 2005). But, what's missing from current training paradigm is the fact that law enforcement officers are all individual humans, with individual abilities to learn and tolerate stress. This is why biofeedback can greatly enhance current tactical training paradigm.

## Biofeedback Training: Adding to the Officer's Skill Set

Training should teach officers how to think and react under pressure. Understanding how the body reacts to stress stimulus and the ability to learn from mistakes to improve performance is essential.

Is it possible to inoculate law enforcement officers from the human stress response? Because *Robocop* is still in the future, the law enforcement profession would be well served to prepare officers to understand and regulate stress response, through biofeedback training.

In a study at California State University Long Beach, researchers defined *biofeedback training* as a "method of helping individuals learn how to control various physiological processes such as muscle tension, blood pressure, breathing, heart rate, brain wave states, skin temperature, and skin conductance" through the use of non-invasive bio-feedback sensors to measure the psycho-physiological process of the individual and provide immediate feedback to him or her. Through biofeedback training, an individual first "gains awareness of the physiological processes occurring within the body and learns to consciously control those processes. Specifically, the individual is trained to modulate the symptoms of stress and anxiety which lead to better functioning for the individual" (Ratanasiripong, Paul, Sverduk, Kevin, Hayasino, Diane & Prince, Judy, 2010, p. 97).

Biofeedback devices are now portable, inexpensive, and the user can be self-taught via device software. It is being used to teach college students to cope with stress, which results in increased student performance. "The current generation of college students enjoys technology and the portable unit fits right into their tech-savvy nature" (Ratana-siripong et al., 2010). As the viability of using biofeedback grows, it is inevitable that law enforcement will study the possibilities to use it for the police.

Biofeedback technology could soon be a part of a law enforcement officer's everyday technology arsenal. The advent of smart wearable systems, such as smart fabrics, will wirelessly connect each officer's biofeedback to a monitoring station (perhaps central dispatch). In a 2012 article discussing advances in smart wearable technology, the authors noted "These systems are able to measure vital signs, such as body and skin temperature, heart rate, arterial blood pressure, blood oxygen saturation, electrocardiograms (ECG), electroencephalograms (EEG), and respiration rate" (Chan, Marie, Esteve, Daniel, Fourniols, Jean-Yves, Escriba, Christophe, & Campo, Eric, 2012, p. 137). The trained para-sympathetic response to stress may even be electronically initiated because of signals received via an officer's "smart wearable system." Abnormal or elevated biofeedback markers during a tactical law enforcement operation could trigger a calming voice instructing the officer to initiate a stress-reducing tactic (Vonk, 2008).

## Smart Wearable Systems: A New Police Officer Uniform Device

In the past decade, wearable technology and integrated systems, so called Smart Wearable Systems (SWS), have demonstrated significant advances in terms of miniaturization, seamless integration, data processing and communication, functionalization and comfort. This is mainly due to the huge progress in sciences and technologies e.g. biomedical and micro and nano technologies, but also to a strong demand for new applications such as continuous personal health monitoring, healthy lifestyle support, human performance monitoring and support of professionals at risk. Development of wearable systems based on smart textiles have, in addition, benefited from the eagerness of the textile industry to develop new value-added apparel products like functionalized garments and smart clothing. Research and development in these areas has been strongly promoted world-wide (European Commission, 2011).

Georgia Tech has developed a "smart shirt" to be worn by combat soldiers. The application of this biofeedback technology could transfer directly to law enforcement

(*Continued*)

applications. Georgia Tech's research is intended to design and develop a "wearable motherboard" for combat casualty care. This "Smart Shirt" has literally created the world's first "intelligent" garment for the twenty-first century. The Georgia Tech Wearable Motherboard uses optical fibers to detect bullet wounds; special sensors also interconnect with the fibers to monitor the body's vital signs during combat conditions. The Smart Shirt provides a versatile framework to incorporate sensing, monitoring and information processing devices. The principal advantage of the Smart Shirt is that it provides, for the first time, a very systematic way of monitoring the vital signs of humans in an *unobtrusive* manner. Smart Shirt is lightweight and can be worn easily by anyone—from infants to senior citizens. It has enormous potential for applications in fields such as telemedicine, monitoring of patients in post-operative recovery, the prevention of SIDS (sudden infant death syndrome), and monitoring of astronauts, athletes, law enforcement personnel and combat soldiers (Georgia Tech, 2014). It is also a suitable platform from which biofeedback data can be monitored and used for the wearer's benefit.

The integration of smart wearable systems into apparel enables law enforcement training to be customized for individuals and improve team dynamics. Biofeedback can be collected and used to customize training from the beginning to the end of a law enforcement officer's career. Trainers can identify stressors for individual officers and address performance issues. As officers progress through their career, biofeedback will enable training to be customized and agencies will have better trained and more resilient officers. The Smart Shirt is just one option to help enhance the health and mitigate the adverse impact of stress. Undoubtedly, there will be other means to accomplish this goal as competing technologies mature.

## Officer Resiliency: Health Monitoring Throughout Career

Training law enforcement officers to regulate stress response should begin day one of the academy. Academic understanding, biofeedback training via gaming or virtual reality, and mapping officers' biofeedback responses to scenario-based training are all viable training strategies. If these training strategies were included in academy curriculum, officers who struggle with stress response and the ability to respond to stimuli could be identified for additional or customized training.

The continued professional training officers receive throughout their career could become meaningful for each individual officer and successful outcomes during tactical law enforcement operations could increase. The potential to reduce post-traumatic stress disorder (PTSD) is also increased because officers understand their sympathetic responses to stimuli and with training can counteract with a parasympathetic response such as slow abdominal breathing (Spira et al., 2006). If officers are exposed to scenario-based training, which triggers sympathetic response and their biofeedback is mapped, they can be taught coping mechanisms. In a study on treatment of PTSD Spira et al. concluded that biofeedback is a useful tool in self-regulation of stress response (2006).

Recent studies have used reality-based training combined with heart rate biofeedback devices to monitor law enforcement officer stress reaction. The military has studied the effects of biofeedback training to alleviate PTSD and increase tactical performance on the battlefield. Training paradigm acknowledges that feedback is essential for learning and improved performance. Law enforcement training currently uses feedback devices such as lasers, which can measure marksmanship accuracy in scenario based training (Placek, 2011), but has not progressed to utilizing biofeedback mapping to obtain optimum performance for individual officers. With the advent of smart wearable systems that wirelessly monitor biofeedback, officers can be trained to regulate their stress response. This should provide an increase in officer performance in tactical law enforcement operations and also significantly contribute to the officer's overall wellness.

The better prepared officer is also an officer who will be more resilient throughout their career. Teaching people about the stress response and its effects on the body helps normalize the sympathetic nervous system response all humans feel when faced with stress. This is often referred to as the 'fight or flight' response. The traditional or cultural way of dealing with these hormone dumps has been to pretend that nervous system response is not occurring. After all, 'cops' are not subject to normal human responses. The problem with this fallacy is that officers pretending they are not human takes a serious toll on long-term health. Officers who do not understand normal responses or why they may feel a certain way tend to develop unhealthy coping mechanisms, such as abusing alcohol, caffeine, or food. Long-term use of biofeedback will enable officers to constantly monitor their health and adjust lifestyle as necessary.

Wellness programs are now institutionalized in many law enforcement agencies because of the recognition that healthy employees perform better, file fewer worker compensation claims, and are able to work effectively as they age. The ability to identify individual stressors via biofeedback data and customize training for the individual could produce added savings due to the increased retention rates of new officers. Biofeedback will also produce officers better prepared to function at optimum levels under stress based on individualized training plans.

## Budgets: The Cost of Not Utilizing Biofeedback

Law enforcement is a service provided by governments. Governments at their essence provide services to the countries, states, counties, and cities they serve. Governments are the business of the people and successful businesses should constantly be looking to improve service models. In this vein, the use of biofeedback data has the potential to produce monetary savings in law enforcement. From recruitment to retirement, law enforcement officers are expensive. In California the cost to produce a qualified law enforcement officer from recruitment to independently functioning officer is well over $100,000; "by some estimates, it costs as much as $170,000 to recruit, run background checks, hire, teach and field train each officer" (Salonga, 2013).

*(Continued)*

The introduction of biofeedback to customize law enforcement tactical training has the potential to reduce trainee failure rate. To date, law enforcement training has been 'cookie cutter.' This is not to say that advancements in equipment and practice have not improved skill and readiness. Law enforcement officers in California are better equipped and trained now than any time in history. However, training advancements are still one size fits all. Recruits going through tactical scenarios are exposed to similar stimulus and they either perform adequately or are dismissed. After failure has occurred, all monies spent to recruit and train the officer are wasted. With the extension of the years necessary to complete a full career, it is even more important that we select and train those who will be well-suited to the task.

The issue of employee resiliency in law enforcement cannot be overstated. In California the minimum retirement age for law enforcement officers has risen to fifty-seven; California law has established eighteen as the minimum age for law enforcement officers. If an individual is employed from 18 to 57 the working career spans thirty-nine years. A long employment career and an older work force demand that employee resiliency be a major priority for law enforcement. Biofeedback information will be integrated into employee wellness programs for early intervention in medical issues and to reduce injuries sustained by working officers.

## What's Next?

Twenty-first-century technology has provided a window to the inner workings of the human body. The information gathered through this window is biofeedback. Law enforcement organizations have the opportunity to use biofeedback to better prepare officers for the beginning to the end of their careers. The following recommendations are intended as a starting point for biofeedback in law enforcement.

1   The instruction and normalization of human stress response during academy training - This will result in a cultural shift away from the "superman" complex and unhealthy coping mechanisms. The proliferation of employee wellness programs has acknowledged the need for resilient healthy officers, but wellness programs face an uphill battle because of cultural norms that start in the academy. This should not be considered a call to abandon the traditional paradigm. Incorporating teaching about stress response and how to effectively deal with the inevitable hormone dump should complement current training paradigm. Knowledge is power; providing officers with data regarding their individual biofeedback will enable customized training plans for success.

2   Continuous monitoring of biofeedback throughout officers' career to facilitate employee wellness - Biofeedback data certainly has potential to complement tactical training; however, employee wellness calls for utilization of biofeedback data. The costs of training an officer and the prevalence of workplace injuries calls for increasing employee resilience. It is often too late to save an officer when a stroke or cardiac event takes place. The goal of long-term monitoring is to increase early intervention in health issues and overcome a cultural 'tuff man' syndrome. Data doesn't lie, and it also removes the stigma of seeking help to deal with health issues.

3    The utilization of biofeedback data to customize tactical training and real time monitoring of officer field performance - Officers have different triggers for their stress response. The ability to identify individual triggers and develop training plans to effectively perform during stress response is invaluable. Officers will not only perform better in actual tactical incidents, they will be better prepared for any post incident stress. The key is to habituate officers to stress triggers. Skills repeatedly performed successfully during stress triggers demonstrate to the officer that their performance was optimum during actual field application, which in turn reduces second guessing of performance and makes incident outcomes easier to accept.

This article is a call to law enforcement trainers and administrators. The bodies that make up law enforcement organizations are talking. The question is, are we listening? If so, is the information provided being used to increase organizational performance and employee wellness?

## References

Andreassi, J. L. (2000). *Psychophysiology: Human Behavior and Physiological Response* (4th ed.). Mahwah, NJ: Lawrence Erlbaum Associates. Retrieved from www.questia.com.

Chan, M., Esteve, D., Fourniols, J., Escriba, C. & Campo, E. (2012). Smart Wearable Systems: Current Status and Future Challenges. *Artificial Intelligence in Medicine, 56 (2012),* 137–156. Retrieved from www.elsevier.com.

Gorman, G. (2005, Spring). Fight, Flight, or Phantom Fatigue? *Nutrition Health Review,* (91), 2+. Retrieved from www.questia.com.

Harkness, T. (2009). Psykinetics and Biofeedback: Abhinav Bindra Wins India's First-Ever Individual Gold Medal in Beijing Olympics. *Biofeedback: 37*(2), 48–52.

Lynch, M. D. (2005, October). Developing a Scenario-Based Training Program: Giving Officers a Tactical Advantage. *The FBI Law Enforcement Bulletin, 74*(10), 1+. Retrieved from www.questia.com.

Placek, C. (2011, August 18). COD Opens '4-D' Police Officer Training Facility. *Daily Herald (Arlington Heights, IL),* p. 4. Retrieved from www.questia.com.

Ratanasiripong, P., Sverduk, K., Hayashino, D., & Prince, J. (2010). Setting Up the Next Generation Biofeedback Program for Stress and Anxiety Management for College Students: A Simple and Cost-Effective Approach. *College Student Journal, 44*(1), 97+. Retrieved from www.questia.com.

Salonga, R. (2013). San Jose Council Proposals Aim to Recover Training Costs From Departing Rookie Cops. *Mercury News* (San Jose, CA.). Retrieved from www.MercuryNews.com.

Spira, J., Pyne, J., Wiederhold, B., Wiederhold, M., Graap, K. & Rizzo, A., (2006). Virtual Reality and Other Experiential Therapies for Combat-Related Posttraumatic Stress Disorder. *Primary Psychiatry: 13*(3), 58–64.

Starkman, R. (2009, October 8). Athletes Wired for Success. *The Toronto Star.*

Vonk, K. (2008, October). Police Performance under Stress. *Law & Order, 56*(10), 86+. Retrieved from www.questia.com.

## Case Study 2
## The Future of Corrections

### How Can Mobile Biometric Technology Revolutionize the Arrest and Booking Process?

*By Jeffrey A. Rose*

The following account is true; only the names were changed to protect the identities of those involved. It was just another day for Deputy Johnson. He was patrolling a high crime area when he noticed a vehicle driving fast through an apartment complex known for drug activity. Deputy Johnson decides to conduct a traffic stop on the vehicle. He approached the driver and immediately senses that something is wrong. The driver is very nervous and is looking around as if he intends to flee from the vehicle. Deputy Johnson asks the driver for his identification. As expected, the driver tells Deputy Johnson that he does not have any identification, but that his name is Clarence Roberson. Johnson suspects that the driver may be lying because he is evasive, nervous and sweating. Something is wrong!

Deputy Johnson believes that the driver must have a warrant or is in possession of narcotics. He decides to run a warrant check on the subject, but no record is found. Deputy Johnson knows something is wrong. He can feel it, but how can he prove it?

Then he remembered about a new piece of technology called Mobile Identification. His station received two Mobile Identification Devices to test in the field. Deputy Johnson contacts his partner, Deputy Smith, who has one of the identification devices with him. Deputy Smith arrives at the location and explains to the subject that because he has no form of identification, he is going to capture a thumbprint on the mobile identification device to see if he is in the system. Roberson places his thumb on the mobile identification device and hears a *beep*, which means the fingerprint was accepted.

Less than one minute later, Deputy Smith gets a response on the mobile identification device. The driver was in fact lying about his name. He has three no bail warrants from a large agency in southern California. He is also considered "armed and dangerous" for attempted murder on a police officer. Deputies Johnson and Smith immediately take the subject into custody without incident. Ironically, the driver later tells Deputy Johnson that he has been stopped on four prior occasions and released with a citation or a warning, avoiding arrest by lying to each police officer. That is until technology caught up with him.

Mobile biometric technology assisted deputies in the apprehension of a dangerous criminal, but what else can this new innovative technology do to help law enforcement officers in the field or in a jail facility? Could mobile biometric technology help with prison overcrowding and efficiency or perhaps save law enforcement agencies thousands of dollars each year in false arrest lawsuits. More importantly, could mobile biometric technology help protect our law enforcement officers on the street? As you read further, law enforcement has only scratched the surface on the many uses for mobile biometric technology.

## The Benefits of New Technology

Technology in criminal justice is advancing at a tremendously rapid pace. Old technology has been integrated into advanced and evolving technology. Fingerprints are one of the oldest and most proven methods of suspect identification. In years past, officers used ink to capture fingerprints during the booking process. Currently officers use computer live scan devices to electronically capture and send the fingerprints to regional or national databases for identification. Increased computing power and carefully crafted algorithms have made it possible to automate the quick and accurate identification of various biometrics including fingerprints, iris, and face. Additionally, as technology and hardware become smaller and more portable, technology companies that specialize in biometric identification have brought a powerful breed of tools to law enforcement.

This emerging technology expands the use of mobile fingerprint devices to include facial recognition and iris identification. The new "multi-modal" technology is revolutionizing law enforcement because it can also be used in a patrol setting (Mayo, 2010). Technologies that integrate biometrics and forensic science are continuing to change how law enforcement officers do their job effectively and efficiently. Biometric identification will significantly enhance an officer's ability to positively identify a subject. This critical capacity will have a significant effect on the entire criminal justice system.

## So What Is Mobile Biometric Identification?

According to the National Law Enforcement and Corrections Technology Center (2007), the term biometrics refers to anatomical, physiological or behavioral characteristics that can be used for automated recognition. Signatures and voice fall into the behavioral category. Blood and DNA are physiological characteristics. Anatomical characteristics such as fingerprints, iris and face are the most frequently used biometrics because they can be measured quickly and easily at a reasonable cost.

Mobile identification devices utilize specialized hardware and software that integrates various biometric characteristics to identify a subject. The devices are hand-held and portable, which makes them a useful tool for law enforcement. The device is basically a smaller version of a fixed live scan fingerprint system, which is used in correctional facilities. Mobile identification devices are equipped to capture fingerprints and photographs, which are electronically sent to computer databases for comparison. The computer search takes only a few seconds and provides the officer with various demographic information about the subject, including name, date of birth, driver's license number photograph and physical description. Some devices are also configured to search county databases for outstanding warrants (NLECTC, 2007). As mobile biometrics moves from the research lab to the field, some law enforcement agencies have already tested and are now using mobile identification devices to positively identify a subject in a patrol setting.

The San Bernardino County Sheriff's Department has one of the largest deployments of mobile identification devices in the country. San Bernardino County is the largest

*(Continued)*

geographical county in the United States with approximately 20,056 square miles (U.S. Census, 2010). Due to the rural size of the county, it may take a deputy several hours to travel to a local jail to verify somebody's identity. Deputies on patrol utilize mobile identification on a regular basis, which saves thousands of dollars each year in staff and travel time alone. For example, a deputy assigned to the Barstow station recently used mobile identification technology to identify a subject traveling through the county to Las Vegas. The subject was stopped for speeding and had no driver's license or form of identification. The deputy quickly identified the subject using mobile identification and arrested him for outstanding warrants. A vehicle search was conducted and a large amount of narcotics were found. Prior to mobile identification, the deputy would have had to drive 1.5 hours to the closest jail to fingerprint and hopefully identify the subject.

Several other law enforcement agencies have already purchased mobile identification devices, including the Los Angeles County Sheriff's Department, the Riverside County Sheriff's Department and the Los Angeles Police Department. The software can be customized based on the needs of a specific agency, and the devices only cost $1,500–$3,000 each. Some departments cannot afford the cost of the devices, so they have formed regional partnerships with larger departments to save money.

## How Can Mobile Identification Help Improve the Arrest and Booking Process?

Historically law enforcement officers are trained to make an arrest and then transport the suspect to a local jail for booking. This is great in theory, but what happens when the jail is already at capacity? In 2011, California Governor Edmund Brown signed Assembly Bill (AB) 109, which reduces the amount of low-level inmates that are incarcerated into state prisons. If an inmate is convicted of a qualifying low–level offense, he/she is sent to a county jail facility for their entire term. AB109 has placed a significant burden on local jail facilities because they will now need to process and house additional inmates within their county jail facilities (CDCR, 2011).

When the jail reaches capacity, inmates are often released early. Some inmates are now being released on the same day they were booked because their booking offense was considered low level or non-violent. In California, local jails have established high bail restrictions for warrant arrests to help mitigate prison overcrowding. The use of mobile biometric technology would not only enhance an officer's ability to identify a suspect in the field, but it could also enhance the overall arrest process because the suspect is positively identified at the beginning of the entire process.

When the suspect is identified, the officer can decide if he or she needs to be transported to a jail for processing. By expanding the mobile identification platform, officers could actually arrest and properly book a suspect in a patrol setting. This would eliminate the need to transport a subject to a local jail and have a serious impact to relieve prison overcrowding.

The police arrest thousands of suspects each year for misdemeanor offenses like petty theft or vandalism. In many cases, they are never fingerprinted or photographed due to jail overcrowding; suspects are usually released from the scene with a citation. This precludes the collection of key biometric data (fingerprints and photographs) that are often used to help solve previous or future crimes.

If more law enforcement agencies started to arrest and actually book and release the subject in the field, we would have fewer inmates incarcerated in local jails and save thousands of dollars each year in staff and transportation costs. For example, the average cost of incarceration for an inmate in California is $47,102 per year or $129.00 per day. This includes housing, healthcare, food and transportation. The average daily inmate population in California is 167,276, which equates to approximately $7.9 billion annually just to take care of prisoners (CDCR, 2009). If law enforcement agencies reduced the amount of non-violent booking by 10,000, the net savings would be over two million dollars each year. Because the police arrest almost a million persons each year for misdemeanor offenses, the actual savings should be significantly higher (CJSC, 2005).

## Improving Efficiency within a Correctional Facility

The standard booking process at a local jail requires the suspect to submit his/her fingerprints. The fingerprints are captured by a computer live scan device and then electronically submitted to an Automated Fingerprint Identification System (AFIS) to positively confirm his/her identity. Some law enforcement agencies also use additional biometric or forensic measures to help identify a subject. They include facial recognition software, IRIS identification systems and DNA testing (Jones, 2006).

One of the biggest complaints from patrol officers is the amount of time it takes to book a prisoner into a local jail. Officers must wait for the booking officer to locate the suspect in a jail information management system (JIMS), verify the booking application information (name, address, etc.) and enter any new changes into the system. This process can keep an officer off the streets for hours depending on the jail. If, however, more law enforcement agencies used biometric technology, the booking process time could be significantly reduced. For example, officers using mobile identification can positively identify a suspect in the field. This will save time at the jail because the suspect has already been identified. The booking officer can quickly locate the suspect by CAL-ID number or other statewide identification number. The net result is officers can return to the field more quickly, thus spending their time where they are best used instead of waiting for administrative processes to be completed.

Fixed biometric fingerprint scanners can also be installed in the intake areas of the jail.

Incoming officers can simply have the suspect place his/her finger on the scanner for immediate identification. The suspect's prior demographic information can be electronically transmitted to the jail information management system. This saves time because the booking officer does not have to re-type the suspect's information. He or she simply adds the new charges, inventories the suspect's property and the suspect is booked.

Single finger fingerprint scanners can be installed at the infirmary, housing units and release window of a jail. The single finger scanners allow jail personnel to quick identify an inmate as they move around the facility and are eventually released from custody. This is important because inmates will often try to conceal their identity by switching

(Continued)

identification cards or wristbands in hopes of being released from custody prematurely (NIJ, 2000). Biometric scanners can also be utilized at local courts to quickly identify subjects that are in custody and out of custody. Biometric technology will allow court personnel to positively link the specific charge or conviction to a specific person. This is very important considering many suspects that appear in court are "long formed" and have never been formally booking into a local jail facility.

In January 2006, the National Institute of Justice (NIJ) conducted an inmate tracking study at the U.S. Naval Consolidated Brig in Charleston, South Carolina. NIJ focused the study on inmate movement within the Brig and wanted to quantify the significance of biometrics in jails. The study concluded that the use of biometric technology improved the overall efficiency of the brig (Miles, 2006). Beyond mere efficiency, however, biometric identification helps to prevent what can be one of the most serious issues of liability, the misidentification of individuals accused of crime.

## Civil Liability Issues

So what happens if an officer comes into contact with someone with the same name and date of birth as someone else and places the subject under arrest for an arrest warrant? Without biometric proof, the officer will never know if they have the correct subject listed on the arrest warrant. This is particularly important, because law enforcement personnel do on occasion make mistakes and arrest the wrong person, which may result in a false arrest lawsuit (Rothiein, 2009). For instance, on August 9, 2006, Heather Williams was arrested by the Vanderburg Sheriff's Department for an outstanding warrant. Williams spent the night in jail and was later released when officials realized that they had arrested the wrong person. Because the officers did not have mobile biometric technology available, they were unable to verify that they had the correct person in custody. They went ahead and arrested Williams based on her name and date of birth only. The family sued for false arrest and settled for an undisclosed amount of money (Braser, 2006).

The use of mobile biometric technology could actually reduce the amount of civil liability claims against a law enforcement agency because the amount of false arrest claims would be reduced. In years past, the courts were lenient on law enforcement agencies if they made a false arrest as long as they acted reasonably. However, with biometric technology, it is possible for magistrates to scrutinize an officer who has the ability to use new technology like mobile identification. The officer must also make sure they arrest the correct person listed on the warrant itself. In most cases, the subject has some type of identification like a driver's license or identification card. However, some subjects hide their identity or use an alias to disguise their true identity. Some individuals have the same name, date of birth or physical features. In San Bernardino County, officers are trained to use mobile identification whenever there is some discrepancy over the true identity of a suspect listed on a warrant. Other agencies like the Riverside County Sheriff's Department and the Los Angeles County Sheriff's Department also use mobile identification to avoid false arrest lawsuits. Law enforcement agencies must adopt thorough and comprehensive policies and procedures to avoid costly mistakes; using biometric identification can be a cornerstone of such policies (Rothiein, 2009).

## Implications for Law Enforcement

The implications of mobile biometric technology on law enforcement are substantial. Some law enforcement agencies are already using mobile identification technology, but on a limited basis. Officers are only using it for identification purposes. Expanding the use of mobile biometric technology statewide will improve the overall efficiency of the criminal justice system and save thousands of dollars each year by eliminating the need to physically house an inmate at a local jail.

Research has clearly shown that the use of fixed or mobile biometric technology can help improve the overall efficiency of the arrest and booking process. Correctional facilities will operate more efficiently and the amount of inmates incarcerated for low-level crimes will also decrease, which will save thousands of dollars each year. The use of mobile biometric technology will also impact and improve officer safety because the officer will be able to identify the suspect within seconds. Suspects often give false information to an officer because they have an outstanding warrant and they do not want to go to jail. Mobile biometric technology will help the officer obtain the truth about the suspects' identity and give the officer added protection. Another important implication of mobile biometric technology is the decrease in civil lawsuits and false arrest claims. The use of mobile biometric technology will eliminate common mistakes made by officers because they will use fingerprints as a way to positively identify a subject before taking them into custody.

Finally, as with any new technology, there may be issues with privacy and the potential violation of the defendant's constitutional rights. The collection of biometric data has many privacy and civil liberty concerns attached to it including scalability, reliability and the security of the data collected. Opponents to this type of technology argue that biometrics was designed for military use and not for domestic use. The potential for misconduct and misuse of this type of technology cannot be overlooked. To prevent misuse, one could argue that police officers should obtain a warrant before collecting any biometric data (Parvaz, 2011). Law enforcement agencies should adopt specific policies when mobile identification devices are used, how the biometric data is kept and for how long. This policy should be reviewed by legal counsel as a precaution.

This type of technology could also have an impact on the community. Generally, the community supports the mission of law enforcement and wants criminals to be kept away from society by housing them in local jails. Mobile biometric technology will challenge that premise because more non-violent criminals will be booked in the field and released while waiting for a complaint to be filed by the District Attorney's office. The public may not feel safe or object to this new procedure because they are used to a "hard stance" on crime and the fact that most suspects are currently taken to a jail facility. However, the community will have more officers in the field handling calls for service because they will not be stuck processing an inmate inside of a local jail. By using mobile biometric technology, law enforcement agencies will become more professional in the eyes of the public and employee morale will also improve.

*(Continued)*

## Conclusion

To increase productivity and efficiency, law enforcement organizations must continue to search for new technology to assist them in crime fighting. Budgetary constraints and the needs from the community are always changing and law enforcement organizations must adapt quickly. Advances in mobile biometric technology can easily revolutionize law enforcement agencies in the next 10–20 years. Ten years ago, nobody thought about capturing a fingerprint in a patrol setting and sending it electronically to a fingerprint database. Today, biometric technology is increasingly expanding and proving to be a great tool for law enforcement.

Law enforcement managers need to consistently look to the future and determine how technology can help keep the community safe by identifying criminals, arresting them when necessary, while protecting the constitutional rights of all subjects at the same time. Law enforcement continues to evolve based on advances in technology. The use of mobile biometric technology in law enforcement is essential and a critical component of the criminal justice system. One might ask, so what role will the police play in the future? A noted futurist named Gene Stephens concluded that "educated police officers with improved people skills and a stronger grasp on emerging technologies will be crucial to successful policing in the future" (Stephens, 2005).

## References

California Department of Corrections and Rehabilitation. (2011). *The Cornerstone of California's Solution to Reduce Overcrowding, Costs, and Recidivism.* Sacramento, Government Printing Office.

California Department of Corrections and Rehabilitation. (2009). *Frequently asked questions: How much does it cost to incarcerate an inmate?* Sacramento, Government Printing Office.

Criminal Justice Statistic Center. (2005). Misdemeanors Arrests 2005–2005. Retrieved June 5, 2014 from www.ag.ca.gov/cjsc/publications/candd/cd05/tabs/2005table25.pdf?.

Jones, P. (2006, August). Using Biometric Technology to Advance Law Enforcement. *Forensic Magazine*, 55–59.

Mayo, K. (2010, July). Mobile Biometrics. The Potential for Real-Time Identification in the Field. Retrieved June 17, 2013 from www.evidencemagazine.com/index.

Miles, C. & Cohn, J. (2006). *Tracking Prisoners in Jail with Biometrics: An Experiment in a Navy Brig.* Retrieved June 5, 2013 from the National Institute of Justice website: www.jij.gov/journals/html.

National Law Enforcement and Corrections Technology Center. (2007). *Biometric Basics.* Washington, DC: Government Printing Office.

Parvaz, D. (2011, August 2). Mobile Biometrics to Hit the U.S. Streets. *Al Jazeera*. Retrieved June 17, 2013 from www.aljazeera.com/.

Rothiein, S. (2009). *Mistaken Identity Warrant Arrests.* Retrieved from www.llrmi.com/articles/legal/.

Stephens, G. (2005, March–April). Policing the Future: Law Enforcement's New Challenges, *The Futurist*, 51–57.

U.S. Census. (2010). *Quick facts.* Retrieved December 1, 2013 from the U.S. Census website: www.quickfacts.census.gov/qfd/states.

## Case Study 3
## Pursuits

### The Good Old Days

*By Greg Garland*

As the police cruiser pulled in behind the stolen Honda, Officer Jordan's heart began to race. "I still get excited, but it's not like the good old days," Jordan said to his partner. "No," his partner replied, "I miss the pursuits." Officer Jordan radioed dispatch, and within a matter of seconds, the Honda became disabled, rolled to a stop and the suspect was apprehended. Could this be a scenario from future law enforcement? Believe it or not, the technology to disable a vehicle before a pursuit begins exists today.

Police pursuits have become a staple of the television news. When the newscast breaks for one, almost everyone stops what they are doing and watches as the helicopter and the patrol cars chase the suspects through a frightening series of near collisions. Usually, the pursuit concludes with a short foot chase and a suspect is taken into custody. But far too often, someone, usually an innocent third party, is injured or killed.

On the pages that follow, you can read how police agencies will stop police pursuits before they happen, and how the televised pursuit will become the vintage re-run in less than 20 years.

### Telematics

The technologies we will use to end police pursuits are derived from the concept of telematics, a combination of Global Positioning System (GPS) and wireless phone technology which interfaces with the vehicle's onboard computer system. In fact, we see uses of telematics systems in many vehicles sold in the past ten years. Telematics has progressed to the point that if all vehicles were manufactured with these systems, law enforcement pursuits could be virtually non-existent.

The first and most popular system is the General Motors OnStar ® System (www.media.gm.com). It uses Telematics to slow down or stop stolen or fleeing vehicles. OnStar has many other selling features, such as air bag deployment for collisions, roadside assistant, vehicle diagnostics, hands free calling, and remote door unlock, to name a few. GM was the first manufacturer to offer such a service in 1996, now boasting five million subscribers on 50 vehicle models. Many other major manufacturers are offering similar systems; Toyota's – Safety Connect ®, Fords – Sync ®, and Mercedes Benz – Mbrace ®, introduced around 2000 offered even more client services than the original OnStar (www.edmunds.com/telematics). OnStar is the only system that has an "ignition block" and "vehicle slow down" feature which is the most valuable telemetric component to law enforcement during pursuit applications. It is this function that can allow the police to intervene to stop or disable a vehicle when necessary for law enforcement action. In a time when pursuits may be "prevented" through legislation, it will never be more timely.

*(Continued)*

## Pursuits and the Law

On May 6, 2009, Mississippi State Senator Terry Burton discovered his OnStar equipped Chevrolet Impala had been stolen. Senator Burton telephoned OnStar and notified the Hinds County Sheriff's Department. Within minutes, a Hinds County Deputy spotted the stolen Impala and a call was made to OnStar. The Stolen Vehicle Slowdown was activated, and the vehicle was safely slowed to a stop. Hinds County Sheriff, Malcolm McMillin, was pleased, saying, "This technology is extremely helpful not only to our officers, but the public as well. I was very pleased with the experience, and the fact that OnStar was able to help us curtail a high-speed chase, which too often has disastrous results" (www.onstar.com/articleID412.536). Of course, this incident was also resolved without the requisite police pursuit and its potential for property damage and death.

Seeing the continued human toll generated by police pursuits, many states have discussed or proposed legislation to ban or restrict police pursuits, others are looking for new federal guidelines to lessen the exposure on pursuits and require vehicle manufacturers to do more to prevent them (www.smartmotorist.com). The FBI reports that about 400–500 people are killed every year in police pursuits (www.kristieslaw.org). According to the National Highway Traffic Safety Administration, more than 1/3 of these deaths were innocent bystanders (www.kristieslaw.org). Tragic statistics, coupled with the fact that the majority of police pursuits begin with a simple vehicle code violation, have many legislators openly questioning their necessity.

A number of states, including California, already have shield laws to protect police agencies and individual officers from liability stemming from a suspect's actions during a pursuit (ABA Journal, Sept. 1998). Groups such as the Council of Civil Liberties and the American Civil Liberties Union, though, are building support for legislation to ban all pursuits, noting that most pursuits are initiated in response to minor infractions, and that 40 percent end in crashes.

Research has shown that Los Angeles has the highest number of pursuits out of 17 large cities surveyed in 2001, recording 781 crashes (vehicle collides with objects), 283 collisions (vehicle collides with other vehicles), 139 injuries and 6 deaths as a result of police pursuits. Police pursuits that end in the tragic deaths of innocent victims catch the eye of the public, the media and even state legislators. Certainly, the astute law enforcement leader would take notice, and then work to mitigate the problem before it is managed without them.

California State Senator Sam Aanestad first introduced Senate Bill 718, known as "Kristie's Law," in 2003 in response to the death of 15-year-old Grass Valley resident Kristie Priano. She was killed when a teenage driver fleeing police crashed into the minivan she was riding in, fatally injuring her. The Bill (which did not pass through the Assembly in 2004) would limit police pursuits in situations where there is an "immediate threat to life or not a serious crime" (www.cnn.com/CNN/Programs/anderson.cooper.360/blog). The purpose of Kristie's Law was to force police into pursuing only those suspects the police believe have committed a violent felony. Also in 2003, State Senator Gloria Romero introduced Senate Bill 719. This legislation was passed in October of 2005 and was signed by Governor Schwarzenegger (www.kristieslaw.org).

This law requires California law enforcement agencies to establish specific policies governing when to initiate a police pursuit, how much training an officer must have in order to begin a pursuit, and mandated routine training. Additionally, Senate Bill 719 requires DMV driver education to obtain a driver's license and enhanced penalties for violations. Also, the victim of fleeing suspects could receive compensation from the State of California's Victim's Restitution Fund. According to staff writer, Larry Mitchell, of Senator Gloria Romero's office, CSSA (Cal-State Sheriff's Association), CPCA (Cal Police Chief Association), and CPOA (California Police Officers Association) assisted with the development and passage of Senate Bill 719. The obvious need for advanced technology in law enforcement, coupled with the desire to pursue and apprehend criminals are a critical component of police work.

Most law enforcement officials oppose such legislation and argue it would severely limit law enforcement's ability to maintain public safety. During the Nominal Group Technique (NGT) Panel Discussion, which convened in 2010 in Rancho Cucamonga, CA, Lieutenant Rick Ells of the San Bernardino County Sheriff's Department stated, "Suspects will do whatever it takes to avoid apprehension. If they know law enforcement will not engage in vehicle pursuits, they will not yield to traffic stops. It really is that simple." Many believe the answer to this dilemma lies in technology already available on today's automobiles. Although LoJack seems to be another obvious choice to assist, it's only designed to locate a vehicle and is not currently capable to disable a vehicle. Specifically, every vehicle on our roadways should be equipped with the OnStar system.

## What Is OnStar and How Does It Works?

The OnStar Corporation was formed in 1995 as a subsidiary of General Motors in a joint venture with Electronic Data Systems and Hughes Electronics. Hughes developed the satellite communication for the system, EDS brought expertise in information management, and GM brought vehicle design and integration to the table.

OnStar debuted at the Chicago Auto Show in 1996 and was first made available to Cadillac models and later the remainder of the GM line. OnStar was also available through a licensing agreement on Audi, Acura, Subaru, Izusu and Volkswagen models (www.wikipedia.org/wiki/OnStar).

Using similar technology as your cellular telephone, OnStar is able to remotely perform a variety of functions on an equipped vehicle. Automobile operators can contact an OnStar representative while in their cars and receive vehicle diagnostics and directions. OnStar can also remotely unlock if you lock your keys in the car. On later models, OnStar is notified if the car is involved in a collision, regardless of airbag deployment, but perhaps the most exciting OnStar feature was introduced in 2009. Stolen Vehicle Slowdown allows OnStar to remotely slow down an equipped vehicle which has been reported stolen (www.onstar.com/stolenvehicleslowdown). For safety reasons, the engine does not immediately shut down, but the car slows to an idle and the power steering and braking remain functional. A companion feature, known as Remote Ignition Block, allows the ignition to be disabled.

*(Continued)*

Current OnStar subscribers pay around $20 each month, depending on the plan they choose. Automakers may oppose any legislation that would make a system such as OnStar mandatory for all new vehicles sold. The cost for such installation could significantly drive up the cost of new vehicles sold. In today's tough economic times, this may result in more purchases of used vehicles without the systems, which could negatively impact the revenue of new vehicle sales. Two factors, however, are causing controversy in automotive manufacturing. First, each manufacturer claims their vehicle technology is better than the others, and manufacturers won't want to pay GM for the use of their copyrighted OnStar System. Additionally, many of the car manufacturers are struggling in this economic climate and required items would drive vehicle costs up which would hurt their bottom line. On the other hand, according to Ezine Articles, having mandatory GPS systems on all financed vehicles could make a significant difference in the amount that is paid out for stolen vehicles (www.eazinarticles.com), thus reducing insurance costs for vehicle discovery. Mandatory GPS systems can not only assist in overall safety, but with theft prevention as well.

The National Transportation Safety Board hands down many requirements to vehicle manufacturers. For safety, as well as theft prevention practices, the NTSB states 65–90 percent of all vehicles on U.S. highways have EDR (Event Data Recorders) already installed. They proposed making this recorder standard in 2008, and are still negotiating what date these would be mandatory. They indicated, to interface with a system to ignition block or auto slow down would only require additional software programs which are currently proprietary by General Motors. One issue not addressed, however, are the privacy implications such systems might present.

During the expert panel's discussion, Lisa Watkins, Nursing Supervisor at Arrowhead Regional Medical Center, voiced concerns regarding confidentiality laws and civil rights violation if certain information was accessible to law enforcement or insurance companies if Event Data Recorders were mandatory. Interestingly, there has been much speculation regarding the ability of law enforcement or criminal organizations to use OnStar for surveillance or eavesdropping, thus lending credence to the fear of "Big Brother."

The "Big Brother" theory does appear to have some valid facts. First, law enforcement and insurance companies would know many things about you and your car that could be disturbing to some people. This includes information such as where your car is parked (inside or outside and at whose house), how many miles you drive, how fast you're driving, characteristics such as number of occupants and much more. Nonetheless, it's obvious that a system like OnStar may be a viable solution to someday ending police pursuits; however, two things must occur to make this happen. Issues remain, such as legislation required to mandate manufacturers to put OnStar technology in all new vehicles. Also at issue are the logistics of equipping police dispatch facilities with OnStar service centers. As far as law enforcement's ability to remotely monitor and manage any car, the fear of misuse or circumventing citizen's rights of not obtaining a judicial search warrant and following phone tapping requirements is of great concern to many watchdog groups. In fact, courts have already denied the FBI permission to use the system due to concerns of possible civil rights violations (www.wikipedia.org/FederalBureauofInvestigation).

Also, if there is a will there is a way for crooks to be crooks. Although most of the Telematic systems are hidden and not quickly accessible to the criminal element, removing the vehicle's battery is similar to removing a cell phone battery. The information is no longer accessible by anyone. Chop shops might still have a way to circumvent the system, but the average suspect fleeing from police will not have spare computers and GPS devices to switch out during a high speed chase.

If OnStar and similar telematic systems can block ignitions, slow and stop fleeing vehicles, law enforcement should strongly consider advocacy to create a cooperative effort to encourage legislators and manufacturers to mandate having an OnStar-like software system on all new vehicles by the end of this decade. This would allow federal grants to give public safety agencies the ability to put systems on patrol vehicles and in dispatch centers. It would also implement a solution that has already seen OnStar dispatchers save hundreds of lives nationally and billions of dollars in damage.

Cost of collisions and injuries should be enough. The technology to put an end to police pursuits is ready and available. The question is whether the willingness of the political realm is ready and available.

## Case Study 4
## Videoconference Police Reporting

Reducing Personnel Costs and Still Providing Personal Service

*By James Hunt*

It's 2018; you get up in the morning, grab a quick breakfast and a cup of coffee in your travel mug to go with you. You are in a hurry because you have a big meeting this morning at work and you have to prepare your presentation. You look for your laptop and realize you must have left it in your car when you got home late last night. You take your coffee and head out to the car.

S@#*, you look at your car and the passenger side window is broken. You quickly assess the damage and look to see what is missing. The laptop is gone along with your GPS unit that was on the dash. You recall the officer at last month's neighborhood watch meeting telling everyone the importance of not leaving any valuables visible in a vehicle. You didn't believe her because you live in such a good neighborhood that you seldom ever worry about locking your doors.

You are in a hurry like always, and you can't wait for an officer to come make a report, so you head off to work. You remember your laptop has a Lojack unit in it, so you know it is important to report this crime right away. You recall the officer describing a videoconference reporting system the police department has and decide to give it a try after you get to work.

A little later that morning, you call the police department using your smart phone. The dispatcher takes your information and gives you a videoconference address to talk to an officer via the smart phone videoconference program. You connect to the officer. "This is great," you think. "I can see the officer and just have a conversation." You use your phone's web cam to show the officer the broken window and the empty cradle where your GPS unit was located on the dash. He records pictures of the damage from his computer, records the Lojack identification information and contacts the company to activate the unit. The officer made an appointment for you to bring your car by the station on your way home for an evidence technician to dust it for fingerprints.

You complete the report in less than fifteen minutes and are back to work. What a great service you think to yourself! An hour later the officer calls to notify you officers have arrested a suspect. They also recovered your laptop along with some additional stolen items from other victims.

Sound like science fiction? The reality is these technologies exist today. In the near future, law enforcement can take advantage of these emerging technologies to create a videoconference police reporting system available to the public. If they are to do this, however, the videoconference programs and high-speed broadband Internet service must be widely available to the public at a cost low enough for the majority of citizens to afford.

## Videoconference Technology

The videoconference scenario described above can become a reality for California law enforcement. Videoconference software programs are currently available for individual users, and simply require a computer with enough processing power to run streaming video. Streaming video over the Internet requires systems that can provide a large amount of data flowing across the line. Fortunately, these systems are already in place. Systems that provide high-speed Internet data flow are called Broadband connections. The FCC defines broadband Internet service as "advanced communications systems capable of providing high-speed transmission of services such as data, voice, and video over the Internet and other networks. Transmission is provided by a wide range of technologies, including digital subscriber line and fiber optic cable, coaxial cable, wireless technology, and satellite. Broadband platforms make possible the convergence of voice, video, and data services onto a single network" (Federal Communications Commission, 2009). It is through this platform that we can transform the way in which we interact with victims of crimes and others needing quick, reliable and proficient police service.

In January of 2008, 96 percent of all households in California already had broadband Internet service available to them, making the State the leader in broadband service availability (Internet Use, 2009). A 2009 survey by the Public Policy Institute of California on Internet use indicates that 62 percent of Californians currently have broadband Internet service in the state, up from 55 percent last year. The survey also indicated 76 percent of Californians use the Internet, up from 70 percent last year. In California, though, there is an income divide on Internet use: 97 percent of those with household incomes over $80,000 use the Internet; 87 percent of households with income between $40,000 and $80,000 also use it. Only 58 percent of those with household incomes under $40,000 use the Internet (Public Policy Institute of California Survey, 2009). To implement efficient videoconferencing protocols for the police, then, we will have to first address the income divide.

As high speed Internet providers compete for customers, the costs of services could decline making it affordable for more lower income users. With current broadband Internet use in California at 62 percent, there are enough citizens with broadband service now to make videoconference police reporting a viable alternative. If the current trends continue the number of citizens able to use videoconference technology will improve into the future as more citizens obtain broadband service. Certainly, police agencies interested in the advantages of such services must become involved in their advocacy as a public safety need. The voice of law enforcement is widely heard, and speaking on behalf of those who cannot easily afford broadband can pay dividends far beyond mere connection with the Internet.

## If We Were to Do It...

If police agencies are going to use a videoconference reporting system, then the computers, webcams and software must be readily available and affordable. Nearly all laptop and desktop computers now sold come with webcams built in. Apple Macintosh computers come with built in webcams and Skype videoconference software already installed. Many PC models also come with this software. For those with older PC systems, aftermarket webcams are available as an add-on to existing computers for a reasonable price.

One option to expand broadband access would be to utilize the growing "netbook" computer. A netbook is a small, light and inexpensive version of a laptop computer. Netbooks have general computing capabilities and are especially suited to be very portable with convenient wireless access to the Internet. Internet providers are using these netbooks as a low cost way to entice consumers to purchase a computer with wireless high-speed broadband Internet service. In December of 2008 Radio Shack and AT&T combined to produce a $99.99 computer netbook. The netbook is offered at this price if you sign up for a two-year AT&T broadband wireless service contract at $60 a month. The netbook is an Acer black Aspire One model with a 160GB hard drive, 1GB of RAM, Windows XP, a webcam, and a built-in 3G modem. This netbook is capable of connecting to the Internet and has the ability to videoconference using a built-in webcam. In 2009, as competition increased for wireless customers, some service providers were even offering free netbooks with a long-term contract for wireless service.

A $100 netbook would certainly make the technology to videoconference available to most Californians as long as they could afford broadband Internet service. AT&T was offering their wireless service on the Radio Shack netbook at $60 a month. "Currently Verizon's service has a starting cost of $140 per month. Cablevision is offering its service at $99.95 a month" (Yao, 2009). The Verizon and Cablevision service prices are for home systems.

The technology for hand-held devices such as smart phones also continues to increase. For example; an iPhone purchased with a broadband wireless contract can be bought for around $199. These phones are capable of doing many things that were years ago reserved only for computers. They can connect to the Internet and stream video. They

*(Continued)*

are capable of taking pictures and some smart phones can take video. They have word processing capability with touchscreen keyboards capable of creating documents or text quickly. Other manufacturers are quickly following suit, developing similar products to the iPhone with the same or more capabilities. It does not take much imagination to realize that these devices will soon be capable of videoconferencing.

Recent technology using cloud servers along with smart phones may allow smart phones to process as much information as a computer. "The problem with mobile phones" says Allan Knies, associate director of Intel Research at Berkeley, "is that everyone wants them to perform like a regular computer, despite their relatively paltry hardware." Byung-Gon Chun, a research scientist at Intel Research Berkeley, thinks he might have the solution to that problem: create a supercharged clone of your smart phone that lives in 'the cloud' and let it do all the computational heavy lifting your phone is too wimpy to handle" (Mims, 2009).

According to a recent article in *Technology Review* magazine, "Clone Cloud, invented by Chun and his colleague Petros Maniatis, uses a smart phone's high-speed connection to the Internet to communicate with a copy of itself that lives in a cloud-computing environment on remote servers. The prototype runs on Google's Android mobile operating system and seamlessly offloads processor-intensive tasks to its cloud-based double" (Mims, 2009). This technology would allow mobile smart phones to perform operations such as videoconferencing at speeds like a computer.

IPhones and other smart phones are selling like crazy. Since the debut in July of 2008 through September of 2008 the iPhone 3G sold 6.9 million units, bringing total iPhone sales for 2008 up to 13 million (Fulton, 2008). IPhone sales continued to increase with over 24 million units sold in 2009. Worldwide total smartphone sales increased to 172 million in 2009 up from 100 million in 2008 (Gartner, 2010).

The trends here are clear. Manufacturers are making computers, netbooks and smart phones more powerful, with faster processers, more memory, more features and at lower prices. Computers, laptops and netbooks are all capable of videoconferencing and it is no stretch of the imagination to envision smart phones in the near future with video-conference capabilities.

## Why Should Law Enforcement Use a Videoconference Reporting Method?

Okay, so the technology is out there, affordable and available. Why would law enforcement want to use a videoconference reporting method? The answer is simple, cost savings and efficiency. Many law enforcement agencies still send officers out in the field to meet the victim and take cold police reports (one where it is reported after the occurrence, and for which there is little or no evidence or investigative leads on the case). Cold reports make up a large portion of the reports that are taken every day by police officers at law enforcement agencies throughout California. A brief case study illustrates the current costs and potential for change.

A six-month review of the reports taken at the Monrovia Police Department from July 2009 through December of 2009 indicates 58 percent of all reports taken were "cold reports." The Monrovia Police Department is a mid-sized agency (60 sworn officers) in Southern California serving an ethnically diverse community of 40,000 citizens.

The ability to take many of these cold reports by a videoconference reporting method has the potential to handle more than half of all the reports taken at this agency using a more efficient and cost effective method. Taking these cold reports using traditional methods is very time consuming. The Monrovia Police Department has the officer drive to the location, interview the victim, collect evidence, and then write or dictate a police report. Because a cold report is the lowest priority call for service often times the victim has to wait an extended period of time before an officer is free from higher priority calls to respond and take the cold report from the victim. All of this results in lost time for proactive patrol by officers and lost time spent by the victim waiting to make a report.

Federal Bureau of Investigation crime data for California indicates 1,265,920 crimes were reported in the state in 2008. Of these the majority, 1,080,747 or 85 percent, were property crimes, which in the FBI report are burglary, larceny and vehicle theft. Property crimes account for a greater percentage of the number of cold reports a police department receives. If the Monrovia Police Department percentages of cold reports were applied to the state statistics for just property crimes, 626,833 reports could potentially be handled by the videoconference method in the state. This could result in a tremendous amount of time saved for the police while also providing a convenience for those we serve.

Videoconference reporting would eliminate the need for the officer to drive to the victim's location. The victim's statement could be recorded and transcribed using voice recognition software. The officer could then dictate and review the report right at his/ her workstation. The victim would be able to have a face-to-face conversation with the officer and have their questions about the case answered. Police departments could use trained civilians to take these reports at a significant cost savings over police officers in the field.

Another cost saving option would be to contract with retired officers to take these videoconference reports from their homes via the Internet. The 3 percent at 50 retirement program has increased the number of highly trained officers that are retired but still looking for options to make additional retirement income. Contracting with these officers would take advantage of their investigative and report writing knowledge to take videoconference reports from their home at a significant savings to the department.

## Conclusion

With the current economic recession hitting California cities hard, police departments must look for cost saving ways to work more efficiently and more effectively. Web-based videoconference police reporting is a way to take cold police reports efficiently at cost savings to a department and still provide a high level of customer service and personal interaction to the victim reporting a crime. As the availability of these technologies grows, the opportunity will be there for a police agency to develop a videoconference reporting system and take advantage of the potential cost savings this program can provide.

*(Continued)*

## References

Fulton, S. (2008, October 22). *13M iPhones sold in total, 2.6M Macs sold last quarter.* Retrieved May 10, 2009, from Betanews: www.betanews.com/article/apple-13-m-iphones-sold-in-total-26-m-macs-sold-last-quarter/1224624147.

Gartner. (2010, February 23). *Gartner Says Worldwide Mobile Phone Sales to End Users Grew 8 Per Cent in Fourth Quarter 2009.* Retrieved March 21, 2010, from Gartner Newsroom: www.gartner.com/it/page.jsp?id=1306513.

*Internet Use.* (2009). Retrieved March 11, 2010, from IT Facts: www.itfacts.biz/96-of-California-households-have-access-to-broadband/9588.

Mims, C. (2009, May 1). *Sending Cell Phones into the Cloud.* Retrieved May 11, 2009, from Technology Review: www.technologyreview.com/communications/22571/.

Public Policy Institute of California Survey. (2009, June 1). *California's Digital Divide.* Retrieved March 10, 2010, from Public Policy Institute of California: www.ppic.org/content/pubs/jtf/JTF_DigitalDivideJTF.pdf.

Yao, D. (2009, April 27). *Cablevision to unveil fastest Internet speeds.* Retrieved April 28, 2009, from MSNBC Technology and Science: www.msnbc.msn.com/id/30442722/.

## Chapter Summary

Public safety agencies must continue to evolve and evaluate how technology will play a role in the future. The aforementioned research papers emphasize the importance of critical thinking, "thinking outside of the box" and learning from other experts in the field. Public safety personnel (at any rank) must continue to use and embrace technology and determine how it will affect the stakeholders in the public safety arena. This chapter discussed four different and specific areas of public safety technology; however, they all have one thing in common: *leadership*. The future of the public safety profession relies on those of you willing to step up and lead. Don't sit back and let technology come to you or your agency. Seek it out. One of the biggest parts of leadership is being an advocate for change and ensuring that future generations of public safety personnel are left with a solid foundation when it comes to technology.

## Command College Articles

1 Gallucci, N. (2015). *Listen to your body.* Command College Program #55, California Commission on Peace Officer Standards and Training, Sacramento, CA. Reprinted with permission from author.

2 Rose, J. (2015). *The future of corrections: How can mobile biometric technology revolutionize the arrest and booking process.* Command College Program #55, California Commission on Peace Officer Standards and Training, Sacramento, CA. Reprinted with permission from author.

3  Garland, G. (2011). *Pursuits: The good old days.* Command College # 48, California Commission on Peace Officer Standards and Training, Sacramento, CA. Reprinted with permission from author.

4  Hunt, J. (2010). *Videoconference police reporting: Reducing personnel costs and still providing personal service.* Command College Program #46, Sacramento, CA. Reprinted with permission from author.

## Key Words or Terminology

| | | |
|---|---|---|
| videoconferencing | biometrics | pursuits |
| biofeedback | smart wearable systems | corrections |
| mobile technology | liability | telematics |
| California Peace Officer Standards and Training (POST) | | |

## Discussion Questions

1.  After reading all four Command College research papers, identify any common themes that were used in the evaluation of technology. Do any of them stand out? Why?

2.  Explain the role of public safety executives, managers, supervisors and line-staff when it comes to the future of technology. What is your role?

3.  You have just read four comprehensive research papers that assess the future trends in public safety technology. You have also read the prior nineteen chapters in this text-book. So what is the future of public safety technology? Identify at least five areas that you consider are the most important parts when dealing with technology. Summarize what you have learned and explain why public safety managers should be part of the technology innovation process.

## Notes

1  *Command college program*, n.d. California Commission on Peace Officer Standards and Training. Retrieved from www.post.ca.gov/command-college.aspx.
2  Ibid.
3  Ibid.

# Appendix 1

# SOCIAL MEDIA TERMINOLOGY

**avatar**—A computer user's representation of himself. This may be a three-dimensional character used in a virtual world or video game.

**blog**—A self-published diary or commentary on a particular subject or topic. A blog allows visitors to post, react or give comments.

**Blogger/blogger**—A blogging platform also known as BlogSpot or someone who blogs.

**Brightkite**—A location-based social media platform.

**cache**—A collection of stored data on a computer that can be accessed quickly if required in the future.

**chat**—An interaction on a website with a number of people adding comments one after the other. This differs from a forum because the conversations happen in "real time."

**click jacking**—A deceptive practice where users are misled into visiting another website, proving information and then spreading the scam to their contacts. This is often done by having visitors click a button that appears to perform another function.

**cloud**—The virtual location of computing resources such as servers, applications and data used in cloud computing. Cloud computing allows traditional IT service to be housed on the Internet: usually to increase capabilities without the need for enhanced physical storage or software.

**Craigslist**—An online classified for posting ads for jobs, housing, services or things for sale.

**crowd sourcing**—The act of a company or institution taking a function once performed by employees and outsourcing it to an undefined network of people in the form of an open call.

**cyber bullying**—Willful and repeated harm inflicted through the use of computers, cell phones and other electronic devices.

**cyber vetting**—An assessment of a person's qualification to hold a position of security clearance using information found on the Internet.

**download**—To transfer data to a computer or device from a larger computer or the Internet. This is the opposite of *upload*.

**emoticon**—A facial expression represented by a combination of punctuation, symbols or letters used to show emotion.

**feed**—A list of a user's recent updates. The feed can be posted on other sites.

**follower**—A person who subscribes to receive tweets from a registered user.

**forum**—A discussion area on a website where people can post messages or comment on existing messages at any time.

**Formspring**—An online forum that allows users to ask and answer questions.

**forum**—A discussion area on a website where people can post messages or comment on existing messages at any time.

**Foursquare**—A location-based social media platform.

**friend**—An individual who is part of another individual's network.

**geolocation/geotagging**—The incorporation of location data. This may be used on social media platforms to notify people where a user is at a given time.

**ghost profile or undercover profile**—A social networking profile created by a person using information that makes the profile appear to be that of someone else for the purpose of online undercover investigations.

**hack**—To gain unauthorized access to a computer system or network.

**hashtag**—The symbol #; precedes a term in a tweet to allow that subject to be more searchable; typically used on Twitter and other social media sites.

**Hoot Suite**—A social media dashboard that allows users to set up team collaboration; schedule updates to Twitter, Facebook, LinkedIn, WordPress, and other social media sites; as well as track trends and conduct searches across social media platforms.

**hyperlink**—Commonly referred to as *links*, hyperlinks allow users to move to other portions of a webpage or document, or to a new webpage or document. A hyperlink is typically activated by clicking on highlighted or different color text or an image.

**impersonate**—To pretend to be someone else. Impersonation with intent to deceive is against the terms of service of several social media sites and may be reported.

**instant messaging**—A form of real-time communication between two or more people based on typed text; the text is conveyed via the Internet or an intranet.

**Internet**—A global system of interconnected computer networks which host a variety of applications that allow users to communicate and interact with each other.

**Internet searching**—A process of locating and retrieving data (written documents and other media such as images, video, and audio files) available on the Internet.

**IP address**—An Internet Protocol (IP) address is a unique numerical label assigned to all devices that are connected to the Internet. Because the number is unique to a device, it can be used to locate a device that has engaged in certain activity on the Internet.

**ISP**—ISP stands for *Internet service provider*, a company that offers customers access to the Internet.

**LinkedIn**—A social network site focused on professional network connections.

**LiveJournal**—A blogging platform.

**mention**—Using the @ symbol to reference another user.

**metasearch engine**—A search engine that submits queries to multiple search engines and returns an aggregate result of multiple searches.

**microblog**—A service that allows users to send short (usually character restricted) messages out to a network of followers; examples include Twitter and Nixle.

**monitoring**—The continuous conducting of searches for any discussions, posts, videos, blogs, online conversations, etc., of your department with the purpose of discovering what is being said about you and being able to correct false information or rumors.

**MySpace**—A social network site.

**Nixle**—A community information service available to local, state, and federal government entities and allows these entities to send messages by text, email, and Internet posts to subscribers.

**page**—The specific portion of a social media website where content is displayed and managed by an individual or individuals with administrator rights.

**phishing**—The fraudulent practice of sending electronic messages claiming to be a legitimate company in order to induce individuals to reveal sensitive data such as user names, passwords, and credit card details.

**platform**—A hardware and/or software architecture that serves as a base.

**podcast**—A Web-based audio broadcast usually available by some form of subscription. Comes from the combination of the acronym POD, play on demand, and broadcast.

**post**—Content, in any format, placed on a website or the act of publishing content on a website.

**privacy settings**—An option many social media sites offer to allow a user to determine the level to which their information is made available to others.

**profile**—Information that users provide about themselves on a social networking site.

**RSS**—Short for *real simple syndication* or *rich site summary*; a format sites can use to indicate they have been updated, people can then subscribe to receive the stream of updates via an RSS reader.

**screencast**—The digital recording of computer screen output.

**screenshot**—An image that shows the contents of a digital screen display; also referred to as a screen capture or screen grab.

**Second Life**—An online virtual community.

**Skype**—A voice over Internet protocol service and software program that allows users to communicate by placing calls, as to telephones, within the computer network; there is also the capability for video calling and conferencing, instant messaging, and file sharing.

**social media**—A category of Internet-based resources that integrate user-generated content and user participation. This includes, but is not limited to, social networking sites (Facebook, MySpace), microblogging sites (Twitter), photo- and video-sharing sites (Flickr, YouTube), wikis (Wikipedia), blogs, and news sites (Digg, Reddit).

**social networks**—Online platforms where users can create profiles, share information, and socialize with others using a range of technologies.

**subscribe**—To authorize to receive or access updates or messages.

**tag**—A label attached to Web content, such as a blog post, to indicate what content is about; tags are also used in HTML coding to format text.

**traffic**—The amount of data sent and received by visitors to a website, webpage, or social media site.

**trending**—A word, phrase, or topic that is popular at a given moment, particularly on Twitter.

**tweet**—A post or status update on Twitter.

**tweetjacking**—Reposting another user's tweet without giving credit and/or leaving out an important part of the original message for your own means or agenda. Tweetjacking can also refer to the act of breaking into someone else's Twitter account and sending messages as that user.

**Twitter**—A microblogging tool that allows users to send short messages (up to 140 characters) that will immediately be distributed to their network of followers.

**typosquatting**—The act of registering the misspelling of a brand name or trademarked term in order to capture the Internet traffic from a legitimate entity.

**upload**—To transfer data from a personal computer or device to a larger entity such as a website.

**URL**—The uniform resource locator; the global address of documents and resources found on the World Wide Web.

**viral**—A term used to describe online content that has become increasingly popular across the Web.

**virtual community**—Online communities that feature computer simulated environments in which users can interact.

**vlog**—A video blog.

**Wall**—The portion of a Facebook page that displays user updates and comments.

**webpage**—A multimedia document (may contain text, images, audio, and/or video) that is accessible on the Internet. A webpage may be static (a user only views) or interactive (a user may input data and alter the content). Webpages often have links which direct users to other webpages.

**website**—A collection of interlinked webpages which are generally authored, hosted and maintained by a single entity. Websites are commonly used to represent entities such as government organizations, businesses or persons, or used as places for individuals with common interests to meet and interact.

**wiki**—Webpage(s) that can be edited collaboratively.

**WordPress**—A blogging platform.

**YouTube**—An online video community that allows users to upload video content, share that content, and view the content uploaded by others.

*Source*: International Association of Chiefs of Police. Social Media Terminology. Retrieved from www.iacpsocialmedia.org/resources.

# Appendix 2

# GLOSSARY OF IT TERMINOLOGY

**acceptance testing**

The process that an agency uses to verify that the delivered and installed product meets the requirements specified in the procurement documents and contract, particularly regarding functionality, reliability and performance.

**activity**

An element of work performed during a project that normally has an expected duration, as well as cost and resource requirements.

**ad hoc working groups**

Groups that are formed as subset to the project's formal decision-making structure to look at specific tasks and business processes that require more in-depth research or analysis, or to carry out research on and development of a variety of project-specific plans, models, policies and directions. Assembled on a temporary basis to address a specific issue or task.

**agreement for extended services**

An exhibit in the contract that should be included if an agency requires continuous vendor product support. It should identify the type of service, the availability and the allowable time frame for responses and correction of various types of problems. The exhibit should detail the pricing that has been negotiated for recurring support.

**assumptions and constraints**

Circumstances and events that can affect the success of the project and are generally out of the control of the project team. Include in the project charter to provide assistance in making/justifying decisions. Consult also when developing the project timeline and risk management plan.

### automated field reporting (AFR) software

AFR automates the incident and other reporting processes from the patrol car. Optimally, AFR allows the capture of incident and report information and then electronically sends the report to a supervisor for approval and for submission to the records management system (RMS).

### automatic vehicle location (AVL) software

Used by law enforcement agencies to remotely track the location of agency units via satellite global positioning systems (GPS). AVL combines GPS technology, wireless communications, street-level mapping and a user interface.

### best practices

Industry-proven processes or methods that, when executed effectively, lead to enhanced or superior project performance and ensure the success of an undertaking (such as planning, procurement, implementation and management).

### bonding costs

Bonds required may include those dealing with performance, maintenance and payment.

### business case

The project's marketing plan that articulates why the project is important in terms of operational benefits to the agency, the justice system in general and the public. Used to educate and inform all project stakeholders.

### business process

A written description of the things that employees do every day in their job functions assessed on a *what, why, when, how* and *where* basis. Business processes are what technology seeks to enhance or improve.

### client/server

An application that runs on a personal computer or workstation and relies on a server to perform some operations. A *thin client* is a client designed to be especially small so that the bulk of data processing occurs on the server.

### communications plan

Formal and agreed-upon strategies for communicating project status and activities to key stakeholders, and methods for developing historical project records and archives.

### computer-aided dispatch (CAD) system

Fully automates the call-taking and dispatching functions of a law enforcement agency and initiates and manages dispatch and incidents.

## consulting costs

Generally, a full-service consultant who provides needs analysis, project planning, procurement assistance, contract negotiations and implementation assistance, and will receive an average of 15 percent of the total project cost.

## contingency costs

Funding that is set aside for unexpected and, therefore, often unbudgeted activities. On the average, contingencies range from 10–15 percent of the hardware and software costs.

## contract

A binding agreement between an agency and a chosen vendor that defines the obligations between the parties, including deliverables, services and responsibilities.

## deliverable

A measurable, tangible, verifiable outcome that must be produced to complete a project or part of a project.

## executive sponsor

The individual who has the ultimate accountability for the project, having authority to sanction the project and make it a priority. Serves as the project's ultimate decision making authority.

## exhibit

Subsets of information related to the contract, usually created by the project team. Includes such documents as: statement of work (SOW); project deliverables; payment schedule; and project timeline.

## external costs

The costs that most agencies associate with procurement, which are generally lumped together in three main categories: hardware, software and services. They also include the staff, resources, supplies, infrastructure, consultants and virtually all project elements that fall beyond the direct financial control of the agency or the parent organization.

## focus groups

A somewhat informal technique that can help to assess user needs while designing the system. Usually six to nine users gather to discuss issues and concerns about the features of the new system.

## functional specifications

Precise descriptions of how a product should operate. These statements should be succinct. A project plan and procurement document often contains numerous such functional requirements. During procurement, vendors should be required to divulge how closely their product matches an agency's functional specifications.

## functionality testing

A type of acceptance testing designed to ensure that the vendor's software is functioning as described in product literature and, possibly, in their response to the agency's RFP.

## funding streams

Variety of means by which an agency may obtain funding for a project, including internal budgets, state and federal grant programs, bond measures, etc.

## geographic information system (GIS)

Stores information about a region in the form of "layers" connected by a common frame of references ($x$-$y$ coordinates). In addition to the specific coordinates, GIS also contains a variety of other geographic references to a specific location. Other data sets include addresses, place names, ZIP codes, phone numbers and indirect references to geography.

## hardware

Tangible devices that enable the use of various software programs. Includes servers, work-stations, laptops, infrastructure (network components) and telecommunications devices (i.e., wireless modems).

## holdbacks

A contract provision that allows an agency to keep a percentage of a vendor's payment until after the vendor successfully completes certain milestones. Useful for keeping the vendor interested in completing all of the tasks associated with a project, even those that are less profitable than others.

## implementation plan

The blueprint that enables project management to define the rules that govern how technology will be installed, tested and managed.

## information system

A purposefully designed system that brings data, computers, procedures and people together in order to manage the information that is important to an organization's mission.

## initial cost

One-time expenses to purchase technology and services for a project. Must be considered in conjunction with recurring costs.

## internal costs

Those cost over which your agency has direct financial responsibility and control, including personnel costs, infrastructure costs, cost recovery fees, etc.

### jail management system (JIMS)
Assists with the full management of a jail or correctional facility, including tracking inmate and facility data.

### license agreement
An exhibit included in the contract that defines what rights the agency has with regard to the use of the vendor's software.

### liquidated damages
A contract provision that compels the vendor to pay the agency if a contracted deadline is missed.

### milestone
A significant event in the project, usually completion of a major deliverable.

### milestone review
A session in which the project team gathers together to review and analyze milestone completion and the process for its completion, and adjust the schedule for future deliverables and milestones, if necessary.

### mobile data computing
Comprised of several hardware and software technologies working together to allow law enforcement officers to access, receive, create and exchange information wirelessly in the field.

### module
A portion of a program that carries out a specific function and may be used alone or combined with other modules of the same program.

### outsourcing
The act of hiring an outside source to perform a service that is beyond the agency's existing resources, usually a consultant.

### performance testing
A type of acceptance testing that is designed to determine the speed of the combined hardware and software package during various transactions.

### performance reports
Provides details about project status, including which deadlines have been met and which have not. Whether prepared by the vendor or internal staff, performance reports should be provided on a weekly or biweekly basis.

### primary agreement
The terms and conditions that govern the agency's relationship with the vendor. The agency's city or county legal staff often prepares the primary agreement document.

### problem escalation and resolution process

A formal and agreed-upon process established by the decision making structure for resolving disputes and problems during a project. Includes documenting any such problems and their disposition.

### project charter

A document developed early in the process (prior to the full Project Plan) that contains an IT project description, complete with scope, objectives, organization and staffing, a decision making structure, the project management approach and initial resource documents. Provides guidance to project staff in planning and designing a system.

### project management

The application of knowledge, skills, tools and techniques to project activities in order to move the project forward to completion and to meet or exceed stakeholder needs and expectations from a project.

### project manager

An individual dedicated to and accountable for all project-related activities and solely responsible for the project's scope, quality and budget. Responsible for virtually all aspects of the initiative and is formally accountable to the steering committee and the executive sponsor.

### project objectives

Quantifiable criteria that must be met for the project to be considered successful. A critical part of scope, objectives must include measures and quality, time, cost, performance, reliability and functionality.

### project planning

A dynamic process that results in a document that guides the entire IT project design, procurement, implementation and future enhancements. The plan is the repository for all project-related research, decisions, deliverables and documents.

### project scope

Clearly defines the boundaries for the project. Scope addresses what users want (functions); how well the user requirements are met (quality of); when and how it must be developed (constraints); and why (the value in the project).

### project timeline

A mechanism to ensure the project is accurately and realistically scheduled so that it can be completed on time within the resources available. The timeline is critical to help avoid delays and associated cost overruns. Includes activities, deliverables and milestones.

### quality assurances (QA)

Tests that ensure the vendor's hardware and software perform according to specification.

## records management system (RMS)

A system that captures, maintains and analyzes all police agency and incident-related event information and is vital to the day-to-day operations of tracking and managing criminal and noncriminal events, investigations and personnel information.

## recurring cost

Continuing cost that must be considered to support, maintain, and enhance hardware and software and user skills. Determined in concert with initial costs.

## reliability testing

A type of acceptance testing designed to determine the "uptime" of a vendor's solution. Typically, this testing focuses on hardware and involves the use of special software that simulates the volume of transactions that the vendor claims to be acceptable.

## request for information (RFI)

A procurement tool used to elicit generalized information about vendor products and services. Pricing, if included at all, is generic and based on averages.

## request for proposal (RFP)

A procurement tool used to obtain actual hardware, software and services proposals from vendors.

## request for qualifications (RFQ)

A procurement tool used to determine whether a vendor meets minimum qualification standards set by the issuing agency. Does not request a proposal response with prices and specific proposal details.

## risk management

A planning process that prepares the agency for dealing with potentially harmful events that could happen in a technology initiative. The risk management plan is prepared by the project manager and steering, user and technical committees.

## schedule management plan

Provides a structured process for documenting, analyzing and approving changes in the project schedule. The schedule management plan should be a formal process that is documented in the project plan.

## scope management plan

Provides a structured process for documenting, analyzing and approving changes in the project schedule. The schedule management plan should be a formal process that is documented in the project plan.

## scope planning

A process to precisely define and document specific activities and deliverables for a particular project. Clarifies and defines the project focus and keeps activities in control and within agreed-upon boundaries. Establishes a formal process for proactively managing changes in project scope.

## scope statement
Defines what is to be included in the project, as well as what is to be excluded. Developed by the project manager and user committee.

## scope-time-cost relationship
The project elements of scope, time and cost are inextricably linked and have a proportional relationship. Should any one of these elements grow or reduce, the other two elements grow or reduce proportionally.

## software
What is required to make a system operational, including operating system software, vendor-supplied application software, third-party software and any network management tools.

## sole-source
A procurement tool used when an agency can show that the chosen vendor is the only vendor capable of supplying the required hardware, software and services in the best interest of the agency.

## stakeholders
Individuals and organizations who are actively involved in the project, or whose interests may be positively or negatively affected as a result of project execution or successful project completion.

## statement of work (SOW)
Included as an exhibit in a contract, the SOW defines each task involved in the entire project. It is the blueprint for implementation.

## steering committee
Members are generally high-level managers and/or supervisors within the agency. This group will ensure that a structured project management process is adopted and followed. Provides constant guidance and oversight to the project, its progress and deliverables, and will make most decisions related to the project.

## SWOT
An acronym sometimes used in referring to a situation assessment, SWOT stands for *strengths, weaknesses, opportunities, threats.*

## systems development lifecycle (SDLC)
A cyclical process regarding IT, with several stages, including planning, procurement, implementation and management.

## technical committee

Includes technical staff from the agency, as well as others from the agency's parent organization (e.g., city, county or state), if such support is provided. This committee's role is to analyze the agency's existing technical environment and to research and propose solutions to the agency's business needs and problems.

## total cost of ownership (TCO)

Used in budget planning, TCO refers to the total costs associated with ownership, usage and maintenance of the system overtime.

## user committee

Includes subject matter and business process experts for the functions to be addressed. This committee's role is to assist and support in creating a project charter and ultimately the project plan. This committee analyzes existing workflows, defines business processes, and looks for efficiencies and establishes the requirements of any new system.

## vision statement

Written by the steering committee, the vision brings a tangible reality to what the agency will address with the new system

*Source:* SEARCH Group Incorporated. Harris, Kelly J., & Romesburg, William H. (2002). *Law Enforcement Tech Guide: How to Plan, Purchase and Manage Technology (Successfully!). A Guide for Executives, Managers and Technologists.* Washington, DC: U.S. Department of Justice, Office of Community Oriented Policing Services. Reprinted with permission.

# Appendix 3

# TECHNOLOGY GRANT

Each grantor has specific information or requirements that must be met before any grant funds are distributed. In Unit 3, Chapter 13, we discussed several key areas that must be addressed during the grant process. The following pages were submitted during a grant solicitation. The grant was a U.S. Department of Justice, Office of Community Oriented Policing Services, technology program.

This is not the complete grant; however, this will give you an overview of what may be required if you decide to pursue grant funding. Public safety personnel should always consult with legal counsel and appropriate elected officials before applying for any grant or federal appropriation funds. Some confidential information has been removed.

*Source:* Courtesy of the San Bernardino County Sheriff's Department.

September 20, 2005

_____, Assistant Attorney General
Department of Justice
Office of Justice Programs
Washington D.C. 20531

Dear Assistant Attorney General _____,

On behalf of the San Bernardino/Riverside Regional CAL-ID consortium, I am submitting this grant request for $2,380,000 to purchase 300 wireless Mobile Identification Devices (MID). The Mobile Identification Devices will allow officers on patrol to identify suspected terrorists and/or criminal offenders by biometric data or fingerprints within minutes. This process also reduces the loss of a wanted person through the suspect's deceit. It also has an added benefit of increasing public safety by putting the officer back on patrol more quickly by reducing the amount of paperwork and time it takes to properly identify and book a prisoner.

The San Bernardino/Riverside Regional CAL-ID consortium is comprised of all law enforcement agencies within San Bernardino and Riverside Counties. This project addresses the issue of Homeland Security and provides an added benefit of keeping our officers safe, while protecting the citizens that we serve.

Enclosed with this letter are an original and copy of our application. If there is any additional information needed to evaluate the San Bernardino/Riverside Regional CAL-ID consortium's proposal, please do not hesitate to contact me. Thank you for your consideration of our application. I look forward to hearing from you.

Sincerely,
Gary S. Penrod, Sheriff
San Bernardino County Sheriff's Department

Contact Person:
Jeffrey A. Rose, Lieutenant
Project Manager / CAL-ID
San Bernardino County Sheriff's Department

## Table of Contents

## Abstract

The need to identify criminals and threats to national safety has always been a priority within the criminal justice system. The tragic events of September 11th once again brought to the forefront our need to properly identify suspected terrorists and other criminals. The ability to identify someone in a patrol setting is crucial. The ability to prevent foreign and domestic terrorism is extremely difficult and solutions are varied; however, a proactive approach is preferable to a reactive one. Handheld wireless Mobile Identification Devices are available to law enforcement agencies, but they are extremely expensive. Unfortunately, law enforcement agencies in San Bernardino and Riverside County do not have enough financial resources to address this issue.

The objective of this proposal is to enable law enforcement officers within the largest geographical county in the United States to quickly identify potential suspects or terrorists by fingerprints in a patrol setting. This proposal will allow the San Bernardino/Riverside CAL-ID consortium to purchase wireless handheld Mobile Identification Devices. The Mobile Identification Devices are easy to use and can be used to identify suspects within 3–5 minutes. The end result of this project is that law enforcement officers will be able to safely identify suspects in the field within a reasonable amount of time. This process also reduces the loss of a wanted person through the suspect's deceit. It also has the added benefit of increasing public safety by putting the officer back on patrol more quickly by reducing the amount of paperwork and time it takes to properly book a prisoner.

The total estimated cost of this project is a one-time purchase amount of $2,380,000 for the purchase of 300 Mobile Identification Devices, dedicated server and software licensing. All training, personnel costs, and maintenance costs will be the responsibility of the San Bernardino/Riverside CAL-ID consortium. San Bernardino/Riverside CAL-ID will donate $458,250 toward this project.

## Introduction

In 1985, the counties of San Bernardino and Riverside embarked on a joint venture to create a regional identification system designed to be shared by all law enforcement agencies in the 27,360 square mile jurisdiction (with a combined population of over 3,250,000). Under the California Identification System (CAL-ID) umbrella, we developed a regional Automated

Fingerprint Identification System (AFIS) and participate in the State of California's Cal-Photo program. The system as it operates today provides fingerprint, photo, and DNA services to all public safety agencies including local police departments, district attorney, school districts, coroner and Sheriff's Departments in Riverside and San Bernardino Counties. It is also available to other state and federal law enforcement agencies that utilize these services on a routine basis.

The tragic events of September 11th once again brought to the forefront our need to properly identify suspected terrorists and other criminals. It caused the country to rethink its permeable borders, the anonymity granted in large cities, and the vastness of the geography that enables anyone to virtually disappear. How often were some of these persons of interest checked by local police agencies through routine checks? How often do known, wanted individuals come in contact with local police agencies and give false identifications?

One solution is to enable competent intelligence gathering networks to provide information to decision-making bodies and to share this intelligence amongst them. However, the lack of interoperability of intelligence systems across law enforcement agencies and jurisdictions is a huge obstacle. This obstacle is well known by law enforcement agencies in our region and we realize that interagency communication is only as effective as its weakest link.

This collaborative project has the ability to address not only Homeland Security concerns, but also the increasing threats to officer safety, and the administrative dangers of prison overcrowding. This comprehensive project will expand on the successful CAL-ID system, by enabling the immediate verification of identification of a subject who cannot prove his or her identity or to verify the positive identification of a prisoner prior to release. The proposed program's technology utilizes the most current and reliable equipment available and will enable the sharing of intelligence amongst all law enforcement agencies in Riverside and San Bernardino Counties.

The monies would fund a collaborative project that will enable officers in the field to fingerprint suspects using handheld Mobile Identification Devices (MID) that transmit information via cellular communication to a regional server capable of handling multiple data requests. This will allow officers the ability to positively identify a subject in the field. This process not only provides increased safety for the officer, it reduces the loss of wanted persons through the suspect's deceit. It also has the added benefit of increased public safety by putting the officer back on patrol more quickly by reducing the amount of paperwork and time it takes to properly book a prisoner into a local jail. Riverside and San Bernardino Counties provide the perfect opportunity to pilot test such a program, which will capitalize on the availability of technology necessary in our fluid and transient environment. The diversity of the bi-county service area is perfect for the replicability of this project: the area encompasses five climatic zones, rural and urban areas, and spans more than 27,360 square miles.

As we work toward the future, a key to our continued success will be the interoperability through the purchase of technology. Given the nature of our current environment and the critical urgency of real-time identification needs for Homeland Security, additional funding will be necessary to equip our officers with the tools necessary to accomplish the mission set before them.

## Problem Statement

The need to identify criminals and threats to national safety has always been a priority within the criminal justice system. Law enforcement officers are the first line of defense against terrorist activity and local street criminal activity. A Regional Identification System will allow officers in a patrol setting to quickly identify a suspect or potential terrorist within minutes. There is sufficient technology available to transmit criminal information and photographs directly to an officer on patrol. By using handheld wireless devices with mobile identification software, an officer can identify a suspect quickly, with minimal training. However, this equipment is very expensive and difficult to manage without the proper resources and personnel. Law enforcement agencies throughout San Bernardino and Riverside County are committed to this project, but lack the financial backing to implement such a large scale, but vital project.

San Bernardino and Riverside County compose the largest geographical region in the United States (27,360 square miles). Both counties are in the top five of the fastest growing counties in the United States. The ability to provide radio and wireless data to an officer in the field is compounded by the intense and rugged terrain that is indicative of both counties. There are five cellular wireless providers that cover both counties and a radio system that is over 30 years old. Many of the law enforcement agencies cannot communicate via radio with another jurisdiction that is only a few miles away.

The infrastructure of San Bernardino and Riverside County has Homeland Security implications because of the presence of high-risk targets. Two of the four main interstate arteries into Southern California run through the San Bernardino/Riverside county region, Interstate 10 and 15. Interstate 15 shares close proximity with two major rail lines as well as fuel and gas pipelines as they traverse the Cajon Pass 15 miles north of the City of Ontario. In addition, three large military bases, Fort Irwin, March Air Force base, and 29 Palms Marine base reside within our region and the remote desert areas hold potential for terrorist training camps and other covert activities. The Mobile Identification Devices could be utilized to identify suspects in the aforementioned locations.

The State of Minnesota and the City of Portland, Oregon, have already implemented a mobile identification system. The system is a tremendous success and has already identified potential suspects and terrorists that would have not been identified under the previous infrastructure.

The tremendous growth of our region has caused a financial drain on both counties to provide adequate public safety services to our citizens. The Regional Identification System has been addressed in our regional strategic master plan. The Regional Identification System is a major priority for the region, however funding is a major setback. The region as a whole is very supportive of this project and has already received support from local, state and federal congressional and law enforcement representatives.

If funding is approved for this project, the current gap or lack of communication interoperability will be significantly reduced. Successes will be judged on our collective ability to identify criminals in the field, but also on our ability to decrease the amount of time it takes to book a prisoner in a local jail. On average it takes approximately 45–60 minutes to book one prisoner into custody. If the suspect is pre-identified with a mobile identification device in the field, the total booking time will be reduced to 10–15 minutes, thus, the officer is back on patrol protecting and serving the public that we serve.

## Goals and Objectives

**GOAL:** Enable law enforcement officers in San Bernardino and Riverside County to quickly identify potential suspects and/or terrorists via the Regional Identification System.

Objectives:
1. Identify and establish the appropriate scope of this project for an RFP for mobile identification software vendors. (By the end of Month #2)
2. Develop standard operating procedures and training programs in accordance with CAL-ID regulations and department policy specific to the mobile identification project. (By the end of Month #3)
3. Begin to utilize the wireless Mobile Identification Devices in the field. (By the end of Month #10)

Activities:
1. Weekly meetings with mobile identification vendors and law enforcement staff.
2. Purchase wireless Mobile Identification Devices and establish a network communication infrastructure.
3. Train law enforcement officers throughout both counties.
4. Evaluate the interoperability of the Mobile Identification Devices and make any necessary adjustments with cellular providers.

**GOAL:** Decrease the amount of time it takes to book a prisoner into custody at a local booking facility.

Objectives:
1. Create a new booking procedure for law enforcement officers in both counties. (By the end of month #12)

Activities:
1. Send appropriate suspect data from a wireless Mobile Identification Device directly to our Jail Information Management System (JIMS).
2. Reconfigure the JIMS software application to accept data from a Mobile Identification Device.

## Plan of Operation

The Regional Identification System will allow all local law enforcement agencies in San Bernardino and Riverside County to access the CAL-ID Automated Fingerprint Identification System (AFIS) via a handheld wireless mobile identification device. The regional AFIS database is already in place and located at the Technical Services Bureau of the San Bernardino Sheriff's Department. The wireless handheld devices will be distributed to local law enforcement jurisdictions at the direction of the CAL-ID board of directors. A sufficient amount of the Mobile Identification Devices will be allocated to cover the various patrol shifts and specialized units. Individual law enforcement agencies will benefit from this project because we have already established a unified network of operational and support personnel, central location for on-site computer infrastructure (hardware) and established policy and procedures for regional CAL-ID projects.

The overall management of this project will be provided by a Sheriff's Lieutenant assigned to oversee the CAL-ID division. The CAL-ID Lieutenant will oversee the development of an RFP, budget, project objectives and ensure that the project progresses efficiently and within policy. Assisting the Lieutenant will be four Systems Support Analysts and two clerical staff. The aforementioned project team is already in place and their salaries are covered by the regional CAL-ID program. The project team will research potential mobile identification vendors and establish the specific policies and procedures necessary for this project. The team will also monitor the specific network infrastructure to ensure that the Mobile Identifications Devices are working properly.

The first stage of this project will involve a Request for Proposal (RFP) for approved mobile identification vendors. Nationwide, there are only three vendors that provide this type of technology for law enforcement. The RFP will be designed to specifically address the needs of the region, any limitations based on our geographical location, and funding restrictions. Part of this process will require CAL-ID staff to evaluate Mobile Identification Devices, "pilot" test the devices in the field and make a formal recommendation to the Regional CAL-ID board for approval. Once a specific vendor has been selected via an RFP, the project team will establish a specific time-table for this project, including internal testing of equipment, training, policy review and the overall distribution of the devices to all law enforcement agencies within the region.

There is sufficient building space at CAL-ID for personnel and equipment. The project team will be responsible for the overall distribution of mobile identification equipment. All equipment will be inventoried according to county policy. The equipment will be internally tested and interface configurations will be completed to AFIS and JIMS. Using a previously established network of law enforcement liaisons from police jurisdictions throughout the region, our project team will be able to provide training, maintenance service and monitor the progress of this project.

Due to the size of the region and the amount of law enforcement officers involved in the project, we will utilize a "train the trainer" concept prior to the initial implementation in the field. Our staff will train agency representatives from all law enforcement agencies within the region and each local representative will then go back to their respective agency and train their personnel. This concept is already being utilized for other large scale projects and is quite successful. Training locations have already been established and agency representatives have been identified.

Once the majority of the law enforcement officers have been trained and the Mobile Identification Devices have been successfully tested by the project team, the devices will be distributed to each agency. The project team and agency liaisons will provide continual support, supervision, and feedback to line officers and command staff.

| Timetable of Events | Time from Grant Award |
|---|---|
| Product demonstration and selection of vendor from RFP | Month #2 |
| Purchase of handheld wireless devices | Month #4 |
| Configuration of wireless devices to search AFIS/JIMS | Month #5 |
| Internal testing of devices | Month #6 |
| "Train the trainer" courses for agency liaisons | Month #7 |
| Roll out of mobile identification devices to agencies | Month #8 |
| Evaluation of project goals and objectives | Ongoing (monthly) |
| Oral and written status reports to CAL-ID board | Monthly |

## Evaluation Plan

### Evaluation Methods and Criteria

The project manager for the San Bernardino/Riverside County CAL-ID program will be responsible for completing the evaluations for this project. The San Bernardino/Riverside Regional Remote Access Network (RAN) board will also receive formal evaluations and provide input on the entire project. Additionally, each law enforcement agency that uses the wireless Mobile Identification Device will have the opportunity to evaluate the entire project both verbally and in writing. The CAL-ID project manager will evaluate whether the project met its stated objectives:

Process Objectives:
* Identify and establish an RFP for mobile identification software vendors by the end of month 2.
* Develop standard operating procedures and department policy on the use of the Mobile Identification Device by the end of month 3.
* Begin to utilize the Mobile Identification Devices in the field by the end of month 6.
* Create a new booking procedure for law enforcement officers in both counties by the end of month 8.

Product Objective:
* Enable law enforcement officers to quickly identify potential suspects via the Regional Identification System.
* Decrease the amount of time it takes to book a prisoner into custody at a local booking facility.

### Data Analysis and Collection

The project manager at CAL-ID will compile the necessary information and specifications necessary in order to submit an RFP to a mobile identification vendor. He will ensure that the RFP responses meet the aforementioned objectives and are within county policy. The RFP itself will be evaluated by the San Bernardino County Board of Supervisors and the

CAL-ID Remote Access Network (RAN) board. If necessary, the project manager will modify or expand on the mobile identification standard operating procedures and department policy based on feedback from command and line staff. Once the wireless mobile identification devices are online and being used in the field, each officer that actually uses the device will complete a written evaluation on the product itself. The officer will evaluate the overall response time, any technical issues with the product, and any officer safety concerns. This information will be sent to the project manager for documentation purposes. The project manager and the selected vendor will make any necessary changes or modifications on the device based on feedback from the individual officer. Additionally, the project manager will receive daily response time journals from the selected vendor in order to ensure that the devices are working properly.

The change in the booking procedure will be evaluated by the decrease in the amount of time it takes to process a prisoner. The total processing time will be compared to current processing times. The success of this project will be evident by our ability to get officers in the field in a timely manner as stated in the project goals.

## Use of Evaluation Results for Program Improvement

The project manager and the individual law enforcement liaisons from each department will meet each week to review the evaluations from the individual officers in the field. Each month, a formal meeting will be held with the Remote Access Network (RAN) board to discuss the overall progress of this project and to ensure that all goals and objectives are met. If any problems or corrections are identified, the problem will be documented and corrected immediately. Each year, the Regional Identification System will be evaluated and compared to other law enforcement jurisdictions throughout the country. The collective evaluation of this project will occur when an officer in the field identifies a potential suspect or terrorist and takes him/her into custody solely based on the information received from the mobile identification device.

## Sustainability Plan

San Bernardino/Riverside CAL-ID has been a successful regional law enforcement organization since 1986. The county department heads, Chiefs of Police and the Sheriff of both counties have supported CAL-ID because of our ability to provide efficient identification services to all law enforcement agencies that we serve. The funds requested for this project will be used exclusively to purchase the necessary infrastructure to start the project. The funds will be used for initial costs only or a one-time expense. CAL-ID already has established revenue sources to provide personnel, training and annual maintenance on any equipment purchased for this project. The revenue sources are secured by California legislative law and not subject to local budget restraints.

The Regional Identification System is a major priority within our county. The ability to identify potential suspects and/or terrorists is on the forefront of all public safety agencies. This project has also received support from Board of Supervisors in both counties.

**TABLE A3.1**   Expanded Budget

## REGIONAL FINGERPRINT IDENTIFICATION PROJECT
## SAN BERNARDINO/RIVERSIDE COUNTY CAL-ID

### BUDGET SUMMARY (One time costs)

| Personnel Costs | Total | Requested | Donated |
|---|---|---|---|
| Project Manager | $1,28,000 | $0 | $1,28,000 |
| System Support Analyst | $74,250 | $0 | $74,250 |
| Clerical Staff (Secretary I) | $41,000 | $0 | $41,000 |
| Personnel Totals: | $2,43,250 | $0 | $2,43,250 |

| Non-Personnel Costs | Total | Requested | Donated |
|---|---|---|---|
| Mobile- ID Software | $3,50,000 | $3,50,000 | $0 |
| Software Licenses | $1,50,000 | $1,50,000 | $0 |
| 300 Mobile- ID devices ($5,000 each) | $15,00,000 | $15,00,000 | $0 |
| 300 Cellular Service Accounts | $2,25,000 | $2,25,000 | $0 |
| Training | $15,000 | $0 | $15,000 |
| Fixed Server for Mobile ID | $1,55,000 | $1,55,000 | $0 |
| Annual Maintenance for project | $2,00,000 | $0 | $2,00,000 |
| Non-Personnel Totals: | $25,95,000 | $23,80,000 | $2,15,000 |
| Sub-Total | $28,38,250 | $23,80,000 | $4,58,250 |
| Total Funds Donated by San Bernardino/Riverside CAL-ID | | | **$4,58,250** |
| Total Funds Requested for this project | | | **$23,80,000** |

Additionally, we have received support from local City Councils, State Legislators and Federal Congressional members.

## Budget Justification

### Personnel Costs

The Project Manager (Lieutenant), Systems Support Analyst and the Secretary are existing personnel assigned to San Bernardino/Riverside CAL-ID. The aforementioned personnel are fully funded each year by existing CAL-ID revenues. The total personnel cost is $243,250 per year.

## Non-Personnel Costs

Mobile Identification software is specific and proprietary to a selected vendor. The actual software and licenses are governed by the State of California CMAS price guidelines. The actual per unit price for a complete Mobile Identification device is $5,750. (Actual unit = $5,000, Cellular service = $750). In order to facilitate the Mobile Identification transactions, a dedicated server will be used. This will be a Dell 7850 rack mount server.

We have also budgeted $15,000 for training. This amount will cover all expenses, including travel, supplies and classroom rental fees.

# Appendix 4

# SAMPLE REQUEST FOR PROPOSAL

This proposal is for a security control and video surveillance system upgrade at a large correctional facility. The original RFP is over 200 pages long. Below are excerpts of some of the key areas for your reference. Some of the material, including name of agency, have been changed or modified for this book.

## I. Introduction

### A. Proposal Submission

Proposals must be received by the designated date and time. An electronic proposal can be submitted through the Electronic Procurement Network (ePro). Submittals in ePro will be opened from the system's "encrypted lock box" after the deadline and evaluated as stated in this solicitation. If the proposal is submitted through ePro, the proposal may also be withdrawn OR retrieved, adjusted and re-submitted by the Proposer at the time prior to the scheduled deadline for submission of the proposal.

Paper responses will also be accepted at the location identified in the solicitation, by mail or in person to the address listed in Section I, Paragraph G and will be time/date stamped when received and can be withdrawn at any time prior to the scheduled deadline for submission of the proposal. If the proposal is submitted through ePro, the proposer acknowledges that its electronic signature is legally binding. **Note: If the proposal is submitted through ePro, the Proposer shall not include Attachment F, "Fee Proposal sheet(s)", as part of Proposer's ePro submittal, but instead shall mail or submit in person Attachment F, in a separate sealed envelope labeled "Fee Proposal Sheet" with the RFP Number and title and the name of the Proposer clearly marked on the outside, to the address stated in Section I. G. In addition, if the proposal is submitted through ePro, Proposer shall also submit the following hard copies to _____ in accordance with Section IX.B.2 of this RFP: one (1) original and** five (5) copies, for a total of six (6), of the complete proposal (excluding Attachment F). The proposal and Attachment F must be received (in separate envelopes) on or before the deadline for proposals. Failure to comply with this requirement shall disqualify the Proposer. ADDITIONAL NOTE: All proposers must register with the ePro system prior to the date and time to receive the proposal or they will be disqualified. Late or incomplete proposals will not be accepted.

## B. Purpose

The County of _____, hereafter referred to as the "County" or "Department", is seeking proposals from interested and qualified Proposers to provide an Intergraded Security Systems Upgrade for _____.

## C. Term of Agreement

Specific services to be provided under this Request for Proposals (RFP) are outlined under Section IV, Scope of Work. The Agreement period will be for approximately three years.

## D. Minimum Proposer Requirements

All Proposers must:
1. Have no record of unsatisfactory performance. Proposers who are or have been seriously deficient in current or recent Agreement performance, in the absence of circumstances properly beyond the control of the Proposer, shall be presumed to be unable to meet this requirement.
2. Proposer, or its sub-consultant identified in the Proposal, must have at the time of submission of a Proposal a California State Contractor's License C-10 (high voltage) or C-7 (low voltage).
3. Identify in Proposal a Project Manager and Project Engineer with the qualifications identified in this RFP.
4. Have the ability to maintain adequate files and records and meet statistical reporting requirements
5. Have the administrative and fiscal capability to provide and manage the proposed services and to ensure an adequate audit trail.
6. Have a minimum of three (3) continuous years of experience providing this type of service.
7. Provide references of a minimum of three (3) other customers, one (1) of which should be a government agency, involving the Proposer's delivery of services that demonstrate the ability of the Proposer to provide a security systems upgrade as outlined in this RFP. All references must have names, titles and phone numbers.
8. Provide evidence Proposer can provide a payment and performance bond equal to the maximum amount of Proposer's cost proposal (i.e. base proposal plus any options/alternates).
9. Meet other presentation and participation requirements listed in this RFP.

## E. Mandatory Job Walk

1. A mandatory Job Walk will be held on: _____

   Location: _____

**Meet in the Administrative Building Lobby**

2. **Attendance at the Job Walk is mandatory. No proposal will be accepted from any Proposer who fails to attend the proposal conference.**
3. All Vendors and sub-consultants that intend to submit a Proposal this Project and who plan to attend the on-site job walk will be required to follow the following Job-walk Rules as listed.
4. **Job-walk Rules:**
   4.1 Proposed Vendors must be on time. Once the Job-walk group leaves the initial meeting location, no additional vendors will be allowed to join the job walk.
   4.2 All attending Vendors will be required to present a company business card with their name on it.
   4.3 All attending Vendors will be required to present photo identification card such as a valid California Driver's License or California Identification card.
   4.4 **No cell phones** will be allowed inside the jail.
   4.5 Cameras will be allowed for project specific photo documentation. Vendors will be allowed to take photographs that pertain specifically to the project. No general photography will be allowed without the consent of the Project Manager. At no time shall any inmates or County employees be photographed.
   4.6 No weapons will be allowed.
   4.7 No smoking, tobacco products, matches or lighters will be allowed.
   4.8 No portable electronic devices will be allowed.
5. Sheriff reserves the right to refuse entry to those who do not comply with the facility rules.

## F. Questions

Questions regarding the contents of this RFP must be submitted in writing on or **before 4:00 P.M. (PST) on** _____ and directed to the individual listed in Section I, Paragraph G. All questions will be answered and both the question and answer will be posted on the County's Web-Site.

## G. Correspondence

All correspondence, **including proposals and questions**, are to be submitted to:

_____

Purchasing Department
Attn:

Fax number and e-mail address may be used to submit questions only. **Proposals will not be accepted by email or facsimile.**

## H. Admonition to Proposers

Once this RFP has been issued, the individual identified above is the sole contact point for any inquiries or information relating to this RFP. Failure to adhere to this policy may result in disqualification of the Proposer. All questions regarding this RFP must be presented in writing as indicated in Section I, Paragraph F.

## I. Proposal Submission Deadline

Proposals must be received no later than **4:00 P.M. (PST), on** _____ Postmarks will not be accepted in lieu of actual receipt. Facsimile or electronically transmitted proposals will not be accepted in lieu of actual receipt. Late or incomplete proposals will not be accepted.

## II. Proposal Timeline

Release of RFP
Mandatory Job Walk
Submission of Questions          _____
Answers to Questions Posted      _____
Deadline for Proposals           _____
Tentative Date for Awarding      TBD
Contract

## III. Proposal Conditions

## A. Contingencies

This RFP does not commit the _____ to award an Agreement. The County reserves the right to accept or reject any or all proposals if the County determines it is in the best interest of the County to do so. The County will notify all Proposers in writing, if the County rejects all proposals. The County also reserves the right to terminate this RFP process at any time.

## B. Evaluation Process

Proposals will be evaluated in compliance with the procedure described in Section VII of this RFP.

## C. Modifications

The County reserves the right to issue addenda or amendments to this RFP if the County considers that additional clarifications are needed. Only those Proposers represented at the

Job Walk will receive addenda or amendments issued after the Mandatory Pre-proposal Conference.

## D. Proposal Submission

To be considered, all proposals must be submitted in the manner set forth in this RFP. It is the Proposer's responsibility to ensure that its proposal arrives on or before the specified time.

## E. Incurred Costs

The County is not obligated to pay any costs incurred by Proposers in the preparation of a proposal in response to this RFP. Proposers agree that all costs incurred in developing this proposal are the Proposer's responsibility.

## F. Negotiations

The County may require the potential Proposer(s) selected to participate in negotiations. This may include cost, technical, or other clarifications needed to make a decision.

## G. Formal Agreement

Proposer will be required to enter into a formal Agreement with the County. This RFP sets forth some of the general provisions which will be included in the final Agreement. In submitting a response to this RFP, Proposer will be deemed to have agreed to each clause unless the proposal identifies an objection and County agrees to a change of language in writing. All objections to any provisions of the final Agreement should be listed on Attachment C – Exceptions to RFP.

## H. Use of Proposals Received

All proposals received shall become the property of the County.

## I. Improper Influence

Proposer shall make all reasonable efforts to ensure that no County officer or employee, whose position in the County enables him/her to influence any award of the Agreement or any competing offer, shall have any direct or indirect financial interest resulting from the award of the Agreement, or shall have any relationship to the Proposer or officer or employee of the Proposer.

## J. Final Authority

The final authority to award Agreements as a result of this RFP rests solely with the County of _____ Board of Supervisors (Board). In certain situations, the Board may authorize the Chief Executive Officer (CEO) and/or the Purchasing Agent to award Agreements.

## IV. Scope of Work

### A. Introduction

The _____ (Sheriff) seeks proposals from qualified Integrated Security Systems Vendors to assist in the design and installation of a security control and monitoring system to upgrade, replace and expand the existing systems at the _____. The Project involves replacing existing hard panels with a graphics user interface (GUI) on interactive display screens, upgrading existing PLC system, replacing the audio systems, the addition of and replacement of existing analog cameras with IP based cameras, controls, and recording, and interfacing to the fire alarm and jail management systems. The Project will involve the reuse of some of the existing Allen Bradley PLC equipment as more fully detailed in this RFP.

### B. Background

The _____ was built in _____ and has undergone several systems upgrades. The security system has a mix of original and upgraded equipment and systems. The Project is intended to upgrade the security system to a uniform level of current technology and equipment.

### C. Project Description

#### 1. Project Objective and Goals

A security systems integrator (Vendor) is sought to assist the Sheriff in the design and installation of an upgraded and expanded security and control system. This will require substantial site investigation, engineering, and working with the Sheriff's staff and consultants to design and implement the systems in a systematic and sequential project schedule in an active and occupied facility. The existing security and control system consisting of control panels, PLC and circuit cards will be replaced using Graphic User Interfaces with PC's and PLC's. Some of the existing PLC equipment will be reused.

This Contract will not include the installation of furniture, conduit and pathways, or the fiber backbone, or the programming of the Jail Management System (JMS). This work will be done by County or County's separate contractor.

The existing intercom and public address headed equipment will be replaced as replacement parts are no longer available. The new headed audio system will be network based and interfaced to the Graphic User Interfaces.

The existing Video Surveillance and Recording System will be replaced and expanded. The new system will be Internet Protocol (IP) based.

## *D. Scope of Work*

1. The scope of work described herein is supplemented with the specifications and drawings included in this RFP (see Attachment G), which includes Section 280500 Common Work Results for Electronic Safety and Security; Section 284800 Sequence of Operations; Section 284600 Integrated Control System; Section 282300 Video Surveillance System; Section 281500 Intercom and Paging System and 3 pages of diagrams). The following descriptions outline the basic work to be performed and the supporting documents provide more detail. The Vendor will provide all components for a complete system. The County or its vendors will provide all conduit and pathways and fiber backbone. Areas included within this project and their respective communications rooms are:

### 1.2 Cell Housing Units
There are 11 Cell housing Units, each with eight (8) Segments (A–H). Segments A–F are for inmate population housing containing sixteen (16) cells. Segment G connects each Housing Unit to the Central Corridor and contains Inmate Visiting Phones, Nurse's Office, and AD SEG Cells. Segment H serves as the Recreation Yard for the Housing Unit. (Housing Units 1–6, 9–12, and 15).

### 1.3 Dorm Housing Units
There are four (4) Dorm Housing Units that have the same structure as Cell Housing Units, but with no individual cells for Inmate Housing. (Housing Units 7, 8, 13 and 14).

### 1.4 Other Control Stations
    1.4.1   Master Control
            Hierarchy: Monitor and take over Control of any Control Room.
    1.4.2   North Control
            Hierarchy: Monitor and take over Control of any Control Room.
    1.4.3   South Control
    1.4.4   Intake Control
    1.4.5   Medical
    1.4.6   Nurse Station
    1.4.7   Law Library
    1.4.8   Releases
    1.4.9   Visiting Deputy
    1.4.10  Visiting Lobby
    1.4.11  Admin Lobby
    1.4.12  Clothing
    1.4.13  Laundry
    1.4.14  Receiving
    1.4.15  Warehouse
    1.4.16  Fiscal
    1.4.17  Booking
    1.4.18  Kitchen

### 1.5 System Interfaces
1.5.1 Fire Alarm
1.5.2 Jail Management Systems

### 1.6 Exclusions from this Contract
1.6.1 Furniture installation
1.6.2 Conduit and pathways.
1.6.3 Fiber backbone
1.6.4 Jail Management System (JMS) programming.

### 1.7 Design
1.7.1 Based on the RFP, Site Investigation, and meetings with the Sheriff's staff the Vendor will provide a system design for approval.
1.7.2 The proposal design shall be presented as a Product Data Submittal and Shop Drawings.

### 1.8 Construction
1.8.1 Based on approved shop drawings the Vendor shall build and shop test the replacement systems. Prior to site installation, a successful hop test and demonstration is required.
1.8.2 Installation of the approved shop tested equipment shall be installed following the approved project schedule.
1.8.3 Training on the new systems shall be conducted prior to the first housing unit being brought online and then per the approved project schedule.
1.8.4 Project completion shall be granted following the 15-Day Continuous Operational Test.

## E. General Information

The Project will require the payment of Prevailing Wages in compliance with all applicable California Laws. Attachment J to this RFP contains the General Prevailing Wage Determination made by the Director of Industrial Relations pursuant to California Labor Code, Part VII, Chapter 1, Article 2, Sections 1770, et seq. and must be complied with for this Project. See Attachment L for additional requirements for this Project.

Payment will be made to Vendor only upon successful completion and acceptance by County of each of the housing or administrative units.

## F. Project Schedule

1. The _____ is in the process of remodeling all 15 housing units, otherwise known as the ADA remodel project. The remodeling requires the demolition of certain cells and fixtures in the day room areas. This project will not affect the housing unit control rooms and should not interfere with the Integrated Security System project as listed in this RFP. All inmates will also be removed from each housing unit during construction. The ADA project contractor anticipates that the remodel time in each housing unit will be approximately 4–6 weeks. The entire project time is approximately 18 months.

2. The security System Vendor will have full access to each housing unit to remove existing equipment and install the Integrated Security System equipment; however, they will only be allowed to work on one housing unit at a time concurrently with the ADA contractor. The Integrated Security System Vendor will not be allowed to work on other housing units until the ADA contractor finishes their work and moves on to another housing unit.
3. The ADA contractor will start work on housing unit #7 on April 7, 2014. The Security System Vendor can begin their site investigation and design phase of the project using housing unit #7 remodel and install their equipment during the 4–6 week period of the next or subsequent housing unit.
4. Once the Integrated Security System equipment AND the ADA remodel is completed in a housing unit, both Vendor and ADA contractor will move to another housing unit and continue with both projects. The project schedule with be coordinated between the Vendor, ADA contractor and WVDC staff. WVDC will determine the actual project schedule.
5. The Security System Vendor will have the opportunity to install most of the Video Surveillance System (VSS) and other Integrated Security Systems of the non-housing units (intake, master control, south control, etc.) on a separate schedule.

## G. Alternates and Options

**Option 1:** Extend recording for Intake and Transportation an additional 13 months:

  **a.** Second Stream: Intake and Transportation: Recording shall be 24/7 at 1 FPS once activated upon motion at 7 FPS for 26 months with a pre and post recording duration of 30 sec.

**Option 2:** Provide a RAID 1 backup system of the video recording storage for all cameras Base Proposal (without Option 1).

**Option 3:** Provide a RAID 1 backup system of the video recording storage for all cameras including Option 1.

## V. Agreement Requirements

It is the County's intent that the contractual relationship between the Proposer and the County shall be substantially as set forth in the attached sample Agreement (Attachment I). In developing the proposal, the Proposer should carefully review the sample Agreement and the contractual requirements listed in Section V and take into consideration the rights, obligations, and costs associated therewith. Any change in the sample Agreement or the contractual requirements in Section V, which the Proposer desires, must be specified in the proposal or the requested change will be deemed to have been waived.

## A. General

### 1. Legality and Severability
The parties' actions under the Agreement shall comply with all applicable laws, rules, regulations, court orders and governmental agency orders. The provisions of this Agreement

are specifically made severable. If a provision of the Agreement is terminated or held to be invalid, illegal or unenforceable, the validity, legality and enforceability of the remaining provisions shall remain in full effect.

## 2. Taxes

County is exempt from Federal excise taxes and no payment shall be made for any personal property taxes levied on Proposer or on any taxes levied on employee wages. The County shall only pay for any State or local sales or use taxes on the services rendered or equipment and/or parts supplied to the County pursuant to the Agreement.

## 3. Representation of the County

In the performance of the Agreement, Vendor, its agents and employees, shall act in an independent capacity and not as officers, employees, or agents of the County of _____.

## 4. Relationship of the Parties

Nothing contained in this Agreement shall be construed as creating a joint venture, part-nership, or employment arrangement between the Parties hereto, nor shall either Party have the right, power or authority to create an obligation or duty, expressed or implied, on behalf of the other Party hereto.

## 5. Vendor Primary Contact

The Vendor will designate an individual to serve as the primary point of contact for the Agreement. Vendor or designee must respond to County inquires within two (2) business days. Vendor shall not change the primary contact without written notification and accep-tance of the County. Vendor will also designate a back-up point of contact in the event the primary contact is not available.

## 6. Change of Address

Vendor shall notify the County in writing of any change in mailing address within ten (10) business days of the change.

## 7. Subcontracting

Vendor agrees not to enter into any subcontracting contracts for work contemplated under the Agreement without first obtaining written approval from the County. Any subcon-tracting shall be subject to the same terms and conditions as Vendor. Vendor shall be fully responsible for the performance and payments of any subcontractor's contract.

## 8. Agreement Assignability

Without the prior written consent of the County, the Agreement is not assignable by Ven-dor either in whole or in part.

## 9. Agreement Modification

Vendor agrees any alterations, variations, modifications, or waivers of the provisions of the Agreement, shall be valid only when reduced to writing, executed and attached to the original Agreement and approved by the person(s) authorized to do so on behalf of Vendor and the County.

## 10. Duration of Terms

This Agreement, and all of its terms and conditions, shall be binding upon and shall inure to the benefit of the heirs, executors, administrators, successors, and assigns of the respective parties, provided no such assignment is in violation of the provisions of this Agreement.

## 11. Time of the Essence

Time is of the essence in performance of this Agreement and of each of its provisions.

## 12. Strict Performance

Failure by a party to insist upon the strict performance of any of the provisions of this Agreement by the other party, or the failure by a party to exercise its rights upon the default of the other party, shall not constitute a waiver of such party's right to insist and demand strict compliance by the other party with the terms of this Agreement thereafter.

## 13. Mutual Covenants

The parties to this Agreement mutually covenant to perform all of their obligations hereunder, to exercise all discretion and rights granted hereunder, and to give all consents in a reasonable manner consistent with the standards of "good faith" and "fair dealing".

## 14. Agreement Exclusivity

This is not an exclusive Agreement. The County reserves the right to enter into an agreement with other proposers for the same or similar services. The County does not guarantee or represent that the Vendor will be permitted to perform any minimum amount of work, or receive compensation other than on a per order basis, under the terms of this Agreement.

## 15. Termination for Convenience

The County for its convenience may terminate this Agreement in whole or in part upon ten (10) calendar day's written notice. Vendor shall immediately stop work in accordance with the notice and comply with any other direction as may be specified in the notice or as provided subsequently by County. County shall pay Vendor for the work completed prior to the effective date of the termination, and such payment shall be Vendor's sole remedy under this Agreement. Under no circumstances will Vendor be entitled to anticipatory or unearned profits, consequential damages, or other damages of any sort as a result of a termination or partial termination under this provision. Vendor shall deliver promptly to County and transfer title (if necessary) all completed work, and work in progress, including drafts, documents, plans, forms, data, products, graphics, computer programs and reports.

## 16. Attorney Fees and Costs

If any legal action is instituted to enforce any party's rights hereunder, each party shall bear its own costs and attorneys' fees, regardless of who is the prevailing party. This paragraph shall not apply to those costs and attorney fees directly arising from a third-party legal action against a party hereto and payable under the Indemnification and Insurance Requirements.

### 17. Venue
The parties acknowledge and agree that this Contract was entered into and intended to be performed in _____. The parties agree that the venue of any action or claim brought by any party to this Agreement will be the Superior Court of California, _____ District. Each party hereby waives any law or rule of the court, which would allow them to request or demand a change of venue. If any action or claim concerning this Agreement is brought by any third-party and filed in another venue, the parties hereto agree to use their best efforts to obtain a change of venue to the Superior Court of California, _____ District.

### 18. Electronic Fund Transfer Program
Vendor shall accept all payments from County via electronic funds transfer (EFT) directly deposited into the Vendor's designated checking or other bank account. Vendor shall promptly comply with directions and accurately complete forms provided by County required to process EFT payments.

### 19. Licenses, Permits and/or Certifications
Vendor shall ensure that it has all necessary licenses, permits and/or certifications required by the laws of Federal, State, County, and municipal laws, ordinances, rules and regulations. The Vendor shall maintain these licenses, permits and/or certifications in effect for the duration of this Agreement. Vendor will notify County immediately of loss or suspension of any such licenses, permits and/or certifications. Failure to maintain required licenses, permits and/or certifications may result in immediate termination of this Agreement.

### 20. Prevailing Wage Laws
By its execution of this Agreement, Vendor certifies that it is aware of the requirements of California Labor Code Sections 1720 et seq. and 1770 et seq. as well as California Code of Regulations, Title 8, Section 16000 et seq. ("Prevailing Wage Laws"), which require the payment of prevailing wage rates and the performance of other requirements on certain "public works" and "maintenance" projects. Section 1720 of the California Labor Code states in part: "For purposes of this paragraph, 'construction' includes work performed during the design and preconstruction phases of construction including, but not limited to, inspection and land surveying work." If the Services are being performed as part of an applicable "public works" or "maintenance" project, as defined by the Prevailing Wage Laws, and if the total compensation is $1,000 or more, Vendor agrees to fully comply with such Prevailing Wage Laws. Vendor shall make copies of the prevailing rates of per diem wages for each craft, classification or type of worker needed to execute the Services available to interested parties upon request, and shall post copies at the Vendor's principal place of business and at the project site. Vendor will also adhere to any other applicable requirements, including but not limited to, those regarding the employment of apprentices, travel and subsistence pay, retention and inspection of payroll records, workers compensation and

forfeiture of penalties prescribed in the Labor Code for violations. Vendor shall defend, indemnify and hold the County, its elected officials, officers, employees and agents free and harmless from any claims, liabilities, costs, penalties or interest arising out of any failure or alleged failure to comply with Prevailing Wage Laws.

### 21. Notification Regarding Performance

In the event of a problem or potential problem that could impact the quality or quantity of work, services, or the level of performance under this Agreement, the Vendor shall notify the County within one (1) working day, in writing and by telephone.

### 22. Conflict of Interest

Vendor shall make all reasonable efforts to ensure that no conflict of interest exists between its officers, employees, or subcontractors and the County. Vendor shall make a reasonable effort to prevent employees, officers, or members of governing bodies from using their positions for purposes that are, or give the appearance of being motivated by a desire for private gain for themselves or others such as those with whom they have family business, or other ties. Officers, employees, and agents of cities, counties, districts, and other local agencies are subject to applicable conflict of interest codes and state law. In the event the County determines a conflict of interest situation exists, any increase in costs, associated with the conflict of interest situation, may be disallowed, by the County and such conflict may constitute grounds for termination of the Agreement. This provision shall not be construed to prohibit employment of persons with whom Vendor's officers, employees, or agents have family, business, or other ties so long as the employment of such persons does not result in increased costs over those associated with the employment of any other equally qualified applicant.

### 23. Material Misstatement/Misrepresentation

If during the course of the administration of this Agreement, the County determines that Vendor has made a material misstatement, misrepresentation or that materially inaccurate information has been provided to the County during the RFP process, this Agreement may be immediately terminated. If this Agreement is terminated according to this provision, the County is entitled to pursue any available legal remedies.

### 24. Ownership of Documents

All documents, data, products, graphics, computer programs, and reports prepared by the Vendor pursuant to this Agreement shall be considered property of the County upon payment for services (and product, if applicable). All such items shall be delivered to the County at the completion of work under this Agreement, subject to the requirements of Section V, Paragraph A, 15 (Termination for Convenience). Unless otherwise directed by the County, Vendor may retain copies of such items.

### 25. Copyright

County shall have a royalty-free, non-exclusive and irrevocable license to publish, disclose, copy, translate, and otherwise use, copyright or patent, now and hereafter, all reports, studies, information, data, statistics, forms, designs, plans, procedures, systems, and any other materials or properties developed under this Agreement including those covered by copyright, and reserves the right to authorize others to use or reproduce such material. All such materials developed under the terms of this Agreement shall acknowledge the County of _____ as the funding agency and Vendor as the creator of the publication. No such materials or properties produced in whole or in part under this Agreement shall be subject to private use, copyright or patent right by Vendor in the United States or in any other country without the express written consent of County. Copies of all educational and training materials, curricula, audio/visual aids, printed material, and periodicals, assembled pursuant to this Agreement must be filed with the County prior to publication.

## 26. Invoices

Vendor shall provide County itemized monthly invoices, in arrears, for services performed under this Agreement within twenty (20) days of the end of the previous month. The County will make payment to Vendor within sixty (60) calendar days after receipt of invoice or the resolution of any billing dispute.

## 27. Release of Information

No news releases, advertisements, public announcements or photographs arising out of this Agreement or Vendor's relationship with County may be made or used without prior written approval of the County.

## 28. Damage to County Property, Facilities, Buildings or Grounds

The Vendor shall repair, or cause to be repaired, at its own cost, all damage to County vehicles, facilities, buildings or grounds caused by the willful or negligent acts of Vendor or employees or agents of the Vendor. Such repairs shall be made immediately after Vendor becomes aware of such damage, but in no event later than thirty (30) days after the occurrence.

If the Vendor fails to make timely repairs, the County may make any necessary repairs. The Vendor, as determined by the County, shall repay all costs incurred by the County for such repairs, by cash payment upon demand or County may deduct such costs from any amounts due to the Vendor from the County.

## 29. Air, Water Pollution Control, Safety and Health

Vendor shall comply with all air pollution control, water pollution, safety and health ordinances and statutes, which apply to the work performed pursuant to this Agreement.

## 30. Drug and Alcohol-Free Workplace

In recognition of individual rights to work in a safe, healthful and productive work place, as a material condition of this Agreement, the Vendor agrees that the Vendor and the Vendor's employees, while performing service for the County, on County property, or while using County equipment:

a. Shall not be in any way impaired because of being under the influence of alcohol or a drug.
b. Shall not possess an open container of alcohol or consume alcohol or possess or be under the influence of an illegal drug.
c. Shall not sell, offer, or provide alcohol or a drug to another person.

This shall not be applicable to a Vendor or Vendor's employee who, as part of the performance of normal job duties and responsibilities, prescribes or administers medically prescribed drugs.

The Vendor shall inform all employees that are performing service for the County on County property, or using County equipment, of the County's objective of a safe, healthful and productive work place and the prohibition of drug or alcohol use or impairment from same while performing such service for the County.

The County may terminate for default or breach of this Agreement and any other Agreement the Vendor has with the County, if the Vendor or Vendor's employees are determined by the County not to be in compliance with above.

### 31. Notice of Delays

Except as otherwise provided herein, when either party has knowledge that any actual or potential situation is delaying or threatens to delay the timely performance of this Agreement, that party shall, within twenty-four (24) hours, give notice thereof, including all relevant information with respect thereto, to the other party.

### 32. Artwork, Proofs and/or Negatives

All artwork, proofs and/or negatives in either print or digital format for this product are the property of the _____. These items must be returned to the _____ within ten (10) days, upon written notification to the Proposer. In the event of a failure to return the documents, the county is entitled to pursue any available legal remedies. In addition, the Proposer will be barred from all future solicitations, for a period of at least six (6) months.

### 33. Environmental Requirements

In accordance with County Policy 11–10, the County prefers to acquire and use products with higher levels of post-consumer recycled content. Environmentally preferable goods and materials must perform satisfactorily and be available at a reasonable price. The County requires Proposers to use recycled paper for proposals and for any printed or photocopied material created as a result of an Agreement with the County. The policy also requires Proposers to use both sides of paper sheets for reports submitted to the County whenever practicable.

Although the County has not committed to allowing a cost preference, if two products are equivalent and the cost is feasible the environmentally preferable product would be selected. The intent is to utilize Proposers that reduce environmental impacts in their production and distribution systems whenever fiscally practicable.

To assist the County in meeting the reporting requirements of the California Integrated Waste Management Act of 1989 (AB939), Proposer must be able to annually report the County's environmentally preferable purchases using a County approved form. Service providers are asked to report on environmentally preferable goods and materials used in the provision of their service to the County.

### 34. Employment Discrimination

During the term of the Agreement, Proposer shall not willfully discriminate against any employee or applicant for employment because of race, religion, color, national origin, ancestry, physical handicap, medical condition, gender, marital status, age, political affiliation, disability or sexual orientation. Proposer shall comply with Executive Orders 11246, 11375, 11625, 12138, 12432, 12250, Title VII of the Civil Rights Act of 1964, the California Fair Housing and Employment Act and other application Federal, State and County laws and regulations and policies relating to equal employment and contracting opportunities, including laws and regulations hereafter enacted.

## 35. Debarment and Suspension
The Proposer certifies that neither it nor its principals or subcontracts is presently disbarred, suspended, proposed for debarment, declared ineligible, or voluntarily excluded from participation in this transaction by any federal department or agency as required by Executive Order 12549.

## 36. Informal Dispute Resolution
In the event the County determines that service is unsatisfactory, or in the event of any other dispute, claim, question or disagreement arising from or relating to this Agreement or breach thereof, the parties hereto shall use their best efforts to settle the dispute, claim, question or disagreement. To this effect, they shall consult and negotiate with each other in good faith and, recognizing their mutual interests, attempt to reach a just and equitable solution satisfactory to both parties.

## 37. Iran Contracting Act
Iran Contracting Act of 2010, Public Contract Code sections 2200 et seq. (Applicable for all Agreements of one million dollars ($1,000,000) or more). In accordance with Public Contract Code section 2204(a), the Proposer certifies that at the time the Agreement is signed, the Proposer signing the Agreement is not identified on a list created pursuant to subdivision (b) of Public Contract Code section 2203 as a person (as defined in Public Contract Code section 2202(e) engaging in investment activities in Iran described in subdivision (a) of Public Contract Code section 2202.5, or as a person described in subdivision (b) of Public Contract Code section 2202.5, as applicable.

Proposers are cautioned that making a false certification may subject the Proposer to civil penalties, termination of existing agreement, and ineligibility to bid on a contract for a period of three (3) years in accordance with Public Contract Code section 2205. Proposer agrees that signing the Proposal and Agreement shall constitute signature of this Certification.

## 38. Records
Proposer shall maintain all records and books pertaining to the delivery of services under this Agreement and demonstrate accountability for agreement performance. All records shall be complete and current and comply with all Agreement requirements. Failure to maintain acceptable records shall be considered grounds for withholding of payments for invoices submitted and/or termination of the Agreement.

All records relating to the Proposer's personnel, consultants, subcontractors, Service/Scope of Work and expenses pertaining to this Agreement shall be kept in generally acceptable accounting format. Records should include primary source documents. Fiscal records shall be kept in accordance with Generally Accepted Accounting Principles and must account for all funds, tangible assets, revenue and expenditures. Fiscal records must comply with the appropriate Office of Management and Budget (OMB) Circulars which state the administrative requirements, cost principles and other standards for accountancy.

### 39. American–Recovery and Reinvestment Act Funding (ARRA)
### Use of ARRA Funds and Requirements

This Agreement may be funded in whole or in part with funds provided by the American Recovery and Reinvestment Act of 2009 ("ARRA"), signed into law on February 17, 2009. Section 1605 of ARRA prohibits the use of recovery funds for a project for the construction, alteration, maintenance or repair of a public building or public work (both as defined in 2 CFR 176.140) unless all of the iron, steel and manufactured goods (as defined in 2 CFR 176.140) used in the project are produced in the United States. A waiver is available under three limited circumstances: (i) Iron, steel or relevant manufactured goods are not produced in the United States in sufficient and reasonable quantities and of a satisfactory quality; (ii) Inclusion of iron, steel or manufactured goods produced in the United States will increase the cost of the overall project by more than 25 percent; or (iii) Applying the domestic preference would be inconsistent with the public interest. This is referred to as the "Buy American" requirement. Request for a waiver must be made to the County for an appropriate determination.

Section 1606 of ARRA requires that laborers and mechanics employed by contractors and subcontractors on projects funded directly by or assisted in whole or in part by and through the Federal Government pursuant to ARRA shall be paid wages at rates not less than those prevailing on projects of a character similar in the locality as determined by the Secretary of Labor in accordance with the Davis–Bacon Act (40 U.S.C. 31). This is referred to as the "wage rate" requirement.

The above described provisions constitute notice under ARRA of the Buy American and wage rate requirements. Proposer must contact the County contact if it has any questions regarding the applicability or implementation of the ARRA Buy American and wage rate requirements. Proposer will also be required to provide detailed information regarding compliance with the Buy American requirements, expenditure of funds and wages paid to employees so that the County may fulfill any reporting requirements it has under ARRA. The information may be required as frequently as monthly or quarterly. Proposer agrees to fully cooperate in providing information or documents as requested by the County pursuant to this provision. Failure to do so will be deemed a default and may result in the withholding of payments and termination of this Agreement.

Proposer may also be required to register in the Central Contractor Registration (CCR) database at www.ccr.gov and may be required to have its subcontractors also register in the same database. Proposer must contact the County with any questions regarding registration requirements.

## Schedule of Expenditure of Federal Awards

In addition to the requirements described in "Use of ARRA Funds and Requirements," proper accounting and reporting of ARRA expenditures in single audits is required.

Proposer agrees to separately identify the expenditures for each grant award funded under ARRA on the Schedule of Expenditures of Federal Awards (SEFA) and the Data Collection Form (SF-SAC) required by the Office of Management and Budget Circular A-133, "Audits of States, Local Governments, and Nonprofit Organizations." This identification on the SEFA and SF-SAC shall include the Federal award number, the Catalog of Federal Domestic Assistance (CFDA) number, and amount such that separate accountability and disclosure is provided for ARRA funds by Federal award number consistent with the recipient reports required by ARRA Section 1512 (c).

In addition, Proposer agrees to separately identify to each subcontractor and document at the time of subcontract and at the time of disbursement of funds, the Federal award number, any special CFDA number assigned for ARRA purposes, and amount of ARRA funds.

Proposer may be required to provide detailed information regarding expenditures so that the County may fulfill any reporting requirements under ARRA described in this section. The information may be required as frequently as monthly or quarterly. Proposer agrees to fully cooperate in providing information or documents as requested by the County pursuant to this provision. Failure to do so will be deemed a default and may result in the withholding of payments and termination of this Agreement.

## Whistleblower Protection

Proposer agrees that both it and its subcontractors shall comply with Section 1553 of the ARRA, which prohibits all non-Federal contractors, including the State, and all contractors of the State, from County of _____ for Proposal. Discharging, demoting or otherwise discriminating against an employee for disclosures by the employee that the employee reasonably believes are evidence of: (1) gross mismanagement of an Agreement relating to ARRA funds; (2) a gross waste of ARRA funds; (3) a substantial and specific danger to public health or safety related to the implementation or use of ARRA funds; (4) an abuse of authority related to the implementation or use of recovery funds; or (5) a violation of law, rule, or regulation related to an agency Agreement (including the competition for or negotiation of an Agreement) awarded or issued relating to ARRA funds.

*Vendor agrees that it and its subcontractors shall post notice of the rights and remedies available to employees under Section 1553 of Division A, Title XV of the ARRA.*

## B. Indemnification and Insurance Requirements

### 1. Indemnification

The Proposer agrees to indemnify, defend (with counsel reasonably approved by County) and hold harmless the County and its authorized officers, employees, agents and volunteers from any and all claims, actions, losses, damages and/or liability arising out of this Agreement from any cause whatsoever, including the acts, errors or omissions of any person and for any costs or expenses incurred by the County on account of any claim except where such indemnification is prohibited by law. This indemnification provision shall apply regardless of the existence or degree of fault of indemnities. The Proposer indemnification obligation applies to the County's "active" as well as "passive" negligence but does not apply to the County's "sole negligence" or "willful misconduct" within the meaning of Civil Code Section 2782.

## 2. Basic Insurance Requirements
### Additional Insured
All policies, except for the Workers' Compensation, Errors and Omissions and Professional Liability policies shall contain additional endorsements naming the County and its officers, employees, agents and volunteers as additional insureds with respect to liabilities arising out of the performance of services hereunder. The additional insured endorsements shall not limit the scope of coverage for the County to vicarious liability but shall allow coverage for the County to the full extent provided by the policy. Such additional insured coverage shall be at least as broad as Additional Insured (Form B) endorsement form ISO, CG 2010.11 85.

### Waiver of Subrogation Rights
The Proposer shall require the carriers of required coverages to waive all rights of subrogation against the County, its officers, employees, agents, volunteers, contractors, and subcontractors. All general or auto liability insurance coverage provided shall not prohibit the Proposer and Proposer's employees or agents from waiving the right of subrogation prior to a loss or claim. The Proposer hereby waives all rights of subrogation against the County.

### Policies Primary and Non-Contributory
All policies required above are to be primary and non-contributory with any insurance or self-insurance programs carried or administered by the County.

### Severability of Interests
The Proposer agrees to ensure that coverage provided to meet these requirements is applicable separately to each insured and there will be no cross liability exclusions that preclude coverage for suits between the Proposer and the County or between the County and any other insured or additional insured under the policy.

### Proof of Coverage
The Proposer shall furnish certificates of insurance to the County Department administering the Agreement evidencing the insurance coverage at the time the Agreement is executed, additional County of _____ Request for Proposal. Endorsements, as required shall be provided prior to the commencement of performance of services hereunder, which certificates shall provide that such insurance shall not be terminated or expire without thirty (30) days written notice to the Department(s) and Proposer shall maintain such insurance from the time Proposer commences performance of services hereunder until the completion of such services. Within fifteen (15) days of the commencement of this Agreement, the Proposer shall furnish a copy of the Declaration page for all applicable policies and will provide complete certified copies of the policies and all endorsements immediately upon request.

## Acceptability of Insurance Carrier
Unless otherwise approved by Risk Management, insurance shall be written by insurers authorized to do business in the State of California and with a minimum "Best" Insurance Guide rating of "A-VII".

## Deductibles and Self-Insured Retention
Any and all deductibles or self-insured retentions in excess of $10,000 shall be declared to and approved by Risk Management.

## Failure to Procure Coverage
In the event that any policy of insurance required under this Agreement does not comply with the requirements, is not procured, or is canceled and not replaced, the County has the right but not the obligation or duty to cancel the Agreement or obtain insurance if it deems necessary and any premiums paid by the County will be promptly reimbursed by the Proposer or County payments to the Proposer(s)/Applicant(s) will be reduced to pay for County purchased insurance.

## Insurance Review
Insurance requirements are subject to periodic review by the County. The Director of Risk Management or designee is authorized, but not required, to reduce, waive or suspend any insurance requirements whenever Risk Management determines that any of the required insurance is not available, is unreasonably priced, or is not needed to protect the interest of the County. In addition, if the Department of Risk Management determines that heretofore unreasonably priced or unavailable types of insurance coverage or coverage limits become reasonably priced or available, the Director of Risk Management or designee is authorized, but not required, to change the above insurance requirements to require additional types of insurance coverage or higher coverage limits, provided that any such change is reasonable in light of past claims again the County, inflation, or any other item reasonably related to the County's risk.

Any change requiring additional types of insurance coverage or higher coverage limits must be made by amendment to this Agreement. Proposer agrees to execute any such amendment within thirty (30) days of receipt.

Any failure, actual or alleged, on the part of the County to monitor or enforce compliance with any of the insurance and indemnification requirements will not be deemed as a waiver of any rights on the part of the County.

## 3. Insurance Specifications
The Proposer agrees to provide insurance set forth in accordance with the requirements herein. If the Proposer uses existing coverage to comply with these requirements and that coverage does not meet the specified requirements, the Proposer agrees to amend, supplement or endorse the existing coverage to do so.

Without in anyway affecting the indemnity herein provided and in addition thereto, the Proposer shall secure and maintain throughout the Agreement term the following types of insurance with limits as shown: County of _____.

### Workers' Compensation/Employers Liability

A program of Workers' Compensation insurance or a State-approved Self-Insurance Program in an amount and form to meet all applicable requirements of the Labor Code of the State of California, including Employer's Liability with $250,000 limits, covering all persons including volunteers providing services on behalf of the Proposer and all risks to such persons under this Agreement.

If Proposer has no employees, it may certify or warrant to County that it does not currently have any employees or individuals who are defined as "employees" under the Labor Code and the requirement for Workers' Compensation coverage will be waived by the County's Director of Risk Management.

With respect to Proposers that are non-profit corporations organized under California or Federal law, volunteers for such entities are required to be covered by Workers' Compensation insurance.

### Commercial/General Liability Insurance

The Proposer shall carry General Liability Insurance covering all operations performed by or on behalf of the Proposer providing coverage for bodily injury and property damage with a combined single limit of not less than one million dollars ($1,000,000), per occurrence. The policy coverage shall include:

a.  Premises operations and mobile equipment.
b.  Products and completed operations.
c.  Broad form property damage (including completed operations)
d.  Explosion, collapse and underground hazards.
e.  Personal Injury
f.  Contractual liability
g.  $2,000,000 general aggregate limit

### Automobile Liability Insurance

Primary insurance coverage shall be written on ISO Business Auto coverage form for all owned, hired and non-owned automobiles or symbol 1 (any auto). The policy shall have a combined single limit of not less than one million dollars ($1,000,000) for bodily injury and property damage, per occurrence.

If the Proposer is transporting one or more non-employee passengers in performance of Agreement services, the automobile liability policy shall have a combined single limit of two million dollars ($2,000,000) for bodily injury and property damage per occurrence.

If the Proposer owns no autos, a non-owned auto endorsement to the General Liability policy described above is acceptable.

### Umbrella Liability Insurance

An umbrella (over primary) or excess policy may be used to comply with limits or other primary coverage requirements. When used, the umbrella policy shall apply to bodily injury/property damage, personal injury/advertising injury and shall include a "dropdown" provision providing primary coverage for any liability not covered by the primary policy. The coverage shall also apply to automobile liability.

**Professional Services Requirements**
**Professional Liability** – Professional Liability Insurance with limits of not less than one million ($1,000,000) per claim or occurrence and two million ($2,000,000) aggregate limits

or

**Errors and Omissions Liability Insurance** with limits of not less than one million ($1,000,000) and two million ($2,000,000) aggregate limits. If insurance coverage is provided on a "claims made" policy, the "retroactive date" shall be shown and must be before the date of the start of the Agreement work. The claims made insurance shall be maintained or "tail" coverage provided for a minimum of five (5) years after Agreement completion.

## C. Right to Monitor and Audit

### 1. Right to Monitor
The County, shall have absolute right to review and audit all records, books, papers, documents, corporate minutes, and other pertinent items as requested, and shall have absolute right to monitor the performance of Proposer in the delivery of services provided under this Agreement. Proposer shall give full cooperation, in any auditing or monitoring conducted. Proposer shall cooperate with the County in the implementation, monitoring and evaluation of this Agreement and comply with any and all reporting requirements established by the County.

In the event the County determines that Proposer's performance of its duties or other terms of this Agreement are deficient in any manner, County will notify Proposer of such deficiency in writing or orally, provided written confirmation is given five (5) days thereafter. Proposer shall remedy any deficiency within forty-eight (48) hours of such notification, or County at its option, may terminate this Agreement immediately upon written notice, or remedy deficiency and off-set the cost thereof from any amounts due the Proposer under this Agreement or otherwise.

### 2. Availability of Records
All records pertaining to services delivered and all fiscal, statistical and management books and records shall be available for examination and audit by County representatives for a period of three years after final payment under the Agreement or until all pending County, State and Federal audits are completed, whichever is later.

## D. Correction of Performance Deficiencies

1. Failure by Vendor to comply with any of the provisions, covenants, requirements or conditions of this Agreement shall be a material breach of this Agreement.

2. In the event of a non-cured breach, County may, at its sole distraction and in addition to any other remedies available at law, in equity, or otherwise specified in this Agreement:

   2.1 Afford Proposer thereafter a time period within which to cure the breach, which period shall be established at the sole discretion of County; and/or

   2.2 Discontinue reimbursement to Proposer for and during the period in which Proposer is in breach, which reimbursement shall not be entitled to later recovery; and/or

   2.3 Withhold funds pending duration of the breach; and/or

   2.4 Offset against any monies billed by Proposer but yet unpaid by County those monies disallowed pursuant to Item "2" of this paragraph; and/or

   2.5 Terminate this Agreement immediately and be relieved of the payment of any consideration to Proposer. In the event of such termination, the County may proceed with the work in any manner deemed proper by the County. The cost to the County shall be deducted from any sum due to the Proposer under this Agreement and the balance, if any, shall be paid by the Proposer upon demand.

## VI. Disclosure of Criminal and Civil Proceedings

The County reserves the right to request the information described herein from the Proposer selected for Agreement award. Failure to provide the information may result in a disqualification from the selection process and no award of Agreement to the Proposer. The County also reserves the right to obtain the requested information by way of a background check performed by an investigative firm. The selected Proposer also may be requested to provide information to clarify initial responses. Negative information provided or discovered may result in disqualification from the selection process and no award of Agreement. County of _____ Purchasing Department Request for Proposal **Integrated Security System Upgrade.**

The selected Proposer may be asked to disclose whether the firm, or any of its partners, principals, members, associates or key employees (as that term is defined herein), within the last ten years, has been indicted on or had charges brought against it or them (if still pending) or convicted of any crime or offense arising directly or indirectly from the conduct of the firm's business, or whether the firm, or any of it partners, principals, members, associates or key employees, has within the last ten years, been indicted on or had charges brought against it or them (if still pending) or convicted of any crime or offense involving financial misconduct or fraud. If the response is affirmative, the Proposer will be asked to describe any such indictments or charges (and the status thereof), convictions and the surrounding circumstances in detail.

In addition, the selected Proposer may also be asked to disclose whether the firm, or any of its partners, principals, members, associates or key employees, within the last ten years, has been the subject of legal proceedings as defined herein arising directly from the provision of services by the firm or those individuals. "Legal proceedings" means any civil actions filed in a court of competent jurisdiction, or any matters filed by an administrative or regulatory body with jurisdiction over the firm or the individuals. If the response is affirmative, the Proposer will be asked to describe any such legal proceedings (and the status and disposition thereof) and the surrounding circumstances in detail.

For purposes of this provision "key employees" includes any individuals providing direct service to the county. "Key employees" do not include clerical personnel providing service at the firm's offices or locations.

## VII. Former County Administrative Official

Proposer agrees to provide information on former County of _____ administrative officials (as defined below) who are employed by or represent Proposer. The information provided must include a list of former County administrative officials who terminated County employment within the last five years and who are now officers, principals, partners, associates or members of the Proposer. Information should also include the employment and/or representative capacity and the dates these individuals began employment with or representation of the Proposer. For purposes of this section, "County administrative official" is defined as a member of the Board of Supervisors or such officer's staff, Chief Executive Officer of the County or member of such officer's staff, County department or group head, assistant department or group head, or any employee in the Exempt Group, Management Unit, or Safety Management Unit.

Failure to provide this information may result in the response to the RFP being deemed non-responsive.

## VIII. Improper Consideration

Proposer shall not offer (either directly or through an intermediary) any improper consideration such as, but not limited to, cash, discounts, service, the provision of travel or entertainment, or any items of value to any officer, employee or agent of the County in an attempt to secure favorable treatment regarding this RFP. The County, by written notice, may immediately reject any proposal or terminate any Contract if it determines that any improper consideration as described in the preceding paragraph was offered to any officer, employee or agent of the County with respect to the proposal and award process or any solicitation for consideration was not reported. This prohibition shall apply to any amendment, extension or evaluation process once a Contract has been awarded.

Proposer shall immediately report any attempt by a County officer, employee or agent to solicit (either directly or through an intermediary) improper consideration from Proposer. The report shall be made to the supervisor or manager charged with supervision of the employee or to the County Administrative Office. In the event of a termination under this provision, the County is entitled to pursue any available legal remedies.

## IX. Proposal Submission

### A. General

1. All interested and qualified Proposers are invited to submit a proposal for consideration. Submission of a proposal indicates that the Proposer has read and understands the entire RFP, to include all County of appendixes, attachments, exhibits, schedules, and addendum (as applicable) and all concerns regarding the RFP have been satisfied.

2. Proposals must be submitted in the format described below. Proposals are to be prepared in such a way as to provide a straightforward, concise description of capabilities to satisfy the requirements of this RFP. Expensive bindings, colored displays, promotional materials, etc., are neither necessary nor desired. Emphasis should be concentrated on conformance to the RFP instructions, responsiveness to the RFP requirements, and on completeness and clarity of content. **Note: If the proposal is submitted through ePro, the Proposer shall not include Attachment F, "Fee Proposal sheet(s)", as part of Proposer's ePro submittal, but instead shall mail or submit in person Attachment F, in a separate sealed envelope labeled "Fee Proposal Sheet" with the RFP Number and title and the name of the Proposer clearly marked on the outside, to the address stated in Section I. G. In addition, if the proposal is submitted through ePro, Proposer shall also submit the following hard copies to County in accordance with Section IX.B.2 of this RFP: one (1) original and five (5) copies, for a total of six (6), of the complete proposal (excluding Attachment F). The proposal and Attachment F must be received (in separate envelopes) on or before the deadline for proposals. Failure to comply with this requirement shall disqualify the Proposer. ADDITIONAL NOTE: All proposers must register with the ePro system prior to the date and time to receive the proposal or they will be disqualified.**

3. Proposals must be completed in all respects as required in this section. A proposal may not be considered if it is conditional or incomplete.

4. All information submitted in the proposal or in response to request for additional information is subject to disclosure under the provisions of the California Public Records Act, Government Code Section 6250 et seq. and the following. Proposals may contain financial or other data that constitutes a trade secret. To protect such data from disclosure, Proposer should specifically identify the pages that contain confidential information by properly marking the applicable pages and inserting the following notice on the front of the response:

NOTICE
The data on pages _____ of this proposal response, identified by an asterisk ($\star$) or marked along the margin with a vertical line, contains information which are trade secrets. We request that such data be used only for the evaluation of our response, but understand that disclosure will be limited to the extent that the County of _____ determines is proper under federal, state, and local law. The proprietary or confidential data shall be readily separable from the Proposal in order to facilitate eventual public inspection of the non-confidential portion of the proposal.

The County assumes no responsibility for disclosure or use of unmarked data for any purpose. In the event disclosure of properly marked data is requested, the Proposer will be advised of the request and may expeditiously submit to the County a detailed statement indicating the reasons it has for believing that the information is exempt from disclosure under federal, state, and local law. The County will exercise care in applying this confidentiality standard but will not be held liable for any damage or injury which may result from any disclosure that may occur.

5. All proposals and materials submitted become the property of the County.

## B. Proposal Presentation

1. Electronic proposals must be received by the deadline for receipt of proposal specified in Section I, Paragraph I (Proposal Submission Deadline). In addition, one (1) original and five (5) copies, for a total of six (6), of the complete proposal must be received by the deadline for receipt of proposal specified in Section II − Deadline for Proposals. The original and all copies must be in a sealed envelope or container stating on the outside; Proposer Name, Address, Telephone Number, RFP number, RFP Title, and Proposal due date. **PROPOSER MUST ALSO COMPLETE THE ATTACHED FEE PROPOSAL SHEET (ATTACHMENT F), AND ENCLOSE IT IN A SEPARATE SEALED ENVELOPE TO BE SUBMITTTED AS PART OF THE PROPOSAL. ATTACHMENT F SHALL NOT BE SUBMITTED IN EPRO, BUT MUST BE MAILED OR SUBMITTED IN PERSON AT THE ADDRESS IDENTIFIED IN SECTION I, PARAGRAPH G.**

2. All proposals must be submitted on 8 ½ x 11 paper, neatly typed, double-sided on recycled paper with normal (1-inch) margins and single spaced. Exhibits/Attachments on larger sized paper is allows as necessary. Each page, including attachments, must be clearly and consecutively numbered at the bottom center of each page.

3. Hand carried proposals may be delivered to the address identified in Section I, Paragraph G, between the hours of 8:00 a.m. and 5:00 p.m., Monday through Friday, excluding holidays observed by the County (provided that the proposal is delivered before the submission deadline state in Section II). Proposers are responsible for informing any commercial delivery service, if used, of all delivery requirements, and for ensuring that the address information appears on the outer wrapper or envelope used by such service.

The County reserves the right to reject any and all proposals or portions of proposal or alternates received by reasons of this request, to negotiate separately with any source whatsoever in any manner necessary to serve its interests.

## C. Proposal Format

Response to this RFP must be in the form of a proposal package, which must be submitted in the following format:

1. **Cover Page** – Attachment A is to be used as the cover page for the proposal. This form must be fully completed and signed by an authorized officer of the Proposer who has the power to bind the firm contractually.

2. **Table of Contents** – All pages of the proposal, including the enclosures, must be clearly and consecutively numbered and correspond to the Table of Contents.

3. **Statement of Experience**
   Include the following in this section of the proposal:
   3.1 Business name of the prospective Proposer and legal entity such as corporation, partnership, etc.
   3.2 Number of years the prospective Proposer has been in business under the present business name, as well as related prior business names.

3.3 A brief summary of the relevant qualifications and experience in providing the services solicited in this RFP.

3.4 List all projects Vendor has completed within the last 3–5 years which are similar to those requested in this RFP.

## 4  Minimum Proposer Requirements

Complete, initial, and sign Attachment B.

## 5  Exceptions to RFP

Complete Attachment C.

## 6  Statement of Certification (Attachment D) – Include the following in this section of the Proposal

6.1 A statement that the offer made in the proposal is firm and binding for 180 days from the date the proposal is opened and recorded.

6.2 A statement that all aspects of the proposal, including the fee proposal, have been determined independently, without consultation with any other prospective Proposer or competitor for the purpose of restricting competition.

6.3 A statement that all declarations in the proposal and attachments are true and that this shall constitute a warranty, the falsity of which will entitle the County to pursue any remedy by law.

6.4 A statement that the Proposer agrees that all aspects of the RFP and the proposal submitted shall be binding if the proposal is selected and an Agreement awarded.

6.5 A statement that the Proposer agrees to provide the County with any other information the County determines is necessary for an accurate determination of the Proposer's ability to perform the services as proposed; and

6.6 A statement that the prospective Proposer, if selected will comply with all applicable rules, laws and regulations.

## 7  References

Provide three (3) references from other agencies, one (1) of which should be a government agency, that you have established an Agreement with on a project of this nature, of same or similar size. Include the name, address, telephone number, and the type/dates of services provided on Attachment E. Please include a contact person who the County can call in order to verify the quality of services your organization/firm has provided.

## 8  Proposal Description

Provide a detailed description of the proposal being made.

8.1 The proposal should address, but is not limited to, all terms in Section IV.

8.2 The proposal should include the following:

8.2.1 A brief synopsis of the Proposer's understanding of the County's needs and how the Proposer plans to meet these.

8.2.2 A concise statement of the services (and product, if applicable) proposed.

8.2.3 An explanation of any assumptions and/or constraints.

9 **Project Team Organization Chart**

Project Team Organization Chart shall clearly show the organization of the team and the hierarchy of the members. It must include:

9.1 Organizational framework for the proposed Project team.

9.2 Company name and key staff name for each role identified in the chart.

10 **Work Plan and Schedule**

Include the following:

10.1 Summary of management/work plan for this Project;

11 **Statement of Qualifications**

Include the following in this section of the proposal:

11.1 Number of years the prospective Proposer has been in business under the present business name, as well as related prior business names.

11.2 Statement that the Proposer does not have any commitments or potential commitments which may impact the Proposer's ability to perform this Agreement.

11.3 Resumes of key Project team members.

11.4 Provide project profiles that directly relate to this Project in terms of size and scope. The project profiles shall clearly indicate the scope of services Proposer provided for that project.

12 **Licenses, Permits and/or Certifications**

Provide copies of all licenses, permits and/or certifications as required under Section V, Paragraph A, 19 and as required in other portions of the RFP.

13 **Cost**

Complete proposed pricing on Attachment F.

14 **Employment of Former County Officials**

Provide information on former County of _____ administrative officials (as defined below) who are employed by or represent your business. The information provided must include a list of former county administrative officials who terminated county employment within the last five years and who are now officers, principals, partners, associates or members of the business and should also include the employment and/or representative capacity and the dates these individuals began employment with or representation of your business. For purposes of this section, "county administrative official" is defined as a member of the Board of Supervisors or such officer's staff, Chief Executive Officer or member of such officer's staff, county department or group head, assistant department or group head, or any employee in the Exempt Group, Management Unit or Safety Management Unit.

Failure to provide this information may result in the response to the request for proposal being deemed non-responsive.

15 **Insurance**

Submit evidence of ability to insure as stated in Section V, Paragraph B, Indemnification and Insurance Requirements.

## X. Proposal Evaluation And Award

### A. Initial Review

All proposals will be initially evaluated by Department staff to determine if they meet the following minimum requirements:

1. The proposal must be complete, in the required format, and be in compliance with all the requirements of this RFP.
2. Prospective Proposers must meet the requirements as stated in the Minimum Proposer requirements as outlined in Section I, Paragraph D. Failure to meet all of these requirements will result in a rejected proposal. No proposal shall be rejected, however, if it contains a minor irregularity, defect or variation and if the irregularity, defect or variation is considered by the County to be immaterial or inconsequential (to be determined by the County in its sole discretion), the County may choose to accept the proposal. In such cases the Proposer will be notified of the deficiency in the proposal and given an opportunity to correct the irregularity, defect or variation or the County may elect to waive the deficiency and accept the proposal.

### B. Evaluation Committee

The County will establish an Evaluation Committee with responsibility for reviewing all proposals that meet the Minimum Proposer requirements outlined in Section I, Paragraph D and conducting the reviews, evaluations, and scoring described in Section X. In addition, the Evaluation Committee, may, in its sole discretion, utilize outside experts and financial consulting or reporting services to assist in the evaluation process.

### C. Evaluation of Proposals

Proposals meeting the requirements of Section X, Paragraph A, will be evaluated by the Evaluation Committee as follows:

1. Qualifications Evaluation – The Evaluation Committee will conduct an evaluation of all proposals under the criteria set forth in Section X, Paragraph D. The Evaluation Committee will rank all proposals and reject any proposals that do not meet the minimum qualifications as stated in this RFP.
2. Fee Proposals – Following a ranking of the proposals, the Evaluation Committee will open all fee proposals (Attachment F). The Evaluation Committee will not alter the ranking of the proposals once the fee proposals have been opened. However, the fee proposals will be used during negotiations with the selected Proposer.
3. Recommendation – Following the completion of evaluations by the Evaluation Committee and the scoring of Proposals in accordance with this Section, the Evaluation Committee will make a recommendation for award of a Proposer Agreement and Department Staff will enter into negotiations with the Proposer. The final decision to award any Agreement as a result of this RFP process rests solely with the County of

_____ Board of Supervisors. In certain situations, the Board may authorize the Chief Executive Officer (CEO) and/or the Purchasing Agent to award Agreements.

## D. Evaluation Criteria

1. No proposal shall be rejected if it contains a minor irregularity, defect, or variation if the irregularity, defect or variation is considered by the County (at the County's sole discretion) to be immaterial or inconsequential. In such cases, the Proposer will be notified of the deficiency in the proposal and given an opportunity to correct the irregularity, defect or variation, or the County may elect to waive the deficiency and accept the Proposal.

2. The successful Proposer will be selected on the basis of demonstrated competence and on the professional qualifications necessary for the satisfactory performance of the services required. The County will use the following criteria in its evaluation and comparison of proposals submitted. The order in which they appear is not intended to indicate their relative importance.

   2.1 Firm Qualifications.

   2.2 Firm Experience

   2.3 References

   2.4 Project Staff

   2.5 Project Work Plan

   2.6 Experience with Similar Projects

   2.7 Demonstration of Understanding of RFP

3. The Evaluation Committee and/or the County may contact any of the Proposer's client references and/or prior similar projects performed by Proposer to discuss the Proposer's qualifications and past performance. The results of any such reference checks and experience with similar projects will be considered in the evaluation and scoring of proposals.

4. The County may also contact any proposer to clarify any response; contact any current or past users of a Proposer's services; solicit information from any available source concerning any aspect of a proposal; request an oral presentation of any or a select few Proposers; and seek and review any other information deemed pertinent to the evaluation process.

## E. Negotiations

1. Following the evaluation process, the most qualified firm will be selected, all fee proposals will be opened and negotiations will be held with that firm. If negotiations are not successful, the County will so notify the firm, and commence negotiations with the next rated firm, and so on.

2. After negotiations are complete, the Agreement will be presented to the County of _____ Board of Supervisors for approval. In certain situations, the Board may authorize the Chief Executive Officer (CEO) and/or the Purchasing Agent to award Agreements. Once the Board has taken action, the selected Proposer will be notified in writing.

## F. Award

Agreement(s) will be awarded based on a competitive selection of proposals received. The contents of the proposal of the successful Proposer will become contractual obligations and failure to accept these obligations in a contractual Agreement may result in cancellation of the award.

## G. Disputes Relating to Proposal Process and Award

In the event a dispute arises concerning the proposal process prior to the award of the Agreement, the party wishing resolution of the dispute shall submit a request in writing to the Director of Purchasing. Proposer may appeal the recommended award or denial of award, provided the following stipulations are met:

1. Appeal must be in writing.
2. Must be submitted within ten (10) calendar days of the date of the recommended award or denial of award letters.

An appeal of a denial of award can only be brought on the following grounds:

1. Failure of the County to follow the selection procedures and adhere to requirements specified in the RFP or any addenda or amendments.
2. There has been a violation of conflict of interest as provided by California Government Code Section 87100 et seq.
3. A violation of State or Federal law.

Appeals will not be accepted for any other reasons than those stated above. All appeals must be sent to:

_____, Director
County of
Purchasing Department

_____

The County Purchasing Agent shall make a decision concerning the appeal, and notify the Proposer making the appeal, within a reasonable timeframe prior to the tentatively scheduled date for awarding the Agreement. The decision of the County Purchasing Agent shall be deemed final.

**SCOPE OF WORK**
**SECTION 284600**
**INTEGRATED CONTROL SYSTEM**

## General

### Related Documents

Drawings and general provisions of the Request for Proposal, including Supplementary Conditions apply to this Section.

## Summary

Section Includes:

> Programmable Logic Controllers (PLC)
> Security Graphics User Interface (GUI) Control Computer
> Programming Laptop Computer
> Power Supplies
> Uninterruptible Power Supply (UPS)
> Data Switches
> Schedule 28460A Equipment Summary

Related Sections:

| | |
|---|---|
| 280500 | Common Work Results for Electronic Safety and Security |
| 280513 | Conductors and Cables |
| 281500 | Intercom and Paging System |
| 282300 | Video Surveillance (CCTV) System |
| 284800 | Sequence of Operations |

## Description of Work

Replace the existing control panels, alarm monitoring system, PLC-5, CompactLogix, UPS, and other equipment for a complete integrated control system to interface to the other systems identified herein. Provide all equipment, cables, and programming for a complete operational system. An equipment summary sheet is provided to identify system requirements.

The new control electronics shall provide Graphics User Interface (GUI) work stations for control and monitoring functions for the systems and interfaces as described on the Drawings and in these Specifications.

## PLC

Replace PLC equipment and reuse existing PLC equipment where indicated to support the control, monitoring and logic required for a complete and operational system. PLC equipment used to replace old equipment in the indicated areas shall offer a one (1) year parts warranty at a minimum.

The controllers shall provide all necessary logic functions, timing functions, memory, software, input/output points and communication capabilities for the operating features required to meet all of the requirements of the Specifications and Drawings.

The controller shall be general purpose in nature and not custom designed and built for this isolated application. The controller shall be generally non-location specific in its construction. The controller shall be made location specific and operationally customized by installing EPROM with applicable software, and making the I/O interface board's system specific and installing the proper I/O modules.

Logic functions shall include, but not be limited to, AND, OR and INVERT functions with sufficient levels to provide operating features required to perform all of the functions required by the Specifications and Drawings.

Timing functions shall include, but not be limited to, on-delay, off-delay, stepping and pulsing. Sufficient variations of programmable timing shall be available to provide all the operating features as required by the Specifications and Drawings.

All new and existing PLC's shall be programmed to correct current issues such as incorrect call-up and sequence of camera displays. See section 284800 for sequences of operations.

Replace all AB PLC-5 and CompactLogix PLCs with ControlLogix PLCs. There are a total of twenty-two (22) PLCs to be replaced.

Single Mode fiber optic cable will be provided by the County from each housing unit penthouse to the main electronics room. Connections to the fiber and all hardware and switches are to be provided by the contractor.

### Graphic User Interface (GUI)

The GUI will be a monitor and PC (operated by mouse) with all system functions centralized on one monitor with multiple screens. It will utilize graphical maps to display, control, and annunciate locations of door control, door status, intercom calls, duress alarms, CCTV controls, and any other miscellaneous functions (including lighting control and other utilities, if necessary).

The architecture for the GUI shall be decentralized with each workstation operating as a server.

Each GUI workstation shall be capable of operating in both run-time and design mode.

Interface with the Jail Management System with a web service protocol to display current inmate information including but not limited to the following;

Name
Inmate photos
Classification
Status
Booking number
Court dates
Money on books
Medical alerts

Refer to section 284800 for sequence of operations for the GUI. This includes functions for the cell/movement intercoms, vehicle gate intercoms, door position statuses, interlocked doors, emergency override, emergency shutdown, emergency access, vehicle gates, swing doors, lighting controls, duress alarms, and other miscellaneous functions.

### Power Supplies

Provide power supplies as required for each system.

Low voltage systems shall operate on 24 VDC or 24 VAC or as determined by each section. Size all power supplies to maintain Class 2 ratings and operation of each system at 150% of the maximum loaded condition.

### Uninterruptible Power Supply (UPS)

Provide UPS to power all the equipment provided by this project in the areas indicated by the attached Specifications and Drawings.

Submit UPS power calculations indicating power consumption by each major equipment component. Size the UPS to operate for 30 minutes on loss of power.

Existing UPS in each housing unit shall be used for the new systems unless otherwise indicated. It is expected that there will be a small net load gain on each UPS as a result of this project.

### Data Switches
Provide data switches to connect the PLC, Audio, Video, GUI, and network in each area. The video switch shall be separate from the PLC, GUI, and Audio switch.

### Submittals
Submit under provisions of Section 280500.

### Quality Assurance
Comply with Section 280500.

Where certifications from the GUI or PLC manufacturers are available, the contractor shall obtain certifications at time of proposal.

### Extra Materials
Deliver the following spare parts at a location to be designated:
  (2) PLC CPUs
  (1) input module per Unit
  (1) output module per Unit
  (2) network modules
  (1) PLC power supply
  (2) 32" GUI Screen
  (2) 24" GUI Screen
  (1) Security GUI Control PC

## Products

### Manufacturers
The _____ currently uses Allen Bradley equipment and does not want to have dissimilar systems throughout the facility. Four of the security control stations already have the latest Allen Bradley PLC equipment and does not need to be replaced (medical, master control, north control, and south control). The _____ also has full time communication technicians specifically trained on Allen Bradley products. No substitute PLC's are permitted. See equipment summary for details.

The control electronics equipment shall be the product of a manufacturer engaged in the production for industrial applications for a minimum of ten (10) years. Only manufacturers with non-proprietary systems and national distribution will be considered.

### Control Electronics Equipment
The PLC products specified in this section shall be used with 'NO SUBSTITUTIONS'.
PLC CPU and Controller ....................................... Allen Bradley Control Logix L6 or L7
PLC Input Module .......................................... Allen Bradley Control Logix 1756-IB32/B

PLC Output Module ........................................ Allen Bradley Control Logix 1756–OB32/A
PLC Network Module ............. Allen Bradley Control Logix EtherNet/IP 1756–ENBT/A
Security GUI Control PC ............................................................................ HP Envy 700
Core Areas GUI PC ......................................................................................... HP Z420
32" GUI Screen ...................................................................................... LG 32LN5300
24" GUI Screen ......................................................................................... LG M2452D
GUI Software ................................................................................. see specifications
UPS ............................................................................................................... Eaton
Data Switch ..................................................... N–Tron7010TX, N–tron EL228

## PLC General Description

General Description:

Environmental ratings for all components of the PLC system, except programming equipment, shall meet or exceed the following requirements:

> Ambient Temperature rating of 0 to 60 C (32 to 140 F) operational and –20 to 70 C (–4 to 158 F) storage.
>
> Humidity rating of 5% to 90% Relative Humidity (non–condensing).
>
> All system modules shall be designed so as to provide for free airflow convection cooling. No internal fans or other means of cooling except heat sinks shall be required.

The PLC shall meet the following standards: UL Listed, CSA Certified, and CE.

The PLC and I/O modules shall be of modular and rack mounted construction.

The system power supplies shall be protected against short circuits.

Programmable controller manufacturer must guarantee the availability of replacement/ spare parts for a minimum of ten (10) years.

All I/O modules and housings must be of a standard type and fully interchangeable with previous PLC series.

All controllers and I/O structures of a single manufacturer shall be capable of being mounted on the same size fixing centers to allow for larger capacity controllers to be installed in the future should the facility require an expansion beyond the limits specified in the original contract documents.

Controllers must be capable of driving local I/O racks, where local is defined as up to one hundred (100) feet from the control unit, without the need for further intelligent interface modules.

When required, the system must be capable of controlling remote I/O up to a distance of 500 meters (1,640 feet) from the controller, using high-speed links with a minimum data rate of one hundred and eighty seven (187) Kbaud. Communications over this link shall be accomplished using twisted-pair wires with an overall shield.

## PLC Central Processing Unit

The central processing unit (CPU) shall be microprocessor based, encased in a shielded enclosure to provide RFI protection, and shall provide the logic control functions and date transfer based upon the program stored in memory and the status of the inputs and outputs. The controller must be able to support up to 5,120 local I/O.

The minimum standard control functions of the CPU shall include:

Relay Ladder Logic

Latching relays

Timer clock pulses (.02s, 0.1s, 0.2s, 1s & 1m) and timers (.01 & 0.1 sec. Increments).

Counters (up/down)

Data comparison (=, <, >), data range comparison, and data table comparison.

Data transfers (single register, blocks of registers, data distribution and collection using pointer).

Synchronous shift registers forward and reverse (multiple channel length bit shifts).

One-shot output and input controls.

Master control relays (interlocks).

Bit reads and moves.

I/O forcing and setting

BCD to Binary or Hexadecimal conversion.

Binary or Hexadecimal to BCD conversion.

I/O Refresh on command, immediate I/O inputs, and scheduled interrupt on command.

On-line program editing.

The following minimum modes of operation of the CPU must be selectable via a key operated switch or programming software commands:

PROGRAM – Processor is not scanning program in memory and all outputs are held OFF.

MONITOR – Processor is executing program and changes in user memory and data memory are allowed.

RUN – Processor is executing program in memory and outputs are controlling to the program. No editing of program or data registers is allowed.

The above settings shall require either a key, a programming console with a key, or programming software loaded on a computer to change the operating mode of the CPU.

The processor shall incorporate extensive self-diagnostic, which will not half the processor. In addition, separate visual indicators will annunciate at the following conditions:

POWER – Logic power is applied to the CPU and I/O rack from the power supply.

RUN – Processor is executing the program in memory outputs are being controlled according to the program.

OUTPUT INHIBIT – Processor is executing program in memory according to input status, but, outputs are being held in the OFF-state.

ALARM – A non-fatal error (such as a low memory battery condition) has occurred in the PLC hardware or program software. The PLC is still running and the outputs are being controlled according to the program.

ERROR – A fatal error (such as a memory parity error) has occurred, the CPU is not scanning the program, and the outputs are held in the OFF-state.

COMM – Indicating the CPU is communicating with the device connected to the peripheral port or RS-232C port.

In addition to visual self-diagnostic indicators (LED's) the processor shall have a specifically designated block of a least 100 words of internal diagnostic words and bits. These shall provide more detailed system status and fault diagnostic information accessible by programming equipment or intelligent peripherals.

The processor must contain an error log area. This area must be able to log what error occurred and when the error happened, giving exact time and date. This area must be able to store a minimum of 1000 records.

At a minimum, the internal diagnostic registers shall the following information:

Type of digital (input or output) or intelligent (analog, ASCII, etc.) I/O unit inserted in a particular slot (I/O table listing). This data should be accessible via programming console or programming software.

If an I/O module is improperly mounted (wrong slot) or not in a slot (I/O verify or I/O bus error).

Error codes for intelligent I/O module errors.

PLC operation mode.

Present and maximum scan time.

Local Area Network operation status and error status.

Local Area Network data Send and Receive verification and error status.

Serial Host Computer interface operation and error status.

Remote I/O rack operation and error status.

Memory Error Area.

Startup time. The start time should be updated every time the power is turned ON.

Power Interruption Time.

A single RS232 or RS422 compatible or Fiber Optic

Differential communication port shall be used for software based ladder logic programming and communications to other compatible devices. The PLC system must support up to three of these ports simultaneously.

The data rate of the serial communications port shall be switch selectable. The following shall be the minimum available data rates: 300, 1200, 2400, 4800, 9600 and 19,200 baud.

### Input/Output Modules

Each input or output module shall be a self-contained unit housed within an enclosure so that no part of its circuit board is exposed to contact by handling.

Input and output units shall be UL listed, CSA certified and CE.

Pressure type screw terminals will accept one No. 12 or two No. 14 stranded or solid wires.

Convenience marker strips shall be provided adjacent to the I/O field wiring terminals for user labeling of all I/O points.

It shall be possible to replace any I/O module without or disturbing user field wiring.

All high-density DC input or output units shall be solid state in nature. The output units shall be transistor type for long life and high DC reliability. Reed relays are not acceptable.

### Network Options

Networking options must include Ethernet, Ethernet IP, Profibus DP, DeviceNet. Ethernet communications must support TCP, UDP, and FTP protocols. The PLC should have the ability to generate e-mail messages to be sent via WAN or LAN, to report errors, provide scheduled maintenance and status reports. In addition, FTP (file transfer protocol) can be used to transfer data files between a host computer and or FLASH memory card and the PLC's memory.

**IDF Network Switch**
Fiber and copper ports
Onboard temperature sensor
ESD and Surge Protection Diodes on all Ports
Redundant power inputs
Configuration backup via SD Card
Redundant N-Ring Coupling
OPC Monitoring
Port Mirroring
Fully managed
MTBF>2 Million Hours

**MDF Network Switch**
IEC 61850 and IEEE 1613 for utility substation automation and other power applications
ANSI/ISA 12.12 and ATEX for Zone 2 hazardous locations
Enter5prise-class functionality and security
Fully managed
Relay contact output to signal alarms

**GUI PC (Non-Core Areas)**
Each GUI PC shall function as the primary means of overall system control and monitoring. The computer equipment shall be arranged to present an efficient and organized appearance.
The computer equipment shall be arranged to present an efficient and organized appearance. The following components shall be located with the workstation:
PC based computer.
32" or 24" Monitor Panel with mount depending on location.
Mouse and keyboard.
Provide computer equipment that meets the following minimum specification requirements
    4th Generation Intel® Core™ i7-4770 processor quad-core [3.4GHz, 8MB Shared Cache]
    8 GB, DDR3-1600MHz RAM memory.
    1 TB 7200 RPM SATA Drive
    Local bus 32-bit IDE controller capable of supporting two (2) hard disk drives.
    ISA expansion bus with three spare expansion slots.
    4 GB NVIDIA Ge Force GT640 Graphics Card
    Dual HDMI Outputs.
    Integrated Sound, Envy Audio; Beats Audio
    Tower type chassis including high capacity power supply with surge suppressor.
    101 key keyboard.
    Microsoft mouse.
Audio tone generator to activate on reception of an alarm. Audio tone shall be capable of being enabled or disabled on operator command.

A control panel monitor shall be the primary means of operator access to the system. They shall provide the operator interface for control of the entire system. The control panel may be an "off-the-shelf" consumer grade panel, but must be secured using custom mounting for adjustable (horizontal, vertical, tilt, with lockable position) movement and minimize shake/torque while in normal operation.

A keyboard and mouse are the secondary means of operator access to the system. To communicate with the direct digital control system, the operator shall input via the keyboard or mouse a command along with a proper alphanumeric identification of the system. Keyboard shall have standard ASCII coded logic outputs, providing full International English language displays and printouts. Auxiliary function keys shall be provided for various functions. These keys shall allow common operations to be performed by punching a single key instead of having to type out the command on the keyboard.

A digital display clock shall display on the monitor at all times. Provision for manually resetting it shall be provided. It shall be a 24 hour real-time clock and seven-day calendar to provide data for logging.

A network control key or software passwords shall allow automatic functions of the system to continue, but prevent unauthorized tampering with any computer pushbuttons or controls while the computer is unattended. This shall not disable the scanning or alarming functions.

### Graphic User Interface (GUI) Software

Software Architecture General Design Features:

The GUI package shall:

Be 32-bit software capable of running on operating systems currently supported by Microsoft Windows and Server 2012, or as recommended by the manufacturer.

Support and take advantage of multiple processors on the same machine (symmetric multiprocessor design). For example, adding another chip to the computer should distribute the load of the GUI software across both chips, thereby increasing performance, etc.

Support and take advantage of multiple threads within the CPU. This multi-threading, among other benefits, aids in multi-tasking for CPU optimization, dependencies, and the like.

Have a scalable architecture such that the user can start with a small application and later grow the application database to any size by upgrading the license.

Embrace and integrate Microsoft Standards including:

Microsoft Access

Microsoft SQL Server

Microsoft Data Engine (MSDE)

Open Database Connectivity (ODBC)

ADO, OLE-DB for Database Interface

Object Linking and Embedding (OLE)

ActiveX Technologies

OLE for Process Control (OPC)

Capable of integrating the following systems:
    CCTV
    Intercom and Paging
    Fire
    Perimeter Fence
    IP Telephony
    Intrusion
    RFID
    Visitation Management
    Body Scan
    Biometrics

Have the ability to write scripts within the package using a non-proprietary language (e.g.: VBScript).

Must support modifications in the driver worksheet to allocate addresses in the PLC (to maintain flexibility on the PLC supplier).

Shall be able to view live video images on door control screens.

Software shall provide off the shelve drivers for integrated systems. All related systems shall be supported through the software without third party custom development.

Networking:
    The GUI package shall:
        Implement Client / Server Distributed Networking.
        Support industry standard network protocols such as Ethernet (TCP/IP and UDP/IP) and Ethernet IP.
        Operate on a network with multiple protocol stacks.
        Plug and Play with standard routers, switches, network Intranets and the Internet.

Be configurable as an independent distributed database regardless of the number of nodes in the system.

Support at least 256 workstations (nodes) simultaneously.

Expansion of the system shall be possible with the addition of non-proprietary PC based off the shelf hardware.

Connect to a large number of I/O Device Interfaces via OPC Servers across the network.

Allow different versions of the development environment to reside simultaneously on the same computer, under different directories.

Have the ability to exchange data with external SQL Relational Databases, via 3$^{rd}$ party ADO providers, without the addition of any add-on packages.

Have the ability to save alarm history and event history to any SQL Relational Database, via 3$^{rd}$ party ADO providers, without the addition of any add-on packages.

Graphic Display Software Module:
    The graphical display module shall have the ability to:
        Allow configuration of highly detailed screens with animation.
        Use an object-oriented design.

Permit using the mouse for object creation, editing, and placing on the screen.

Show object properties for customization with either menu choices, right-clicking, pop-up menus, or double-click shortcuts.

Offer floating, dockable tool bars with drawing and animation tools for building the display.

Provide a grid that can be displayed on screen to assist in aligning objects precisely.

Permit re-sizing of the grid in both the X and Y direction (independently) in one-pixel increments.

Allow "Snap to Grid" functionality to be turned on/off during configuration.

Not require compilation of the displays before use; a simple "save" is all that is needed for use.

Offer Password Protection of displays created.

Provide language switching "on the fly"; with the ability for user-created displays to change languages, as well as the menus and tools employed by the graphics package itself.

Display the graphic interface in 2 monitors connected to the same computer (CPU). The graphic interface available on each monitor must provide independent screen navigation.

Run more than one instance of the graphic interface on the same computer (Thin Client solution) without any additional configuration on the Server station.

Create tags as structures/classes of at least on member.

Create array tags and configure another tag as its index when configuring objects on the screen.

Alarms and Events:

The alarm system shall provide complete alarm and event management with a user-definable message structure.

The alarm system shall provide 16 message sub-classes and 16 message types.

The alarm system shall provide the ability to condense system alarming by the provision of group messages/alarms.

The alarm system shall be programmed to alarm any change of state that the system detects, including:

The failure of communications channels used by the system.

The failure of system's hardware which results in an automatic fail-over of the system's functions from the active to standby server.

The alarm system shall be capable of annunciating alarms, including, but not limited to:

Activation of an audible alarm or light.

Alarm display updated with the current alarm.

Alarm banner updated on configured process displays.

The alarm system shall display alarm messages in a manner to facilitate easy interpretation of current alarms, including, but not limited to:

Different text color and background color for those points that are in alarm, those that have been acknowledged, and those that are no longer in alarm.

Flashing of the current alarm message(s) in the alarm list.

The alarm system shall provide capability to acknowledge alarm message when data point enters and/or exits alarm state. The system shall permit alarm acknowledgement, including, but not limited to:
On an individual point.
On a filtered group of points.
On all alarms.
The alarm system shall provide filtering to control the alarms display. The filtering shall include, but not be limited to:
Date.
Time.
Alarm class.
Alarm type.
Alarm priority.
Status (in alarm, out of alarm, or acknowledged).
Any defined alarm message field.
Alarm colors vary by equipment served. Alarms colors shall visually annunciate to meet site requirements.

Security:
The software shall provide a security component for restricting access to different areas of the system.
It shall be possible to configure different sets of individual users (range at least 1 to 1000 users) as well as categorizing those users (e.g., engineers, operators, supervisors, etc.) into groups (range at least 1 to 100 groups).
It shall be possible to assign a person to more than one group (e.g., Engineer and a Supervisor).
For each individual user, and for each group, it shall be possible to define:
Name.
Password, including such parameters as minimum length required, time allowed before it must be changed, and uniqueness over time).
Data Points which can and cannot be written to.
Which screens they have access to.
It shall be possible to configure an Auto-Logout period, whereby the user is automatically logged out of the system after a specified amount of time has elapsed.
Restrictions on software module interaction shall be configured on a per-user and per-group basis. Items to lock out include:
Exiting the applications.
Printing.
Entering Configuration Mode.
Switching Languages.
Starting/Stopping of Alarm and/or Data Logging.
Acknowledgement of Alarms.
Alarm Filtering.
Changing Zoom Factors in Graphics and Trends.

Modifying and Executing Trend Reports.

Adding, Editing and/or Deleting Trend Pens.

Running a Script.

Accessing the Windows Desktop.

If a user fails to successfully log in after a configurable number of times, it shall be possible to lock that account out until either an administrator clears it, or after a preset amount of time has elapsed.

A utility shall be provided to show which users are logged into the system (both on the local machine, and on networked machines).

Internet Connectivity:

The GUI software will be accessible only through a hard line connection between the Security Network Switch and the County LAN. Coordinate with County IT for IP, network bridging, and all other security protocols.

OPC Data:

If OPC databases are used, must be able to import OPC tags

The OPC Browser shall list all registered OPC Data Servers when making a connection to I/O data, and OPC Alarm and Event Servers when configuring alarms, and OPC Historical Data Access servers when configuring trending applications.

It shall be possible to browse OPC Servers installed on the local machine as well as those installed on any node visible on the network.

Ability to keep OPC tags on scan to optimize communications to commonly used data items.

On-line OPC Data Configuration changes (e.g., adding a new tag on-line) shall be supported by the GUI package.

OPC Data Ranges shall be read in and used to configure limits on graphic dynamics, trend limits, data entry field ranges, and so on.

OPC Quality Flags shall be used in graphic dynamics (degrees of communication quality shall be indicated by change in color used for objects), data logging, and alarm presentation.

A component for bridging/mapping OPC Data from one server to another shall be provided (e.g., map a PLC data point to a Modbus register).

Historical Data:

The system shall provide a complete historical subsystem providing the user the capability to capture and analyze historical data. The system shall allow for historical logging capabilities to be done at each PC within the single software platform.

There shall be no limit (other than storage capacity) on the number of archives that can be created. The system shall also allow selection of any point in the system to be added/configured for archiving.

The historical subsystem shall use standard Windows tree/list view presentation techniques to facilitate the display and editing of archive timers, archive types, graphical data displays and tabular data displays.

The historical subsystem shall promote the visualization of historical data in both tabular and graphical form. This includes the capability to view historical data via a web-enabled interface as specified herein.

Reports:

The system shall provide an integral reporting subsystem used to report both current and archived data.

The reporting subsystem shall provide the capability define reports for both visualization and printed format.

The reporting subsystem shall provide the capability to define both the dynamic and static properties reports, including, but not limited to:

Inclusion of archived data, alarm data or event data.

Customization of the format, layout, and graphical images, included on a report.

Configuration of automatic report generation, including frequency, destination of the report, and a prioritized list of alternate system resources should problems be encountered during automatic production.

The system shall be supplied with pre-configured reports, including, but not limited to:

Graphic display documentation.

Historical archiving.

Alarm archiving.

Control logic/scripting configuration.

User and group security configuration

The reporting subsystem shall not impose limits on the number of reports that can be configured.

Database:

The system shall utilize a real-time relational database for storage of all process related data.

The database shall be based on an accepted industry standard database technology.

Tag names should be able to support up to 255 characters

The database subsystem shall provide the capability of "browsing" an application database, independent of the application.

The database system shall support both internal (computational) and external tags (real world). Use of internal tags shall be unlimited.

The database system shall provide the ability for each tag (dependent on type) to have high and low limits, start and substitute values.

The database system shall provide for event driven execution for data processing. Systems that require external data sources (PLCs) be polled for complete database update shall not be accepted.

Client/Server:

The software shall employ native client-server architecture. The architecture shall promote the use of multiple server and multiple client (i.e., workstation) configurations.

Any server computer shall be able to be dedicated to specific process functionality (i.e., Alarm Service, Historical Data Collection, etc.)

All clients shall have the capability to locally store and utilize process displays, as well as local control actions. Should a requested display and/or control action not exist locally at the client level; the client will access the data for the server. This operation will be transparent to the user.

All clients shall have complete visibility to all servers, and all servers shall have visibility at the peer level.

The software shall promote portability of applications between computers without any redevelopment or modification.

It shall be possible for the user to monitor and control the process from client or server. This includes, but is not limited to:

View the same or different displays simultaneously.

Make process adjustments and acknowledge alarms.

View alarms, events, trends, and reports.

The development and runtime environments shall be decoupled allowing the user to configure run-time only clients without any development capabilities. Modification of a client from run-time only, to runtime/development, shall be achieved as a simple license upgrade. Reinstallation or new installation of software will be permitted to achieve this functionality.

Run time and design mode shall be possible on each GUI PC. Execution

### Installation

Comply with Section 280500.

Comply with manufacturer's recommendations, procedures and standards for the assembly and operation of the Control Electronics.

Common functions such as sally port interlocks shall be wired to a single PLC system. This type of function shall not be networked.

Provide Category 6 cables, patch panels, and patch cords unless otherwise noted.

Provide Category 6a cords for 10GBASE-T applications with a distance over 40 meters. Exception: When fiber optic cable is used.

Comply with ANSI, TIA, EIA, and BICSI Standards for Category cable, Fiber cable, and related fixtures installation.

All patch cords to be factory made and tested.

### UPS

Connect new and existing UPS's to data network.

Program GUI System to monitor and report UPS trouble and alarm signals.

Program GUI/PLC Administration Workstation to monitor UPS's status and alarm signals.

### Training

Comply with Section 280500, TRAINING.

### Field Quality Control

Testing: Comply with Section 280500.

★★★ END OF SECTION ★

# INDEX